A POLITICAL COMPANION TO
John Steinbeck

Edited by
Cyrus Ernesto Zirakzadeh
and Simon Stow

UNIVERSITY PRESS OF KENTUCKY

Scholarly publisher for the Commonwealth,
serving Bellarmine University, Berea College, Centre
College of Kentucky, Eastern Kentucky University,
The Filson Historical Society, Georgetown College,
Kentucky Historical Society, Kentucky State University,
Morehead State University, Murray State University,
Northern Kentucky University, Transylvania University,
University of Kentucky, University of Louisville,
and Western Kentucky University.
All rights reserved.

Editorial and Sales Offices: The University Press of Kentucky
663 South Limestone Street, Lexington, Kentucky 40508-4008
www.kentuckypress.com

The Library of Congress has cataloged the hardcover edition as follows:

A political companion to John Steinbeck / edited by Cyrus Ernesto Zirakzadeh
and Simon Stow.
      pages   cm. — (Political companions to great American authors)
   Includes bibliographical references and index.
   ISBN 978-0-8131-4202-9 (hardcover : alk. paper) —
ISBN 978-0-8131-4203-6 (epub) — ISBN 978-0-8131-4204-3 (pdf)
   1. Steinbeck, John, 1902-1968—Political and social views. 2. Politics and literature—United States—History—20th century. I. Zirakzadeh, Cyrus Ernesto,
1951– editor of compilation II. Stow, Simon, editor of compilation
   PS3537.T3234Z787 2013
   959.704'3373--dc23

                         2013003757

ISBN 978-0-8131-4739-0 (pbk. : alk. paper)

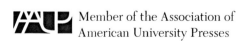

I believe that out of the whole body of our past, out of our differences, our quarrels, our many interests and directions, something has emerged that is itself unique in the world: America—complicated, paradoxical, bullheaded, shy, cruel, boisterous, unspeakably dear, and very beautiful.

—John Steinbeck, *America and Americans*

I did not need or want to be a citizen of this gray and dangerous country.

—John Steinbeck, *The Winter of Our Discontent*

Contents

Series Foreword

THOSE WHO UNDERTAKE a study of American political thought must attend to the great theorists, philosophers, and essayists. Such a study is incomplete, however, if it neglects American literature, one of the greatest repositories of the nation's political thought and teachings.

America's literature is distinctive because it is, above all, intended for a democratic citizenry. In contrast to eras when an author would aim to inform or influence a select aristocratic audience, in democratic times public influence and education must resonate with a more expansive, less leisured, and diverse audience to be effective. The great works of America's literary tradition are the natural locus of democratic political teaching. Invoking the interest and attention of citizens through the pleasures afforded by the literary form, many of America's great thinkers sought to forge a democratic public philosophy with subtle and often challenging teachings that unfolded in narrative, plot, and character development. Perhaps more than any other nation's literary tradition, American literature is ineluctably political—shaped by democracy as much as it has in turn shaped democracy.

The Political Companions to Great American Authors series highlights the teachings of the great authors in America's literary and belletristic tradition. An astute political interpretation of America's literary tradition requires careful, patient, and attentive readers who approach a text with a view to understanding its underlying messages about citizenship and democracy. Essayists in this series approach the classic texts not with a "hermeneutics of suspicion" but with the curiosity of fellow citizens who believe that the great authors have something of value to teach their readers. The series brings together essays from varied approaches and viewpoints for the common purpose of elucidating the political teachings of the nation's greatest authors for those seeking a better understanding of American democracy.

Patrick J. Deneen
Series Editor

John Steinbeck in the 1930s: Living Under the Gun

Rick Wartzman

IN ONE OF HIS MORE obscure works, *The Acts of King Arthur and His Noble Knights,* John Steinbeck asserts that in any fight "the final weapon is the brain. All else is supplemental." Perhaps. This analysis, however, didn't stop Steinbeck from packing a pistol in the late 1930s, just in case he needed a little protection beyond what resided between his ears.[1]

It isn't entirely clear what kind of firearm he had. But records suggest that he owned a Colt automatic, maybe two. In any case, beyond doubt is that Steinbeck felt his life was in danger—as stark a sign as any of the deep divide between Far Left and Far Right in California during the Great Depression and of the central role that Steinbeck played in this schism.

As one account has it, Steinbeck was attending a picnic with some old friends from Salinas High during those hungry years when a white pickup truck jumped the curb and sent everyone scattering. Two men leaped out, and one thrust a gun into Steinbeck's chest. The assailant told Steinbeck that "he better stop writing what he was writing—or else," one of the picnic goers would recall much later.[2]

Over time, Steinbeck grew afraid that he might be set up for charges of drunk driving or falsely accused of rape. "I went to my attorney, and he said there was no way of stopping a charge but advised me of keeping a diary containing names of people I saw and when so that I could call an alibi if I had to," Steinbeck explained, adding that his enemies were "capable of anything."[3]

A few years later, after Steinbeck had moved to the East Coast, the menacing evidently continued. According to one story, he took a phone c in New York, and the voice on the other end of the line told him, "You may think you're safe 3,000 miles away, but we're coming for you."[4]

It is difficult to think of another author—aside perhaps from Salman Rushdie, on whose head a *fatwa* would be placed a half century after Steinbeck's struggles—who has come under siege like this. And it certainly raises the question, Why would anyone want Steinbeck dead?

The short answer, of course, boils down to four words: *The Grapes of Wrath.* Steinbeck's 1939 classic, more than any book of its day, laid bare the inequities of capitalism and the mistreatment of migrant laborers who toiled in California's farm fields. But it did so in a style that, for many readers, was more compelling and accessible than the proletarian literature of Dos Passos, Farrell, or Caldwell. The result: *The Grapes of Wrath* catapulted to the top of the national best-seller list in 1939 (with some 430,000 copies sold), and it was also one of America's top-ten favorites for 1940, when the film version of the novel appeared.[5] Tom Joad, the book's protagonist, was quickly on his way to becoming an indelible American icon. Men of the day even took to donning a hat called the "Joad Cap."[6]

Yet it wasn't simply Steinbeck's gripping prose or his immense popularity that incensed those on the right. Their intense reaction was very much the product of a particular time and place. California had been boiling over politically and ideologically for the better part of a decade.[7]

The state has always been the home of extremes—like the rest of America, "only more so," as Wallace Stegner famously put it. In 1934 this quality manifested itself in the gubernatorial campaign of Upton Sinclair, the muckraking writer and longtime Socialist who promised to end poverty in California. At the heart of this pledge was a quixotic fiscal scheme that involved putting private factories under government supervision and allowing workers to own what they had manufactured. Small farmers, for their part, would then bring crops to the city, where they'd be "made available to the factory workers in exchange for the products of *their* labor."[8]

Although everyone from William Randolph Hearst to President Franklin D. Roosevelt derided Sinclair's plan, Uppie (as he was called) won the Democratic primary and almost triumphed in the general election. All in all, said Jerry Voorhis, who would eventually become a Democratic congressman from the Golden State, it was "the nearest thing to a mass movement toward Socialism that I have heard of in America."[9]

Those on the right—those with a stake in the system—celebrated Sinclair's defeat, but not for long. Four years later a state senator from Los Angeles and Sinclair protégé named Culbert Olson was elected California's governor—the first Democrat to hold that office in the twentieth century—and he immediately took steps that unnerved and enraged the conservative establishment.[10]

For starters, he let out of prison Tom Mooney, the militant labor leader who had been convicted of planting a bomb that killed ten and injured forty at a San Francisco parade more than twenty years earlier. It had become widely apparent over the years that Mooney had been framed. But none of Olson's Republican predecessors would intervene in the case. Just before his release and still in shackles, Mooney marched to the floor of the state assembly and declared, "I understand those common elementary laws that govern all life. They are simple. In the biological world, they are conception, birth, growth, decay, and death . . . and so it is with our present economic system."

"It was conceived like we were," Mooney continued. "It was born, it grew to maturity, and now it is in a state of decay . . . and in its place, just as in our place, it will be replaced by a new and I hope better social order."[11]

One of Olson's next acts seemed to put flesh on Mooney's rhetoric. The governor appointed as head of state farmworker policy another writer, Carey McWilliams, whose book *Factories in the Field* was seen as the nonfiction counterpart to *The Grapes of Wrath*. If California's agricultural barons hated one person more than Steinbeck it was McWilliams; they branded him the most dangerous pest they'd ever seen, "worse than pear blight or boll weevil."[12]

He, too, was full of radical ideas—including pushing for the Soviet-style collectivization of all private farms in the state. "The final solution," McWilliams wrote, "will come only when the present wasteful, vicious, undemocratic, and thoroughly antisocial system of agricultural ownership in California is abolished."[13] Now a public official, McWilliams began to hold hearings in California's farm belt with the intention of lifting workers' wages—a bold intervention in the marketplace.[14]

Into this mix stepped John Steinbeck, who was keenly aware that, as he described it, there seemed to be "a revolution going on."[15] "There is little question in my mind that the principle of private ownership as a means of production is not long with us," Steinbeck observed. "This is not in terms of what I think is right or wrong or good or bad, but in terms of what is inevitable."[16] Steinbeck wasn't a member of the Communist Party. (Neither, for that matter, was McWilliams or Olson.) But he was unabashedly what Yale University's Michael Denning has characterized as a communist, "using the term with a small *c*"—a proud part of the Popular Front, in league with countless other artists and intellectuals.[17]

Even before *The Grapes of Wrath* was released, Steinbeck had helped California's beleaguered farmworkers. He had conducted a considerable amount of research in the state's bountiful fields, witnessing firsthand both the terrible conditions under which the migrants suffered and the level of aggression that some growers were willing to unleash to maintain their riches.[18] This nexus—the linking of one man's profit to another's privation—fueled a series of reports that Steinbeck wrote for the *San Francisco News* in 1936 and later became a primary theme in *The Grapes of Wrath.*[19]

Meanwhile, Steinbeck—already famous for *Of Mice and Men*—allied himself with a number of liberal groups eager to unionize California's farmworkers. One group even took his name: the John Steinbeck Committee to Aid Agricultural Organization, with the author serving as state chairman.[20]

The efforts of the Steinbeck Committee—along with the election of Culbert Olson and the appointment of Carey McWilliams—emboldened the United Cannery, Agricultural, Packing, and Allied Workers of America. Its leaders (some of them Communists, with a capital *C*) were active in the San Joaquin Valley throughout the late 1930s, urging cotton workers to walk off the job and hold out for higher pay.[21]

Through all of this, Steinbeck's chief adversary was the Associated Farmers of California, Inc., a confederation of the state's biggest growers and their financial backers from San Francisco. The group denounced *The Grapes of Wrath* as "a pack of lies" and "communist propaganda," but its members fought with more than words.

Launched after a series of bloody agricultural strikes in Central California in 1933, the Associated Farmers became a political power, lobbying for the passage of antipicketing ordinances and other measures designed to defeat organized labor. Associated Farmers leaders and their vigilante friends also wielded bats, pickaxe handles, and guns to keep laborers in line—a record of ruthlessness that the *Nation* magazine called "organized terrorism in agriculture."[22]

Nor was the violence confined to the fields. In 1934 the city of San Francisco was shut down by a general strike, spearheaded by Harry Bridges of the International Longshoremen's Association. On July 5 of that year thousands of pickets faced off against eight hundred uniformed police. The clash left scores injured and two workers dead.[23]

For much of the 1930s, California was a tinderbox. *The Grapes of Wrath* was truly scary for those who possessed a lot of land or owned a big business because it looked as if Steinbeck's novel might be the match that would ignite the flames. "When property accumulates in too few hands," Steinbeck wrote in one of the inter-chapters of the book, "it is taken away. And that companion fact: when a majority of people are hungry and cold they will take by force what they need."[24]

If Steinbeck wasn't calling for open revolt, he was surely tiptoeing close to that edge. And those on the Far Right were terrified by his vision—a vision that suddenly didn't seem so far-fetched in a world led by Culbert Olson and Carey McWilliams.

In the minds of conservatives, the America they knew and loved was being destroyed not only by Communists but by others who were, as one Associated Farmers official saw it, part of the same "family tree": "a Socialist, a parlor pink, a minister who thinks he's working for the brotherhood of man, a college professor who thinks it is an indication of mental courage to teach that our government is old fashioned."[25] In turn, John Steinbeck believed that the America he knew and loved was being destroyed by what he termed "a type of Fascist psychology."[26]

In the end, the two ends of the political spectrum could not agree on anything, least of all common goals. But make no mistake: they did share at least a few things in common—fear, anger, and guns.

Notes

1. Steve Hauk details Steinbeck's gun ownership during this period in "Steinbeck Armed: (A Colt Revolver) with the Truth," *Steinbeck Review* 5, no. 1 (2008): 91–96.

2. Ibid.

3. From a March 4, 1939, letter from Steinbeck to his literary agent, Elizabeth Otis. The letter is quoted in Rick Wartzman, *Obscene in the Extreme: The Burning and Banning of John Steinbeck's* The Grapes of Wrath (New York: Pub-

licAffairs, 2008), 74. It's also quoted in Jackson Benson, *The True Adventures of John Steinbeck, Writer* (New York: Viking Press, 1984), 394.

4. Hauk, "Steinbeck Armed."

5. Wartzman, *Obscene in the Extreme*, 72, 237.

6. The popularity of the "Joad Cap" is cited in Bryant Simon and William Deverell, "Come Back, Tom Joad: Thoughts on a California Dreamer," *California History* 4 (Winter 2000–2001): 182.

7. For more on this tumultuous decade in the Golden State, see Rick Wartzman, "New Deal, No Deal," in *A Companion to California History*, ed. William Deverell and David Igler (West Sussex, UK: Wiley-Blackwell, 2008), 292–309.

8. Ibid. Also see Greg Mitchell, *The Campaign of the Century: Upton Sinclair's Race for Governor of California and the Birth of Media Politics* (New York: Random House, 1992), 22–23.

9. Wartzman, *Obscene in the Extreme*, 31.

10. Olson's background and policies are detailed in Robert E. Burke, *Olson's New Deal for California* (Berkeley: University of California Press, 1953), 4–13.

11. Curt Gentry, *Frame-Up: The Incredible Case of Tom Mooney and Warren Billings* (New York: W. W. Norton, 1967), 422–23. For more on Mooney and his release by Olson, see Burke, *Olson's New Deal*, 48–58.

12. Mark Arax and Rick Wartzman, *The King of California: J. G. Boswell and the Making of a Secret American Empire* (New York: PublicAffairs, 2003), 173.

13. Carey McWilliams, *Factories in the Field* (Boston: Little Brown, 1939), 324–25.

14. Wartzman, *Obscene in the Extreme*, 102–5.

15. From a July 28, 1939, letter from Steinbeck to Elizabeth Otis. It is quoted in Robert DeMott, ed., *Working Days: The Journals of* The Grapes of Wrath, *1938–1941* (New York: Viking Penguin, 1989), 154. The full quotation, referring to *The Grapes of Wrath*, is: "This is a rough book, as rough as the people it deals with. It deals with them in their own terms. So in choosing a publisher (if you must) be sure there are neither moral traits nor reactionary ones, because a revolution is going on and this book is revolutionary. And I wouldn't want it changed to fit the policy of an old house."

16. Wartzman, *Obscene in the Extreme*, 194–95.

17. Michael Denning, *The Cultural Front: The Laboring of American Culture in the Twentieth Century* (London: Verso, 2000), xviii.

18. Wartzman, *Obscene in the Extreme*, 75–94.

19. These reports would later be collected and published as *The Harvest Gypsies* (Berkeley, Calif.: Heyday Press, 2002).

20. Wartzman, *Obscene in the Extreme*, 97–98.

21. Ibid., 98–99, 106–8.

22. Herbert Klein and Carey McWilliams, "Cold Terror in California," *Nation*, July 24, 1935. For more on the history and tactics of the Associated Farmers, see Wartzman, *Obscene in the Extreme*, 23–25. Among the richest sources of documentation on Associated Farmers activities are the reports of the hearings of the La Follette Committee, in U.S. Senate, Committee on Education and Labor, *Violations of Free Speech and Rights of Labor: Hearings Pursuant to S. Res. 266*, 76th Cong., 3rd sess., 1940.

23. Wartzman "New Deal, No Deal." For more on this episode, also see David F. Selvin, *A Terrible Danger: The 1934 Waterfront and General Strikes in San Francisco* (Detroit: Wayne State University Press, 1996).

24. John Steinbeck, *The Grapes of Wrath* (New York: Viking, 1939; reprint, New York: Penguin 1976), 306.

25. Wartzman, *Obscene in the Extreme*, 37.

26. Ibid., 87.

The Dangerous Ambivalence of John Steinbeck

Simon Stow

AT A TIME WHEN the United States is enduring a severe economic crisis caused by the unregulated lending practices of major financial institutions, decades of antilabor policies, and rampant globalization; when that crisis has driven families from their homes; and when the gap between the rich and poor in America is, by some measures, larger than at any point in its history, a volume on the political work of John Steinbeck could not, perhaps, be more apropos. Steinbeck will be forever known as the author of *The Grapes of Wrath*, the 1939 novel in which he chronicled in fiction what had occurred in fact: the devastation of the American way of life by a faceless economic system in which empathy, pity, and understanding were seen as market failures rather than the basis of a decent human society. It is therefore unsurprising that many commentators have turned to Steinbeck as a lens through which to view the contemporary crisis.[1]

In the popular imagination, Steinbeck's Joad family has become shorthand for the consequences of economic downturn, faceless corporate capitalism, and social and political inequality. In this, perhaps, the book has become the specter that haunts Steinbeck scholarship.

Clearly *The Grapes of Wrath* is Steinbeck's most important and most influential novel, and the great majority of essays in this volume reference the text in one way or another. It is, nevertheless, but one text from a lifetime of writing and activism largely committed to political critique and social change. John Steinbeck was, as Rick Wartzman reminds us in his prologue, a dangerous writer. Part of what made Steinbeck so dangerous—and such a threat to capital, communists, school boards, and library patrons up and down the country—was the coexistence within both him and his writings of contradictory attitudes toward a multitude of modern phenomena, including, but not limited to, his nation.[2] Steinbeck was a staunch critic of capitalism but despised its state-centered alternatives; he championed community but feared the mob; he embraced his nation's wars but mourned their cost; he celebrated American ingenuity but criticized the society it created; he advocated for humanitarian intervention but recognized its costs to indigenous peoples; he sought solace and insights in nature but lamented the cruelties it inflicted on humanity. Steinbeck was, and remains, dangerous precisely because it is impossible to pin him down to any single position. Capitalists called him a communist, communists a capitulator. Critics do not like to be confounded in their attempts to compartmentalize.

For if John Steinbeck was ambivalent about America, it is also clear that America has been ambivalent about John Steinbeck. The decision of the Nobel Committee to award Steinbeck the 1962 prize for literature crystallized the vapors of disapproval that had swirled around his work from the very beginning of his career. Many suggested that while Steinbeck had achieved something of note in his most famous novel, this success was more a product of the times than of his artistry; many dismissed his subsequent work as either didacticism or folly. Yet Steinbeck remains remarkably popular among the reading public, both nationally and internationally. All of his novels remain in print, and *East of Eden* received perhaps the highest imprimatur in modern American publishing when it was chosen as an Oprah's Book Club selection in 2003, with the host declaring that it was possibly the best novel she had ever read.[3]

Writing about his own simultaneously loved and reviled position within American letters, Richard Rorty once observed that "if there is anything to the idea that the best intellectual position is one that is attacked with equal vigor from the political right and the political left, then I am in good shape."[4] As in Rorty's case, some see in Steinbeck's work only a contrarian streak or confusion rather than a coherent position or complex philosophy. The notion that what some perceive as a productive ambivalence is merely inconsistency and sloppiness is a persistent meme among Steinbeck's critics. The essays in this volume attempt to block that meme's transmission. Their very variety is a testament to the depth and breadth of interests Steinbeck expounded in his political work and activism. Indeed, the volume draws on expertise from a multiplicity of disciplines—political theorists, literary critics, and scholars of theater, film, music, and photography—to capture the many, frequently overlapping, layers of Steinbeck's politics. Unlike, perhaps, other volumes in this series of political companions to great American authors, *A Political Companion to John Steinbeck* seeks to address not only Steinbeck's writing but also his influence and activism, both artistic and political. While we might talk about Melville's or Whitman's art, it is perhaps more fitting to refer to Steinbeck's "work." For Steinbeck—to borrow a phrase from Ishmael Reed—"writin' is fightin'."[5]

The volume is divided into four parts. The first situates Steinbeck within his most familiar role as social critic. Locating Steinbeck within his personal and historical context, the opening essay by Cyrus Ernesto Zirakzadeh tackles *The Grapes of Wrath* head on. Zirakzadeh identifies both the ambivalent picture of America that Steinbeck offers in the novel and the ambivalent response it generated, disliked as it was by both communists and conservatives. The essay offers an account of the radicalism of Steinbeck's political vision and his commitment to collective action while simultaneously noting the ways in which this vision was predicated on a conservative understanding of the role of women and the family. The essay exposes and explores the tensions in Steinbeck's approach to the politics of social protest to argue that these very ambivalences invite the reader into the political debates that the novel depicts.

In the second essay in this section, Zoe Trodd situates Steinbeck firmly within a tradition of American protest literature that includes Harriet Beecher Stowe's *Uncle Tom's Cabin,* Upton Sinclair's *The Jungle,* and the hortatory writings of Ida B. Wells. Identifying the persistent disparity in enthusiasm for Steinbeck's work between critics and readers, Trodd takes on and transforms this binary. She—like Zirakzadeh—shows that by inviting the reader into his work and "demanding a responsibility that extends beyond the page," Steinbeck provokes a deep reflection in his audience. The supposed weaknesses that many literary critics identify in his work are, Trodd suggests, strengths when that work is understood as part of a tradition concerned with provoking debate and dialogue.

Donna Kornhaber also situates Steinbeck within a distinct literary tradition complementary to that identified by Trodd, not least because it too demands the active participation of its audience in political dialogue and social change. Kornhaber broadens our understanding of Steinbeck's role as social critic by highlighting his often-overlooked role as playwright. She situates Steinbeck within an American theatrical tradition that not only included such contemporaries as Eugene O' Neill, Elmer Rice, and Hallie Flanagan of the Federal Theater Project but also stretched back to Michael Gold, James A. Hearne, and the agitprop plays of the suffrage and temperance movements. Kornhaber notes that although Steinbeck was a capable playwright and much respected by his peers, critics were typically backhanded in their praise. In Kornhaber's account, however, Steinbeck was concerned more about the response of his audience than that of his critics. Indeed, she suggests that Steinbeck's genre-expanding innovation of the playable novel confounded even the most trenchant artistic critiques of his work.

The final essay in the opening section explores Steinbeck's ambivalences about his self-assumed role as a social critic and the role's impact on the world beyond the page. Offering a reading of *The Pearl*—an important but frequently ignored text in the Steinbeck canon—Adrienne Akins Warfield details the dialogue that Steinbeck had both with his friend Ed Ricketts and with himself about the nature and costs of social progress for ostensibly primitive societies. Unlike Ricketts, who seemed to idealize the primitive, Akins Warfield argues, Steinbeck embraced many of the social and technological changes of modernity while remaining acutely aware of modernity's considerable costs. In this, Akins Warfield suggests, *The Pearl* expresses a tragic worldview that underpinned Steinbeck's literary activism, confounding those who would see him as a mere literary didact.

The second section of the book examines the cultural roots of Steinbeck's political vision and highlights the ways in which he drew on the conflicts and complexities of nature as well as traditional American myths to identify and express his social critique. In the first essay, Charles Williams interrogates the political ramifications of Steinbeck's phalanx theory. Williams demonstrates the ways in which the theory, drawn from Steinbeck's observations about nature, embodies many of the tensions in Steinbeck's political work. He discerns a conflict between Steinbeck's awareness of the need for a political group and his fear of the mass man of fascism and communism. Likewise, while noting the importance of the theory to Steinbeck's embrace of New Deal liberalism, Williams shows how the theory nevertheless led the author to reject excessive state power both at home and abroad.

Although his argument is predicated on a reading of *In Dubious Battle,* Williams traces how the theory of the phalanx shaped Steinbeck's political sympathies throughout his career.

In his essay Michael T. Gibbons notes Steinbeck's depiction of nature's inhospitality to humanity in two very different literary worlds: those of *The Grapes of Wrath* and *Cannery Row.* Steinbeck's view, Gibbons argues, is not that nature precludes what Gibbons calls an "authentic" life—that is, one in which social relations are largely transparent, the causes of injustice and inequality are understood, and progress is possible. Rather, humanity creates institutions to cope with nature that then inadvertently make an authentic life difficult to achieve. Depicting the dark side of capitalism in *The Grapes of Wrath,* Steinbeck enmeshed the Joads in a world over which they had no control, while in *Cannery Row* the good life promised in post–World War II America came at the expense of one's safety, health, and control over one's own existence. Gibbons connects Steinbeck's ideas about the economic crisis of the 1930s and the false promise of the postwar boom to today's crises of capitalism and contemporary challenges to fashioning an authentic existence.

In the final essay in this section Roxanne Harde explores the importance of the story of Exodus to *The Grapes of Wrath.* Detailing the myriad ways in which Steinbeck fashioned his novel around one of the central stories of the American founding, Harde shows how Steinbeck embraced an American literary tradition of borrowing from, refashioning, and extending the nation's myths for political purposes. Her close reading of the novel and its literary forebear shows, furthermore, that Steinbeck not only drew on this American literary tradition but added to it, thereby providing opportunities for other artists, including Woody Guthrie and Bruce Springsteen, to do the same.

Fittingly, the third section of the book discusses Steinbeck's considerable influence on other American artists working in diverse media. James R. Swensen describes how Dorothea Lange—whose black-and-white images of the great westward migration from the Dust Bowl later become synonymous with Steinbeck's early work—recorded the political impact of Steinbeck's name on working-class protests against the inequalities of capitalism. Examining Lange's photographs of the John Steinbeck Committee to Aid Agricultural Organization, Swensen establishes Steinbeck's influence on mass political action during the late 1930s and provides further evidence of the ways in which the American protest literature tradition identified by Trodd emboldened its readers to seek social change.

Marijane Osborn, in calling Steinbeck's work "participatory parables," coins a phrase that succinctly captures a common theme across many of the essays in this volume: the demand that the reader, or the viewer, do something to alleviate the conditions depicted by the artist's work. Her chapter on the cinematic adaptations of Steinbeck's Mexican trilogy—*The Forgotten Village, The Pearl,* and *Zapata*—discusses how these films, and the books they either spawned or drew on, anticipate questions of colonialism and intervention that would inspire later postcolonial thought and writing. Addressing some of the concerns raised by Adrienne Akins Warfield in her essay, Osborn shows how Steinbeck's struggles with the complexities surrounding modernity provided opportunities and impetus for other artists to struggle with the same questions in different media.

In her essay on John Steinbeck and Bruce Springsteen, Lauren Onkey shows how Steinbeck provided the musician with a model as he struggled with the issues of mass popularity and its potentially negative effect on his work. After describing several similarities between Steinbeck and Springsteen, which, as she notes, Springsteen has deliberately cultivated, Onkey argues that Springsteen endeavors, as did Steinbeck, to create a community committed to social justice. Moreover, Onkey argues that Springsteen's music constitutes what she calls a "gospel response" to Steinbeck's work that both engages and expands the political community Springsteen is seeking. Similar to the cultural borrowing described by Roxanne Harde in her essay, Springsteen borrowed from, reformulated, and extended the political lessons in Steinbeck's literature. Onkey contends that Springsteen in particular addressed a relative lacuna in Steinbeck's work: the treatment of migrant workers.

Combining discussions of literature, film, and music, Cyrus Ernesto Zirakzadeh's second essay in the volume explores the ways in which Steinbeck's *The Grapes of Wrath* has been employed by different artists to advance different political agendas. Zirakzadeh observes that the cinematic version of *The Grapes of Wrath* portrays a constructive role for government in reestablishing the conditions under which social justice and capitalism can flourish simultaneously. This is quite different from the more ambiguous depiction of government action in the novel. The novel questions both the viability of America's capitalist economy and the possibilities for a state responsive to the dispossessed, whereas the film places its faith in the New Deal liberalism identified and discussed by Charles Williams earlier in the volume. Looking at one of Bruce Springsteen's performances and his retelling of the story of the Joads, Zirakzadeh shows how the ongoing conflict between these two visions of social change continues to resonate in contemporary politics and culture.

In the last section of the volume the authors consider Steinbeck's relationship to his country—both real and imagined. That topic raises the always vexed question of what it means to love one's country. Mimi R. Gladstein and James H. Meredith's essay notes the ironies of Steinbeck's attempts to serve his country during World War II. His efforts to serve were frequently rebuffed because of suspicions about his political sympathies arising from his novels' depictions of America. As did Wartzman in his essay, Gladstein and Meredith discuss the fears that Steinbeck's writings generated in others, in this case the FBI and other government agencies. The authors argue that by struggling—and later managing—to serve his country as a wartime correspondent, Steinbeck displayed a love for his nation that transcended the narrowly political concerns of his government. The essay thereby suggests ways in which love of country can move beyond nationalistic sentiments and embrace both service and critique.

Robert S. Hughes's essay on Steinbeck's final two books—*Travels with Charley* and *America and Americans*—recounts Steinbeck's last attempts to understand a nation from which, in many ways, he had become alienated. Hughes notes that the two volumes—published only four years apart—differ in tone. *Travels with Charley* depicts a nation populated by malcontents and the complacent, he argues. The most redeeming character is, perhaps, the eponymous dog Charley. The disappointments and scolding tone of *Travels,* Hughes suggests, are tempered in *America and Americans* by a recognition of the nation's virtues, not least of which are the ongoing dissatisfaction and restlessness that move the country forward despite its many faults. In both the juxtaposition of the two works and his account of paradoxes of American life in *America and the Americans,* Hughes uncovers Steinbeck's ambivalence about the country of his birth. He concludes, however, that Steinbeck's final vision of the nation's future was, overall, a positive one.

In the concluding essay of the volume, Simon Stow tackles Steinbeck's final literary work, *The Winter of Our Discontent,* and finds in it evidence that supports Gladstein and Meredith's and Hughes's claims about Steinbeck's patriotism. Stow, however, suggests that Steinbeck is hopeful rather than optimistic about his nation. Moreover, the novel's final act—which is widely seen as redemptive of humanity and nation—is actually more ambiguous than many critics have suggested. In the final act Stow sees a tragic, ambivalent sensibility. Steinbeck recognizes that even as a nation aspires to greatness, it may fail, and even if it were to succeed, such success would come with significant costs. Stow employs Steinbeck's tragic vision to address a recent debate among political theorists about the efficacy and dangers of patriotism in a democratic community.

In March 2011 Paul LePage, the Republican governor of Maine, ordered the removal of a mural depicting the history of workers in the state—including colonial-era shoemakers, lumberjacks, Rosie the Riveter, and a 1986 paper mill strike—from the Department of Labor Building in the state capital of Augusta. The mural, LePage declared, was too prounion and, as such, contrary to the probusiness goals of his administration.[6] In the middle of a battle about austerity measures, workers' rights, and the role of unions in the economies of both the state and nation, when the mere *depiction* of workers is considered hostile to businesses interests, John Steinbeck could not be more important. He remains a dangerous writer, hostile to political cant on both the Left and the Right, and therefore an author whose political vision remains worthy of our attention.

Notes

1. In August 2009 journalist Chris McGreal of the British newspaper the *Guardian* wrote a series of articles in which he retraveled the route of Steinbeck's Okies across America and reported in prose, photographs, video, and audio on the economic ravages of the new recession. See McGreal's introduction to the series and days one through four on the series website, "*The Grapes of Wrath* Revisited," accessed July 18, 2011, http://www.guardian.co.uk/world/series/grapes-of-wrath-revisited. Additionally, see Robert Gottlieb, "The Rescue of John Steinbeck," *New York Review of Books,* April 17, 2008; and Rachel Dry, "A Recession Only Steinbeck Could Love," *Washington Post,* March 22, 2009. According to Dry, this newfound interest in Steinbeck is not confined to journalists and critics. In 2009 the National Endowment for the Arts Big Read program received twice as many applications for reading groups on *The Grapes of Wrath* as it had in the previous year.

2. Rick Wartzman, *Obscene in the Extreme: The Burning and Banning of John Steinbeck's* The Grapes of Wrath (New York: PublicAffairs, 2008).

3. "Your Guide to *East of Eden*," Oprah's Book Club Collection, June 18, 2003, http://www.oprah.com/oprahsbookclub/Oprahs-Book-Club-East-of-Eden-by-John-Steinbeck.

4. Richard Rorty, *Philosophy and Social Hope* (New York: Penguin, 1999), 27.

5. Ishmael Reed, *Writin' Is Fightin': Thirty-Seven Years of Boxing on Paper* (New York: Atheneum, 1988).

6. Steven Greenhouse, "Mural of Maine Workers Becomes Political Target," *New York Times,* March 23, 2011, http://www.nytimes.com/2011/03/24/us/24lepage.html; Peter Catapano, "The Mural Vanishes," *Opinionator* (blog), *New York Times,* April 1, 2012, http://opinionator.blogs.nytimes.com/2011/04/01/the-mural-vanishes.

PART I

Steinbeck as Social Critic

CHAPTER 1

Revolutionary Conservative, Conservative Revolutionary? John Steinbeck and *The Grapes of Wrath*

Cyrus Ernesto Zirakzadeh

IN 1939 JOHN STEINBECK finished *The Grapes of Wrath,* his sixth novel.[1] It is, among other things, a political saga about the Joads, an imaginary family of heavily indebted tenant farmers who are suddenly evicted from the land that their forebears had seized from Indians and Mexicans and then proudly cultivated.[2] Rather than remain in Oklahoma and become servile machine tenders, the family decides to purchase a used jalopy and head for California. The male members of the family envision the West as a pristine Eden, with abundant and fertile land and without heartless bankers who bedevil small farmers. The women, however, fear that even in California "lobos" (southwestern slang for wolves) roam.

The women's worries prove well founded. After arriving in California, the family confronts an impersonal agricultural economy that treats wage laborers as throwaway tools. The family further discovers a political system that openly sides with the wealthy and that denies the rural have-nots their rights of free speech and assembly. Police and middle-class vigilantes harass the Joads and thousands of other transient harvesters who have little food and clothing and no permanent dwelling place.

Steinbeck uses the Joads as a case study with which to illustrate the fate of a larger group of down-on-their-luck Americans. He sprinkles sociological commentary throughout the story, in which he elaborates on the economic processes prompting the cruel behavior. Owners of enormous farms, needing pickers quickly for very brief harvesting seasons, lure the recently dispossessed to fields with promises of lucrative wages.[3] Then, when the number of workers exceeds the number of jobs, the owners pay less-than-subsistence wages and impose harsh working conditions. Once the harvest is over, local police and health inspectors expel the field hands from the local community, purportedly to preserve order and to maintain community cleanliness for the permanent residents. Having helped big businesses protect their profit margins, the itinerant families find themselves "on the road" again, homeless, hungry, without work, and without a political home.

During their trek, the Joad family gradually grows smaller. The grandparents die of age and heartbreak. Frustrated, three younger adult males individually abandon the family. One, having killed a vigilante in a burst of righteous anger, hides in a marsh. Another, having read popular magazine ads about career opportunities, deserts his pregnant young wife in order to find his fortune. The third, finding life outside Oklahoma too bewildering, simply leaves the family at the roadside and vanishes in the forest.

By the novel's closing, only the indefatigable altruism of Ma Joad and her daughter, Rose of Sharon, holds the family together. Malnourished, Rose delivers a stillborn baby in an unused railcar, which the family soon must abandon because of a drenching rain and coming flood. To escape the gully washer, the family members climb a hill. But the waters continue to rise. Atop the hill, the Joads discover a frightened, hungry child and father in a dilapidated barn. Spurred by a tacit sense of responsibility to humankind, Rose overcomes her adolescent bashfulness and breast-feeds the man, who lacks strength enough even to raise his head. Cradling the stranger, Rose gazes into the air and "smiles mysteriously."[4] And then the story ends.

Steinbeck's literary depiction of the seemingly endless sufferings caused by what today are called agribusinesses immediately generated controversy. On the floor of the U.S. House of Representatives, the Honorable Lyle Boren of Oklahoma declared, "I cannot find it possible to let this dirty, lying, filthy manuscript go heralded before the public without a word of challenge or protest."[5] Boren was not the only nationally renowned politician to take a stand. On the wireless, both the president and the first lady defended the accuracy and value of Steinbeck's novel.[6] Meanwhile, many local officials in California, Oklahoma, Missouri, and Kansas denounced the book for its fueling of class hatred and undermining of respect for private property and property owners. In some farming communities in the Midwest and on the West Coast, citizens either compelled municipal governments to remove the book from public libraries or destroyed copies in bonfires. Lobbied heavily by California's big businesses, the Federal Bureau of Investigation gathered

information on Steinbeck's political activities and potentially subversive beliefs. Business associations also urged politically conservative artists to write
responses. It wasn't long before saccharine novels with romantic depictions
of rural life on California farms were published with such titles as *Grapes
of Gladness*.[7] (For additional reflections on local responses to the novel, see
the prologue, by Rick Wartzman.) *? ?, ?.*

    The controversy never ended. *The Grapes of Wrath* continues to be
one of the most commonly banned books in U.S. public schools and libraries.[8] Its translation into other art forms has often been opposed and greeted
with derision. During the 1940s Eric Johnston, who served as president of
both the Motion Picture Producers Association and the U.S. Chamber of
Commerce, denounced the novel and its film adaptation before screenwrit-
ers: "We'll have no more 'Grapes of Wrath,' we'll have no more 'Tobacco
Roads,' we'll have no more films that deal with the seamy side of American
life. We'll have no more films that treat the banker as a villain."[9] To assure
parents that the minds of their children would not be tainted, Twentieth
Century Fox announced that nonadults would not be able to purchase tick-
ets to the motion-picture version of *The Grapes of Wrath*.[10]

    Despite the many attempts to dissuade audiences from taking *The
Grapes of Wrath* seriously, large portions of the American reading public
were, and remain, fascinated by it. The book topped the best-seller lists of
1939 and 1940. Sales tapered off during the Cold War decades, but only
moderately. More than two million hardbacks and paperbacks had been sold
by 1975.[11] By the end of the twentieth century Steinbeck's story, in terms of
total sales, had become one of the most widely read novels in U.S. history.
The novel's impact on Americans' imaginations has never been measured
through surveys, but ad hoc observations attest to its fecundity. The book's
characters and plotlines have inspired three generations of screen- and
playwrights, theater troupes, muralists, and composers, as well as musicians
from Woody Guthrie to Bruce Springsteen. (For further discussion of Steinbeck's influence on Bruce Springsteen, see chapter 10, by Lauren Onkey.)
Playwright Arthur Miller—himself a twentieth-century political writer of
considerable influence—recalled that "there was a time" when Steinbeck's
novel "would rouse Congress to pass legislation to ameliorate conditions
in the transient labor camps of the West."[12] The late radical historian and
magazine columnist Howard Zinn once argued that *The Grapes of Wrath*
was a primary source of his understanding of class conflict in the United

comments on cultural influence

States because it gave his working-class experiences theoretical coherence.[13] Thousands of educators still regularly assign *The Grapes of Wrath* to high school, college, and graduate students. When at the end of the twentieth century panels of American artists and literary critics were asked to list the one hundred most important and influential "novels of the century," *The Grapes of Wrath* repeatedly appeared near the top, alongside such works as James Joyce's *Ulysses*, Vladimir Nabokov's *Lolita*, James Baldwin's *Go Tell It on the Mountain*, and George Orwell's *1984*.[14]

Given the book's enduring popularity and its impact on American artists, politicians, and citizens for almost eighty years, we are prompted to ask, Why has there been ongoing controversy? And, if the political ideas in the book are truly outrageous, what explains its popularity? Probably, the answers lie partly in the interests, worries, and desires that readers bring to the novel. The answers also lie partly in the book's message, which evokes readers' interests, worries, and desires in the first place. Something in the book ignites readers' interests and concerns.

The text itself offers clues. But the deciphering of literature more than seven decades old poses the challenge of anachronism. If we casually impute our latter-day political experiences, beliefs, and values to the author, we can easily misread the intended message (and find some unintended messages, as well). Hence, let us first recall some of Steinbeck's circumstances, experiences, and philosophic beliefs prior to the composition of *The Grapes of Wrath*. Then we will be in a better position to discern the political lessons embedded in the story.

The Political Education of John Steinbeck

Biographers and historians agree that three sets of experiences and circumstances shaped Steinbeck's vision of the United States: his preadult life in Salinas, California (where he observed his parents' indefatigable efforts to climb its social ladder), his courtship and ten-year marriage to the radical activist Carol Henning, and his earliest journalistic assignments.[15] Each set drew Steinbeck toward a slightly different political orientation. Together, they fostered ambivalence within him about the trajectory of his country.

Steinbeck was born in 1902 to a former schoolmarm and a hardworking yet financially unlucky small shopkeeper who, after losing his store (and subsequently becoming acutely depressed), found employment as a middle-level manager for a large sugar corporation. The business failure emotionally scarred Steinbeck's father, whose suffering Steinbeck vividly remembered. Steinbeck received a more positive image of property owner-ship from his two pairs of grandparents, who had emigrated from Europe in the late nineteenth century and then cleared land, raised cash crops and cattle, and helped found small towns in the then-new state of California. As a child Steinbeck eagerly visited his grandparents' ranches and avidly listened to tales about crossing the continent and confronting Indians and wild beasts.

Steinbeck's parents liked gardening and other outdoor activities but did not fully share their son's admiration of sodbusting. Both, having been raised on farms, had fled the fields for the opportunities and challenges of what at the time was urban life. Shortly after they married, they bought a home in Salinas, one of the more bustling small towns in central California, with a permanent population of roughly four thousand. They promptly opened a feed and grain store that soon went out of business (partly because mechanical farm equipment replaced horse-drawn buggies and mule-pulled plows).

Devastated by his business loss, the elder Steinbeck sat quietly for long hours in the dark. Friends helped the proud and deeply embarrassed man land an office job in the sugar-processing plant in Spreckels, a town that abuts Salinas. At the time Spreckels was a company town designed and managed by the Spreckels Sugar Company, one of the world's wealthiest ag-ricultural firms. The company provided family housing, public transporta-tion, and places of worship and recreation for its work force. Its mechanized irrigation systems and electrified trolley system were considered among the technological marvels of international capitalism. Steinbeck's father commuted to Spreckels from the family's mildly upscale Victorian home in Salinas.

Although Steinbeck's parents originally sought the pleasures of town life, they were hardly libertines. Steinbeck's grandparents were deeply reli-gious (one pair had been missionaries in Palestine). They passed their beliefs to Steinbeck's parents, who sincerely believed in the virtues of hard work and self-discipline, feared temptations of the flesh, and held that success in secular labor was a reflection of the quality of one's soul and a portent of ascension to heaven. The parents assiduously read from the Bible, took John and his sisters to church (where John served as an altar boy), and during the summers vacationed in the Episcopalian enclave of Pacific Grove on the Monterey Bay coast. To nurture more refined tastes in their children, the parents played operatic music on the phonograph and enrolled young John in dancing classes.

The flip side of Steinbeck's spiritual upbringing was the crass materialism of his hometown. Steinbeck later recalled that Salinas "had misers, lots of misers. . . . One of our rich men used to sweat with nervousness when he had to pay a bill in gold. Paper saved him considerable painful emotion because it didn't really seem like money to him."[16] Town boosters hoped that one day soon Salinas would rival San Francisco and cited Chicago as their model of urban growth.[17] They advocated the development of transportation infrastructure that would attract investors and the promotion of mass entertainment, such as the town's yearly rodeo, to attract tourists. Local merchants sold manufactured and nondurable goods to the farmers scattered throughout the hundred-mile valley. The rail station allowed both small entrepreneurs and larger agribusinesses to transport perishable crops via refrigerated cars to cities across North America. Many of the town's property owners soon became wealthy thanks to the tonnage Salinas exported in grain, potatoes, sugar beets, lettuce, artichokes, and other "green gold." Meanwhile, the town's saloons and bordellos entertained weekend visitors from as far away as San Francisco.

The wealthier folks in Salinas often looked down on the ethnic enclaves on the city's outskirts because non-Caucasian residents reportedly indulged in exotic cultural practices, including the smoking of opium. In memoirs and autobiographical accounts, Steinbeck describes having ridden his bike through Salinas's red-light district and Chinatown in hopes of observing scandalous goings-on. He maintains that the practices he observed were indeed deliciously untamed: "I wonder whether all towns have the blackness—the feeling of violence just below the surface."[18] Although his memories possibly contain a touch of tall tales, they probably also have some basis in reality, especially if we recall that one of Salinas's claims to fame in the 1920s was a widely reported shoot-out between federal agents and local bootleggers.

During Steinbeck's youth the Democratic Party ran Salinas through patronage and favors. According to oral histories, the party machine was in cahoots with owners of bars and bordellos. The party's commitment to long-term material prosperity satisfied the town's many churchgoers, who frowned upon (but seldom actively opposed) the town's rough-and-tumble side. The leaders of the town's Democratic Party also met with Republican leaders from nearby communities, and the two parties jointly oversaw Monterey County through a system of prearranged election competitions that assured each party plenty of offices.

Steinbeck's parents were active in the town's political affairs and social organizations. When Steinbeck's father was getting back on his feet after losing the store, Democratic leaders appointed him to the paid office of Monterey County treasurer (the previous officeholder had been accused of embezzlement and resigned in ignominy). Information on his subsequent political history is slender. In one letter Steinbeck brags that his father carried substantial sums of public money at least twice a year ("it amounts to something over a million dollars this time") and periodically drove with hired gunmen to protect him and the unregistered bonds from "highwaymen."[19] Biographers thus far have not explored the role of Steinbeck's father within the Salinas Democratic machine. Newspapers of the time suggest that he was considered a person of moderate political weight.[20] Although a few residents recall in recorded oral histories questioning the propriety of his hiring family members to do the local government's clerical work, it appears that he was generally above reproach.[21]

Mrs. Steinbeck was civic-minded before the days of female suffrage. Her behavior strikingly fits stereotypes of early twentieth-century Progressives.[22] She participated in innumerable community organizations and projects, including campaigns to beautify the streets and to develop a municipal opera company. She considered it government's job to nurture civilization and to deter slovenly, savage, and selfish behavior. She pressured the local government to put in place ordinances that would punish homeowners who did not maintain tidy yards. Steinbeck's mother was highly sensitive about the family's status among the town's well-to-do families and was also a tad prudish (which occasionally led her to question her son's artistic career—although, in fairness, it must be noted that she came to his defense when neighbors expressed outrage at his "filthy" writings). Strong-willed and outspoken, Mrs. Steinbeck often violated Victorian norms of female decorum. For example, she flew with a stunt pilot during a daredevil air show—an unprecedented act for a woman that drew the attention of the town newspaper.[23]

Steinbeck was not politically involved during his teenage and early adult years. He apparently found local politics uninteresting—perhaps even dangerous and distasteful. In his later years he would portray the Salinas government ranks as a home for scoundrels: "There were whispers of murders, covered up and only hinted at, of raids on the county funds. When the old courthouse burned down it was hinted that the records would have been dangerous to certain officeholders."[24] There is no record of his working on election campaigns or talking at length about politics with his father. He did not, according to biographers, join the political clubs in his high school and college despite the many exciting events of his day, from the entry of the United States into World War I, to the Russian and Mexican revolutions, to the rise and fall of California's Progressive movement. Later, when he could not secure a steady income early in his writing career, his mother urged him to enter local politics as his father's assistant. The younger Steinbeck refused. No ambitious politician was he.

Steinbeck might have remained an apolitical offspring of small-town bourgeois parents if not for Carol Henning, who hailed from the San Francisco Bay region and who sympathized with myriad left-wing movements and causes, including feminism, trade unionism, and socialism. Steinbeck met Henning by chance in his early twenties. At first he was smitten by Henning's beauty, humor, and vitality—certainly not her political beliefs. As they became romantically involved, she pressured him to attend political gatherings and study circles. At these events she exuberantly spoke with other activists and sympathizers, while her beau, according to observers' reports, alternately moped and scowled in the corners.[25]

Thanks to Henning's persevering and outgoing personality, Steinbeck eventually met Marxist propagandists, union organizers hiding from the law, and radical muckrakers, among them Lincoln Steffens. Steffens took an interest in the younger, withdrawn, and thus far unsuccessful writer and encouraged him to use his literary talents to write about the conditions of the dispossessed. He also helped Steinbeck, during those lean years, to land a paying job, writing about the rural poor for the left-leaning *San Francisco News*. This assignment provided Steinbeck with an unexpected set of experiences that became the subject matter of several so-called proletarian stories that he wrote in the late 1930s, including *The Grapes of Wrath*.[26]

In the course of gathering information for the news stories, Steinbeck became more familiar with the class structure of California. Steinbeck had never been ignorant of the nonbourgeois world. As a child, he had sometimes roamed the poorer neighborhoods of Salinas, and during high school and his aborted college career, he had worked part-time for Spreckels. In the company's fields, canneries, and bunkhouses, he had carefully observed how its manual workers—generally unmarried males from Mexico, the Philippines, Japan, and China—lived, talked, and thought. Steinbeck, however, was largely ignorant of a new wave of transient laborers whom property owners derogatorily called "Okies." These dispossessed family farmers began arriving in California during the 1930s from Arizona, Oklahoma, Arkansas, Kansas, and other farm-belt states. The "Okies" were a new breed of worker in terms of social habits and backgrounds. They were born and raised in the United States, were Northern European in moral beliefs and cultural habits, traveled with families, and were hungry to own land again.

Steinbeck contacted the government agencies responsible for helping seasonal field hands and visited the new camps for the rural unemployed. There he talked to residents, watched government officials make rounds, read officials' dossiers about conditions and activities, and visited the migrant workers in nearby shantytowns to compare the lives of the two groups. While gathering information for his news stories, he saw firsthand the difficulty of finding even short-term jobs. He was dismayed by watching the once-proud property owners slowly but surely lose their confidence, health, and will to live. He watched them valiantly fend off floods, endure oppressive heat, and fight illnesses in rickety, unsanitary shacks. Recalling the workers' defining traits, he notes in a later autobiographical essay, "I liked these people. They had qualities of humor and courage and inventiveness and energy that appealed to me. I thought that if we had a national character and a national genius, these people, who were beginning to be called Okies, were it. With all the odds against them, their goodness and strength survived."[27]

Steinbeck was stunned, but not surprised, when strikes and shootouts broke out in the California countryside in the late 1930s. He had sincerely believed that the social order was about to change, and he lay blame for the unrest at the feet of California's peculiar system of production that, in his opinion, depended on the ruthless exploitation of the have-nots: "I don't know whether you know what a bomb California is right now or not. . . . There are riots in Salinas and killings in the streets of that dear little town where I was born. I shouldn't wonder if the thing had begun. I don't mean any general revolt but an active beginning aimed toward it, the smouldering."[28] In another letter: "I must go over into the interior valleys. There are about five thousand families starving to death over there, not just hungry but actually starving. The government is trying to feed them and get medical attention to them with the fascist group of utilities and banks and huge growers sabotaging the thing all along the line and yelling for a balanced budget. . . . I'm pretty mad about it. No word of this outside because when I have finished my job the jolly old associated farmers will be after my scalp again."[29]

Philosophic Orientations

By the time that Steinbeck had begun to write in earnest about the former farmers from Oklahoma and elsewhere, he had been married for roughly five years. Because of Henning's various jobs and an allowance from his father, Steinbeck had the financial resources to be a full-time author. Each day, he spent his first waking hours carefully composing letters, some of which recorded his most private speculations about human nature, psychology, and history. After those hours, he turned to writing for publication.

We know from his letters and also from his lively conversations with mostly male friends that Steinbeck viewed himself as an economically marginalized, avant-garde intellectual.[30] In the evenings he frequented a local oceanographic laboratory where young scientists, artists, and scholars living around Monterey met to socialize over drinks. There he immersed himself in discussions and debates with the likes of cultural anthropologist Joseph Campbell about the basis of knowledge, the nature of human beings, the logic of history, and the status of moral judgments.

As early as 1933 Steinbeck confided to close friends that he wanted his fiction to express a new, ambitious understanding of America—a theoretical outlook that at times he called "group-man theory" and at other times the "phalanx theory." (For additional discussion of this aspect of Steinbeck's work, see chapter 5, by Charles Williams, and chapter 12, by Mimi R. Gladstein and James R. Meredith.)[31] He thought that his vision synthesized his contemporaries' best insights into the nature of human beings and society and also offered an alternative to most Americans' cheery optimism, which he personally disliked. For the remainder of the decade, Steinbeck emphasized in correspondence his intention to incorporate his theoretical outlook into both his fiction and nonfiction. He contended that he wished to become not a popular and well-paid writer but a writer whose philo-sophic vision would puncture fashionable but misleading myths about the world and provide an unadorned view of reality. Referring specifically to *The Grapes of Wrath,* he wrote, "I tried to write this book the way lives are being lived not the way books are written."[32] And in another letter he wrote, "This book wasn't written for delicate ladies. If they read it all they're messing in something not their business. I've never changed a word to fit the prejudices of a group and I never will. . . . I've never wanted to be a popular writer—you know that. And those readers who are insulted by normal events or language mean nothing to me."[33]

Steinbeck's group-man theory rested on what one might call a bifurcat-ed (or perhaps a two-story) view of human psychology and on a Darwinian understanding of cultural evolution. Both components reflected Steinbeck's exposure to currents of European thought that had arrived in the United States around the turn of the century.

According to Steinbeck's letters, our minds have two analytically sepa-rable sides that are engaged in different activities.[34] One side calculates how best to achieve a given goal. We often privately feel that we control this side's workings—for example, when we talk about the reasons for our deci-sions and choices, in such quotidian sentences as "I decided to buy groceries at this store because the vegetables are fresher than in the other store." But there is another part of our minds—something like a second, locked room in an apartment or the lower floor of a two-story house—that we feel that we do not consciously control. Instead, we feel driven by powerful physical urges and haunting voices of the past. This side of our mind provides us with the aims and goals that privately seem compelling and imperative.

Our goals and aims are partly a set of universal biological demands—such as urges to rest, eat, and mate—that are required for our individual survival and for the reproduction of the species. But we also are driven by worries and warnings that we inherit from our ancestors and that we experi-ence as mysterious preferences and arbitrary values and directives thrust upon us. Even though the original conditions that prompted our forebears to embrace these ideas no longer exist and no longer are remembered, their judgments about right and wrong conduct, good and evil circumstances, and wise and foolish actions retain their emotive power across generations and, in some cases, over centuries.[35]

Steinbeck perceived the relationship between our biological needs and our inherited normative codes as complex and, sometimes, discordant. If we always give higher priority to biological needs and dismiss our inherited norms, we suffer guilt and pay the social price of neglecting the wisdom of ages. One alternative is to revere the voices from the past and obey without equivocation our inherited values and priorities—say, those of a self-reliant farmer, a devoted mother, or an enterprising banker. But, Steinbeck argues, a heavy psychological price is paid for this ability to control our biological drives. The suppressed desires for food, sleep, shelter, and sex never fully disappear. They quietly percolate in the corners of our minds and then unexpectedly swamp our minds with passion, especially when we feel either physically exhausted or overly giddy about a pleasant turn of events. At such moments the internalized norms feel like heavy chains that we yearn to throw off, and we are tempted to engage in what our inherited normative voice normally considers reckless, sinful, and criminal conduct—such as infidelity, blasphemy, and even mob violence.[36]

Steinbeck derived his understandings about divided minds, the socialization of traditional norms, and the repression of physical drives from the ideas of Freud, Jung, and their followers. He found modern psychological speculations (especially the Jungian tradition) inspiring and illuminating. Conversely, he found implausible the so-called realistic view, popular in the United States, that humans act simply according to personal calculations of pleasure and pain and that they can apprehend the world without preconceptions and the mediation of cultural baggage from previous generations.

Steinbeck believed that we seldom clearly see either ourselves or our circumstances because our minds are the repositories of inherited norms and beliefs, which Steinbeck sometimes calls our "fantasies," and because our values are constantly warring with our repressed desires. Whenever we try to think rationally about our goals and to choose our aims, our minds confront the waxing and waning of biological needs and the demands of inherited norms and beliefs, some of which no longer make sense in present circumstances. Psychotherapy, which rests on the hope that individuals can know and thereby partly rise above the pull of their deep emotional currents, is too puny to corral our biological drives and cultural demands. It is Pollyannaish to think that the deep movements within our souls can be directed. In Steinbeck's words, "I don't think you will like my late work. It leaves realism farther and farther behind. I never had much ability for nor faith nor belief in realism. It is just a form of fantasy as nearly as I could figure. Boileau was a wiser man than Mencken. . . . There are streams in man more profound and dark and strong than the libido of Freud. Jung's libido is closer but still inadequate."[37]

In pondering the social origins of our ancestrally transmitted fantasies, Steinbeck applied elements of Darwinian social thought—another avant-garde fashion that he had first discovered in college and then in the 1930s revisited with his artistic and scientific friends.[38] Members of his Darwinist-leaning circle denied the existence of eternal and universal principles of right and wrong. They instead believed that every local human community devises a unique code of conduct for biological reasons, as a way to cope with immediate, visible threats. The local environment (and the multiple threats that it poses to human existence) inevitably changes over time. To avoid extinction, human groups endlessly tinker with their cultural inheritances, without totally jettisoning their pasts. Humans always retain some of the beliefs and prescriptions of their forebears, for these provide time-tested moorings from which to face the world.

Steinbeck called this understanding of the local origins of morals "non-teleological thinking" because it refuses to assume the existence of a human "telos"—a single, eternal, and objectively correct set of moral rules and social arrangements that all human societies ought to move toward. Non-teleological thinking instead celebrates normative diversity and views revisions of normative beliefs as natural and healthy.[39]

Steinbeck and his circle were not so-called Lamarckians in their think-ing about cultural evolution.[40] That is, they did not believe that all local groups are successful in their efforts to adapt their cultures to changing environments. Over time, some die because their gradual accumulation of cultural traits becomes inappropriate. Extinction of human communities is as much part of the natural cycle of change as is continued cultural diversity.[41]

Steinbeck's attraction to non-teleological thinking casts light on his constant diatribes against morally self-righteous and ideological thinking— regardless of whether it was expressed by partisans of the political Left or of the political Right. In his opinion, too many people who wish to improve the world begin with unshakable faith in an abstract, utopian blueprint. Instead, they should patiently and carefully study local communities, the threats to the communities' survival that the local environments pose, and the communities' experiments with incremental cultural change as a way to alleviate suffering. Steinbeck conceded that he had come across flexible, pragmatic, nonauthoritarian adherents to almost every political persuasion, including Communists.[42] But many reformers are morally self-righteous, dismiss locally accumulated wisdom, and adopt a dictatorial approach to remaking the world. They are fanatics who behave almost hysterically when their prescriptions are not adopted. In a letter concerning some dogmatic Communists whom he had met, Steinbeck railed, "I don't like communists either, I mean I dislike them as people. I rather imagine the apostles had the same waspish qualities and the New Testament is proof that they had equally bad manners. . . . Some of these communist field workers are strong, pure, inhumanly virtuous men. Maybe that's another reason I personally dislike them and that does not rebound to my credit."[43]

Images of Rebellion in *The Grapes of Wrath*

With the above sketch of Steinbeck's life and philosophic beliefs in mind, let us turn to *The Grapes of Wrath* and explicate the embedded arguments about the family's responses to unwanted social conditions. In extracting a Steinbeckian vision, we first will look at some details involving the setting of the story and then will examine particular actors and events.

One striking aspect of Steinbeck's book is its depictions of the multiple cultures that coexist in North America. Unlike some twentieth-century writings about a so-called American way of life, Steinbeck's novel does not assume the existence of a single national culture. Nor does he portray American society in terms of a coherent class war between a self-conscious nationwide bourgeoisie and a self-conscious nationwide proletariat. Instead, the novel presents the United States as a vast collection of local settlements and meeting places—such as roadside coffee shops, used-car lots, and family farms. Each encourages and reinforces distinctive values and habits. Because of the large number of local social settings, U.S. culture resembles a quilt, with an amazing variety of hues, patterns, and textures.

Steinbeck spends much of the book constructing sometimes amusing and sometimes uneasy encounters between people from different local environments. One of his vignettes takes place at a roadside diner along Route 66. Steinbeck imagines a Midwestern businessman and his wife stopping for a short rest after a long drive. Steinbeck contrasts the wife's thoughts and behavior with those of the waitress laboring behind the counter.[44] Although both characters live in a world in which men and women have different social roles and privileges, the customer and the server appear as radically different beings with few, if any, common concerns. In a another episode, the Joads try to repair a jalopy at a roadside gas station.[45] The attendant nervously wants to obey rules and serve his boss, while the Joad men, raised in settlements of small farms, value spontaneity and self-reliance. The temporary gas station attendant and the dispossessed family farmer—regardless of their comparable economic vulnerability and similar alienation from the instruments of production—see the world differently and therefore approach it differently.

Of course, the various local cultures in the United States, when viewed abstractly, arise from a common biological imperative: the need to live. In this sense, all humans are basically the same. But the similar imperative spawns different cultural responses. Steinbeck, usually in the role of the omniscient narrator, discusses the biological roots of what some readers might prematurely judge as gratuitous, misanthropic behavior. He reinterprets the gestures and remarks of the rich as expressions of acquired habits of survival. The aforementioned vignette about well-heeled customers at a roadside hamburger stand illustrates the novelist's Darwinian approach to culture. The waitress and the truckers, who are sitting at the counter, despise the arrogance and close-fisted behavior of the bourgeois couple that stops at the eatery. The pair's effronteries include grimacing at the food and refusing to give the tired waitress a reasonable tip. After the couple leaves, the waitress and the patrons call the visitors "shitheels."[46] But in the middle of the passage Steinbeck offers readers insight as to the origins of the rude behavior of the bourgeoisie. The narrator explains that years of dog-eat-dog competition for sales and customers had turned the pair into people who, despite their relative wealth, mistrust hired help, instinctively pinch pennies, and readily see scams where none exist. Their excessive frugality and suspicion are the byproducts of years of trying to avoid bankruptcy and want—they are not signs of amoral character flaws, of unprovoked meanness and rudeness, as the other patrons in the diner mistakenly presume.[47]

Steinbeck's novel relies on the local cultural diversity within the United States to explain both why rebellions do not often happen and why (in his opinion) they soon will occur. Steinbeck is far from being an immiseration theorist who contends that material suffering, if intense enough, will automatically provoke rebellious behavior. The novel describes in detail the hard times facing many kinds of nonwealthy people, including truckers, clerks, gas-station attendants, and Native Americans who have been forcibly expelled from their lands. In the story most nonwealthy Americans live in misery and feel discontent, but they endure hard times in silence. Only one social group refuses to accept its fate: recently evicted small farmers.

In Steinbeck's story, the capacity for rebellion of the dispossessed small farmers has two equally important taproots: yeoman-farmer lifestyles and the threat of imminent death.[48] Having worked their own property without supervision or orders from outsiders and having lived for decades on the frontier with minimal public services and government directives, the so-called Okies have acquired over the years a self-reliant, willful outlook lacking among other poor people. These are, the narrator informs us, "families which had lived on a little piece of land, who had lived and died on forty acres, had eaten or starved on the produce of forty acres. . . . There in the Middle- and Southwest had lived a simple agrarian folk who had not changed with industry, who had not farmed with machines or known the power and danger of machines in private hands. They had not grown up in the paradoxes of industry. Their senses were still sharp to the ridiculousness of the industrial life."[49]

According to the book, the nation's much-vaunted "Jeffersonian" democratic culture of widespread confidence, open-mindedness, and versatility is not found among all classes and in all places. Wealthy Americans are too greedy, satiated, and fearful of losing privileges to want to share power with the propertyless and less well off. The prosperous become close-minded and hard-hearted. Members of the proletariat, meanwhile, suffer from patterns of mechanized production, habits of obedience, and fears of unemployment. They tend to be timorous—at least in Steinbeck's story.

Small farmers, however, have cultivated a spirit of initiative and self-reliance that is derived from years of self-directed production with hand tools. The daily challenges of taming the soil produce lifestyles that lack hierarchy, diffidence, or conformity. The resultant mind-set, according to Steinbeck, can be seen in the ritualized family meetings of small farmers, where all adults—male and female, elders and young folks—confidently express their opinions and vote on proposals.[50]

Penniless and starving, the former farming families in the novel meet serendipitously on roadsides and in makeshift camps. In such short-lived, intimate settings and without any appointed leader or organizer, they talk about their similar problems and gradually acquire a new outlook on social institutions. "Because they were all going to a new mysterious place, they huddled together; they talked together; they shared their lives, their food, and the things they hoped for in the new country."[51] Over time, the small acts of kindness become habitual among these nomads, and social thought and affection stretch accordingly: "In the evening a strange thing happened: the twenty families became one family, the children were the children of all."[52]

Steinbeck (again, in the role of the narrator) tells us that as they struggle to survive, families quietly jettison some of their older notions of right and wrong behavior, which no longer seem appropriate, and, conversely, experiment with novel moral values and social duties: "And the families learned, although no one told them, what rights are monstrous and must be destroyed. . . . And as the worlds moved westward, rules became laws, although no one told the families."[53] The threat of starvation unleashes the migrants' imaginations. The yearning onetime farmers sometimes even contemplate sharing property and collectively owning machinery in the future: "If this tractor were ours it would be good—not mine, but ours. . . . We could love that tractor then as we have loved this land when it was ours."[54] They occasionally even wonder about seizing land from absentee landlords.[55]

Alongside these grassroots changes in popular ideas about right and wrong conduct, moral outrage over the broader organization of American society mounts. The personal feelings of disappointment and worry turn into a collective anger at current economic arrangements. Former farmers look at corporate-owned land, which is kept fallow to keep prices high, as "a sin and the unused land a crime against the thin children."[56] The narrator contends that the fermentation of righteous wrath among the small farmers, which is spontaneously communicated, inevitably leads to a willingness to challenge authorities and to seize property. The narrator predicts that in the coming battle, large landowners must lose, partly because of their small numbers: "Here is the node, you who hate change and fear revolution. Keep these two squatting men apart; make them hate, fear, suspect each other. Here is the anlage of the thing you fear. This is the zygote."[57]

In the novel, the narrator expects that big businesses will try to intimidate the poor through the laws against the migrants and vigilante violence. But repression against the dispossessed farmers must backfire because it reinforces collective anger rather than breeding timidity. Vigilante attacks and police raids, ironically, do not help the wealthy but are the "means that in the long run would destroy them. Every little means, every violence, every raid on a Hooverville, every fat-assed deputy swaggering through a ragged camp put off the day a little and cemented the inevitability of the day."[58]

Steinbeck, as narrator, seems to accept (and perhaps even approve of) the coming violence between the former small-scale farmers and the agribusinesses, for he declares that there is no point in attempting to reason with rich folks and to build reform alliances across classes. The plutocracy in California foolishly believes that radicals from abroad plant seditious ideas in the otherwise patient and grateful American workers. The rich, furthermore, cannot comprehend that their incomes and status depend on the suffering of others: "If you who own the things people must have could understand this, you might preserve yourself. If you could separate causes from results, if you could know that Paine, Marx, Jefferson, Lenin, were results, not causes, you might survive. But that you cannot know."[59] The rich cannot know because decades of inordinate comfort and privilege, alongside daily scheming and life-and-death struggles against fellow entrepreneurs, preclude appreciation of the sufferings and sacrifices of wage earners.

The narrator's periodic prophecies of capitalism's inevitable doom at times resemble the grave-digging passages of Marx and Engels's *Communist Manifesto*. For instance, Steinbeck writes that "the companies, the banks worked at their own doom and they did not know it."[60] This may explain why some scholars and commentators criticize *The Grapes of Wrath* on the grounds that it resembles old-fashioned Communist art. Leslie Fiedler, for one, contends that the novel's vision would please "the Cultural Commissars in Moscow." [61]

Steinbeck's tack, however, is different from those of theorists of vanguard parties and proletarian revolutions. He insists that desires to remake American society arise, in the last analysis, from the biological need to survive and then from habits and outlooks fostered in local communities, not from political organization by outsiders. As the narrator puts it, "Need is the stimulus to concept, concept to action."[62] In the novel, political education by "bolshevisky" organizers is marginal to the former farmers' predilection toward activism.[63] The need to survive provides sufficient motivation for those with self-reliant lifestyles to question authority, and frontier-based norms provide a sufficiently strong cognitive and emotional foundation for imaging a new social order. On their own, the farmers have the ability to imagine and experiment with new institutions and norms.

One reason that the former farmers can rebel against corporate capitalism involves the gender roles spawned in frontier communities. Mother figures abound in *The Grapes of Wrath* and dominate its final scenes; fathers and sons become less salient.[64] The prominence of maternal figures relates to their distinctive capacity to imagine what Ma Joad calls the human "fambly."[65] Having been raised on farms to be tenacious, self-directing, and self-reliant, the males are infatuated with the opportunities that they believe a market economy offers enterprising individuals. Only after repeated failures to find employment do some men dare to alter their thinking. Mothers and grandmothers on family farms, in contrast, toil day in and day out without monetary compensation or public honors. In the shadows and corners of the farmstead, they develop an ethic of service and self-sacrifice. They come to see themselves as patient nurturers of helpless children and of bruised and tired men. This outlook, inherited from past generations and reinforced daily, inoculates rural women from the men's grandiose dreams of personal success within a market economy. The eager, risk-taking ethos, bubbling within an ambitious "man on the make," is absent from the women's consciousness. They are cautious and protective of others and value social interdependence. In the words of Ma Joad, "Man, he lives in jerks—baby born an' a man dies, an' that's a jerk—gets a farm an' loses his farm, an' that's a jerk. Woman, its all one flow, like a stream, little eddies, little waterfalls, but the river, it goes right on. Woman looks at it like that."[66]

The significance of this maternal culture perhaps is best illustrated in Ma Joad's refusal to allow the men of the family to leave in small numbers to search for lucrative jobs and then reassemble in a few months with high wages in hand. Steinbeck, as the narrator, perhaps to highlight the political lessons of the incident, twice calls Ma Joad's defiance of the males' wishes a "revolt."[67] Ma, finding the money-gathering strategy destructive of the family's collective identity, seizes a jack handle and threatens to bash her husband if he and the others go through with their plan. The men in the novel find her intense distrust of market opportunities irrational, akin to the seemingly thoughtless motions of a wild jackrabbit. They nonetheless believe that she means what she says and, therefore, may well use the potential murder weapon. They defer in exasperation.

If one equates politics with government, Steinbeck's vision is arguably antipolitical and even anarchistic. The book says very little about the role of municipal and state government in promoting justice or serving citizens or initiating social reform. With the partial exception of Weedpatch camp, no government initiative is presented in a positive light.[68] Rather, government is portrayed overwhelmingly as a corrupted tool of powerful, self-interested, and well-organized business groups. Officials—from police officers to health inspectors—throw derogatory language at the migrants and other desperately poor people. When large landowners request police support, it is available at a moment's notice. If, however, seasonal workers are starving or have no shelter, government officials do little, citing bureaucratic regulations and red tape as their justification for inaction.[69]

Throughout the story, local property owners—to prevent the poor from settling, sharing resources, and acquiring power—sponsor antiloitering laws, lobby for health codes that are biased against the impoverished transients, deploy armed sheriffs and deputies, and fund extralegal violence (including the tarring and feathering of suspected union organizers). After repeatedly being ignored and rebuffed by public officials, the migrants begin to distrust the political system. They see it as a tool of organized interests and as only superficially democratic. The migrants conclude that they can trust only themselves. In the words of Ma Joad, "I'm learnin' one thing good. . . . Learnin' it all a time, ever'day. If you're in trouble or hurt or need—go to poor people. They're the only ones that'll help—the only ones."[70]

According to statements by both the narrator and the fictional Okies in the novel, anger among former yeoman farmers is on the verge of fulmination. The impending rebellion against corporate capitalism will evolve in shantytowns and temporary roadside gatherings—not in conventional hallways of power. And onetime farmers alone will launch it, without help from government institutions.

Steinbeck's Legacy: Conservative Roots of Revolution

The Grapes of Wrath was, among other things, Steinbeck's effort to understand the origins of a revolution that he believed was already taking place. He thought that his group-man approach—with its social-psychological and

Darwinist logic—gave him insight that academics and other political commentators lacked. Shortly after the novel's publication he wrote to a friend, "I have too a conviction that a new world is growing under the old, the way a new finger nail grows under a bruised one. I think all the economists and sociologists will be surprised some day to find that they did not foresee nor understand it. . . . Communist, Fascist, Democrat may find that the real origin of the future lies on the microscope plates of obscure young men, who, puzzled with order and disorder in quantum and neutron, build gradually a picture which will seep down until it is the fibre of the future."[71] Steinbeck believed that he had discovered a new, nonromantic method of analyzing American history. His scientific starting points and field observations jointly told him that a new world was already emerging. *The Grapes of Wrath* was his public forecast.

A geographically dispersed revolution by restive yeoman farmers and dutiful mothers never occurred, however. Steinbeck's non-teleological reasoning and phalanx theory missed something. Perhaps his interest in biological determinism had led him to underestimate the roles of utopian visions and of deliberative, well-organized parties in the construction of new institutions and goals? Perhaps his admiration for the independent traditions of small property owners in the United States and for the self-effacing culture of their wives had led him to misjudge both the political capacities of nonagrarian folk and the actual dreams and nightmares of America's rural workers, many of whom still dreamt of one day owning private property? As a scientific account (albeit in fictional guise) of upcoming social upheaval and political change in the United States, the story is wanting.

But the book's embedded political lessons also can be approached in terms of its genre, independently of our awareness of Steinbeck's scientific principles and aspirations. The book, after all, is a novel; and like many novels, *The Grapes of Wrath* has a subversive side. The book openly questions the purported benefits of America's new economic order. It predicts (and implicitly endorses) an uprising by recently dispossessed small farmers. It celebrates a nonindividualist, antimarket ethic through the words and deeds of its female protagonists, Ma Joad and Rose of Sharon. The novel challenges readers' faith in the fairness of local government and maintains that political democracy in the United States is an illusion. It insists that in the near future the economically and politically last shall be first. In all these ways the book culturally challenges the political status quo, provoking critics and pundits to make statements in this vein: "If only a couple of million overcomfortable people can be brought to read it, John Steinbeck's *The Grapes of Wrath* may actually effect something like a revolution in their minds and hearts."[72] Or as an editorial in *Collier's* put it, *The Grapes of Wrath* "is propaganda for the idea that we ought to trade our system for the Russian system."[73]

Even so, alongside such subversive notions are some strikingly conservative messages. First of all, the novel obscures the ways that rural gender roles might oppress women. Instead, it depicts domestic housekeeping and maternal self-sacrifice as intrinsically rewarding. Ma Joad's countenance is "controlled, kindly" and Rose "smiles mysteriously" after they complete exhausting chores and endure intense physical trials.[74] The book says nothing about the potentially liberating effects for women of working outside the home or about the value of developing identities independent of maternal status. Early on, Steinbeck portrays Rose's early desires for physical pleasure, for a suburban house with labor-saving appliances, and for urban entertainment and excitement as the silly dreams of an immature girl; she triumphantly outgrows the fantasies by the book's conclusion. But might she have had a point in seeing the traditional life of an altruistic farm mother as stultifying, tiring, and constrictive?

The novel, in addition, devalues participation in conventional politics. Few political scientists, political sociologists, or political historians would question the thesis that interest-group politics in the United States has an upper-class bias.[75] But the episodes in Steinbeck's novel cumulatively advance a more extreme position—that local and state governments are responsive *only* to business interests. Might the novel's cynicism dissuade readers from participating in conventional politics and thereby tend to further entrench interest-group power?

Finally, the book's celebration of preindustrial farming culture, when combined with its negative portrayal of the cultural habits of the industrial and urban poor, leads to potentially paternalistic conclusions. In the story, only one class (the former yeomen farmers) appears worthy of political power; other groups of poor folk evoke pity from readers but do not appear deserving of political power. Consider Tom Joad's impatient outburst toward an introspective and fragile gas-station attendant, which is not seriously criticized by anyone in the book (including the narrator) but, to the contrary, appears to be praiseworthy tough love.[76] Throughout the book, truck and tractor drivers and other machine tenders are depicted as drugged into despondency by their dependency on distant bosses and by their monotonous, repetitive labor. Steinbeck writes of an anonymous machine handler on a large corporate farm, "The driver's hands could not twitch because the monster that built the tractor, the monster that sent the tractor out, had somehow got into the driver's hands, into his brain and muscle, had goggled him and muzzled him—goggled his mind, muzzled his speech, goggled his perception, muzzled his protest."[77] The book implies that industrial culture has imposed a natural limit on the number of poor people who will have the self-esteem and abilities necessary to act for themselves. Those who are not from small-farm backgrounds are, for better or worse, doomed to be the playthings of their time. They can be helped, but it is presumed that they should not be expected to be the agents of their own liberation.[78]

The Grapes of Wrath, in sum, fosters political ambivalence within readers when it is read closely. The book is sacrilegious about some common ethical and political beliefs that Americans hold dear (such as the democratic workings of local government and the beneficence of a free-market economy). In that sense, it carries a radical political message that runs against the American grain. Yet the book's tone is reverential toward other conventional habits and beliefs, such as the proper social duties of women and the purported cultural benefits of freely laboring on one's own land.[79] This perennially popular novel, while relentlessly attacking the ideological defenses of laissez-faire industrialization and growing concentration of capital, reaffirms a nostalgic view of preindustrial America and contributes to negative stereotypes of industrial wage earners. Its defense of female domesticity, its celebration of small plots of private property, its fierce attack on municipal and state government, and the distinctions in political capacity that it draws between different classes of poor folk not only constitute important parts of a complex argument about the need for radical social change but also reflect and reinforce some long-standing American predilections. Stated differently, the book's call for wholesale economic change rests on socially conservative grounds. Therein lies its fascination for past and future generations of American readers, who for the most part are not radicals.

Notes

This chapter is a revision and expansion of an argument that appeared in a previously published essay, "John Steinbeck on the Political Capacities of Everyday Folk: Moms, Reds, and Ma Joad's Revolt," *Polity* 36 (July 2004): 595–618. I thank Simon Stow, Michael Meyer, and the two anonymous reviewers for the University Press of Kentucky for their useful comments on earlier drafts.

    1. All quotations are from the Library of America edition of the novel: John Steinbeck, The Grapes of Wrath *and Other Writings, 1936–1941* (New York: Library of America, 1996), 207–692.

    2. The symbolic and sociological readings of the novel are legion. This chapter does not question the value and importance of such readings and, in fact, borrows from some of the nonpolitical interpretations of the text. It chooses, however, to focus on the novel primarily as a political rumination on the state of American democracy. For a sympathetic survey of alternative ways of reading *The Grapes of Wrath,* see Louis Owens, The Grapes of Wrath: *Trouble in the Promised Land* (Boston: Twayne, 1989).

    3. Commentators for decades have debated the historical accuracy of Steinbeck's portrayal of hiring practices in rural California. For a sample of the different opinions that abounded shortly after the publication of the book, see Frank J. Taylor, "California's Grapes of Wrath," *Forum* 102 (November 1939): 232–38; and Carey McWilliams, "California Pastoral," *Antioch Review* 2 (March 1942): 103–21. For a history of the early debates over the accuracy of Steinbeck's story, see Rick Wartzman, *Obscene in the Extreme: The Burning and Banning of John Steinbeck's* The Grapes of Wrath (New York: PublicAffairs, 2008).

    4. Steinbeck, *Grapes of Wrath,* 692.

    5. Martin Shockley, "The Reception of *The Grapes of Wrath* in Oklahoma," *American Literature* 15 (January 1944): 357.

    6. David Wyatt, introduction to *New Essays on* The Grapes of Wrath, ed. David Wyatt (Cambridge: Cambridge University Press, 1990), 3.

    7. The classic scholarly study of *The Grapes of Wrath*'s political reverberations within the United States is Shockley, "Reception of *The Grapes of Wrath*," 351–61. For a contemporary view from the political left, see Samuel Sillen, "Censoring *The Grapes of Wrath*," *New Masses* 32 (September 12, 1939): 23–24. For more recent accounts of the book's reception, see Wyatt, introduction; and Wartzman, *Obscene in the Extreme.*

    8. Nicholas J. Karolides, Margaret Bald, and Dawn B. Sova, *100 Banned Books: Censorship Histories of World Literature* (New York: Checkmark Books, 1999), 43–56.

9. Quoted in Lary May, *The Big Tomorrow: Hollywood and the Politics of the American Way* (Chicago: University of Chicago Press, 2000), 177.

10. Stephen Schwartz, *From West to East: California and the Making of the American Mind* (New York: Free Press, 1998), 310.

11. Donald L. Siefker, "Steinbeck and Best Sellers," *Steinbeck Quarterly* 11 (Summer–Fall 1978): 106; Wyatt, introduction, 3.

12. Arthur Miller, *Echoes down the Corridor: Collected Essays, 1944–2000* (New York: Viking Press, 2000), xi.

13. Howard Zinn, *The Future of History: Interviews with David Barsamian* (Monroe, Me.: Common Courage Press, 1999), 87–88, 144–45.

14. *The Grapes of Wrath* ranked tenth on the Modern Library list of "100 Best Novels of the 20th Century" and third on the Radcliffe Publishing Program's "100 Best Novels of the 20th Century."

15. The following historical summary draws on Jackson J. Benson, *The True Adventures of John Steinbeck, Writer* (New York: Viking Press, 1984); Thomas Kiernan, *The Intricate Music: A Biography of John Steinbeck* (Boston: Little Brown, 1979); Anne Loftis, *Witnesses to the Struggle: Imaging the 1930s California Labor Movement* (Reno: University of Nevada Press, 1998); Jay Parini, *John Steinbeck: A Biography* (New York: Henry Holt, 1995); and Kevin Starr, *Endangered Dreams: The Great Depression in California* (Oxford: Oxford University Press, 1996). Some additional information comes from the taped oral history collection at the National Steinbeck Center in Salinas, California, and from newspaper holdings at the Salinas Public Library.

16. John Steinbeck, "Always Something to Do in Salinas," in *America and Americans and Selected Nonfiction*, ed. Susan Shillinglaw and Jackson J. Benson (New York: Viking Press, 2002), 8–9.

17. For political histories of Salinas during the first third of the twentieth century, see Robert B. Johnston, *Salinas, 1875–1950: From Village to City* (Salinas, Calif.: Fidelity Savings and Loan Association, 1980); Jennie Dennis Verardo and Denzil Verardo, *The Salinas Valley: An Illustrated History* (Sacramento, Calif.: Windsor, 1989).

18. Steinbeck, "Always Something to Do in Salinas," 6.

19. Steinbeck to George Albee, May 1931, in *Steinbeck: A Life in Letters*, ed. Elaine Steinbeck and Robert Wallsten (New York: Viking Penguin, 1975), 41.

20. *Salinas Daily Index*, February 26, 1933, 1.

21. Josephine Dorneidon Cahill, interview with Pauline Pearson, November 7, 1974; and William Pellissier, interview with Pauline Pearson, May 19, 1975. Pearson's interviews are part of the oral history collection at the National Steinbeck Center, Salinas, California.

22. For an introduction to the topic of women's public roles during the Pro-

gressive period, see Theda Skocpol, *Protecting Soldiers and Mothers: The Political Origins of Social Policy in the United States* (Cambridge: Harvard University Press, 1992), chap. 6.

23. *Salinas Daily Index*, April 25, 1919, 1.

24. Steinbeck, "Always Something to Do in Salinas," 6.

25. Daniel and Lilth James, interview with Pauline Pearson, March 1, 1988. See also Benson, *True Adventures*, 146–47; Parini, *John Steinbeck*, 77, 89–90.

26. Steinbeck's other "proletarian" novels about California's rural poor are *In Dubious Battle* (1936) and *Of Mice and Men* (1937).

27. John Steinbeck, "A Primer on the '30s," in America and Americans *and Selected Nonfiction*, 25.

28. Steinbeck to George Albee, 1936, in Steinbeck, *Life in Letters*, 132.

29. Steinbeck to Elizabeth Otis, February 1938, ibid., 158.

30. Steinbeck took great pleasure in writing letters. A small sample of his correspondence can be found in *Steinbeck: A Life in Letters.* Many letters remain in university collections or in the private possession of Steinbeck's friends.

31. For an introduction to Steinbeck's phalanx theory and its uses in *The Grapes of Wrath*, see Owens, Grapes of Wrath: *Trouble in the Promised Land*, 65–76. For biographical interpretations of the development of the phalanx theory, see Benson, *True Adventures*, 200–10, 234–50, 265–70; and Parini, *John Steinbeck*, 101–11, 136–37, 152–59, 162–69.

32. Steinbeck to Pascal Covici, January 16, 1939, in Steinbeck, *Life in Letters*, 178.

33. Steinbeck to Pascal Covici, January 3, 1939, ibid., 175.

34. Steinbeck to Carlton A. Sheffield, June 21, 1933; to George Albee, 1933; and to George Albee, 1934, ibid., 74–77, 79–82, 92–94.

35. For Steinbeck's fictional depictions of the painful process of childhood socialization and indoctrination, see chapters 5, 8, and 10 of *The Pastures of Heaven*, which is included in John Steinbeck, *Novels and Stories, 1932–1937* (New York: Library of America, 1994). For a fictional illustration of the mysterious voices of our ancestors that we hear and that control our priorities, see *To a God Unknown*, which is also included in *Novels and Stories, 1932–1937*.

36. See, for instance, the short stories titled "The Harness," "The Vigilante," and "Johnny Bear" in *The Long Valley* (which is included in The Grapes of Wrath *and Other Writings*) and *Pastures of Heaven*, chapter 5. The topic of psychological repression and biological resistance also appears in *The Grapes of Wrath*, when Al Joad, Jim Casy, and Uncle John describe the anxiety and guilt that they suffer as they try to reconcile their biological drives with normative demands.

37. Steinbeck to Carl Wilhelmson, August 9, 1933, in Steinbeck, *Life in Letters*, 87. Modern readers may find Steinbeck's statement about Freud's and Jung's

"inadequate" accounts of libido astonishing. Because Steinbeck never published a study on the concept of libido, it is difficult to discern his exact meaning. One possibility is that in the 1920s and 1930s both Freud and Jung were read in the United States primarily as therapists who believed that humans have the ingenuity to channel their periodically unhealthy flows of libido in healthy directions. Perhaps Steinbeck, who at the time suffered acutely from what he called "melancholy" and who wrote in a letter that his wife "was ready for a breakdown," had doubts about the ego's strength vis-à-vis unruly emotions and conjectured that some self-destructive movements of libido are simply irresistible? For a personal letter that supports such an understanding, see Steinbeck to Carl Wilhelmson, 1933 (day and month unknown), in Steinbeck, *Life in Letters*, 86. For an example of Steinbeck's earliest historical fiction, in which settlers of California are represented as barely able to master their wild flows of libido, see *To a God Unknown* (1933), which, interestingly enough, Steinbeck composed while he and Joseph Campbell were jointly analyzing and contrasting the ideas of Freud and Jung. See Parini, *John Steinbeck*, 119.

38. For more on Steinbeck's use of Darwinian theories, see Brian E. Railsback, *Parallel Expeditions: Charles Darwin and the Art of John Steinbeck* (Moscow: University of Idaho Press, 1995).

39. Steinbeck's most sustained discussion of non-teleological thinking appears in *The Log from the Sea of Cortez*, in The Grapes of Wrath *and Other Writings*, 820–23, 858–75, 886–87, 948–52, 963–64.

40. For an elaboration of some differences between Darwinian and Lamarckian visions of social change, see Michael R. Rose, *Darwin's Spectre: Evolutionary Biology in the Modern World* (Princeton, N.J.: Princeton University Press, 1998), 35–36, 75–78.

41. The death of human communities fascinated Steinbeck during the 1930s and was a central theme in several of his books that preceded *The Grapes of Wrath*, including *Pastures of Heaven* (published in 1932), *To a God Unknown* (1933), and *Tortilla Flat* (1935).

42. Steinbeck to Elizabeth Otis, April 1935, in Steinbeck, *Life in Letters*, 109–10.

43. Steinbeck to Louis Paul, February 1936, ibid., 120.

44. Steinbeck, *Grapes of Wrath*, 374–75.

45. Ibid., 400–404.

46. Ibid., 375.

47. Ibid., 374–75.

48. For other opinions about Steinbeck's views on yeoman farmers, see Chester E. Eisinger, "Jeffersonian Agrarianism in *The Grapes of Wrath*," *University of Kansas City Review* 14 (Winter 1947): 149–54; Horst Groene, "Agrarianism

and Technology in Steinbeck's *The Grapes of Wrath*," *Southern Review* 9 (1976): 27–31; Owens, Grapes of Wrath: *Trouble in the Promised Land*, 51–54.

49. Steinbeck, *Grapes of Wrath*, 510.

50. Ibid., 315–19, 356–58, 386–91.

51. Ibid., 416.

52. Ibid.

53. Ibid., 417.

54. Ibid., 370.

55. Ibid., 458–64.

56. Ibid., 459.

57. Ibid., 370.

58. Ibid., 464.

59. Ibid., 371.

60. Ibid., 512.

61. Leslie Fiedler, "Looking Back after 50 Years," *San Jose Studies* 16 (1990): 56.

62. Steinbeck, *Grapes of Wrath*, 371.

63. Ibid., 415. In the novel, a former minister—Jim Casy—teaches one of the Joad men the value of union organizing, but Casy's political insights are derived from neither a formal Christian nor communist ideology but primarily from living alongside and observing the Joads (Ma Joad, in particular). Casy is less an outside agitator than a mouthpiece for the people. For different perspectives on Steinbeck's views of labor organizing, see Helen Lojek, "Jim Casy: Politico of the New Jerusalem," *Steinbeck Quarterly* 15 (Winter–Spring 1982): 30–37; Richard S. Pressman, "'Them's Horses—We're Men': Social Tendency and Counter-Tendency in *The Grapes of Wrath*," *Steinbeck Quarterly* 19 (Summer/Fall 1986): 71–79.

64. For further discussion of matriarchy in *The Grapes of Wrath*, see Warren Motley, "From Patriarchy to Matriarchy: Ma Joad's Role in *The Grapes of Wrath*," *American Literature* 54 (October 1982): 397–412; Nellie Y. McKay, "'Happy[?]-Wife-and-Motherdom': The Portrayal of Ma Joad in John Steinbeck's *The Grapes of Wrath*," in Wyatt, *New Essays*, 47–69.

65. The promotion of nonindividualist thinking is not women's only cultural function in Steinbeck's pre-1940s short stories and novels. Strong wives and mothers also help men stay focused on laboring and earning money (and not spending it on bodily pleasure). See, for example, Steinbeck's "The Harness" and "Johnny Bear" in *The Long Valley*.

66. Steinbeck, *Grapes of Wrath*, 660.

67. Ibid., 389.

68. Weedpatch camp provides a temporary refuge for the Joads and other migrant farmworkers. The camp is run democratically, with the families ruling

themselves through a system of elections, committees, and assemblies. The camp, however, owns neither fields nor farm machinery and therefore does not have the power to provide work and jobs for the rural poor. Ma Joad quickly recognizes the inadequacy of the camp. At her behest, the family leaves. Steinbeck, *Grapes of Wrath*, 513–94.

69. Ibid., 437–38, 463, 469, 670.

70. Ibid., 610.

71. Steinbeck to Carlton A. Sheffield, November 13, 1939, in Steinbeck, *Life in Letters*, 194.

72. Quoted in Parini, *John Steinbeck*, 220.

73. Quoted in Sillen, "Censoring *The Grapes of Wrath*," 24.

74. Steinbeck, *Grapes of Wrath*, 288, 692.

75. See, for example, E. E. Schattschneider's seminal work on interest-group politics, *The Semisovereign People: A Realist's View of Democracy in America* (New York: Holt, Rinehart and Winston, 1960).

76. Steinbeck, *Grapes of Wrath*, 400–404.

77. Ibid., 246.

78. The racist implications of Steinbeck's distinction (between poor people who are ready for democracy and poor people who are not) remain latent in *The Grapes of Wrath*. They are much more manifest in Steinbeck's 1930s journalistic essays, where he talks about the superior political capacities of "white" laborers, in contrast to the cultural submissiveness of Mexican workers and other "little brown men." See, for example, his newspaper articles that were later published as a booklet, *Their Blood Is Strong*, and that are included in The Grapes of Wrath *and Other Writings*, 991–94, 1015–19, 1022. See also the discussions of "degenerate groups" in Steinbeck, *Log from the Sea of Cortez*, 823, 921–23, 950–52. For additional discussions of Steinbeck's distinctions between active and quiescent poor folk, see Jackson J. Benson and Anne Loftis, "John Steinbeck and Farm Labor Unionization: The Background of *In Dubious Battle*," *American Literature* 52 (1980): 194–223; Kevin Hearle, "These Are American People: The Spectre of Eugenics in *Their Blood Is Strong* and *The Grapes of Wrath*," in *Beyond Boundaries: Rereading John Steinbeck*, ed. Susan Shillinglaw and Kevin Hearle (Tuscaloosa: University of Alabama Press, 2002), 243–55; Louis Owens, "Writing 'in Costume': The Missing Voices of *In Dubious Battle*," in *John Steinbeck: The Years of Greatness, 1936–1939*, ed. Tetsumaro Hayashi (Tuscaloosa: University of Alabama Press, 1993), 77–94.

79. Stephen Railton holds a different interpretation of Steinbeck's view of private property and maintains that "Steinbeck's antagonist in the novel is not the group of large owners, but rather the idea of ownership itself." Railton cites several passages in *The Grapes of Wrath* where characters express longing for a vaguely

communal existence. Railton's interpretation of Steinbeck as a sentimental socialist contains at least a grain of truth but, in my opinion, fails to appreciate Steinbeck's repeated celebration of the salutary effects of small holdings on farmers. Stephen Railton, "Pilgrims' Politics: Steinbeck's Art of Conversion," in Wyatt, *New Essays*, 31; Steinbeck, *Grapes of Wrath*, 248–49.

CHAPTER 2

Star Signals: John Steinbeck in the American Protest Literature Tradition

Zoe Trodd

Canons and Culture

> "They ain't gettin' rid a me."
> —Muley, in *The Grapes of Wrath*

"A WRITER . . . IS TRYING to communicate like a distant star sending signals," observed John Steinbeck in 1955—"to tell a story begging the listener to say—and to feel—'Yes, that's the way it is, or at least that's the way I feel it. You're not as alone as you thought.'"[1] Although he did not anticipate a widespread and explosive response to *The Grapes of Wrath* (1939), he did hope to achieve more with its publication than a place in America's literary canon. After researching squatter camps in August 1936, he published a series of seven newspaper articles titled "The Harvest Gypsies" for the left-leaning *San Francisco News*. Then, in February and March 1938, he saw flooding in Visalia. "I want to put a tag of shame on the greedy bastards who are responsible for this," he noted in a letter denouncing "the fascist group of utilities and banks and huge growers."[2] To his literary agent, Elizabeth Otis, he explained, "Four thousand families, drowned out of their tents are really starving to death. . . . The newspapers won't touch the stuff but they will under my byline. The locals are fighting the government bringing in food and medicine. I'm going to try to break the story hard enough so that food and drugs can get moving. Shame and a hatred of publicity will do the job to the miserable local bankers."[3]

He intended to "see if I can't do something to help," and though in one letter of February 1938 he acknowledged how "mean and little books become in the face of such tragedies," in another letter the following month he rejected "the argument that one person's effort can't really do anything."[4] His newspaper articles and the Visalia experience formed the core of *The Grapes of Wrath*. As Steinbeck explained, he was trying with the novel to "write history while it is happening"—to send star signals that readers might see and understand.[5]

Once released, the book was a publishing sensation, the only protest novel of the 1930s to reach a mass audience. "I have read a book recently; it is called *The Grapes of Wrath*," said President Franklin D. Roosevelt in a radio address of January 1940. There were five hundred thousand Americans living in the book's covers, Roosevelt added, proclaiming, "I would like to see the California Columbia Basin devoted to [their] care."[6] His copy of Steinbeck's novel was one of 428,900 sold in its first year of publication. *The Grapes of Wrath* stayed atop of best-seller lists through 1940, and more than 543,000 copies were sold by 1941. The Farm Security Administration (FSA) photographer Russell Lee set out to find a real version of the Joad family and eventually published a westward narrative of the Elmer Thomas family; *Look* magazine published a series of FSA images captioned with *Grapes of Wrath* quotations. Some agreed with Steinbeck that an individual *could* help. "If there are transient camps, and better working conditions, and a permanent agency seeking to help migratory workers," wrote documentary filmmaker Pare Lorentz in 1941, then "Steinbeck [and Dorothea Lange] . . . have done more for these tragic nomads than all the politicians of the country."[7]

The public response exploded *against* Steinbeck, as well. The executive council of the Associated Farmers of California said the novel was factually incorrect and that it created "antagonism and class hatred." Others termed it "the most damnable outrage ever perpetrated in California."[8] The novel was ritually burned, publicly banned, and, as with Harriet Beecher Stowe's *Uncle Tom's Cabin* (1852) and Edward Bellamy's *Looking Backward* (1888), was attacked in spin-offs, including a pamphlet (*Grapes of Gladness*), a film (*Plums of Plenty*), and a novel (*Of Human Kindness*). (For more on the diverse political responses to Steinbeck's book, see the prologue, by Rick Wartzman, and chapter 1, by Cyrus Ernesto Zirakzadeh.)

Although the novel no longer prompted this kind of political outrage by the turn of the twenty-first century, it *had* become literary cannon fodder—repeatedly attacked by scholars. In 2002, the centennial year of Steinbeck's birth, Martin Arnold observed in the *New York Times* that Steinbeck's writing was considered "too sentimental for great art, his writing simply not good enough." Steinbeck has never been "too popular among the higher academics of literature," Arnold added, going on to note that Harold Bloom considers Steinbeck "a poorer Hemingway," not worthy of inclusion in the canon's American division.[9] Other journalists took up the same theme that year. Henry Kisor wrote that "high-minded professors of literature" disdained Steinbeck, and Jessica Winter concluded that while he might be taught in American high schools, his work makes a "surreptitious exit once budding scholars pack their bags for college."[10]

Long before the centennial examination of Steinbeck's literary legacy, scholars had periodically acknowledged his marginalized place in the Western canon. In 1970 Robert Richards questioned the lasting value of *The Grapes of Wrath,* and in 1995 Benjamin Griffith claimed that Steinbeck had been banished to literary obscurity.[11] In 1993 Jackson J. Benson insisted that the "chances of reading Steinbeck in an English class in a major university are very low, and in the Ivy League practically zero," and in 2000 Mary Brown reported that less than 20 percent of 150 university English departments were teaching *The Grapes of Wrath* (largely because the book is not "good enough").[12] Some commentaries on Steinbeck's literary positioning suggest that this rejection by canon makers is due to the political nature of his work. For example, Benson points to the "original categorization [of *The Grapes of Wrath*] as a propaganda novel or social document."[13]

But precisely *because* of its categorization as a "social document," *The Grapes of Wrath* continues to excite those with an "interest in the relationship between radical politics and . . . fiction" (as Alan Trachtenberg observed to Arnold for his 2002 *New York Times* article). For scholars of cultural history and American studies, *The Grapes of Wrath* stands alongside *Uncle Tom's Cabin* and Upton Sinclair's *The Jungle* (1906) as one of the most important American novels ever published. If there was a Steinbeck revival under way, wrote Arnold, then the "new evangelism comes from American studies programs and their examinations of history's disinherited."[14]

Perhaps, declared Susan Shillinglaw and Kevin Hearle in their centennial volume of essays, Steinbeck's "place in the much-debated literary 'canon'" had become "unsettled, uncertain."[15]

In fact, even before these centennial reassessments of Steinbeck's legacy critics had positioned him in a *different* canon, what Jane Tompkins might term a canon of "cultural work."[16] In 1963 Granville Hicks called *The Grapes of Wrath* "an almost perfect example of social protest" and one of three novels of the 1930s that deserves to be remembered.[17] In 1996 James Gilbert argued that Steinbeck's work might have influenced public opinion on the justice system and shifted attention from gangsters to corrupt public officials in the 1930s, and in 2000 Carl Jensen celebrated *The Grapes of Wrath* as, quite simply, a book that "changed America."[18]

Steinbeck's rejection by literature's canon makers and his celebration by scholars of "cultural work" leaves him between two extremes—trapped in the seemingly unclosable blank space between "literature" and "protest." As John Stauffer argued in 2006, in an essay defining the "protest literature" genre, there has been "no common understanding of protest literature; the term has been used to mean virtually all literature . . . or no literature." Either, Stauffer explained, "all novels [are] a form of protest," and so the term *protest literature* becomes tautology, or else "literature [is] a hermetic text, divorced from politics and ideology"—the term "something of an oxymoron."[19] Sure enough, even when scholars *have* mentioned Steinbeck's place within some kind of protest canon, they have neglected to define that canon's boundaries. John Seelye, for example, discusses Steinbeck in the tradition of sentimental protest, asserting along the way that the term "sentimental novel" is complex and worth defining but that the term "protest novel" can be taken for granted: "surely all of us can agree what a protest novel is."[20]

Theorizing Steinbeck in the tradition of American protest literature reveals the coherent and unique qualities of that genre. It also reveals the relationship between literary form and political content in his work and shows that he fused aesthetics and ideologies to create a *politics of form.* That is, his aesthetic choices—symbols, rhythms, echoes, and syntax—express both cultural change and social conflict. This politics of form moves Steinbeck beyond the either/or tensions of Western canon versus cultural history. It reestablishes his place within a canon of cultural work, repositions him as a writer of literary sophistication, and establishes his place as not either/or but both: as a writer within the canon of American protest literature.[21]

The Politics of Form

> Storytellers . . . spoke in great rhythms. . . . Listeners became great
> through them.
> —John Steinbeck, *The Grapes of Wrath*

American protest writers try to remake their country. Living in a partially
achieved nation and asking America to *be* America, they take "a role beyond that of entertainer," as Ralph Ellison once put it. "American fiction
has played a special role in the development of the American nation," he
argued. Protesting the failed promises of the democratic experiment, artists redraw its blueprints—sensing, like Ellison's character in *Juneteenth*
(1999), that "'in this great, inventive land man's idlest dreams are but the
blueprints and mockups of emerging realities.'"[22]

That process of redrawing America's blueprints involves balancing the
exigencies of protest and aesthetics. Alain Locke described this balancing
act in 1928, advising that beauty is literature's "best priest" and that psalms
are "more effective than sermons," though "propaganda itself is preferable to
shallow, truckling imitation."[23] Similarly attuned to the need to balance politics and form, Glenway Wescott said in 1938 of Walker Evans's photographs,
"For me this is better propaganda than it would be if it were not aesthetically
enjoyable. It is because I enjoy looking that I go on looking until the pity and
the shame are impressed upon me, unforgettably."[24] While Evans and other
protest artists did take on a "role beyond . . . entertainer," they also offered
pleasure in the moment of confrontation and expressed faith in the power of
literature's form to heighten that confrontation with its protest content.

Making form central to political protest, for example, Stowe represents
a black woman and a white woman as equals when she describes both *as*
the food they prepare: the black slave Aunt Chloe is shown trussing chicken
with a face "so glossy as to suggest . . . she might have been washed over
with white of eggs, like one of her own tea rusks" and the white Quaker Rachel Halliday first appears "sorting some dried peaches" with a face "round
and rosy . . . suggestive of a ripe peach."[25] In the twentieth century, Tim
O'Brien's collection of Vietnam stories, *The Things They Carried* (1990),
has a politics of form in the looping from story to story. "Though each
protest medium has its place, *this* form of Vietnam literature matches its
looping subject—the circular war," explained O'Brien.[26]

Steinbeck, on the other hand, suggests in *The Grapes of Wrath* that the literary form itself is untrustworthy. Tom knows that Pa "don't even like word writin'," because "ever' time Pa seen writin', somebody took somepin away from 'im" and when Tom returns from prison, Ma reads his face "for the answer that is always concealed in language."[27] The trucker distrusts people who use "big words," and the Wilsons can barely understand a lady from Massachusetts at all.[28] At times, language seems to be entirely stripped of meaning. It is an empty shell: during the prayer offered by Casy, Granma times her responses to the pauses, for it was "so many years since she had listened to or wondered at the words used," and the others are "trained like dogs" to raise their heads at "Amen."[29] The word *Okie* is also intrinsically meaningless: "Okie means you're scum," explains one man. "Don't mean nothing itself, it's the way they say it." This explanation is immediately followed by an observation about California: "I can't tell you nothin'. You got to go there."[30]

But as the novel progresses, Steinbeck conveys more faith in the power of expressive forms to transform the self and then society. Casy advises Muley to talk because "a sad man can talk the sadness right out of his mouth . . . a killin' man can talk the murder right out of his mouth."[31] Similarly, Ma expresses a belief in language's meaningfulness when she tells Tom to rewrite the death note for Grampa: "Long's you're gonna put one down, it might's well mean somepin'."[32] Then, at the novel's midpoint—during the scenes in the makeshift camp along the highway where a new world is born in miniature ("a world created" by the families themselves) and the people change "as in the whole universe only man can change"—the families speak softly of their homes, their tragedies, their futures and are welded as "one unit" by the songs of a guitar player.[33] Later Casy explains to Tom that he's listening "all the time . . . to people talking. . . . I hear 'em an' I feel 'em."[34] The migrants listen to stories around the campfire and "became great through them."[35] The Joads then offer a last communication to the world in the form of Rose of Sharon's dead baby—released into the water to "[g]o down an' tell 'em," to "talk."[36]

This last communication, and the example of Casy's listening, reveal three major elements of American protest literature's politics of form: shock value (the dead baby will "rot," imagines Uncle John, and shock people into knowledge), empathy ("I hear 'em an' I feel 'em"), and symbolic action (the dead baby scene is a repetition-with-difference of Exodus 2:3, where the *living* baby Moses is placed in a basket on the Nile). (For more on the relationship between *The Grapes of Wrath* and the book of Exodus see chapter 7, by Roxanne Harde.) Protest writers, including Stowe, O'Brien, and Steinbeck, construct their American blueprints through a politics of form comprising these three elements, as Stauffer explains:

> Protest literature employs three rhetorical strategies in the quest to convert audiences. The first two are empathy and shock value. Empathy is central to all humanitarian reform, and protest literature encourages its readers to participate in the feelings of the victims, to "feel their pain." Shock value inspires outrage, agitation, and a desire to correct social ills. The third characteristic of protest literature is "symbolic action," to borrow a term from Kenneth Burke. Symbolic action implies indeterminacy of meaning, rich ambiguity, and open-endedness in the text, which goes beyond the author's intent. It invites dialogue, debate, and interpretation among readers. It points to a distinction between what an author displays and what he betrays. It prevents protest literature from becoming an advertisement, or propaganda, whose purpose is strictly teleological. Advertisements send a clear message and seek to convert their audiences. Symbolic action produces open-ended symbols, giving the text subtlety and nuance, providing an aesthetic experience for readers.[37]

To these three elements can be added a fourth: radical folk memory. Writers have long appropriated the master's tools to dismantle the master's house, but they have also borrowed the tools of earlier protest movements as they redraw America's blueprints.[38] They have made protest literature a kind of radical bricolage: ideas, images, and language stored across time, then transformed by new contexts into a living protest legacy. Steinbeck's politics of form incorporates all four elements.

From Sentiment to Empathy

> "Use' ta be the family was fust. It ain't so now. It's anybody."
> —Ma Joad, in *The Grapes of Wrath*

Comparing *The Grapes of Wrath* to *Uncle Tom's Cabin*, Seelye calls Steinbeck's novel a "work of sentimental fiction, which attempts to enlist our sympathies, to draw from us tears of grief."[39] Like Stowe, "Steinbeck wanted to move his readers, and he could only do so by engaging them with the predicaments of the Joads."[40] The "sentimental impulse is essential to novels of social protest," he concludes, and Steinbeck's is "the greatest sentimental novel of protest of the twentieth century."[41] According to Seelye, readers of Steinbeck's novel were supposed to be moved "to action"—to "enlist" in the migrants' struggle and weep "tears of anger" that are not "idle tears."[42] Seelye, however, fails to expand upon Steinbeck's design: the devices by which tears might become action and the attempt to move readers beyond passive sympathy to the active solidarity of *empathy*.

Beyond Seelye, some critics have dismissed the sentimental elements of the novel as "maudlin . . . overblown," in Leslie Fiedler's famous words, and akin to "the sentimental symbolism of Hollywood," as Edmund Wilson put it.[43] Other critics simply praise Steinbeck's compassion. Charles Poore pointed to his "remarkable sympathy and understanding" for his characters; Peter Monro Jack gushed that "Steinbeck has written a novel from the depths of his heart with a sincerity seldom equaled"; and Louis Kronenberger celebrated the novel's "great indignation and great compassion" and its "largely and tragically felt" theme.[44] In part, this praise is a response to Steinbeck's location of the labor problem within the domestic sphere. As the Joads lose Grampa, Granma, Noah, Connie, Tom, and Rose of Sharon's baby from their unit, the novel appeals to readers' identities as family members themselves—taking care to universalize familial loss when the shopkeeper remarks to Tom, "Seems like you people always lost somebody."[45]

In the protest tradition, however, writers call for empathy (feeling *with*) rather than sympathy (feeling *for*).[46] They propose sharing another's suffering in order to help end it. For example, the opening of *Uncle Tom's Cabin* aligns readers with slaves: we're in the ranks of the slaves from the start, and all evil done is done unto us. On forty-three occasions Stowe directly addresses her readers and emphasizes our bonds to her slave characters.[47] Similarly, James Agee observed in an unpublished passage of *Let Us Now Praise Famous Men* (1941) that he was trying to close the gap between readers and farmers with his circular, repetitive prose style. He wanted readers to experience the boredom of tenant farmers' work. He was asking that "a little might be set upon you of the unspeakable weight, and monotonies of the work itself."[48] Ida B. Wells likewise asks her reader to reach across difference in the last paragraph of her antilynching pamphlet *Southern Horrors* (1892). Demanding a responsibility that extends beyond the page, she concludes, "Nothing is more definitely settled than he must act for himself. . . . by a combination of all these agencies can be effectually stamped out lynch law. . . . 'The gods help those who help themselves.'" The phrase "by . . . all these agencies can be effectively stamped out lynch law" reverses the expected syntax, asking the stumbling reader to work harder and participate in the "stamping out."[49]

Some artists also imagined themselves *as* their subjects. Walt Whitman famously declared that "whoever degrades another degrades me. . . . I do not ask the wounded person how he feels, I myself become the wounded person," and Agee notes in the published version of *Let Us Now Praise Famous Men*, "I become not my own shape and weight and self, but that of each of them . . . so that I know almost the dreams they will not re-member."[50] Authors also often experienced empathy as painful. Lewis Hine needed "spiritual antiseptic" to survive; Sinclair described the "tears and anguish" that went into *The Jungle;* and Steinbeck noted that his visits to Visalia and Nipomo were "heartbreaking."[51]

Steinbeck was participating in a tradition that demands active empa-thy rather than passive sympathy, asking his readers to employ *Einfühlung* ("feeling into") as the starting point for action. His strategy echoes Stowe's arousal of "motherly sympathies" in order that the Mrs. Birds of America might use the long arm of parlor authority to persuade their husbands to resist the Fugitive Slave Act of 1850.[52] He reached for what social scientist C. Daniel Batson terms "perspective taking": the imaginative identification with another's vantage point followed by the stimulation of moral action.[53] *The Grapes of Wrath* offers a form of empathy described by Johann Got-tlieb Fichte. "My wish," wrote Fichte, "is that the reader may become the 'I' who speaks—that readers may understand what is said here . . . actively talk with themselves while reading, pause to consider here and there, draw reckonings, and form decisions. . . . For, thus, by their own work and re-flection, purely out of themselves, readers may develop the actual ways of thinking for which a blueprint is set forth in this book, and build them in their hearts."[54]

With its contrapuntal structure, comprising narrative chapters (even-numbered chapters except 12 and 14, plus chapter 13) and synecdochal inter-chapters (odd-numbered chapters except 13, plus 12 and 14), *The Grapes of Wrath* offers space where, in Fichte's words, readers might "ac-tively talk with themselves while reading, pause to consider here and there, draw reckonings, and form decisions." The inter-chapters were intended, Steinbeck said in a letter of 1953, to "hit the reader below the belt" by offering "the rhythms and symbols of poetry." They would "open him up" and then "while he is open introduce things on a [*sic*] intellectual level."[55] These "rhythms and symbols of poetry" in chapters 1, 3, 7, 9, 11, 23, 27, and 29 include a passage that imitates in prose the rhythms of the square dance that it describes: "Look at that Texas boy . . . with the Cherokee girl."[56] And if the inter-chapters (along with the Joads' story in the narrative chapters) grabbed readers' "hearts," as Fichte puts it, then they also asked readers to pause and "draw reckonings" when confronted by banks, owners, cotton prices, "labor unity," strikes, the theft of land from Mexicans, the "changing economy," and direct questions ("Where does the courage come from?" and "How can a man without property know the ache of ownership?").[57]

Employing what Fichte describes as active participation, Steinbeck seeks to make his reader into the "'I' who speaks." Events in inter-chapters anticipate similar events in narrative chapters: anonymous farmers are pushed off their land, then Tom returns to find his family gone; we witness exploitation in California before the Joads arrive; rain floods camps generally before the Joads begin their struggle with the water level. Readers experience the growing awareness of an inevitable disaster *with* the migrants: the sensation of being caught in an unstoppable flow toward a failed Promised Land is produced through these foreshadowings and thus includes us in Steinbeck's *we*.[58]

Steinbeck continues to create this participatory reader by repeating the second-person *you* in the inter-chapters: "you're buying a sorrow that can't talk," "you may know when the bombs plummet," "you who hate change and fear revolution."[59] This draws us closer to the Joad family, letting them gradually dominate our consciousness. The first narrative chapter is only ten pages long, the same as the first inter-chapter, but by chapter 26 the ratio has become seventy pages to four. The voices of the Joads take over, and readers—now carrying the broader histories and political theories of the earlier, editorializing inter-chapters—can shift from macro to micro, rather than the reverse. No longer asked *first* to care about the family and *then* to receive the narrator's editorializing "message" (as in the unpopular last section of *The Jungle*), readers can now apply the earlier "intellectual levels" as he or she enters the final, grueling episode of chapter 30. With the migrants themselves we have been addressed by Floyd Knowles, "They's stuff ya got to learn."[60] And eventually, in response to the stillbirth and final tableau, we might move beyond a mere heartstrings response to experience the *knowl-*

edgeable empathy of both head and heart—Fichte's "ways of thinking" that are built in the "hearts" and the learned "stuff" mentioned by Floyd.

Our reasoned empathy matters. Steinbeck explained in 1939—echoing Fichte's description of readers who pull meaning "purely out of themselves"—that "the reader must bring the implication to it."[61] But in trying to "make the reader participate in the actuality," as he put it in the same letter, Steinbeck expressed a faith in the reader's capacity for change and in the capacity of that changed individual to change others. Many of the novel's pivotal moments take place in private: Casy's revelation in jail, Tom's revelation when hiding out, the private look between Ma and Rose of Sharon at the novel's end, and Rose of Sharon's private exchange with the sick man. Having witnessed Tom's private conversion in response to Casy's martyrdom—as akin to George's conversion by Uncle Tom in Stowe's novel—the solitary reader might achieve a similar transformation. Like Stowe's readers, Steinbeck's must "see to it that *they feel right*," as Stowe put it in her conclusion to *Uncle Tom's Cabin*.[62] Like Casy, we might move beyond the mere slumming (symbolized in chapter 23 by the movie in which a rich couple "purtend like they's poor") and "hear 'em an . . . feel 'em." Like the migrants who hear stories around a campfire, we might "become great through them."[63]

From Sensation to Shock

> The break would never come as long as fear could turn to wrath.
> —John Steinbeck, *The Grapes of Wrath*

"The ultimate question," argued Allen Ginsberg in 1989, is "how to make poetry that will make people cry." But was "tender heart enough?" he wondered.[64] Fifty years earlier, Richard Wright had wondered the same thing. Troubled by the response to his *Uncle Tom's Children* (1938), he questioned the protest value of sympathy, observing in 1940, "When the reviews of that book began to appear, I realized that I had made an awfully naïve mistake. I found that I had written a book which even bankers' daughters could read and weep over and feel good about. I swore to myself that if I ever wrote another book, no one would weep over it; that it would be so hard and deep that they would have to face it without the consolation of tears."[65] Five years later, in his autobiography *Black Boy* (1945), Wright elaborated on this possible alternative to the "consolation of tears." In the works of H. L. Mencken he had encountered language used "as a weapon": "I pictured the man as a raging demon, slashing with his pen, consumed with hate. . . . yes this man was fighting, fighting with words. He was using words as a weapon, using them as one would use a club." Wright was, he recounted, "jarred and shocked by the style."[66]

Across time, protest artists such as Ginsberg and Wright have slashed at the "tender heart" response with the weapon of shock value. Whether through Hugh Wolfe's suicide in Rebecca Harding Davis's *Life in the Iron Mills* (1861), the meatpacking scenes in *The Jungle,* or Agee's descriptions of masturbation in *Let Us Now Praise Famous Men,* writers have combined shock value with empathy to create their protest readers. Even Stowe employs shock value in her depictions of violence (including Legree striking Tom with a cowhide until "blood . . . trickled down his face"). After one scene in which a slave trader separates mother and child, she warns the reader against becoming desensitized to such alarming scenes: "[The trader's] heart was exactly where yours, sir, and mine could be brought, with proper effort and cultivation. . . . You can get used to such things, too, my friend."[67] Explaining the importance of shock value to protest literature, Tim O'Brien claims that the shock value in his work "awakens the reader, and shatters the abstract language of war." He adds, "So many images of war don't endure for the reader—it's the effect of a TV clip followed by a Cheerios ad. But my fiction asks readers not to shirk or look away."[68]

Anticipating Wright's resistance to the "consolation of tears," Steinbeck utilized the shock-value technique of the protest tradition. The desire to cause "hatred" motivated his first attempt at the novel, he acknowledged to his agent in 1938.[69] He observed in another letter in October of that year, "I think that to large numbers of readers it will be an outrageous book."[70] He considered printing a foreword "warning sensitive people to let [the novel] alone," and upon finishing it, noted to his publishers, "I am not writing a satisfying story. I've done my damnedest to rip a reader's nerves to rags, I don't want him satisfied." Even his own nerves were "tattered" by the book, he added.[71] Sure enough, early reviewers responded to the book's use of shock value. One critic pointed to its "graphic style." Kronenberger wrote that it burned "with no pure gemlike flame, but with hot and immediate fire," and Malcolm Cowley called it one of the "great angry books."[72]

As an act of "literary terrorism," observes Seelye, the book is the equivalent of "John Brown's raid."[73] Spliced amongst the lyrical descriptions of landscape, the rhythms of folk music, and the echoes of newsreels, ad copy, and the Old Testament are the moments that caught the attention of the novel's censors: Grampa scratching his privates, Casy discussing sex with girls in the grass, Ma sitting with Granma's corpse in the desert, Pa assessing toilet facilities at the Weedpatch camp. And beyond these moments, unforeseen violence jolts the reader out of any complacency caused by the novel's foreshadowings—whether the turtle's sudden collision with a truck in the opening pages ("the driver saw the turtle and swerved to hit it") or the swift murder of Casy ("the heavy club crashed into the side of his head").[74]

Most reliant of all on shock value, however, are the climactic scenes in which Uncle John releases Rose of Sharon's baby into the water to "rot an' tell 'em that way" and Rose of Sharon breast-feeds a dying stranger.[75] Here, observed one early reviewer, was a "touch of new . . . horror" before Steinbeck "abruptly halts."[76] Steinbeck's publishers were troubled by what they considered an "abrupt" ending. They told him to revise it—to make the dying stranger an acquaintance and to plant clues earlier that the breast-feeding tableau was on the horizon. But he insisted that it must be "quick" and without "sentiment."[77] Like the terrible swift sword in Julia Ward Howe's hymn from which his title is taken, the ending must strike suddenly.

Steinbeck's readers, with nerves ripped to rags, are therefore asked to experience more than the easy sympathy of those "reformers" mentioned earlier in the novel who "don't bite enough into living to know."[78] The dead baby, a "blue shriveled little mummy," is Steinbeck's ultimate offering to those readers. Placed into an apple box, it symbolizes the anticipated decay of all the shriveling fruit in California ("forced to rot" in the orchards) and of the stillborn myth of an American Eden.[79] Its release by Uncle John into the water brings *him* a release from the guilt he felt over his role in his wife's death. Cursed instead is the society that bore this fruit, and Uncle John presents society with its tree of knowledge and its judgment. Traveling out to "tell 'em," the dead baby offers any witnesses—and by implication readers—a transformation, like John's, from mere guilt to shocked action. Just as Eva's death gives her "the power to work in, and change, the world," as Tompkins notes of *Uncle Tom's Cabin*, so the death of the Joad baby might be a revelation and an incitement to the previously passive reader.[80] Unable to "bite enough into living to know," Steinbeck's middle-class readers have experienced instead the shock of biting into death.

From Symbolism to Symbolic Action

> "Maybe Tom'll kill the fatted calf like for the prodigal in Scripture."
> —Casy, in *The Grapes of Wrath*

In 1957 Steinbeck offered Annie Laurie Williams some advice about the staging of a musical play based on *Of Mice and Men.* "Let your audience *almost* recognize something familiar, and out of that go to your freshness," he noted.[81] Like empathy and shock value, the creation of something "almost" familiar has been a common strategy among protest writers. Seizing the master's tools to dismantle the master's house, they revised the Declaration of Independence in "The Working Men's Party Declaration of Independence" (1829), the "Seneca Falls Declaration of Sentiments" (1848), the "Declaration and Protest of the Women of the United States" (1876), and the "Declaration of Interdependence by the Socialist Labor Party" (1895)—on each occasion using the Founding Fathers' tools to dismantle their house of inequality. Equally, Stowe challenged the dominant discourse while using its tools. *Uncle Tom's Cabin* echoes the Bible and incorporates the sermon, the captivity narrative, the spiritual autobiography, the confession, and the conversion narrative. Putting herself firmly in the prophetic tradition, Stowe used familiar and undeniable biblical home truths and helped turn abolitionism into a divinely sanctioned blueprint for the new, free American interior. Within the antilynching tradition, Ida B. Wells used a similar strategy of appropriation. Fashioning her protest from material generated by lynchers themselves, she quotes white newspapers at length in her pamphlets and explains, "Out of their own mouths shall the murderers be condemned."[82]

These strategies of appropriation create what Stauffer (borrowing from Kenneth Burke) describes as "symbolic action": a "distinction between what an author displays and what he betrays."[83] Displaying the rhetoric of equality, love, and honor in their protest texts that signify upon the Declaration, the Bible, and lynching practice, writers betrayed the hollowness of that rhetoric. They unveiled the "distinction" between the Declaration's language of equality and America's reality, Christianity's doctrines of love and the fact of slavery, lynchers' justifications for violence and the real motivation. In the gap between blueprint and reality—between what *should be* and what *is*—is Stauffer's "indeterminacy of meaning," or what Steinbeck terms the "almost" familiar.

Steinbeck's own symbolic action plays out in two ways in *The Grapes of Wrath*. First, he draws upon America's narrative convention of endless progress and even makes his migrants literal—as well as symbolic—descendants of America's frontiersmen. One migrant shares his experience of fighting Indians; another reiterates, "When grampa came—did I tell you?—he had pepper and salt and a rifle. Nothing else."[54] But these are *strange* descendants of pioneer heroes. Their frontier spirit is thwarted as they move west to find no promised land. Using familiar mythology, Steinbeck challenges it—and offers an alternative to the migration story of movement, conquest, and success.

Second, he sets up a series of Christian symbols and biblical analogies. His migration story refashions the story of Exodus as well as the pioneer narrative. Rose of Sharon is named from Song of Solomon; the novel's title comes from Revelations 17–20 and the "Battle Hymn of the Republic"; Tom tells Ma he'll be "aroun' in the dark . . . ever'where—wherever you look," like the Holy Spirit; Casy shares Christ's initials and has twelve disciples in the Joads, as well as a Judas (Connie); Casy's prayer for Grampa echoes Jesus's command to "let the dead bury their own dead," in Luke 9:60; and Casy dies with the words "You don' know what you're a-doin'," a paraphrase of Jesus's words on the cross in Luke 23:34 ("forgive them for they know not what they do").[85] Finally, the novel's ending—which Steinbeck termed "huge and symbolic" in a journal entry of June 1938—is a Eucharist scene, complete with the Madonna's mysterious smile.[86]

But like his frontier mythology, Steinbeck's Christian symbolism functions ironically—moving beyond symbolism to become symbolic action because it is only *"almost . . . familiar."* The ironically named Noah doesn't witness the flood and abandons the Joads' ark, and unlike Christ, Casy doesn't forgive his murderers. Casy himself further introduces the irony of self-consciousness when he notes the parallels to Christ: "I been in the hills, thinkin', almost you might say like Jesus went into the wilderness to think His way out of a mess of troubles."[87] And the novel's ending is an *anti*-Eucharist, Rose of Sharon an anti-Madonna. Her baby is a dead Moses released onto the river as well as an Old Testament symbol of America's sin (abandoned to rot in an apple box) rather than a New Testament baby Jesus. Instead she holds in her arms, in that "whispering barn," an old man.[88]

As Stephen Railton argues, Steinbeck "insinuates his revolutionary vision by presenting it in the familiar guise of Christianity. . . . Every novel of purpose must make some compromises with its audience if it wants to reach and move them."[89] But when that "familiar guise" becomes what Steinbeck termed the "almost . . . familiar," the novel goes even further than "compromises" and calls for change. It demands that readers close the gap between ideal and reality—between what Frederick Douglass once termed "what is" and "what ought to be." "Poets, prophets, and reformers are all picture-makers, and this ability is the secret of their power and achievements," wrote Douglass in 1864; "they see what ought to be by the reflection of what is, and endeavor to remove the contradiction."[90]

Invited to achieve a knowledgeable empathy with the Joads, shaken alongside that empathy by the novel's shock value, and now floundering in the gap between absolute symbolism and thwarted mythology, readers can "endeavor to remove the contradiction." Casy hopes that people "see it." When he speaks to Tom about the possibility of labor unity, he observes, "I wisht they could see it. I wisht they could see."[91] And having seen the contradiction ("a million people hungry . . . and kerosene sprayed over the golden mountains"), readers might now resolve it by turning symbolic action into *action*. Like an anonymous tenant early in the novel, readers might know that "we've got a bad thing made by men, and by God that's something we can change."[92]

From Amnesia to Memory

> How will we know it's us without our past?
> —John Steinbeck, *The Grapes of Wrath*

Claiming a heritage of dissent, writers arguably have made America a protest nation and have made protest literature the most American of forms. Alongside their strategies of empathy, shock value, and symbolic action, writers have emphasized an American protest tradition and recycled earlier protest literature. They have refused to discard history or participate in what D. H. Lawrence termed "the true myth of America": the "sloughing of the old skin, towards a new youth." Instead, writers have consistently debunked the myth of American history and literature as a series of fresh starts, of America as a perpetual New World.[93] And, with its chosen and reshaped ancestry, protest literature has challenged the pervasive ideas that leftist writing is without memory, never putting down roots, and that only conservatives draw on tradition. Protest literature has been a folk process, old tunes with new words in new circumstances.

For example, Sinclair set out in *The Jungle* to write the *Uncle Tom's Cabin* of wage slavery. He compared chattel slavery to wage slavery and claimed that abolitionism was an early form of socialism. Eugene Debs looked to the abolitionists as his heroes and demanded a John Brown for wage slavery. Ralph Chaplin rewrote the Civil War marching song "John Brown's Body" as "Solidarity Forever" (1915). Ginsberg wanted to speak the unspeakable and called on Whitman as his forebear, Farm Security Administration photographers returned to Hine's survey tradition, and second-wave feminists looked back to feminism's first wave. Numerous other socialist, civil rights, women's rights, abolitionist and antilynching activists, artists, and writers connected their movements to the Revolution and the country's founding and argued that if dissent was treason then Americans were traitors in 1776. Though protesters sought and found new countries, then set sail for better ones, they carried fragments of their past along. Summing up this process in 1920, Floyd Dell argued for an acknowledgment of America's protest heritage: "We do not even know that the literature of America is above everything else a literature of protest and of rebellion. . . . Not knowing the past, we cannot learn by its mistakes. . . . We only slowly come to learn that what we sometimes contemptuously call 'American' is not American at all: that it is, astonishingly enough, *we* who are American: that Debs and Haywood are as American as Franklin and Lincoln."[94]

Steinbeck entered this tradition of radical folk memory; he was keen to fashion *The Grapes of Wrath* into what he called in his journal a "truly American book."[95] He wanted the whole of Julia Ward Howe's hymn (sung to the tune of "John Brown's Body") as a preface. He explained to his editor that "the fascist crowd will try to sabotage this book because it is revolutionary. They try to give it the communist angle. However, The Battle Hymn is American and intensely so. . . . if both words and music are there the book is keyed into the American scene from the beginning."[96] The novel establishes the Americanness of protest. The narrator at one point mentions "Paine,

Marx, Jefferson, Lenin" in one breath—further linking (like Floyd Dell) the American revolutionary tradition with socialism. After all, as Ma explains, the Joads' ancestors "fit in the Revolution."[97]

Continuing to plant fragments of American history—and its history of radical protest—Steinbeck includes folk songs and protest tunes in his novel, such as "Ten-Cent Cotton and Forty-Cent Meat," about the poverty of cotton farmers, sung in South Carolina during the 1920s. Or, moving back to antebellum America, he makes an explicit connection between migrants and slaves, noting that the landowners "imported slaves, although they did not call them slaves: Chinese, Japanese, Mexicans, Filipinos."[98] Further evoking slavery, a boy laboring over some bills of sale repeats the rhetoric of nineteenth-century pseudoscience: "Okies . . . ain't human. . . . They ain't a hell of a lot better than gorillas."[99] Then, a few pages after these examples, Steinbeck prophesizes another civil war: "three hundred thousand—if they ever move under a leader—the end. Three hundred thousand, hungry and miserable; if they ever know themselves, the land will be theirs and all the gas, all the rifles in the world won't stop them."[100]

Material embodiments of folk history appear in the novel. In 1852 Stowe had crafted a vision of folk history when Mrs. Bird looks through her collection of objects: "Mrs. Bird slowly opened the drawer. There were little coats of many a form and pattern, piles of aprons, and rows of small stockings; and even a pair of little shoes, worn and rubbed at the toes, were peeping from the folds of a paper. . . . leaning her head on her hands over it, wept till the tears fell through her fingers into the drawer; then suddenly raising her head, she began, with nervous haste, selecting the plainest and most substantial articles, and gathering them into a bundle."[101] Steinbeck describes a similar situation involving Ma Joad:

> Ma . . . brought out a stationery box, old and soiled and cracked at the corners. She sat down and opened the box. Inside were letters, clippings, photographs, a pair of earrings, a little gold signet ring, and a watch chain of braided hair and tipped with gold swivels. . . . She bit her lower lip, thinking, remembering. And at last she made up her mind. She picked out the ring, the watch charm, the earring, dug under a pile and found one gold cuff link. . . . She lifted the stove lid and laid the box gently among the coals. Quickly the heat browned the paper. A flame licked up and over the box.[102]

Both women gather articles for flight: Mrs. Bird for the fugitive Eliza, Ma

Joad for her own family. And both women pause to acknowledge the significance of their rummaging through the archives. Mrs. Bird is "leaning her head on her hands," while Ma Joad is biting her "lower lip, thinking, remembering." Throughout their novels, Stowe and Steinbeck engage the folk process of protest literature, whether George's memory of the Revolution when he insists, "If it was right for [the Founding Fathers], it is right for me!" or Steinbeck's nuggets of labor songs and abolitionism. Mrs. Bird's and Ma Joad's confrontations of memory's concrete form is that folk process writ large.[103]

But while Mrs. Bird transforms her archive's useless items into Eliza's treasure, Ma Joad burns her treasure as trash. Mrs. Bird uses the dead relics of her drawer to assist the living Eliza and her living son, but Ma Joad cannot transform *her* mementos into tools for the future. The Joads set out for California without many of their memory fragments. Denied the ability to recycle history as they move westward, the Joads succumb to the frontier mythology that Frederick Jackson Turner pithily described in 1893: "American social development has been continually beginning over again on the frontier. This perennial rebirth, this fluidity of American life . . . furnish[es] the forces dominating American character."[104] While seeking that rebirth on California's frontier, the Joads experience it as destructive. They lose members of their group—and lose them as easily as Ma's box of family memories—and they find no new life in Rose of Sharon's stillborn baby.

Steinbeck insists on the importance of memory when a character in an inter-chapter cries, "How can we live without our lives? How will we know it's us without our past?"[105] Like Stowe, he asserts the importance of recycling memory. The Joads have tried to start afresh on the frontier, and failed. Instead, the novel ends with a redemptive act of recycling. Just as Mrs. Bird sees the importance of a *living* past and gives her dead child's clothes to Eliza, so Uncle John gives the stillborn baby as a witness—to "tell 'em"—and Rose of Sharon gives her otherwise useless breast milk to the dying man. The barn scene amends the forced amnesia when the Joads left their home. What Ma gave to the fire, which had "sighed up and breathed over the box," Rose of Sharon now reclaims in the rain, with its "soothing swish." And, while Ma's "lips parted" in the act of burning her family mementos, Rose of Sharon's "lips came together." Ma's abandonment of the family's past is redeemed through Rose of Sharon's recycling of her own brief past as a mother.[106]

If Steinbeck entered a protest tradition with his use of empathy, shock value, symbolic action, and radical folk memory, then he was also reclaimed in the protest tradition that followed. The Native American protest poet Sherman Alexie has always claimed Steinbeck as a major influence on his writing, and in 1995 Bruce Springsteen released his song "The Ghost of Tom Joad." (For a discussion of Steinbeck's influence on Springsteen, see chapter 10, by Lauren Onkey.) Taking up this idea of Tom's ghost, Bryant Simon and William Deverell explained in 2000 that "Tom Joad is still dangerous, or at least frightening, to those counties and schools and school boards that still flirt with banning *The Grapes of Wrath* from classrooms." After all, they added, "in the bans, which still take place, we see the ghost of Tom Joad. There's power there, there's the sixty-year-old Tom Joad still breathing fire."[107]

But within the protest tradition, the ghost of Tom Joad has breathed the most fire through Woody Guthrie. On March 3, 1940, Guthrie played in a "Grapes of Wrath Evening" to benefit the John Steinbeck Committee agricultural workers. (For a discussion of the Steinbeck Committee, see chapter 8, by James Swensen.) A *Daily Worker* piece promoted the benefit with a photo of Guthrie captioned "Woody—that's the name, straight out of Steinbeck's *The Grapes of Wrath*—sings People's Ballads."[108] Days later Guthrie wrote a ballad that really *was* straight out of *The Grapes of Wrath*. The ballad, "Tom Joad" (1940), includes the line "Wherever men are fightin' for their rights, / That's where I'm gonna be."[109] As late as 1954 Guthrie was still invoking Steinbeck. He wrote a play about Tom Joad, who again promises to organize—to fight for "folks . . . fightin f'r their rights." Guthrie, for one, saw in *The Grapes of Wrath* a blueprint for the protest future.[110]

Notes

An earlier version of this chapter appeared as Zoe Trodd, "Star Signals: John Steinbeck in the American Protest Literature Tradition," *Steinbeck Review* 5, no. 2 (2008): 11–37. © 2008 The Martha Heasley Cox Center for Steinbeck Studies/ Wiley Periodicals, Inc.

1. The quote is from a 1955 interview with Steinbeck, collected in *Writers at Work: The* Paris Review *Interviews*, fourth series, ed. George Plimpton (New York: Viking, 1976), 183. See also Audre Lorde, "Sisterhood and Survival," *Black Scholar*, March/April 1986, 5–7: "I am a black feminist lesbian poet, and I identify

myself as such because if there is one other black feminist lesbian poet in isolation somewhere within the reach of my voice, I want her to know she is not alone." For another echo of Steinbeck, see Howard Zinn, afterword to *American Protest Literature*, ed. Zoe Trodd (Cambridge, Mass.: Harvard University Press, 2006), 517: "Protest literature should move people to think more broadly, feel more deeply, and begin to act; perhaps alone at first, but then with others. It works on the supposition that social change comes through the combined and cumulative actions of many people. . . . Protest literature says to the reader, have hope—you are not alone."

2. John Steinbeck, *Steinbeck: A Life in Letters*, ed. Elaine Steinbeck and Robert Wallsten (New York: Viking Press, 1975), 162, 158. "The Harvest Gypsies" was republished in 1938 by a prolabor organization called the Simon J. Lubin Society, as a pamphlet titled *Their Blood Is Strong*, with an eighth chapter. The series is collected in *The Harvest Gypsies: On the Road to* The Grapes of Wrath (Berkeley, Calif.: Heyday, 1988).

3. Steinbeck, *Life in Letters*, 159.

4. Ibid., 158, 159, 161.

5. Ibid., 162. For more on the origins of *The Grapes of Wrath*, see Jackson J. Benson, "The Background to the Composition of *The Grapes of Wrath*," in *Critical Essays on Steinbeck's* The Grapes of Wrath, ed. John Ditsky (Boston: G. K. Hall, 1989), 505–25, and Cyrus Ernesto Zirakzadeh, chapter 1, this volume.

6. Roosevelt cited in David Wyatt, ed., *New Essays on* The Grapes of Wrath (Cambridge: Cambridge University Press, 1990), 3.

7. Pare Lorentz, "Dorothea Lange" (1941), in Milton Meltzer, *Dorothea Lange: A Photographer's Life* (New York: Farrar Straus Giroux, 1978), 203.

8. "Farmers Hit Steinbeck's Latest Book," *Monterey (Calif.) Peninsula Herald*, August 26, 1939, 7. See also Marci Lingo, "Forbidden Fruit: The Banning of *The Grapes of Wrath* in the Kern County Free Library," *Libraries and Culture* 38, no. 4 (2003): 351–77. For a discussion of the outrage that erupted in Oklahoma, see Martin Staples Shockley, "The Reception of *The Grapes of Wrath* in Oklahoma," *American Literature* 15, no. 4 (1944): 351–61; and Marsha L. Weisiger, "The Reception of *The Grapes of Wrath* in Oklahoma: A Reappraisal," *Chronicles of Oklahoma* 70, no. 4 (Winter 1992): 394–415.

9. Martin Arnold, "Making Books: Of Mice and Men and Novelists," *New York Times*, February 7, 2002, E3. Arnold terms Bloom "a chancellor of the Western literary canon."

10. Henry Kisor, "Disdained by the Literati," *Chicago Sun-Times*, February 24, 2002, 14; Jessica Winter, "The Ghost of John Steinbeck," *Village Voice*, April 17–23, 2002, 12.

11. Robert F. Richards, "Literature and Politics," *Colorado Quarterly* 19

(Summer 1970): 97–106; Benjamin Griffith, "The Banishing of Caldwell and Steinbeck," *Sewanee Review* 103, no. 2 (Spring 1995): 325–28.

12. Jackson J. Benson, "The Favorite Author We Love to Hate," in *The Steinbeck Question: New Essays in Criticism*, ed. Donald R. Noble (Troy, N.Y.: Whitston, 1993), 8–22 (11); Mary M. Brown, "*The Grapes of Wrath* and the Literary Canon of American Universities in the Nineties," in *The Critical Response to John Steinbeck's* The Grapes of Wrath, ed. Barbara A. Heavilin (Westport, Conn.: Greenwood Press, 2000), 285–98. See also Leslie A. Fiedler, *Waiting for the End* (New York: Stein and Day, 1964), which argues that *The Grapes of Wrath* is "hoked up with heavy-handed symbolism" and represents "the preparation for a new middlebrow literature" (57, 61). For an early critique of Steinbeck's work as low-quality literature, see Philip Rahv, "A Variety of Fiction," *Partisan Review* 6 (Spring 1939): 111–12. Rahv argues that the book is didactic and long-winded.

13. Benson, "Favorite Author," 21.

14. Arnold, "Making Books," E3.

15. Susan Shillinglaw and Kevin Hearle, "Rereading John Steinbeck," in *Beyond Boundaries: Rereading John Steinbeck*, ed. Susan Shillinglaw and Kevin Hearle (Tuscaloosa: University of Alabama Press, 2002), 1–10 (1).

16. See Jane Tompkins, *Sensational Designs: The Cultural Work of American Fiction, 1790–1860* (New York: Oxford University Press, 1985).

17. Granville Hicks, "The Thirties: A Reappraisal," *Saturday Review*, May 4, 1963, 27–28.

18. James N. Gilbert, "The Influence of John Steinbeck on American Social and Criminal Justice," *Platte Valley Review* 24, no. 1 (Winter 1996): 89–99; Carl Jensen, *Stories That Changed America: Muckrakers of the 20th Century* (New York: Seven Stories Press, 2000), 89–94. For another critic positioning Steinbeck in a canon of "cultural work," see Morris Dickstein, "Steinbeck and the Great Depression," *South Atlantic Quarterly* 103, no. 1 (Winter 2004): 111–31. Dickstein observes, "With the exception of Harriet Beecher Stowe in *Uncle Tom's Cabin*, Upton Sinclair in *The Jungle*, and perhaps Richard Wright in *Native Son*, no protest writer had a greater influence on how Americans looked at their own country" (112).

19. John Stauffer, foreword to Trodd, *American Protest Literature*, xi–xvii (xii).

20. John Seelye, "Come Back to the Boxcar, Leslie Honey: Or, Don't Cry for Me, Madonna, Just Pass the Milk: Steinbeck and Sentimentality," in Shillinglaw and Hearle, *Beyond Boundaries*, 11–33 (13).

21. For one previous articulation of what this chapter calls the "politics of form," see Ralph Ellison, *The Collected Essays of Ralph Ellison*, ed. John F. Callahan (New York: Modern Library, 2003), 708: "From the beginning our novelists

have been consciously concerned with the form, technique and content of the novel, not excluding ideas. . . . The major ideas of our society were so alive in the minds of every reader that they could be stated implicitly in the contours of the form. . . . The form of the great documents of state constitutes a body of assumptions about human possibility which is shared by all Americans, even those who resist violently any attempt to embody them in social action."

22. Ralph Ellison, "The Novel as a Function of American Democracy" (1967), in *Collected Essays*, 759–69 (767); Ellison, *Juneteenth* (New York: Vintage, 1999), 17.

23. Alain Locke, "Art or Propaganda?" *Harlem* 1 (November 1928): 12–13.

24. Glenway Wescott, *U.S. Camera* 1 (1938): 67.

25. Harriet Beecher Stowe, *Uncle Tom's Cabin* (1852; reprint, New York: Penguin, 1988), 66–67, 215.

26. Tim O'Brien, interview with Zoe Trodd, July 12, 2005.

27. John Steinbeck, *The Grapes of Wrath* (1939; reprint, New York: Penguin, 1992), 74, 103.

28. Ibid., 15.

29. Ibid., 110.

30. Ibid., 280.

31. Ibid., 72.

32. Ibid., 195.

33. Ibid., 265, 267.

34. Ibid., 340.

35. Ibid., 445.

36. Ibid., 609.

37. Stauffer, foreword, xiii.

38. See Audre Lorde, "The Master's Tools Will Never Dismantle the Master's House" (1979), in *Sister Outsider* (Trumansburg, N.Y.: Crossing Press, 1984), 110–13.

39. Seelye, "Come Back to the Boxcar," 12. Kisor, in "Disdained by the Literati," is another critic who compares Steinbeck to Stowe, calling them both "unabashed sentimentalists" (14).

40. Seelye, "Come Back to the Boxcar," 21–22.

41. Ibid., 20.

42. Ibid., 13, 15, 12.

43. Leslie Fiedler, "Looking Back after 50 Years," *San Jose Studies* 16, no. 1 (1990): 54–64 (55); Edmund Wilson cited in Louis Owens, "The Culpable Joads: Desentimentalizing *The Grapes of Wrath*," in Ditsky, *Critical Essays*, 101–15 (109).

44. Charles Poore, "Books of the Times," *New York Times*, April 14, 1939,

27; Peter Monro Jack, "John Steinbeck's New Novel Brims with Anger and Pity," *New York Times Book Review*, April 16, 1939, 2; Louis Kronenberger, "Hungry Caravan," *Nation*, April 15, 1939, 440–41 (440). See also Edward Weeks, "A Year the Writer Made Good," *New York Times Book Review*, December 2, 1962, 1. Weeks notes that Steinbeck's *Travels with Charley* "exposed once more the power of sympathy" that had been expressed in his earlier novels and added "an extra cubit to Steinbeck's stature."

45. Steinbeck, *Grapes of Wrath*, 374.

46. What this chapter discusses as "empathy" is mentioned as a different form of "sympathy" by literary scholar Neville Hoad. He notes that sympathy can be a "self-consolidating experience" but also a "way of putting [oneself] at risk . . . in the interest of a collective rather than a personal good." See Neville Hoad, "Cosmetic Surgeons of the Social: Darwin, Freud, and Wells and the Limits of Sympathy on *The Island of Dr. Moreau*," in *Compassion: The Culture and Politics of an Emotion*, ed. Lauren Berlant (New York: Routledge, 2004), 187–218 (191). See also Jeff Goodwin, James Jasper, and Francesca Polletta, eds., *Passionate Politics: Emotions and Social Movements* (Chicago: University of Chicago Press, 2001). The editors of *Passionate Politics* argue that an "under-studied aspect" of social movements is the "emotions and experiences that prepare individuals for political action" (23).

47. Emphasizing the importance of *feeling* to abolitionism, Stowe explained in *Uncle Tom's Cabin*, "An atmosphere of sympathetic influence encircles every human being; and the man or woman who *feels* strongly, healthily and justly, on the great interests of humanity, is a constant benefactor to the human race. See, then, to your sympathies in this matter!" (624).

48. James Agee, unpublished "Works" chapter, typescript and carbon copy typescript with corrections, n.d., James Agee Collection, Harry Ransom Humanities Research Center, University of Texas at Austin, 6, 12–15.

49. Ida B. Wells, *Southern Horrors* (1892), in *Southern Horrors and Other Writings: The Anti-Lynching Campaign of Ida B. Wells, 1892–1900*, ed. Jacqueline Jones Royster (Boston: Bedford Books, 1997), 72.

50. Walt Whitman, *Leaves of Grass* (1855; reprint, New York: T. Y. Crowell, 1902), 55, 39; James Agee and Walker Evans, *Let Us Now Praise Famous Men* (Boston: Houghton Mifflin, 1941), 52.

51. Lewis Hine, field note, 1910, in *America and Lewis Hine: Photographs, 1904–1940* (New York: Aperture, 1977), 91; Upton Sinclair cited in Christopher Wilson, *The Labor of Words* (Athens: University of Georgia Press, 1985), 115; Steinbeck, *Life in Letters*, 161.

52. Stowe, *Uncle Tom's Cabin*, 108.

53. See C. Daniel Batson et al., "Perspective Taking: Imagining How Another

Feels versus Imagining How You Would Feel," *Personality and Social Psychology Bulletin* 23, no. 7 (1997): 751–58. See also A. D. Galinsky et al., "Perspective-Taking and Self-Other Overlap: Fostering Social Bonds and Facilitating Social Coordination," *Group Processes Intergroup Relations* 8, no. 2 (2005): 109–24; and C. Daniel Batson et al., "As You Would Have Them Do unto You: Does Imagining Yourself in the Other's Place Stimulate Moral Action?" *Personality and Social Psychology Bulletin* 29, no. 9 (2003): 1190–201.

54. Johann Gottlieb Fichte, "Die Bestimmung des Meschen," in *Johann Gottlieb Fichte's Sämmtliche Werke* 1.2 (Berlin: Veit, 1845), 168.

55. Steinbeck (1953) cited in Paula Moya, *Learning from Experience: Minority Identities, Multicultural Struggles* (Berkeley: University of California Press, 2002), 191. For more on the inter-chapters in *The Grapes of Wrath*, see Barbara Foley, *Radical Representations: Politics and Form in U.S. Proletarian Fiction, 1929–1941* (Durham, N.C.: Duke University Press, 1993), 398–441.

56. Steinbeck, *Grapes of Wrath*, 449.

57. Ibid., 204, 325, 165, 386.

58. See Steinbeck's description in an inter-chapter of a shift from "'I' to 'we,'" in *Grapes of Wrath*, 206. Pointing to the power of combining macro- and micro-level stories in 1941, Steinbeck offered an explanation for the power of his film *The Forgotten Village* (1941), which is structured in a similar fashion to *The Grapes of Wrath*: "It means very little to know that a million Chinese are starving unless you know one Chinese who is starving. Our story is centered on one family in one small village [and] from association with this little personalized group, the larger conclusion concerning the racial group can be drawn with something like participation." *The Forgotten Village* (New York: Viking, 1941), preface, n.p. Steinbeck's interest in inevitability means he is sometimes placed in the naturalist tradition. For more on this, see Horace P. Taylor Jr., "The Biological Naturalism of John Steinbeck," *McNeese Review* 12 (Winter 1960–1961): 81–97. For further discussion of *The Forgotten Village*, see Adrienne Akins Warfield, chapter 4, this volume.

59. Steinbeck, *Grapes of Wrath*, 118, 205, 206.

60. Ibid., 355.

61. Steinbeck, *Life in Letters*, 178.

62. Stowe, *Uncle Tom's Cabin*, 624.

63. Steinbeck, *Grapes of Wrath*, 446, 340, 445.

64. Allen Ginsberg, "Revolutionary Poetics" (1989), in *Civil Disobediences: Poetics and Politics in Action*, ed. Anne Waldman and Lisa Birman (Minneapolis: Coffee House Press, 2004), 243–67 (263).

65. Richard Wright, "How 'Bigger' Was Born" (1940), in *Native Son* (New York: HarperPerennial, 1992), 531. As early as 1937 Wright had protested the "consolation of tears," writing bitterly in a newspaper column, "Negro, with 3 week

old baby, begs food on streets . . . if you are the type to weep you can have a good cry over this and then feel good, 'purged,' you know." See Wright, *Daily Worker,* August 4, 1937, 3.

66. Wright, *Black Boy* (1945; reprint, New York: Harper Perennial, 1993), 248.

67. Stowe, *Uncle Tom's Cabin,* 386, 142.

68. O'Brien interview.

69. Steinbeck, *Working Days: The Journals of* The Grapes of Wrath, *1938–1941,* ed. Robert DeMott (New York: Viking, 1989), xl.

70. Steinbeck, *Life in Letters,* 172.

71. Ibid., 168, 178.

72. "Grapes of Wrath," *Collier's,* September 2, 1939, 54; Kronenberger, "Hungry Caravan," 440; Malcolm Cowley, "American Tragedy," *New Republic,* May 3, 1939, 382–83 (383).

73. Seelye, "Come Back to the Boxcar," 30.

74. Steinbeck, *Grapes of Wrath,* 22, 527.

75. Ibid., 609.

76. Kronenberger, "Hungry Caravan," 441.

77. Steinbeck, *Life in Letters,* 177, 178. For more on Steinbeck's ending, see Jules Chametzsky, "The Ambivalent Ending of *The Grapes of Wrath,*" *Modern Fiction Studies* 11 (1965): 34–44.

78. Steinbeck, *Grapes of Wrath,* 447.

79. Ibid., 603, 477.

80. Tompkins, *Sensational Designs,* 130.

81. Steinbeck, *Life in Letters,* 563.

82. Wells, *A Red Record* (1895), in *Southern Horrors and Other Writings,* 82.

83. Kenneth Burke discusses the novel in his discussion and definition of "symbolic action," commenting on the turtle in particular. See Burke, *The Philosophy of Literary Form: Studies in Symbolic Action* (Jackson: Louisiana State University Press, 1941), 36–37, 81, 84, 87, 90–91, 126.

84. Steinbeck, *Grapes of Wrath,* 120.

85. Ibid, 572, 527.

86. Steinbeck, *Working Days,* 36. For more on Christian symbolism in the novel, see Stephen Bullivant, "'That's him. That shiny bastard': Jim Casy and Christology," *Steinbeck Studies* 16, nos. 1 and 2 (2005): 14–31. Earlier reviewers mentioned the Christian symbolism. Cowley remarks on Casy's transformation into "a Christ-like labour leader" ("American Tragedy," 382) and Charles Lee refers to "Christ-like Casy" in "*The Grapes of Wrath:* The Tragedy of the American Sharecropper," *Boston Herald,* April 22, 1939, 7. For a discussion of parallels between *The Grapes of Wrath* and the Old Testament, see Roxanne Harde, chapter 7, this volume.

87. Steinbeck, *Grapes of Wrath*, 109.

88. Ibid., 618.

89. Stephen Railton, "Pilgrims' Politics: Steinbeck's Art of Conversion," in Wyatt, *New Essays*, 27–46 (40).

90. Frederick Douglass, "Pictures and Progress," manuscript fragment, n.d. [ca. late 1864], Frederick Douglass Papers, Manuscript Division, Library of Congress, Washington, D.C., box 28, reel 18 (page 18 of 22).

91. Steinbeck, *Grapes of Wrath*, 524.

92. Ibid., 476, 52.

93. D. H. Lawrence, *Studies in Classic American Literature* (1923; reprint, New York: Penguin, 1977), 60.

94. Floyd Dell, "Our America," *Liberator*, January 1920, 46.

95. Steinbeck, *Working Days*, 29.

96. Steinbeck, *Life in Letters*, 174.

97. Steinbeck, *Grapes of Wrath*, 206, 420.

98. Ibid., 316.

99. Ibid., 301. For more on Steinbeck's approach to ethnicity and race in the novel, see Susan Shillinglaw, "Steinbeck and Ethnicity," in *After the Grapes of Wrath: Essays on John Steinbeck*, ed. Donald V. Coers, Paul D. Ruffin, and Robert J. DeMott (Athens: Ohio University Press, 1995), 40–57.

100. Steinbeck, *Grapes of Wrath*, 325.

101. Stowe, *Uncle Tom's Cabin*, 153–54.

102. Steinbeck, *Grapes of Wrath*, 148.

103. Ibid., 187. Readers and reviewers have often juxtaposed the novels by Stowe and Steinbeck and thereby remembered America's protest history when reading Steinbeck's novel. The first reviews of *The Grapes of Wrath*, by Clifton Fadiman for the *New Yorker*, Louis Kronenberger for the *Nation*, and Malcolm Cowley for the *New Republic*, all paired *The Grapes of Wrath* with *Uncle Tom's Cabin*. See also the review headlined "*Grapes of Wrath* May Be the *Uncle Tom's Cabin* of Our Day," *Milwaukee Post*, April 22, 1939, 5. Critics also have compared Steinbeck to other writers in the American protest tradition. Railton compares him to Whitman ("Pilgrims' Politics," 45); Alexander Saxton compares him to Edward Bellamy in "*In Dubious Battle*: Looking Backward," *Pacific Historical Review* 73, no. 2 (May 2004): 249–62; and Kurt Hochenauer compares him to Thomas Paine in "The Rhetoric of American Protest: Thomas Paine and the Education of Tom Joad," *Midwest Quarterly* 35, no. 4 (Summer 1994): 392–404.

104. Frederick Jackson Turner, *The Significance of the Frontier in American History* (1893; reprint, New York: Ungar, 1963), 2–3.

105. Steinbeck, *Grapes of Wrath*, 120.

106. Ibid., 120, 617, 148, 619.

107. Bryant Simon and William Deverell, "Come Back, Tom Joad," *California History* 79, no. 4 (Winter 2000): 180–91, 232–33 (191). For more on Steinbeck's legacy in Native American protest writing, see Paul and Charlotte Hadella, "Steinbeck's Influence upon Native American Writers," in Shillinglaw and Hearle, *Beyond Boundaries*, 87–97. For more on Bruce Springsteen and Steinbeck, see Gavin Cologne-Brookes, "The Ghost of Tom Joad: Steinbeck's Legacy in the Songs of Bruce Springsteen," in Shillinglaw and Hearle, *Beyond Boundaries*, 34–46; and Lauren Onkey, chapter 10, and Cyrus Ernesto Zirakzadeh, chapter 11, this volume.

108. *Daily Worker* cited in John Greenway, *American Folk-Songs of Protest* (Philadelphia: University of Pennsylvania Press, 1953), 289. See also Bryan K. Garman, *A Race of Singers: Whitman's Working-Class Hero from Whitman to Springsteen* (Chapel Hill: University of North Carolina Press, 2000).

109. Woody Guthrie, "Tom Joad," in Trodd, *American Protest Literature*, 317–19 (319).

110. Guthrie, "Tom Joad," February 12, 1954, typescript, Woody Guthrie Archives, New York, Manuscripts, box 8, folder 22. Of the ballad Guthrie explained, "I wrote this song because the people back in Oklahoma haven't got two bucks to buy the book, or even thirty-five cents to see the movie, but the song will get to them and tell them what Preacher Casy said." Woody Guthrie, *Pastures of Plenty: A Self-Portrait* (New York: HarperCollins, 1990), 7. Guthrie told *Daily Worker* readers that the story shows "the dam bankers men that broke us and the dust that choked us, and comes right out in plain old English and says what to do about it. It says you got to get together and have some meetins, and stick together, and raise old billy hell till you get youre job, and get your farm back." See Guthrie's column for *People's World* (1940) in *Woody Sez* (New York: Grosset & Dunlap, 1975), 133. For more on Guthrie and Steinbeck, see Elaine S. Apthorp, "Steinbeck, Guthrie, and Popular Culture," *San Jose Studies* 16, no. 1 (Winter 1990): 19–39; Harry R. Stoneback, "Rough People . . . Are the Best Singers: Woody Guthrie, John Steinbeck, and Folksong," in Noble, *Steinbeck Question*, 143–70; Stoneback, "Songs of 'Anger and Survival': John Steinbeck on Woody Guthrie," *Steinbeck Quarterly* 23, nos. 1–2 (Winter–Spring 1990): 34–42; and Stoneback, "Woody Sez: Woody Guthrie and *The Grapes of Wrath*," *Steinbeck Newsletter* 2, no. 2 (Summer 1989): 8–9.

CHAPTER 3

The Novelist as Playwright: Adaptation, Politics, and the Plays of John Steinbeck

Donna Kornhaber

THE AUTHOR OF SOME twenty-seven novels and works of nonfiction, John Steinbeck was unmistakably committed to prose. Yet according to Brooks Atkinson, theater critic for the *New York Times*, he could have easily been one of America's greatest playwrights, crafting works designed for performance and not simply for private reading. Steinbeck's "first play," Atkinson writes, "is the quintessence of commercial theatre and it is also a masterpiece."[1] The occasion for Atkinson's praise was the 1937 Broadway premier of *Of Mice and Men*, the first of three plays Steinbeck would pen over his lifetime. The second would be an adaptation of his 1942 novel *The Moon Is Down*, which opened on Broadway in the same year, and the third an adaptation of *Burning Bright* in 1950. Curiously, Steinbeck attempted playwriting only three times in his prolific career. Despite his avowed affinity for prose, both fiction and nonfiction, he had no aversion to the dramatic form as such. He would see no fewer than seventeen of his novels turned into films and would garner three Academy Award nominations for his efforts in screenwriting. By all accounts, Steinbeck could have easily enjoyed similar success in what was then known as the "legitimate" stage. But Steinbeck's engagement with the theater was a strategic one, more of an attempt to add a component of political action to his writing than an investment in the world of the theater as such. For a writer often criticized for declaiming high principles without offering any means of achieving them, Steinbeck's stage adaptations offered a kind of direct political outlet: a way to communicate his perspectives to a mass audience, rousing them to new understandings and to new action. Writing theater was, for Steinbeck, not just a matter of working in another artistic mode; as for many of his contemporaries, it was also a political act unto itself.

Of Mice and Men, his first theatrical effort, appeared well before Steinbeck had reached the height of his fame as a novelist (indeed, several of the New York theater critics who reviewed the play, including Atkinson, were not previously familiar with Steinbeck's fiction). It opened at one of the premier theaters in New York—Broadway's Music Box Theatre—and ran for an impressive 207 performances before transferring to London. What is more, it was directed by George S. Kaufman, coauthor of some of the most popular comedies of the 1920s and 1930s, including *Dinner at Eight* and *You Can't Take It with You,* and one of the most acclaimed theatrical directors of the era. Critic Russell Rhodes described Kaufman as "the theatre's miracle man."[2] Yet Steinbeck did not even leave his home in California to attend the New York production.

Commentators who have considered Steinbeck's theatrical efforts—perhaps one of the most understudied aspects of his heavily scrutinized career—have regarded them largely as a side interest and ultimately a trivial pursuit. It was not disgust that kept Steinbeck from his first Broadway premier, as was sometimes the case with other playwrights of the era—occasionally even Eugene O'Neill. He is known to have had a good rapport with Kaufman. They spent several months perfecting the final script, and Steinbeck is said to have been quite proud of their final product.[3] Most commentators have therefore simply attributed to Steinbeck a lack of interest in the stage. But to disregard or downplay Steinbeck's theatrical pursuits is to overlook a powerful key to his thoughts as a political writer. Although theater may have largely lost its political function today, in the 1930s it was perhaps the political-literary form par excellence—far more left-leaning and politically engaged as a medium than either prose fiction or film. To understand the politics of the theatrical world that Steinbeck entered is to better understand the political import of his work as a whole. Far more than a vanity project or side pursuit, Steinbeck's theatrical efforts constitute an attempt to harness the political power of the stage: to add an *active* political dimension to some of his most politically minded works. Insofar as a writer in the first third of the twentieth century could ever hope to turn political narrative into political action, the stage was the means by which to do it. Steinbeck's entry—and return—to the theater must, therefore, be regarded as among the most politically informed moments in an already politically charged life.

To recognize that Steinbeck could have been a successful playwright, one need only read the reviews of *Of Mice and Men. Literary Digest* declared, "A great play has reached Broadway—a play of lowly, cast-off men, whose stark emotions have tamed testy critics and tired audiences into stunned reverence."[4] This was a common response among the literati in New York and beyond. As an article in the *San Francisco Chronicle* recounts, "The play, as you doubtless know, opened in New York on November 23, and was almost unanimously voted a fine thing by the critics."[5] Atkinson's admiration for the play led him to revise his entire outlook on the 1937 Broadway season. "After speaking contemptuously of the commercial theatre on many occasions," he wrote, "this column is prepared to eat its words. . . . When the theatre falls on lean days it retreats to Shakespeare and adaptations of novels. The recrudescence of Shakespeare, the staging of new versions of old plays and of plays based on novels are signs of the theatre's loss of spontaneity. *Of Mice and Men,* however, is no product of weariness."[6] Not just Steinbeck's text but the entire production received high acclaim. As Joseph Wood Krutch wrote in the *Nation,* "What one gets in the theatre is almost the total effect of the short novel plus the additional vividness of fine, imaginative sets, expert direction, and highly accomplished performances. No wonder then, that the play is already established as the solidest dramatic success of the season."[7]

The reviews, nevertheless, offered a tempered estimation of the author's craftsmanship. Comparing the play to Jack Kirkland's 1933 Broadway adaptation of Erskine Caldwell's novel *Tobacco Road,* about Georgia share-croppers, Stark Young wrote in the *New Republic,* "It has far less bounce, gusty relish, scope and trenchant humor; and less of the outline of significant fable."[8] Critic after critic would question the validity of Steinbeck's play as a work of art. Krutch would write, "*Of Mice and Men* puts its author in the topmost class of popular writers. It does not, I think, lift him out of that class."[9] This was not, oddly enough, a criticism of the technical elements of Steinbeck's script, new as he was to the stage. On technical matters of dialogue or character development many of the critics found Steinbeck wholly suited to the task. Krutch would remark that Steinbeck "writes with great technical adroitness," while Rhodes would declare the author to have "a shrewd sense of theatre unusual in a novelist."[10] Rather, what many critics found missing from the play was an artfulness—a dramatic construction and arrangement of the basic narrative so as to achieve a transcendent artistic and emotional effect, an overall impression that escapes the fundamentals of the situation presented on stage. "[The play] has no general significance," Atkinson would write. "Compare it with O'Neill's dour and gnarled *Desire under the Elms*, in which the characters are larger than life and the morbid passions are expressions of man in conflict with nature. *Of Mice and Men* is tragedy without that much compass."[11] Surprisingly, the same critic who declared Steinbeck's work "a masterpiece" also found his work to be "lacking in scope and universal meaning."[12]

What most critics admired in Steinbeck's piece was not its artfulness but something else entirely: its realism. Steinbeck brought to the stage a side of American life rarely seen in New York. "*Of Mice and Men* bristles with profanity and the vulgar speech of drifting vagabonds," Rhodes wrote. "But its honesty pierces, for this is vastly more than a shocker from the garbage heap of lost men."[13] Atkinson would similarly observe, in a column titled "Episode in the Lower Depths," that "the dialogue could be scandalous if it were a less honest expression of male life in a ranch bunkhouse. . . . The supreme virtue of the story, on stage as well as in print, is the lyric perfection of all these rude materials—the violence springing naturally out of the situation and the bawdy dialogue tumbling without self-consciousness out of the mouths and minds of 'bindle-stiffs.'"[14] For some, Steinbeck's vision was a little "too" real. Grenville Vernon wrote in *Commonweal* that the dialogue "is true to life, at times poetic, utterly dramatic, but is nonetheless appalling. It is unquestioned that the people of Mr. Steinbeck's creation would use the language allotted them, but are such people fitted for dramatic representation unexpurgated in their speech?"[15]

But for the majority, verisimilitude lay at the heart of Steinbeck's achievement. As Atkinson wrote in the first paragraph of his review, Steinbeck's play "makes no artistic pretensions, it is art in the keenness of its expression. Mr. Steinbeck has caught on paper two odd and lovable farm vagrants whose fate is implicit in their characters. . . . Although many people may shy away from the starkness of the fable, every one will admire the honesty of the author's mind and the clarity of its statement in the theatre."[16] Margaret Shedd would echo similar sentiments in her own account of the play's San Francisco premier: "One expects a great deal from a play about the living, wandering men who plant crops they never see harvested. . . . All the exciting dramatic realities are in the theme, and when the curtain goes up on *Of Mice and Men* the play seems authentic: characters who demand we learn all about them, situations which we feel impelled to follow through to a consummation."[17]

Underlying such praise is, even amongst the highbrow New York literati, a none-too-subtle political sensitivity. They praise Steinbeck's realism not because they are merely curious or sociologically minded. They do not laud Steinbeck for bringing to them an interesting specimen of the American milieu. They laud him for bringing to light American injustice. The reaction of many theater critics to Steinbeck's laborers ranged from expressions of curiosity to near disgust: they are "odd and lovable" in Atkinson's words and barely "fitted for dramatic representation" in Vernon's account. Yet alongside such blunt reactions to the characters is a romanticized respect for the nobility and suffering of these figures: they are "characters who demand we learn all about them" and who live in "situations which we feel impelled to follow through to a consummation," in Shedd's review. As Vernon writes of Steinbeck's characters, "His people have fled the city, and yet have found no rest or haven in their rural stopping places. . . . They suffer, not only in their bodies but in their souls. It is this realization that a human being has a soul which raises Mr. Steinbeck head and shoulders as a thinker and an artist."[18] Steinbeck's realism, in such accounts, involves his commentary on injustice—a commentary on what Shedd calls "what is inherent in the tragic saga of the itinerant agricultural worker."[19] Critics acquired only an abstract understanding of the daily suffering of agricultural laborers, to be sure, but it was a powerful reaction nonetheless. In merely depicting the conditions of California's migrant workers—in giving tangible reality to and an occasion for sympathy with a segment of the underclass that was poorly understood in New York—Steinbeck had made a substantial contribution to the New York stage. The critics' praise resides on the level of representation and not on the level of artistic workmanship. They praised Steinbeck's work as "a high spot of the current Broadway season" on political, rather than artistic, grounds.[20]

To comprehend why so many critics, supposedly committed to assessing the artistic integrity of the works before them, could slip into political judgment, one must recall the political context and history of theater in the 1930s. Steinbeck himself drew on this very history and context in his writing for the stage, and his efforts can best be understood in relationship to the other politically minded playwrights of the era.

Many have argued that the 1930s was perhaps the greatest period of political engagement in American theater. But it is a common misconception that the political agenda of this period arose solely from the Great Depression. "The struggle to create a committed theatre of the Left," writes C. W. E. Bigsby, "was principally a product of the 1930s."[21] To be sure, the 1930s spawned a leftist turn in almost all artistic genres of the period—a cultural consequence of the decade's increasing unionism and the solidification of the antifascist Popular Front, as Michael Denning recounts in *The Cultural Front*. But the political dimension of the theater differed fundamentally from that of other genres. While all genres, from the novel to film, saw their fair share of politically engaged work in the 1930s, the theatrical community focused almost exclusively on political matters. The main artistic competitors to the New York unit of the Federal Theatre Project (FTP) were the Workers' Drama League, explicitly created as a workers' theater; the Workers' Laboratory Theatre, which aimed to "be a theatre where the worker may be inspired to fight for his liberation"; and the Theatre Union, which declared itself "a united front theatre organized to produce plays that all honest militant workers and middle-class sympathizers can support."[22] The FTP, created by the Works Progress Administration in 1935, was closed down by Congress in 1939 for what Bigsby calls "political reasons"—that is, the increasingly left-leaning agendas of its plays.[23] Unlike the other artistic arms of the federal work projects—such as the Federal Writers Project, the Federal Music Project, or the Federal Art Project—the FTP became almost immediately an active, even subversive, political organization. Hallie Flanagan, director of the FTP, proclaimed that her objective was the "birth of a politically and economically literate theatre in America."[24] Thus the term *political theater* was, in the era of Steinbeck's Broadway forays, redundant: the two terms were synonymous.

The chief reason for the theater's emphasis on political engagement and political action was that, in twentieth-century America in particular, the theater had *always* been political. Politics was the wellspring from which modern American drama developed. American theater had existed prior to the early twentieth century, to be sure, but it was largely derivative of European models. It wasn't until the early twentieth century that an American drama emerged that critics deemed distinctly American, largely because of the incorporation of political subjects and purposes. Indeed, Louis Broussard calls the early twentieth century "the period of emergence" for American playwriting, while Jordan Miller and Winifred Frazer compare the rapid developments in American drama in the early twentieth century to the transformation in English drama that began with the Restoration in 1660.[25]

According to critics like Michael Cotsell, the roots of this emergence lie squarely in the realm of politics: specifically, in the politically informed and socially conscious dramas of the early Progressive Era, which Cotsell defines as "roughly the 1890s to World War I."[26] Evincing a concern for issues of social justice alongside a highly developed sense of the traumatic, not just the melodramatic, these plays, Cotsell argues, provided the basis for all later developments in American theater. The social realist work of James A. Hearne—whose 1890 play *Margaret Fleming* addressed the plight of American women—to the short "agitprop" plays of the suffrage and temperance movements captivated audiences and inspired debate through dramatic presentations of political issues.[27]

But American plays were more than mere political agitation. In the Progressive Era, observes Cotsell, "American dramatists, like their European contemporaries, uniformly attempted to treat subjects from the perspective of psychology, that is, not just externally, but internally."[28] In 1905 George Pierce Baker taught the world's first collegiate playwriting class at Harvard University—a move that, according to Bigsby, was of paramount importance to the development of American drama. From Baker's "Harvard 47" class emerged some of the most important American playwrights of the early twentieth century, including Eugene O'Neill and FTP director Hallie Flanagan. Baker's groundbreaking course was contemporaneous with a newfound public awareness of the theater's political function. Indeed, the theater was repeatedly employed *as* a political tool during the reform campaigns of the Progressive movement.[29]

Steinbeck inherited this dual legacy of American drama. Although people today often associate political theater with the 1930s, it was actually a persistent aspect of American culture. As early as 1914, playwright Michael Gold declared himself a revolutionary. In 1921 he wrote in "Towards a Proletarian Art" that "we are prepared for the economic revolution of the world, but what shakes us with terror and doubt is the cultural upheaval that must come."[30] Politics was salient even in the most purely artistic works by Eugene O'Neill, perhaps the least overtly political of the great dramatists of the 1920s and one who was inspired primarily by the philosophical ideas of Friedrich Nietzsche and Sigmund Freud. But one can find pressing political questions in his plays, such as the condition of the modern industrial worker in *The Hairy Ape* or racism and the consequences of slavery in *The Emperor Jones.* Indeed, O'Neill's theatrical career began—not unlike Steinbeck's—with dramatic depictions of the lives of the working class. He wrote about the common sailors he came to know during his youthful years as a seaman. *Bound East for Cardiff* is a character study of an unschooled sailor set on the fictional vessel *Glencairn* and was O'Neill's first play. What would sometimes be known as O'Neill's "Glencairn Plays" would be the hallmark of his early career.

Elmer Rice best represents the politicization of even artistically minded dramatists during the early twentieth century, and his career arc intimates how Steinbeck himself would come to approach theater. During the early 1920s Rice established himself as one of the foremost stylistic innovators on the American stage. His landmark 1923 play *The Adding Machine* is often regarded as, in the words of Broussard, "this country's first mature drama," and it introduced to Broadway many of the hallmarks of nonrealist, symbolic staging that had been hallmarks of the European avant-garde.[31] Yet even in its stylistic innovations Rice's work remained politically committed. The play tells the story of a man who has dedicated twenty-five years of his life to the same unskilled job and who, when he learns he is to be replaced by a simple adding machine, murders his boss in a fit of rage. It is, writes Frank Durham, a cautionary tale about a society in which the individual "is dehumanized, turned into a machine."[32]

Not long after revolutionizing the American stage with *The Adding Machine,* Rice went on to embrace a more straightforward realism, which increasingly exposed his political motives. His 1929 *Street Scene,* for instance, included some stylistic innovations but focused mostly on contemporary social and economic conditions, what Durham calls "lower middle-class characters trapped in a seemingly hopeless environment."[33] By the 1930s Rice's work became even more explicit in its political message, and he jettisoned all stylistic pretensions. He openly described his 1933 play

We, the People as "an exposé of the forces of reaction which stand in the way of a better life for the masses of the American people."[34]

Rice's career reveals not so much a change in focus but a shift in emphasis, one that effectively set the scene for the theatrical environment that Steinbeck ultimately entered. The American theater had always been a place for political statements. But whereas such concerns were balanced against artistic interests and experiments in the more politically tranquil 1920s, they came unabashedly to the forefront during the political turmoil of the 1930s. For writers like Rice—and his more avowedly revolutionary predecessors like Gold—the theater had always been a vehicle for political action, whatever other artistic functions it may have served. Rice wrote in the *New York Times* that he had always seen the theater as a means for "liberation from political autocracy," even in his most experimental works.[35] What Rice labeled the *functionality* of the theater became a common way in which the theater was conceived of and utilized in the 1930s. It was an outgrowth of drama's status in the 1920s rather than a new departure, and it would motivate the new crop of playwrights who emerged in the 1930s, including Steinbeck himself.

Indeed, Steinbeck wrote about the theater as a revitalizing force for the modern writer and about its inherently political character. He often remarked in his letters of the 1930s that the novel was dead or dying but that the theater was "waking up."[36] The reasons for this were manifold. Steinbeck believed that the economy of the dramatic form was well suited for some of the most important political issues of the day. In an essay titled "The Play-Novelette" (originally titled "The Novel Might Benefit . . ." and published in *Stage* magazine), Steinbeck writes that "in a play, sloppy writing is impossible because an audience becomes restless."[37] The terseness and directness of the dramatic form prompted a direct confrontation with the facts: "the vehicle exactly adequate to the theme," according to one of his letters. This is true if the themes are the lives of agricultural laborers, as in *Of Mice and Men*, or World War Two resistance fighters, as in *The Moon Is Down*.[38] (In *Burning Bright*, written much later in his career, Steinbeck began to explore a more symbolic side of stage drama, sometimes likening his work to the medieval morality play *Everyman*).[39] More than that, Steinbeck believed that the nature of theatrical performance necessarily inspired a kind of political awareness and call to group action. Plays, Steinbeck opined, allow you "to feel drawn into the group that was playing" and are thus best suited to "themes which are most poignantly understood by a group."[10] As he writes in "The Play-Novelette,"

> The recent tendency of writers has been to deal in those themes and those scenes which are best understood and appreciated by groups of people. There are many experiences which cannot be understood in solitude. War cannot be understood by an individual. . . . A mob cannot be understood by a person sitting alone in an armchair, but it can be understood by that same person in the mob. . . . A man alone under a reading light simply cannot experience *Waiting for Lefty* on anywhere near the same plane as he can when the whole audience around him is caught in the force of that play.[11]

By the mid-1930s Steinbeck came to view the novel as largely unsuited for some of the material he found most compelling, beginning with his intimate story of itinerant laborers in *Of Mice and Men*. One drawback of the dramatic form is the limited size of local theater audiences, as compared to the national readership of a novel. Another drawback is the general difficulty of reading a play rather than seeing it. "The reading of plays is a specialized kind of reading, and the technique of reading plays must be acquired with some difficulty," he writes. "The small distribution of plays intended to be read indicates the almost aversion most people have for reading them."[12] Thus Steinbeck envisioned *Of Mice and Men* to be what he called a "playable novel"—readable as a novel but immediately transferable to the stage for live performance. As he wrote to his agents in 1936, "The work I am doing now is neither a novel nor a play but is a kind of playable novel. Written in novel form but so scened and set that it can be played as it stands. It wouldn't be like other plays since it does not follow the formal acts but uses chapters for curtains. . . . Plays are hard to read so this will make both a novel and play as it stands."[13] For Steinbeck, not all novels were suited to the theater or to his new hybrid approach: "The novel of contemplation, of characterization through analysis, of philosophic discussion is not affected at all by this form," he explains.[14] But for works that explore current social, economic, or political realities, the theater was both the model and the ultimate objective. "For some years," Steinbeck writes, "the novel has increasingly taken on the attributes of the drama. Thus the hard-finish, objective form which is the direction of the modern novel not only points in the direction of the drama, but seems unconsciously to have aimed at it. . . . This experiment, then, is really only a conclusion toward which the novel has been unconsciously heading for some time."[45] For Steinbeck, to write with a political outlook and political agenda was, in many ways, to write for the theater.[46]

Clifford Odets also focused on the political functionality of the stage. He is the dramatist with whom Steinbeck arguably has the most in common and whose play *Waiting for Lefty* Steinbeck references directly in "The Play-Novelette." Unlike Rice or O'Neill, whose careers began in the 1910s and 1920s, Odets was, artistically speaking, a product of the Depression era. He was a founder of the Group Theatre—an influential avant-garde troupe in New York that incorporated the naturalistic acting theories of Constantin Stanislavski into a politically informed, wholly realist theatrical style. His first play premiered in 1935 at the depth of the Depression. Odets's *Awake and Sing* tells the story of a large Jewish family struggling to survive in Depression-era New York. In many ways it is a continuation of the kind of family drama O'Neill inaugurated in *Desire under the Elms.* But *Awake and Sing* is also a work of engaged art that calls for a radical vision of collective action. Protagonist Ralph declares at the very end of the work, after a slew of economic and personal misfortunes, "I'll get along. Did Jake die for us to fight about nickels? No! 'Awake and sing,' he said. . . . I saw he was dead and I was born! I swear to God, I'm one week old! I want the whole city to hear it—fresh blood, arms. We got 'em. We're glad we're living."[47] As Bigsby observes, Odets's "radical character is allowed a perception which never moves from language to action," yet the endorsement of change is there nonetheless.[48] Odets's impulse to create political action on stage would at last be realized in *Waiting for Lefty,* completed in 1935. Inspired by the New York taxi strike of the year before (though Odets would claim to have had no knowledge of the event in his 1953 testimony before the House Un-American Activities Committee), he bridges the gap between representation and action. The play moves from a fictional depiction of taxi workers debating whether to strike to a participatory rally in favor of the strike (and strikes in general) directly involving the audience. The Group Theatre's cofounder Harold Clurman wrote that the audience's impassioned cries of "Strike! Strike!" at the close of the play were "the birth of the thirties. Our youth had found its voice. It was a call to join the good fight for a greater measure of life in a world free of economic fear, falsehood, and craven servitude to stupidity and greed."[49]

This impulse to treat theater primarily as a venue for political action would be the major cause of both the success and the decline of the greatest theatrical experiment of the 1930s, the FTP. Designed to resuscitate the country's failing theater industry—by 1933 half of New York's theaters had closed and more than half of the city's actors were unemployed—the project quickly became a hotbed of radical activity. Controversies surrounded such high-profile productions as *The Cradle Will Rock,* Orson Welles's production of Marc Blitzstein's musical review about efforts to form a steel union (the government attempted to block the performance by padlocking the theater and surrounding it with armed soldiers). But the greatest difficulties the FTP encountered arguably arose from the attempts of its "Living Newspapers" to inspire political engagement among audience members. Elmer Rice headed the Living Newspaper project, which was one of the five original divisions of the FTP. Living Newspapers provided dramatized accounts of contemporary local events. Besides recounting recent news items, the artists agitated the audience. Directly connected to the economic and political problems facing the country, the Living Newspapers were well suited to exploit the functional aspects of American theater. Witness the conclusion to one Living Newspaper project, titled *One Third of a Nation:* "Wait a minute! Hold it! Don't blackout on that yet! Bring those lights up—full! That's better. This scene isn't over yet! Now, Mister Landlord, we know that the conditions you showed us exist. They were a little exaggerated perhaps, but they exist. . . . But we can't just let it go at that. We can't let people walk out of this theatre, knowing the disease is there, but believing there's no cure. *There is a cure! . . . Government Housing!*"[50] Statements like these generated the greatest controversies surrounding the FTP. They are perhaps more explicit than other statements in the American dramatic tradition. But they convey the shared sense that drama could be used for political ends, not just for entertainment or purely aesthetic goals as artistic creation.

This same impulse motivated Steinbeck's ventures into the theater. He recognized its political function from his first foray into the genre. It is intriguing, and significant, that with the exception of the unrealized *God in the Pipes*—an early version of the material that would appear in *Cannery Row*—Steinbeck never attempted to write an original work for the stage. Rather, his stage plays were addenda to already completed prose works, his so-called playable novels. Indeed, for the original production of *Of*

Mice and Men—presented not in New York but at San Francisco's Theatre Union—Steinbeck did little more than hand over chapter manuscripts to a theater director. According to Shedd's account of that original production, the Theatre Union "believed it should have plays about local current history. Wellman Farley, the president, said this to John Steinbeck and forthwith Steinbeck handed him an as yet unpublished manuscript, *Of Mice and Men*."[51] Unlike the professional ensemble that would attempt Steinbeck's play in New York, Farley's Theatre Union was an avowedly "proletarian theatre" that drew its cast and crew from the working classes and rehearsed for months during the workers' spare time.[52] The cast included a garage repairman, milkman, and store salesperson, some of whom, according to Shedd, were born and raised in the very agricultural communities Steinbeck depicted in the play. Thus the first attempt to bring *Of Mice and Men*—a story about California's migrant workers—to the stage was enacted, if not by migrant workers, then by fellow laborers and former migrants. Steinbeck was in essence offering his story (quite literally the manuscript pages) as an opportunity for California's workers to give voice to their own stories. Steinbeck's play might not have included a call to strike like Odets's *Waiting for Lefty* or a call for government housing like *One Third of a Nation*, but it communicated a political message to an audience that otherwise might not ever see the flesh-and-blood workers whose suffering his novella depicted. The play was intended to give a politically charged "reality" to the written tale.

In New York Steinbeck was unable to replicate the unique conditions offered by the Theatre Union. No California workers stormed the stages of Manhattan. Yet his political motivations remained largely the same. As has been noted, the artistic qualities of Steinbeck's play were roundly criticized, even by its most ardent supporters. Yet if Steinbeck's drama is seen as an attempt to give authenticity to a written story, then the kind of dramatic and narrative perfection sought by critics like Atkinson becomes irrelevant. Steinbeck worked with Kaufman to revise the play after its relatively unsuccessful reception in San Francisco. Had he crafted a work along the lines of *Madame Bovary, Ethan Frome,* or *Desire under the Elms,* replete with "morbid passions," "expressions of man in conflict with nature," and "universal meaning," as Atkinson suggested, he would have enveloped his narrative in another layer of artistic craftsmanship and compromised its documentarian impact by making it too artistic.[53] Atkinson's conception of tragedy would have rendered Steinbeck's work "safe" by taking it out of the realm of life and into the realm of art. But the production Steinbeck actually offered was anything but "safe." Witness the response of Vernon: "To say everything violates the canons not only of good taste but of art itself. *Of Mice and Men* is an unusual play, but it would have been an even better one had it allowed less license to its language."[54] Broderick Crawford and Wallace Ford, who performed the roles of Lennie and George, were not themselves farmworkers. However, in the estimation of many reviewers, they were as real as could be expected on the New York stage—perhaps even, in Vernon's account, too real. Their performances, according to Atkinson, were "patient and subdued"—in other words, not melodramatic or histrionic.[55] Speaking of "the most difficult acting assignment in recent years," the reviewer for *Literary Digest* praised the "fine and moving" performances.[56] As in the California production, Steinbeck had succeeded in making plausible the fictional characters whose plight he had chronicled and in informing audiences of the suffering around them. His project in *Of Mice and Men* was the inverse of the FTP's Living Newspapers. The latter fictionalized real events in order to make the need for political action more understandable. Steinbeck's play made fictional characters and events as real as possible to emphasize the need for political action.

Steinbeck's political purposes are also evident in his theatrical adaptation of *The Moon Is Down*. The work is unique among Steinbeck's early compositions in that he conceived it as a novel-play endeavor from the outset. (Steinbeck would repeat the attempt in 1950 with *Burning Bright*. In contrast, *Of Mice and Men,* Steinbeck would claim, was conceived of as "a play in the form of a novel.")[57] Steinbeck, working in both formats simultaneously, hoped to release the book and premier the play at approximately the same time.[58] Roy Simmonds observes that the novel has several unseemly hallmarks of this dual construction: "The play origin of the work seeps through occasionally into the text of the published novel in some of the descriptions of the rooms in the mayor's palace and of Molly's living room. These descriptions are of rooms as they would be seen by an audience through the proscenium arch."[59] Some theater critics, such as John Gassner, found the reasoning behind Steinbeck's decision obscure. The product was neither a fully realized novel nor a fully realized play. "If Mr. Steinbeck could be charged with writing the mere outline of a novel in his published book," Gassner writes, "it could be maintained, with greater

justification, that he created the mere sketch of a play. . . . The play produces a confusing alignment of forces, a divided effect, and a somehow
incompletely precipitated dramatic experience."[60] Others, like Simmonds,
wondered what was added thematically by revisiting the book's material
in dramatic form. The book, which appeared shortly before the play's New
York premier, had stirred controversy because of its seemingly sympathetic
portraits of the militaristic occupiers of a small town in an unnamed country. As Simmonds relates, "The drama critics reiterated and developed all
the old arguments and counterarguments over the portrayal of the Nazis."[61]
Mark Van Doren wrote in the *Nation* that "John Steinbeck's *The Moon is
Down* gets nowhere with its novelty, which consists in the suggestion that a
Nazi conqueror may be a man with a heart and human memories after all,"
while an unsigned review in *Time* declared Steinbeck's decision to "make
his Nazis human beings rather than monsters" to be "over-reassuring"
and "still-too-optimistic."[62] Only Brooks Atkinson in the *New York Times*
discerned Steinbeck's primary purpose: "Mr. Steinbeck apparently feels
that a free people do not have to be manipulated by half-truths and tactful
evasions. Without raising his voice or playing tricks on a plot, he has put
down some of the fundamental truths about man's unconquerable will to
live without a master. . . . All this Mr. Steinbeck tells in terms of ordinary
people who are face to face with realities."[63]

Steinbeck considered his seemingly sympathetic portraits of Nazis
absolutely necessary for his work to be as realistic as possible. The work was
not a parable, it was a manual—a tool for understanding the actual process
of resistance rather than simply an abstract exercise in moral or spiritual
reflection. According to Simmonds, Steinbeck had originally "set the work
in an American town that had been invaded, and it had been conceived by
him as a 'blueprint' to the people of America, 'setting forth what might be
expected and what could be done about it.'"[64] The original proposal horri-
fied Steinbeck's superiors at the government's Foreign Information Service,
where he worked during the war. Steinbeck quickly relocated the events
to an unnamed country—and in an unnamed war—to quell concerns over
propriety.[65] Yet the premise and the political purpose remained the same.
The work was to serve as a political manual for his country as a whole.
The novel's format facilitated wide dissemination, but the play would also
help Steinbeck achieve his goal of turning political instruction into political
action. On stage occupation and resistance could be seen in an embodied

form. The audience could see, hear, and feel what such an event might be like, all the better to prepare them for such an eventuality—to contemplate "those themes and those scenes which are best understood and appreciated by groups of people," as Steinbeck put it in "The Play-Novelette." The characters on stage modeled paths of resistance for the audience, and with far more immediacy than a book could ever achieve.

Steinbeck's *The Moon Is Down* project, however, failed to achieve its goals. Troubled by casting and production concerns from the very start, Steinbeck continued to revise and rewrite the script until just three days before the Broadway opening. The production was, for the most part, a disaster. *Newsweek* called it "one of the major disappointments of a disappointing theater season," and *Time* declared that the work "never really comes to life."[66] The failure was almost inevitable because Steinbeck was attempting to turn what he called a "blueprint" into art. Such attempts, writes Bigsby, are almost always bound for failure: "The language of theatre stands at another extreme from the language of action. The framing of that language by the context of the stage is a protection against the consequences of its own meaning."[67] In other words, the characters on stage, no matter how realistic they may seem, are merely *performing* their actions: there is no real-world consequence to their actions or statements. To bridge the gulf between staged performance and real-world action, as Bigsby observes, is a notoriously difficult affair. Yet by using the theater to convey the political subtext of his novels, Steinbeck was also making a statement about the role of politics in his work. He was not simply a politically minded documentarian wishing merely to chronicle injustice. Steinbeck wanted to spur political action.

Steinbeck's political understanding of the theater helps to explain why he turned only occasionally to the stage, despite his initial success in the genre. He had little interest in the theater as a purely artistic medium. His singular attempt to separate his efforts on the stage from any overt political purpose yielded one of the most disastrous projects of his career. The 1950 stage adaptation of *Burning Bright*—an exploration of love, marriage, and parenthood rather than politics—garnered not a single sympathetic review and played on Broadway for only thirteen performances before closing at a loss. Without a political agenda, Steinbeck had little to offer the stage that he had not already presented in his novels. The very first reviews of *Of Mice and Men*, after all, criticized the author's artistic accomplishments even as they extolled his political ones. Like *Waiting for Lefty* and *One Third of a Nation*, Steinbeck's theatrical works turned ideas into action and gave his fiction the air of reality. That Steinbeck felt his work deserving of such transformation speaks volumes not just of his playwriting career but of his relationship to fiction, of his belief that fiction needed the theater to help it "wake up" and confront "themes which are most poignantly understood by a group."[68] As Steinbeck writes in "The Play-Novelette," the modern novelist only "limits the possibility of being understood by making it impossible for groups to be exposed to his work."[69]

To call Steinbeck a politically informed and politically engaged writer is hardly a new observation but, as with many politically minded writers, Steinbeck is not infrequently criticized for presenting lofty ideals and proposing no concrete means of achieving them. Bigsby, for one, compares Steinbeck's *The Grapes of Wrath* with Odets's *Waiting for Lefty* and writes that "this play is no clearer than Steinbeck's novel about the means of translating rhetoric into action. It is a call to arms, to spiritual renewal, but the way in which that renewal is to express itself is left unexamined."[70] Steinbeck rarely spells out specific methods for changing the realities he presents (*The Moon Is Down* being a partial exception). His involvement in the theater indicates his desire to convert his political ideas into political action and to allow his themes to be received and understood by groups and thereby to be experienced as they can only be "when the whole audience . . . is caught in the force of that play."[71] "There are many experiences which cannot be understood in solitude," Steinbeck writes, with political issues such as those expressed in *Waiting for Lefty* foremost among them.[72] Steinbeck believed that his readers needed to see with other audience members certain realities performed in front of them. Witness the theatrical corollary to the "blueprint" of *The Moon Is Down*. The play, which follows the novel in almost every detail, adds nothing to the book except a kind of reality— the reality of a live performance with live actors, which in the 1930s was believed to be capable of actually creating political change, from calling for strikes in *Waiting for Lefty* to demanding government housing in the FTP. Even if Steinbeck was not entirely successful in using the theater to incite his audience members he was not alone in the belief that the theater could do such a thing. This had always been the fundamental project of American drama, from the Civil War onward. By moving back and forth between the world of fiction and the world of the stage, Steinbeck indicated that he did not merely want to inform, but he also wanted to instigate change. And, in common with many writers of the period, he saw the theater as the clearest means for turning art into action.

Notes

1. Brooks Atkinson, "Episode in the Lower Depths," *New York Times*, December 12, 1937, 3.

2. Russell Rhodes, "The Stage at Eve," *Where to Go* (New York), December 1, 1937, 7.

3. Warren G. French, "The First Theatrical Production of Steinbeck's *Of Mice and Men*," *American Literature* 36, no. 4 (January 1965): 525.

4. "Theatre: A Completely Satisfying American Play," *Literary Digest*, December 18, 1937, 34.

5. Joseph Henry Jackson, "A Bookman's Notebook," *San Francisco Chronicle*, December 18, 1937, 8.

6. Atkinson, "Episode," 3.

7. Joseph Wood Krutch, "Oh, Hell, Said the Duchess," *Nation*, December 11, 1937, 663.

8. Stark Young, "Two from the Novel," *New Republic*, December 15, 1937, 170.

9. Krutch, "Oh, Hell, Said the Duchess," 663.

10. Ibid., 664; Rhodes, "Stage at Eve," 7.

11. Atkinson, "Episode," 3.

12. Ibid.

13. Rhodes, "Stage at Eve," 7.

14. Atkinson, "Episode," 3.

15. Grenville Vernon, review of *Of Mice and Men*, *Commonweal*, December 10, 1937, 191.

16. Brooks Atkinson, "John Steinbeck's *Of Mice and Men* in a Production Staged by George S. Kaufman," *New York Times*, November 24, 1937, 20.

17. Margaret Shedd, review of *Of Mice and Men*, *Theatre Arts*, October 1937, 774.

18. Grenville Vernon, "The Prize Plays," *Commonweal*, June 3, 1938, 161.

19. Shedd, review of *Of Mice and Men*, 774.

20. Rhodes, "Stage at Eve," 7.

21. C. W. E. Bigsby, *A Critical Introduction to Twentieth-Century American Drama: 1900–1940* (Cambridge: Cambridge University Press, 1982), 193.

22. Malcolm Goldstein, *The Political Stage: The American Drama and Theatre of the Great Depression* (New York: Oxford University Press, 1974), 32, 60.

23. Bigsby, *Critical Introduction*, 211.

24. Jane De Hart Matthews, *The Federal Theatre, 1935–1939: Plays, Relief and Politics* (Princeton, N.J.: Princeton University Press, 1967), 58.

25. Louis Broussard, *American Drama: Contemporary Allegory from Eugene O'Neill to Tennessee Williams* (Norman: University of Oklahoma Press, 1962), 4; Jordan Y. Miller and Winifred L. Frazer, *American Drama between the Wars: A Critical History* (Boston: Twayne, 1991), viii.

26. Michael Cotsell, *The Theater of Trauma: American Modernist Drama and the Psychological Struggle for the American Mind, 1900–1930* (New York: Peter Lang, 2005), 9. Although Cotsell doesn't draw the connection explicitly, theater of the Progressive Era in many ways grew from the theater of the antebellum abolitionist movement—in particular, the variety of stage adaptations of Harriet Beecher Stowe's *Uncle Tom's Cabin*. For further reading on abolitionist theater, see S. E. Wilmer, *Theatre, Society, and the Nation: Staging American Identities* (Cambridge: Cambridge University Press, 2002).

27. For further reading on suffrage and temperance plays, see Sheila Stowell, *A Stage of Their Own: Feminist Playwrights of the Suffrage Era* (Ann Arbor: University of Michigan Press, 1994); and John W. Frick, *Theatre, Culture, and Temperance Reform in Nineteenth Century America* (Cambridge: Cambridge University Press, 2000).

28. Cotsell, *Theater of Trauma*, 9.

29. For studies that consider the political theater of the Progressive Era, see Andrew Chamberlain Rieser, *The Chautauqua Moment: Protestants, Progressives, and the Culture of Modern Liberalism* (New York: Columbia University Press, 2003); and David Krasner, *Resistance, Parody, and Double Consciousness in African American Theatre, 1895–1910* (Basingstoke, UK: Palgrave Macmillan, 1997).

30. Quoted in Bigsby, *Critical Introduction*, 189.

31. Broussard, *American Drama*, 46.

32. Frank Durham, *Elmer Rice* (New York: Twayne, 1970), 41.

33. Ibid., 128.

34. Ibid., 126.

35. Quoted in Bigsby, *Critical Introduction*, 127.

36. Quoted in Susan Shillinglaw, introduction to *Of Mice and Men*, by John Steinbeck (New York: Penguin Classics, 1994), xvi.

37. John Steinbeck, "The Play-Novelette," in *America and Americans and Selected Nonfiction* (New York: Penguin Classics, 2003), 156.

38. Quoted in Shillinglaw, introduction, xvii.

39. Robert E. Morsberger, "Steinbeck and the Stage," in *The Short Novels of John Steinbeck*, ed. Jackson J. Benson (Durham, N.C.: Duke University Press, 1990), 285.

40. Steinbeck, "Play-Novelette," 157.

41. Ibid., 156.

42. Ibid., 155.

43. Quoted in Shillinglaw, introduction, xvi.

44. Steinbeck, "Play-Novelette," 156.

45. Ibid.

46. Although Steinbeck never confronts the issue in his published writings on the theater, an obvious limitation here is the ability of the stage to capture stories that combine epic scope and political import, such as Steinbeck's own *Grapes of Wrath*. Steinbeck seems to have had an intuitive understanding of this limitation and declined a dramatic adaptation of *In Dubious Battle* even as he was beginning to work on the play version for *Of Mice and Men*, in large part due to the sprawling nature of the book.

47. Clifford Odets, *Awake and Sing*, in Waiting for Lefty *and Other Plays* (New York: Grover Press, 1979), 100–101.

48. Bigsby, *Critical Introduction*, 129.

49. Quoted in ibid., 200.

50. Ibid, 231.

51. Shedd, review of *Of Mice and Men*, 774.

52. Ibid., 778.

53. Atkinson, "Episode," 3.

54. Vernon, "Prize Plays," 192.

55. Atkinson, "Episode," 3.

56. "Theatre: A Completely Satisfying American Play," 34.

57. French, "First Theatrical Production," 525.

58. Roy Simmonds, *John Steinbeck: The War Years, 1939–1945* (Lewisburg, Penn.: Bucknell University Press, 1996), 97.

59. Ibid., 99–100.

60. John Gassner, "*The Moon Is Down* as a Play," *Current History*, May 1942, 232.

61. Simmonds, *John Steinbeck*, 119–20.

62. Mark Van Doren, "Monster Modified," *Nation*, April 18, 1942, 468; "New Play in Manhattan," *Time*, April 20, 1942, 36.

63. Brooks Atkinson, review of *The Moon Is Down*, *New York Times*, April 8, 1942, 22.

64. Simmonds, *John Steinbeck*, 97.

65. Despite the anonymity of the locales, critics generally took Steinbeck's depiction to be of Norway.

66. "Steinbeck's Faith," *Newsweek*, April 20, 1942, 72; "New Play," 36.

67. Bigsby, *Critical Introduction*, 207.
68. Steinbeck, "Play-Novelette," 157.
69. Ibid.
70. Bigsby, *Critical Introduction*, 201.
71. Steinbeck, "Play-Novelette," 157.
72. Ibid.

CHAPTER 4

Steinbeck and the Tragedy of Progress

Adrienne Akins Warfield

JOHN STEINBECK LEARNED in late 1962 that he had won the Nobel Prize for Literature. Fearing that the award would prove to be an "epitaph" for his writing career, he hesitated to embrace the accolades of the literary establishment. Shortly afterward, critics who believed his writings were unworthy of the award spoke up. Steinbeck complained to his friend Bo Beskow, a Swedish artist, "I suppose you know of the attack on the award to me not only by *Time* magazine with which I have had a long-lasting feud but also from the cutglass critics, that grey priesthood which defines literature and has little to do with reading. They have never liked me and now are really beside themselves with rage."[1]

One such critic, Cornell professor and Fitzgerald scholar Arthur Mizener, published a scathing commentary in the *New York Times Book Review* on December 9, just a day before Steinbeck accepted the prize in Stockholm. In the article Mizener deems *The Grapes of Wrath* Steinbeck's best novel, after which "most serious readers seem to have ceased to read him." Mizener attributes this novel's success to the emotional atmosphere of the late thirties, when Americans were "responsive to even feeble renderings" of suffering induced by unemployment and poverty "and, with the typically impatient idealism of Americans, eager to be offered a course of action that sounded, however superficially, as if it would remedy the situation."[2] Mizener is particularly critical of what he calls Steinbeck's tendency to explore "idea[s] for solving a social problem or explaining human nature."[3] He claims that the author's "theory of what human nature ought to be has made him forget all he has observed of what men are."[4] Like many later critics of Steinbeck, Mizener assumes true art should stay detached from political commitments: art should concern itself not with what should be, but with what is.[5]

Steinbeck's Nobel Prize acceptance speech was in many ways a response to critics like Mizener. In his letter to Beskow, Steinbeck said of the speech, "I should like to make it as near to the truth as possible."[6] In a letter to longtime friend Carlton Sheffield, Steinbeck spoke of his struggles to formulate a "suave and diplomatic" speech and his final rejection of such an approach: "Last night I got mad and wrote exactly what I wanted to say. I don't know whether it's good but at least it's me."[7] After initial thanks to the Swedish Academy, Steinbeck's Nobel speech quickly moves to an examination of the role of the writer: "It is customary for the recipient of this award to offer personal or scholarly comment on the nature and the direction of literature. At this particular time, however, I think it would be well to consider the high duties and the responsibilities of the makers of literature." These "makers of literature," Steinbeck asserts, should not be "a pale and emasculated critical priesthood singing their litanies in empty churches—nor is [writing] a game for the cloistered elect, the tinhorn mendicants of low calorie despair." Rather, the "functions," "duties," and "responsibilities" of the writer are "decreed by" the needs of the human race for hope, improvement, and survival. For Steinbeck, the particular need of the hour is for the writer to address "the present universal fear" that "has been the result of a forward surge in our knowledge and manipulation of certain dangerous factors in the physical world," most specifically the threat of nuclear weapons. Steinbeck acknowledges that humanity's ethical understanding and environmental concerns have not progressed at the same rate as discoveries and developments in science and technology but contends that "there is no reason to presume that they cannot or will not draw abreast. Indeed it is a part of the writer's responsibility to make sure that they do."

Situating his argument within the context of the life of Alfred Nobel, Steinbeck refers to Nobel's realization of "the cruel and bloody misuses of his inventions" and to his efforts to "invent a control, a safety valve" for the destructive power of dynamite and other such inventions. According to Steinbeck, Nobel found such control "only in the human mind and the human spirit," as evidenced by the categories of the Nobel Prize awards. Steinbeck, agreeing with Nobel, states that the writer "is charged with exposing our many grievous faults and failures, with dredging up to the light our dark and dangerous dreams for the purpose of improvement." In other words, the writer should illuminate threats to humanity's survival posed by the selfish and violent sides of human nature, particularly when these negative impulses manifest themselves under the guise of progress. Steinbeck adds, however, that the writer must celebrate "man's proven capacity for greatness of heart and spirit—for gallantry in defeat—for courage, compassion and love."[8] For Steinbeck, the role of the writer involves truthful representation of the human capacity for evil, as exemplified in the "cruel and bloody misuses" of technological developments for destructive purposes; the writer also must emphasize humanity's aptitude for overcoming this negative capacity and for harnessing new discoveries that serve the collective good of the human race, especially those who are vulnerable and oppressed.

Steinbeck's acceptance speech reflects his disdain for critics and his refusal to be cynical about the possibility of positive social change. However, both within his speech and in many of his earlier writings, Steinbeck exhibits an awareness of the dangers of unchecked confidence in knowledge and progress. He was also not blind to the possibility that particular political commitments could skew the truthfulness of artists, including himself. An acute consciousness of such risks and possibilities undergirds Steinbeck's view of the role of the writer in society and informs many of his fictional works.

In chapter 14 of this anthology Simon Stow argues that Steinbeck's final novel, *The Winter of Our Discontent*, published the year before he won the Nobel Prize, expresses a tragic vision of the world, though not one without hope. Stow emphasizes the "distinction between tragedy as condition and tragedy as response. Tragedy as condition entails an understanding of the world as one of irreconcilable conflicts, frustrated agency, human suffering, and paradoxical demands. Tragedy as response shares this worldview and seeks to provide humanity with a coping strategy for the inevitable circumstances of its existence." Stow connects the tragic worldview of the novel to "the wartime experiences of both John Steinbeck" and the novel's protagonist Ethan Hawley, who is a veteran of World War II.

Steinbeck's Nobel speech likewise strikes a tragic tone in its treatment of questions of war, violence, and technological change. The tone echoes in Steinbeck's assessment of his work as a war correspondent on the European front during World War II. In his 1958 introduction to the collection of his wartime writings *Once There Was a War,* Steinbeck anticipates the argument in his Nobel Prize speech about the destructive capacity of technologically sophisticated weapons. "Once upon a time there was a war," but this war was "so long ago" that "even people who were there are apt to forget. This war that I speak of came after the plate armor and longbows of Crécy and Agincourt and just before the little spitting experimental atom bombs of Hiroshima and Nagasaki." Steinbeck further warns that "the next war, if we are so stupid as to let it happen, will be the last of any kind. There will be no one left to remember anything."[9] Sounding remarkably like those who criticized his 1930s novels as propagandist, he characterizes his wartime writings as "period pieces, the attitudes archaic, the impulses romantic, and, in the light of everything that has happened since, perhaps the whole body of work untrue and warped and one-sided." He admits that "the events set down here did happen" but adds that much else happened that was not reported because "there was a huge and gassy thing called the War Effort. Anything which interfered with or ran counter to the War Effort was automatically bad."[10] Near the end of the introduction, Steinbeck anticipates another key theme of his Nobel Prize speech, the human capacity for good even amid the horrors of war: "Although all war is a symptom of man's failure as a thinking animal, still there was in these memory-wars some gallantry, some bravery, some kindliness. . . . Now for many years we have suckled on fear and fear alone, and there is no good product of fear. Its children are cruelty and deceit and suspicion germinating in our darkness. And just as surely as we are poisoning the air with our test bombs, so are we poisoned in our souls by fear, faceless, stupid, sarcomic terror."[11] The similarities between Steinbeck's ruminations here and the warnings in his Nobel speech suggest that his reflections on his wartime journalism contributed to his later artistic philosophy and his vision of the relationship between the tragic results of human failure and the hope of human progress. (For a further discussion of Steinbeck's wartime writings, see chapter 12, by Mimi Gladstein and James H. Meredith.)

After completing his job as a war correspondent in December 1943, Steinbeck "return[ed] to the United States in poor shape physically and emotionally."[12] During the next month Steinbeck embarked on a trip to Mexico with his wife, Gwyn, and planned *The Pearl,* which was published under the title "The Pearl of the World" in the December 1945 issue of

Woman's Home Companion before its novella-form publication in December 1947.[13] The timing of *The Pearl*'s composition is significant because of the close proximity to that of two other works also set in Mexico: *Sea of Cortez* (published jointly with Steinbeck's closest friend, marine biologist Edward F. Ricketts, in 1941) and *The Forgotten Village* (1941). Steinbeck loved Mexico but believed it was sorely in need of technological and sociopolitical development. Each of these works was important in Steinbeck's philosophical development, as he explored in very different ways the possibility of progress and, in doing so, raised significant questions about the role of the writer in society.

Although many have discussed the influence of Ricketts on Steinbeck, few have considered the implications of this influence for *The Pearl*. While a number of literary critics, most notably Charles R. Metzger, interpret the message of *The Pearl* as congruent with the philosophical views expressed in *Sea of Cortez,* they fail to note that much of *Sea of Cortez*'s narrative content, and all of the philosophically central musings on "'is' thinking," were derived from Ed Ricketts's journal and unpublished essays.[14] By interpreting *The Pearl* only in the context of what Richard Astro terms "premises stated in *Sea of Cortez* believed to be [Steinbeck's], but actually developed by Ricketts," Metzger and similar critics fail to explore the ways in which Steinbeck differed philosophically from Ricketts.[15] These differences are evidenced in, among other works, *The Forgotten Village*, a movie script so offensive to Ricketts that it provoked him into writing an opposing "anti-script." A thorough analysis of *The Pearl* and Steinbeck's evolving views on progress, tragedy, and the social role of the writer must include consideration of *The Forgotten Village* as well as investigation of Ricketts's role in the composition of *Sea of Cortez.*

Sea of Cortez: A Leisurely Journal of Travel and Research consists of a 277-page narrative presented as a "travel log" and a 302-page appendix of biological data on marine specimens collected and classified by Steinbeck and Ricketts during their five-week voyage down (and back up) Baja California. Steinbeck, Ricketts, and crew departed from Monterey Harbor in a ship called the *Western Flyer* on March 11, 1940, and returned on April 20. After their return Steinbeck revised and expanded a travel log kept by Ricketts during the expedition. Steinbeck incorporated an unpublished essay by Ricketts on what the biologist termed "non-teleological or 'is' thinking," as well as portions of some of Ricketts's unpublished essays.[16] The revised and expanded log became the narrative portion of *Sea of Cortez.*

Sea of Cortez was not Steinbeck's only project in 1940. He temporarily stopped working on *Sea of Cortez* during the summer of 1940 in order to work on the documentary film *The Forgotten Village* with producer-director Herb Kline.[17] *The Forgotten Village* tells a story about the indigenous people of Santiago, a rural mountain community in Mexico. The main character is a Mexican Indian boy named Juan Diego whose brother Paco dies from illness. Juan Diego learns from the village schoolteacher that the children are dying not from evil spirits, as almost all the local people believe, but from diseases caused by germs. However, due to the strong and oppressive influence of the *curandera,* or "Wise Woman," as Steinbeck translates the term, the villagers refuse to sign a petition to bring doctors to the village.[18] Juan Diego brings city doctors to his home, but the villagers drive them away. *The Forgotten Village* advocates a philosophy of progress through learning and enlightenment, which together will enable a "long climb out of" the "darkness" of superstition and resistance to medical and technological advancement.[19] This climb is facilitated by the education provided in "government schools," from which "the boys and girls from the villages will carry knowledge back to their own people."[20]

The themes of *The Forgotten Village* emerged from Steinbeck's experiences in rural Mexico. (Further discussion of *The Forgotten Village* is offered in chapter 9, by Marijane Osborn.) According to Robert E. Morsberger, while Steinbeck and Kline were researching material for a planned antifascist documentary, they learned about the struggles of the Mexican Rural Service to control disease among village children. Steinbeck and Kline "were often thwarted by the hostility of *curanderas* and the fatalism of the Indians." This prompted Steinbeck to write the script for *The Forgotten Village.*[21] He hoped not only to improve public health but also to instigate social change, encourage technological development in Mexico, and influence Mexican views of the United States and the Allied war effort. Donald V. Coers notes that, while traveling through Mexico in 1940, Steinbeck "became troubled about what he perceived as an inadequate U.S. response to Nazi Bund activities in Latin America."[22] In a letter to his uncle Joseph Hamilton, Steinbeck argued that "the life of an Indian village is tied up with the life of the Republic. The Germans have absolutely outclassed the Allies in propaganda. If it continues, they will completely win Central and South America away from the United States."[23] Similarly, on June 24, 1940, shortly after returning from Mexico and immediately after learning that France had surrendered to Germany, Steinbeck wrote to President Roosevelt explaining that "in light of this experience [of filming *The Forgotten Village* in Mexico] and against a background of the international situation, I am forced to the conclusion that a crisis in the Western Hemisphere is imminent, and is to be met only by an immediate, controlled, considered, and directed method and policy."[24]

The divergent philosophies in *The Forgotten Village* and *Sea of Cortez*, two works that Steinbeck composed at the same time, make it especially challenging to deduce Steinbeck's views on the best approach for responding to the international conflicts of the early 1940s. *The Forgotten Village*'s celebration of technological progress and call for government intervention stand in direct opposition to the philosophy espoused throughout *Sea of Cortez*, the worldview that Ricketts referred to as "non-teleological or 'is' thinking." In Ricketts's view, non-teleological thinking is a system of thought that is contingent upon accepting natural and social phenomena "as is." According to non-teleological thinking, all attempts to identify cause-effect relationships between conditions and events, as well as attempts to change conditions for the better, are seen as futile and even counterproductive. Such attempts are often based on a "very superficial" understanding of what is "better" because the rush to improve human conditions obstructs full comprehension of these conditions as they exist.[25] As Astro has noted, *Sea of Cortez* suggests that "our quest for progress may ultimately end in our extinction as a species."[26] While the bulk of Steinbeck's reflections on "'is' thinking" can ultimately be traced back to Ricketts, certain positions in *Sea of Cortez* appear elsewhere in Steinbeck's personal writings—for example, in a letter to his publisher, Pascal Covici, in January 1941: "I asked Paul de Kruif once if he would like to cure all disease and he said yes. Then I suggested that the man he loved and wanted to cure was a product of all his filth and disease and meanness, his hunger and cruelty. Cure those and you would have not man but an entirely new species you wouldn't recognize and probably wouldn't like."[27] This sentiment is echoed in the *Sea of Cortez*, where Steinbeck states that all humans are ultimately "products of disease and sorrow and hunger and alcoholism. And suppose some all-powerful mind and will should cure our species so that for a number of generations we would be healthy and happy? We are the products of our disease and suffering. . . . To cure and feed would be to change the species, and the result would be another animal entirely."[28] Such ideas conflict with the optimism about overcoming ignorance, curing disease, and mitigating poverty evident in *The Forgotten Village*, but they anticipate the tragic mode of *The Pearl* and other of Steinbeck's later writings.

Ricketts was outraged by *The Forgotten Village*'s betrayal of ideas from *Sea of Cortez*, and he argued openly with Steinbeck during the film shoot. He later expressed his disapproval of *The Forgotten Village* through a proposal for an alternative screenplay titled "Thesis and Materials for a Script on Mexico Which Shall Be Motivated Oppositely to John's 'Forgotten Village.'" In the anti-script Ricketts contrasts cultures that value material progress with cultures that value human relationships. Ricketts characterizes the Mexican people as superior to those who own "outward possessions" (by which he means both physical possessions and "mental acquisitions" such as technology, medicine, and education "in the formal and usual sense, as emphasizing the acquisition of facts and skills, and in which the teaching is by rule, more or less impersonal, and in quantity production") because of the Mexicans' "inward adjustments": love and dignity. Ricketts associates "inward adjustments" with "teaching in the old sense," which emphasized the inward development of the mind and spirit "through personal relationship between master and pupil."[29] His anti-script decries the effects of technological modernization in Mexico on the grounds that such development corrupted humans' relationships with nature and with each other. In Ricketts's alternative script, the chief character is "some wise and mellow old man" who guides a troubled adolescent grandchild during the construction of a high-speed road through a "primitive" community. The wise old man points out "the evils of the encroaching mechanistic civilization to a young person."[30] In the subsections of his script Ricketts cites his past experiences in Mexico and offers conjectures about the future to support his negative assessment of the impact of technology on rural societies.

Ricketts's script romanticizes the often arduous lives of rural Mexicans, citing "the curiously illuminating smiles, of especially the younger poor country people, on the rare occasions when you are able to get contact with them, as evidence of their internal adjustment and happiness in a life normally involving almost unbelievable rigors of poverty and disease."[31] Nonetheless, many of his points are compelling when juxtaposed with the unchecked optimism about scientific knowledge and progress in *The Forgotten Village.* Joel W. Hedgpeth speculates that Steinbeck must have recognized the validity of his friend's critique.[32] This becomes evident in Steinbeck's subsequent work about Mexico, *The Pearl,* which depicts the tragic consequences of what is labeled "progress," "civilization," and education.[33] Steinbeck first heard the folk story that serves as the basis of *The Pearl* during his expedition with Ricketts, and the story is briefly recounted in *Sea of Cortez.* In the original folktale, a Mexican Indian boy finds an unbelievably large pearl. He plans to sell the pearl to buy drink, court women, and purchase masses to ensure places in heaven for himself and his dead relatives. But the boy is unable to obtain a fair price because all the pearl dealers work for one man. Later he is attacked by people who want to steal the pearl. The tale ends with the boy joyfully throwing the pearl into the sea.[34]

The novella version of *The Pearl* centers on Kino, an indigenous fisherman and pearl diver living on the outskirts of the Mexican village of La Paz; his wife, Juana; and their baby, Coyotito. At the story's opening, Coyotito is stung by a scorpion, and the town doctor refuses to treat the baby because the family has no money. The family's luck appears to change when Kino finds a large and beautiful pearl. He dreams of the new life he will purchase. He hopes to finance the education of his son and to free his family from hardship. But ironically, the pearl brings only new hardships to Kino and Juana. Kino becomes a target for thieves and a target for exploitation by a doctor, a priest, and a number of pearl merchants. Dreaming about a better life for his family, Kino grows so attached to the pearl that he refuses to give it up despite its threat to his family's safety. Juana insists that the pearl is "evil" and that they must rid themselves of it. After Coyotito is killed during the family's journey to the capital, Kino finally recognizes his wife's wisdom and throws the pearl back into the sea.

The Pearl, unlike *The Forgotten Village,* depicts the negative effects of modernization and of knowledge divorced from human relationships and ethical concerns. In *The Forgotten Village* education is portrayed as a beneficent force, as indicated by the story's closing sentences: "'The change will come, is coming, as surely as there are thousands of Juan Diegos in the villages of Mexico.' And the boy said, 'I am Juan Diego.'"[35] The name of the story's main character matches that of St. Juan Diego of Mexico, who, according to Catholic and folk tradition, saw the Virgin Mary in 1531, when she appeared as a dark-skinned woman and asked him to build a church for her. He recounted Mary's request to Bishop Juan de Zumárraga, but the bishop demanded proof of the encounter. The Virgin Mary then reappeared to Juan Diego and commanded him to pick roses, put them in his cloak, and deliver them to the bishop as a sign. When Juan Diego opened his cloak before the bishop, an image of the dark-skinned Virgen de Guadalupe was emblazoned on it.[36] The closing lines of *The Forgotten Village* are thus highly symbolic. They signify that, in the words of John Ditsky, "miracles are brought . . . less by faith than by the enlightened human mind engaged in an inquiring pursuit of knowledge."[37]

The Pearl, by contrast, attributes no miraculous power to its educated characters, only laziness, cruelty, and greed. Unlike the doctor in *The Forgotten Village,* a potential savior who is rejected by the villagers, the doctor in *The Pearl* uses his knowledge and skills to exploit those with less education. Upon hearing that Kino has found the great pearl, the doctor visits Kino's hut and claims that although Coyotito looks almost well, sometimes babies stung by scorpions show apparent improvement before the toxins take effect. Steinbeck describes Kino's predicament: "He did not know, and perhaps the doctor did. And he could not take the chance of pitting his certain ignorance against this man's possible knowledge."[38] In an ironic reversal of the plot from *The Forgotten Village,* in which the villagers refuse to let the doctor medicate their children, the doctor tricks Kino and then gives Coyotito a powder that makes the baby violently ill. The doctor's callousness and dishonesty are manifestations of the lack of "inward adjustments"—of care, concern, and integrity within "the field of human relationships"—that Ricketts claims is prevalent in more technologically advanced nations.[39] Conversely, Kino's moral code when he, needing to escape, discovers that his canoe has been broken ("It did not occur to [Kino] to take one of the canoes of his neighbors. Never once did the thought enter his head, any more than he could have conceived breaking a boat"), illustrates the "inherent honesty" that Ricketts argues is characteristic of rural Mexicans.[40]

Ricketts's alternative script cites examples of Mexican virtue, including a description of an American restaurant owner in Mexico who insisted on the safety of the area around her restaurant. The restaurateur allegedly said, "You're not in the States. Leave your car parked here for several days if you want, nobody'll take anything."[41] Ricketts also tells a story about "the nieve seller at Puebla" who did not require his customers to pay for their trays of ice cream until after they had finished eating. Ricketts asks himself, "What if the nieve-seller tried to conduct business with Americans along those lines, or even with United States resident Mexicans, who had acclimated themselves to our ways? Your brisk, ethical American would not only not bother to pay the nieve-seller (since doing so would entail some trouble), he wouldn't even bother to return the glass and spoon. 'Such lack of business acumen!' the American would think."[12] Ricketts's hypothetical Americans display the same character traits as Steinbeck's doctor in *The Pearl*: callousness and dishonesty. Ricketts wrote that "in an inward sense, the Mexicans are more advanced than we are, but they can be corrupted by a virus so powerful as that of the present United States mechanistic civilization."[13]

In Steinbeck's novella the effects of the pearl on the residents of La Paz can indeed be likened to those of a virus. The greed occasioned by the pearl's discovery rapidly spreads and corrupts the desires of the populace: "The essence of the pearl mixed with the essence of men and a curious dark residue was precipitated. . . . The news stirred up something infinitely black and evil in the town; the black distillate was like the scorpion, or like hunger in the smell of food, or like loneliness when love is withheld."[14] The last two similes are especially significant because Steinbeck defines the intensity of the evil in terms of the goodness of what is denied. Hunger is intensified by the smell of food that prompts memory of its taste, while loneliness is intensified by the memory of love before it was withheld. Similarly, the violence and greed that follow the pearl's discovery stand in sharp relief to the peace (La Paz) and generosity (as demonstrated by the assembly of villagers who follow Juana and Kino as they seek medical care for their sick baby, Coyotito) that previously existed in the community.

Steinbeck also uses biblical symbolism in *The Pearl* to convey the dangers and illusory nature of knowledge. The idea that knowledge, particularly scientific knowledge, can be pernicious is an important theme in *Sea of Cortez*, particularly in the following passage, which does not appear in Ricketts's essays or in the journal from the expedition:

> It would be interesting to try to explain to one of these [Gulf] Indians our tremendous projects, our great drives, . . . the defense of the country against a frantic nation of conquerors, and the necessity for becoming frantic to do it; the spoilage and wastage and death necessary for the retention of the crazy thing; the science which labors to acquire knowledge, and the movement of people and goods related to the knowledge obtained. How could one make

an Indian understand the medicine which labors to save a syphilitic, and the gas and bomb to kill him when he is well, the armies which build health so that death will be more active and violent. It is quite possible that to an ignorant Indian these might not be evidences of a great civilization, but rather of inconceivable nonsense.[45]

In *The Pearl* a scorpion, like the serpent in Genesis, enters the world of Kino and Juana. Steinbeck uses the Old Testament language of *evil, enemy, death,* and *fell* when describing the scorpion, and Kino's crushing and stamping the "enemy" scorpion into the dirt recalls the prophecy that the serpent would eat dust and be crushed by Eve's offspring.[46] The humans' desire for knowledge is an especially important aspect of *The Pearl*'s lapsarian imagery. Kino associates knowledge with freedom and empowerment. After his brother Juan Tomás asks him what he will do with the riches from the pearl, "Kino's face shone with prophecy. 'My son will read and open the books, and my son will write and will know writing. And my son will make numbers, and these things will make us free because he will know—he will know and through him we will know.'"[47] However, Kino's desire for knowledge tragically leads not to freedom, but to Coyotito's death.

A number of influential Christian theologians, including Augustine, have argued that the Fall led not only to death and moral corruption but also to the corruption of human reason.[48] Steinbeck's symbolism in *The Pearl* draws on the Pauline idea that human beings see the world as if "through a glass, darkly."[49] Steinbeck's description of the gulf air on the morning Kino finds the pearl reflects this idea: "The uncertain air that magnified some things and blotted out others hung over the whole Gulf so that all sights were unreal and vision could not be trusted. . . . Thus it might be that the people of the Gulf trust things of the spirit and things of the imagination, but they do not trust their eyes."[50] Even though Kino has seen the pearl, he still hesitates to open the oyster shell for fear that his eyes have tricked him, because "in this Gulf of uncertain light there were more illusions than realities."[51] Kino's fear of distorted and misleading vision foreshadows the destructive illusions that are to come.

Steinbeck's conveyance of the fallibility of human perception and reasoning through optic symbols follows a long literary tradition associated with tragedy. According to Christopher Rocco, *Oedipus the King* is "a paradigmatic articulation of the triumphs and failures of enlightened thinking, an exemplary (and tragic) tale of enlightenment and its highly ambivalent consequences."[52] Rocco points out that Sophocles dramatically portrays the illusory nature of knowledge and vision through sight-related imagery.[53] Steinbeck similarly uses representations of skewed sight and Edenic imagery to explore the implications of the pearl's promises and dangers. Trying to sell the pearl in the capital city, Kino rambles nervously to Juana, "Beware of that kind of tree there. . . . Do not touch it, for if you do and then touch your eyes, it will blind you."[54] The association of the Fall with damaged vision is developed further a few lines later.

> And Juana said, "Perhaps the dealers were right and the pearl has no value. Perhaps this has all been an illusion."
>
> Kino reached into his clothes and brought out the pearl. He let the sun play on it until it burned in his eyes. "No," he said, "they would not have tried to steal it if it had been valueless."
>
> "Do you know who attacked you? Was it the dealers?"
>
> "I do not know," he said. "I didn't see them."
>
> He looked into his pearl to find his vision. "When we sell it at last, I will have a rifle," he said, and he looked into the shining surface for his rifle, but he saw only a huddled dark body on the ground with shining blood dripping from its throat. And he said quickly, "We will be married in a great church." And in the pearl he saw Juana with her beaten face crawling home through the night. "Our son must learn to read," he said frantically. And there in the pearl Coyotito's face, thick and feverish from the medicine.[55]

This passage juxtaposes Kino's deepest hopes with the horrors of his post-pearl life (the attacker he killed; his beating of Juana when she tried to throw the pearl back into the sea; the sickness of Coyotito caused by the "medicine" of the greedy doctor) and thereby emphasizes both his flawed sight and the pearl's false promise of happiness. Whereas *The Forgotten Village* describes knowledge and progress as a "long climb out of darkness," Kino's desires for knowledge and progress lead him to the tragic betrayal of his deepest values. His desire to possess the pearl, with its illusory capacity to improve his family's educational opportunities and quality of life, results in Kino abusing his wife, neglecting his child, and taking the life of a fellow human being.

The Pearl nonetheless expresses more than resignation and pessimism. Steinbeck's unflinching descriptions of the hardships and oppression endured by the uneducated challenge Ricketts's romanticized portrayals of rural Mexican life. The director of *The Forgotten Village* film, Herb Kline, expressed his aggravation at Ricketts's fascination "with Rousseau and the joys of the primitive man while [Mexican women and children] were dying unnecessarily from the inadequate treatment of witch doctors."[56] Echoing Kline's sentiments, Steinbeck told Ricketts that "keeping the Indians around as Mexican curios may be very nice for the tourists to look at and be amused," but he considered the protection of their lives and health more important.[57]

Such hope for progressive social change is not the same as blind optimism. Indeed, Steinbeck's focus on the tragic suffering in rural Mexico contrasts sharply with Ricketts's narrowly optimistic vision. In both *The Forgotten Village* and *The Pearl* Steinbeck depicts societal marginalization. During his journey to the city, Juan Diego hears that doctors would not come to his village of Santiago because it "was too far away and it was a waste of time."[58] This idea is echoed in *The Pearl.* When Juana seeks a doctor for Coyotito, neighbors say that "he would not come" because he is attending to the rich people who live in town.[59] In *The Pearl* Steinbeck depicts the shame that can accompany oppression, poverty, and neglect. When visiting a doctor's office, Kino hesitates at the door because, "as always when he came near to one of this race, Kino felt weak and afraid and angry at the same time. . . . He could kill the doctor more easily than he could talk to him, for all of the doctor's race spoke to all of Kino's race as though they were simple animals."[60] The doctor's servant asks if Kino has money to pay for the treatment, and he pulls out "eight small misshapen seed pearls, as ugly and gray as little ulcers, flattened and almost valueless." The servant then tells Kino that the doctor has gone out. A sense of shame spreads among the people who had accompanied Kino and Juana. They depart "so that the public shaming of Kino would not be in their eyes."[61] In Steinbeck's story indigent life is not replete with the "illuminating smiles" that Ricketts describes.

The Forgotten Village and *The Pearl* also address the issue of mortality. In both stories children die. In addition, Steinbeck highlights Kino's own mortality. Kino repeatedly proclaims, "I am a man." This statement can be interpreted on at least three levels. First, it expresses Kino's machismo and his belief in his superiority to Juana. Second, the statement is an attempt to assert his dignity within a society that often treats Kino as subhuman. Finally, the statement ironically reveals Kino's desire to deny his own mortality. When Kino asserts, "We will have our chance. . . . We will not be cheated. I am a man," Juana replies, "Kino . . . I am afraid. A man can be killed. Let us throw the pearl back into the sea."[62] Kino's bravado evokes the sentiments of a *Peninsula Herald* (Monterey, Calif.) editorial that Ricketts cites in his alternative script. The editorial writer praises those who die "for causes they consider to be just, for ideals that are in their own minds, or even for the sake of carrying a man's part among their fellows" and declares that "these things are not vain things for which men have died. . . . However such men die, they rise superior to those that live in vain."[63] Kino embodies the type of honorable abandon that Ricketts applauds when citing the editorial, but Juana's hope for survival is grounded in her deeper understanding of the tragic and inescapable realities of life and death.

A final problem that appears in both *The Forgotten Village* and *The Pearl* is the exploitation of illiteracy. In the earlier work the *curandera*, knowing that the presence of physicians would hurt her business, urges the villagers to hide their children from doctors. *The Pearl* portrays a similar situation. The absence of formal education among the indigenous people leads to their exploitation by pearl buyers, the doctor, and the priest. To persuade Kino to give money to the Church, the priest says, "Thy namesake tamed the desert and sweetened the minds of thy people, didst thou know that? It is in the books."[64] The narrator describes Kino's predicament: "He was trapped as his people were always trapped, and would be until, as he had said, they could be sure that the things in the books were really in the books."[65] Ricketts, in contrast, downplays the economic benefits of literacy through the use of irony:

> A group of assembly line workers, spending their day of rest in the State Museum (of the future), as all good workers should do, passing before the painting shown in the prelude, smiles all gone now, significantly and sadly reading the words (now *all* the workers can read):
>
> > "*La verdadera civilizacion sera la harmonia de los hombres in* [sic] *la tierra y de los hombres entre si.*"[66]

Ricketts implies that literacy is unimportant and irrelevant for the uneducated poor, who live in harmony with the land. Steinbeck, however, insists that Kino is subjected to exploitation because of his illiteracy.

Though Steinbeck acknowledges the dangers that arise from misapplication of knowledge, the story line of *The Pearl*, tragic though it is, nonetheless justifies the protagonist's desire to learn and thus improve the lot of his family. James A. Hamby argues that the novella does not repudiate change per se. Rather, the story finds problems with Kino's approach to change: "Kino's flaw rests in his belief that tradition can be replaced by progress in a single, swift alteration."[67] The transformation of Juana's character over the course of the story can be seen as an acknowledgement of the dangers of "single, swift alteration." At the beginning of the story Juana, not Kino, challenges the traditionally marginalized status of the indigenous by first sending for the doctor and then, in response to the resigned declarations that "he would not come," asserting proactively, "Then we will go to him."[68] After the doctor refuses to treat the baby, Juana prays that they will find a pearl "with which to hire the doctor to cure the baby."[69] When she observes the greed and violence prompted by the pearl, however, she reverses her position. Unlike Kino, Juana can accurately assess and reject the pernicious road to "progress" offered by the pearl. In the view of Kyoko Ariki, Juana "serves as an alter ego of the writer."[70] Juana's realistic hope for the future, grounded in her tragic awareness of human mortality, leads her both to challenge Kino's blindly optimistic devotion to a simplistic image of progress and to urge him to consider the importance of his own survival.

Echoing Juana's position, Steinbeck asserts in his Nobel Prize speech that the role of the writer is to "dredg[e] up to the light our dark and dangerous dreams" in order to improve life.[71] In *The Pearl*, Steinbeck acknowledges the difficulties and dangers of knowledge and technological progress but affirms the need for both. His experiences in Mexico and as a war correspondent, his dialogues with Ricketts, and his continuing exploration of the complexities of life led Steinbeck to temper his admiration for rapid development. He expanded his perspective to include a tragic vision of the world and humanity while holding fast to his belief that a writer's skills should be used to improve the lives of fellow human beings. Such commitment, I would argue, is a prerequisite for what Mizener terms the "most distinguished of literary prizes."[72]

Notes

1. John Steinbeck, *Steinbeck: A Life in Letters*, ed. Elaine Steinbeck and Robert Wallsten (New York: Vintage, 1975), 754.

2. Arthur Mizener, "Does a Moral Vision of the Thirties Deserve a Nobel Prize?," *New York Times Book Review*, December 9, 1962, 43.

3. Ibid.

4. Ibid., 44.

5. As Morris Dickstein has noted, Steinbeck's "success as a protest writer undermined his literary standing, especially after the war, when such commitment came to be seen as limiting and simplistic." See Morris Dickstein, "Steinbeck and the Great Depression," *South Atlantic Quarterly* 103, no. 1 (2004): 112.

6. Steinbeck, *Life in Letters*, 754.

7. Ibid., 758.

8. John Steinbeck, "Nobel Prize Acceptance Speech," in *America and Americans and Selected Nonfiction* (New York: Penguin, 2002), 173–74.

9. John Steinbeck, *Once There Was a War* (New York: Penguin, 1958), x.

10. Ibid., xi.

11. Ibid., xx.

12. Li Luchen, ed., *John Steinbeck: A Documentary Volume*, vol. 309 of *Dictionary of Literary Biography* (Detroit: Gale, 2005), 125.

13. Ibid.

14. Charles R. Metzger, "Steinbeck's *The Pearl* as a Nonteleological Parable of Hope," *Research Studies* 46 (1978): 98–105. See Richard Astro, "Steinbeck and Ricketts: Escape or Commitment in the *Sea of Cortez*?," *Western American Literature* 6 (1971): 109–21; Richard Astro, *John Steinbeck and Ed Ricketts: The Shaping of a Novelist* (Minneapolis: University of Minnesota Press, 1973); and B. L. Perez, "The Collaborative Roles of John Steinbeck and Edward F. Ricketts in the Narrative Section of *Sea of Cortez*" (PhD diss., University of Florida, 1973).

15. Astro, *John Steinbeck and Ed Ricketts*, 14.

16. John Steinbeck and Ed Ricketts, *Sea of Cortez: A Leisurely Journal of Travel and Research* (New York: Viking Press, 1941), 132.

17. Astro, *John Steinbeck and Ed Ricketts*, 15.

18. John Steinbeck, *The Forgotten Village* (New York: Viking, 1941), 10.

19. Ibid., 141.

20. Ibid., 140.

21. Robert Morsberger, "Steinbeck's Films," in *John Steinbeck, from Salinas to the World: Proceedings of the Second International Steinbeck Congress held in Salinas, California*, ed. S. Yano, T. Hayashi, R. F. Peterson, and Y. Hashiguchi (Tokyo: Gaku Shobo, 1986), 54.

22. Donald V. Coers, *John Steinbeck as Propagandist: The Moon Is Down Goes to War* (Tuscaloosa: University of Alabama Press, 1991), 4.

23. Steinbeck, *Life in Letters*, 205.

24. Ibid., 206.

25. Steinbeck and Ricketts, *Sea of Cortez*, 140.

26. Astro, "Steinbeck and Ricketts," 114.

27. Steinbeck, *Life in Letters*, 163.

28. Steinbeck and Ricketts, *Sea of Cortez*, 117.

29. Ed Ricketts, "Thesis and Materials for a Script on Mexico Which Shall Be Motivated Oppositely to John's 'Forgotten Village,'" in *The Outer Shores*, part 2, *Breaking Through (from the Papers of Edward F. Ricketts)*, ed. J. W. Hedgpeth (Eureka, Calif.: Mad River Press, 1978), 174.

30. Ibid., 177.

31. Ibid.

32. Hedgpeth, *Outer Shores*, part 2, 6.

33. Adina Cruz regards *The Pearl* as the crystallization of Steinbeck's philosophical creed. See Cruz, "Similitud y Contraste en Las Novelas *Huasipungo* y *The Pearl*," *Literatura Inglesa* 4, no. 2 (1980): 114. While Cruz's thesis may be overstated, *The Pearl* does illustrate both the impact of Ricketts on Steinbeck's philosophy and the ways in which Steinbeck differed philosophically from his friend.

34. Noburu Shimomura has demonstrated that the novella *The Pearl* began as a script for the 1947 movie of the same name. See Noburu Shimomura, "Guilt and Christianity in *The Pearl*," *Studies in American Literature* 16 (1980): 19. The fact that both *The Forgotten Village* and *The Pearl* began as movie scripts makes comparison between the two works especially appropriate.

35. Steinbeck, *Forgotten Village*, 142–43.

36. The cloak with the frequently reproduced image is currently housed in La Basilica de Guadalupe (three miles northeast of Mexico City).

37. John Ditsky, *John Steinbeck and the Critics* (Rochester, N.Y.: Camden House, 2000), 141.

38. John Steinbeck, *The Pearl* (New York: Penguin, 1994), 36.

39. Ricketts, "Thesis and Materials," 174.

40. Ibid., 69.

41. Ibid., 178.

42. Ibid., 180.

43. Ibid., 181.

44. Steinbeck, *Pearl*, 29.

45. Steinbeck, *Forgotten Village*, 208.

46. Steinbeck, *Pearl*, 9.

47. Ibid., 31.

48. See Augustine, *The City of God* 19.4, *Confessions* 10.35, *De libero arbitrio* 3.20, and *De vera religion* 4. Peter Harrison summarizes Augustine's position on human knowledge: "As for knowledge in a fallen world, Augustine emphasized the fact that Adam's lapse was not merely a moral loss but one that had plunged the human race into an irremediable epistemological confusion. As a consequence of

original sin, individuals not only habitually make wrong moral choices but consistently confuse error for truth." Harrison, *The Fall of Man and the Foundations of Science* (New York: Cambridge University Press, 2007), 32.

49. 1 Corinthians 13:12 (King James version).

50. Steinbeck, *Pearl*, 19.

51. Ibid., 25.

52. Christopher Rocco, *Tragedy and Enlightenment: Athenian Political Thought and the Dilemmas of Modernity* (Berkeley: University of California Press, 1997), 19.

53. Ibid., 43.

54. Steinbeck, *Pearl*, 76.

55. Ibid., 76–77.

56. Astro, *John Steinbeck and Ed Ricketts*, 59.

57. Cited in ibid., 116.

58. Steinbeck, *Forgotten Village*, 98.

59. Steinbeck, *Pearl*, 13.

60. Ibid., 15.

61. Ibid., 17.

62. Ibid., 61.

63. Cited in Ricketts, "Thesis and Materials," 175–76.

64. Steinbeck, *Pearl*, 33.

65. Ibid., 36.

66. Ricketts, "Thesis and Materials," 182; emphasis in original. Ricketts here slightly misquotes a statement from a mural by Mexican artist Diego Rivera, "La verdadera civilización será la armonía de los hombres con la tierra y de los hombres entre si," which roughly translates, "The true civilization will be the harmony of men with the land and among themselves."

67. James A. Hamby, "Steinbeck's *The Pearl:* Tradition and Innovation," *Western Review: A Journal of the Humanities* 7, no. 2 (1970): 65.

68. Steinbeck, *Pearl*, 13.

69. Ibid., 20.

70. Kyoko Ariki, *The Main Thematic Current in John Steinbeck's Works: A Positive View of Man's Survival* (Osaka, Japan: Osaka Kyoiku Tosho Press, 2002), 154.

71. Steinbeck, "Nobel Prize Acceptance Speech," 173.

72. Mizener, "Moral Vision," 45.

PART II

The Cultural Roots of Steinbeck's Political Vision

CHAPTER 5

Group Man and the Limits of Working-Class Politics: The Political Vision of Steinbeck's *In Dubious Battle*

Charles Williams

JOHN STEINBECK'S *IN DUBIOUS BATTLE* was initially praised for its political objectivity and realism. Most reviewers judged Steinbeck as broadly sympathetic toward the striking apple pickers and Communist organizers portrayed in the novel yet deemed *In Dubious Battle* devoid of bald propaganda. As William Rose Benét wrote in the *Saturday Review*, "The author's attempt has been to bring out heroic motive and action in those whom the newspapers denounce as 'Reds,' and at the same time to state events as they would naturally happen as logically and fairly as possible." "Here are no puppets of propaganda," he concluded, "here are real men of flesh and blood." Similarly, *New York Times Book Review* critic Fred T. Marsh simultaneously admired Steinbeck's restrained approach and anticipated the novel's positive contribution to labor's cause: "Steinbeck keeps himself out of the book. There is no editorializing or direct propaganda. His purpose is to describe accurately and dramatize powerfully a small strike of migratory workers, guided by a veteran Communist organizer, in a California fruit valley." Such integrity might disappoint committed partisans of either side, but it also meant that "these strikers and their leaders and their arguments and actions will . . . win the admiration and sympathy of many middle-grounders."[1]

Subsequent scholarship, however, has often viewed *In Dubious Battle* in another light and has identified a very different "objective" concern as the motivation for the novel. On this account, Steinbeck ultimately wished to convey a theory of human behavior grounded in a particular kind of biological naturalism.[2] Here the strikers are illustrations of "group-man," a mob driven by animal instincts and acting violently and independently of individual consciousness. According to what Steinbeck calls his "Argument of Phalanx," such groups have emerged throughout history and can explain invasions, mass migrations, and other mysteries of human life. *In Dubious Battle* merely describes this recurrent phenomenon through the story of a strike. To impart specific political meaning to the novel, then, is to disregard Steinbeck's more universal intent. His theme, furthermore, accounts for the divergences of his narrative from the actual strikes on which he based his story. His revisions of history should be interpreted not in political terms but in terms of the author's philosophical commitments and artistic techniques.[3]

Steinbeck's own remarks lend weight to a nonpartisan reading of *In Dubious Battle.* In a letter to friend and writer George Albee he claimed that "I'm not interested in strike as means of raising men's wages, and I'm not interested in ranting about justice and oppression." Such things were "mere outcroppings" of an underlying human dynamic that concerned him.[4] In light of this assertion we might ask whether it remains valid to relate *In Dubious Battle* to the politics of the 1930s. One affirmative response is offered by Alexander Saxton. He argues that the novel's underlying sympathy for the strikers is both unquestionable and all the more revealing precisely because it conflicts with Steinbeck's scientific ambitions and naturalist philosophy. As Saxton puts it, "Scientific detachment in the midst of the Great Depression was not a role Steinbeck could adhere to." His subject matter was "not blobs of organic chemicals in a tide pool" but rather "sentient beings, some of whom suffer, while others deliberately (and unnecessarily) impose suffering. Detached though he might try to make himself, Steinbeck was obligated to choose sides." For Saxton, *In Dubious Battle* stands as a transitional work, pointing the way to the political commitments evident in *The Grapes of Wrath:* "Its importance for the Steinbeck repertory is that it traces the transition from strategies of denying or transcending suffering to those of accusation and confrontation."[5]

This notion of competing levels of meaning in *In Dubious Battle* is illuminating. Scholars have discerned allusions in the novel to the Bible, *Paradise Lost,* and Arthurian legend.[6] (For further discussion of the biblical allusions in Steinbeck's work, see chapter 7, by Roxanne Harde.) This additional tension between objective naturalism and partisan social protest further helps us to understand Steinbeck's evolution as a writer. Yet a more substantial political reading of the novel (and one that greatly complicates the initial reviews noted above) requires that we consider how Steinbeck's "scientific" observations on the phalanx were also linked to a political vision that informed his subsequent work, including *The Grapes of Wrath.* That is, rather than seeing his account of group man as removed from and in conflict with the political commitments revealed in *In Dubious Battle,* we ought to recognize that Steinbeck's anxieties over the dangers of group man shaped his sympathies for workers and the downtrodden and that this orientation persists in his later writing.

For Steinbeck, actions undertaken by the apple pickers in *In Dubious Battle* constitute a danger to humanity. They constrict human freedom by releasing animal urges that threaten the autonomous and rational individual. Far from viewing the problem of mass man abstractly, Steinbeck recognized it as a political danger visible in contemporary fascist and communist movements and regimes. Accordingly, Steinbeck endorsed reforms that would (he hoped) preserve human dignity and improve the lives of the farmworkers who were his immediate point of reference. In this sense he supported the New Deal philosophy of the 1930s, which was intent on upholding American democracy and capitalism through a pragmatic government response to the crisis of the Depression that would foreclose the possibility of destructive mass politics. That said, Saxton and others correctly point to the growing support for collective political struggle in *The Grapes of Wrath.* Here, and in his related journalism, Steinbeck analyzes the Okies as special bearers of America's agrarian democratic traditions. This offered one possibility for reconciling his two potentially conflicting concerns, group struggle and individual autonomy and reason. Yet Steinbeck's political vision was not exclusively defined by this particular solution. At times, as in *The Grapes of Wrath,* he made more universal claims about "the people" as a positive social force united by similar experiences of suffering that set them against the propertied classes, particularly as such classes exhibited "fascist" propensities. Steinbeck's views on the significance of mass movements during social crisis thus reveal the political anxieties and ambiguities that marked American liberalism in the New Deal era.

The Phalanx, *In Dubious Battle,* and Class

To see the evolution of Steinbeck's political concerns, we need to begin with the phalanx theory that informs *In Dubious Battle.* Steinbeck's theory arose in part from frequent discussions with close friend and marine biologist Edward F. Ricketts, whose ideas led Steinbeck to revisit his own earlier interest in natural science and its philosophical implications. Ricketts, drawing on the ideas of his mentor, University of Chicago biologist W. C. Allee, developed a worldview based on the interdependence of living organisms and the automatic character of natural interactions. As Jackson Benson summarizes, Allee's insight that "social behavior . . . among the lower animals is not the result of conscious decision" led Ricketts to reject the normal human tendency to ask why things happen in favor of a philosophy of simple acceptance, what he termed "non-teleological thinking."[7] This moral position provided an important starting point for *In Dubious Battle.*

Steinbeck detected ideas similar to those of Ricketts in anthropology, history, psychology, and physics. Particularly inspiring were the efforts of philosopher John Elof Boodin, who combined evolutionary theory with a belief in a greater force (with religious, and for Steinbeck also Jungian, overtones) that united individual minds into "a larger whole with properties of its own."[8] As Steinbeck excitedly wrote in a letter to his college roommate Carlton Sheffield, such insights had convinced him that the phalanx was a naturally occurring human organism distinct from the individuals that compose it: "All of the notations I have made begin to point to an end—That the group is an individual as boundaried, as diagnosable, as dependent on its units and as independent of its units' individual natures, as the human unit, or man, is dependent on his cells and yet is independent of them." Linking such groups to the non-teleological perspective of Ricketts, Steinbeck concluded that the phalanx reduces humans to an animal or even insect level. In his words, "As individual humans we are far superior in our functions to anything the world has born—in our groups we are not only not superior but in fact are remarkably like those most perfect groups, the ants and bees."[9]

The phalanx could produce destructive behavior because group man responds involuntarily to natural stimuli. Observing that "sometimes a terrible natural stimulus will create a group over night," Steinbeck extrapolated to the larger historical claim that the phalanx would "explain how

Genghis Khan and Attila and the Goths suddenly stopped being individual herdsmen and hunters and became, almost without transition, a destroying creature obeying a single impulse." Similarly, he concluded from a case in Mendocino County where "a whole community turned against one man and destroyed him although they had taken no harm from him" that "it is quite easy for the group, acting under stimuli to viciousness, to eliminate the kindly natures of its units." As he elaborated in a letter to Albee a short time later, "The phalanx has emotions of which the unit man is incapable. Emotions of destruction, of war, of migration, of hatred, of fear."[10] Steinbeck thus saw a powerful force standing above individual men that made them components of a bigger entity, even as it threatened or debased their existence by destroying their individuality and working in nonrational ways they could not understand or control. As we will see in relation to *The Grapes of Wrath* (and as Richard Astro has emphasized), not all group behavior associated with the phalanx was judged negatively. Nonetheless, the concept of the phalanx exceeded mere factual description or detached observation and carried potentially ominous significance for human society.

According to Steinbeck, the subordination of individuality applied even to the apparent leaders of the phalanx, who were ultimately its products rather than its creators. "Hitler did not create the present phalanx in Germany," Steinbeck explained to Albee, "he merely interprets it."[11] As this quote suggests, the theme of mass irrationality linked Steinbeck to contemporary political debates on both the left and the right regarding the meaning of fascism (a link particularly visible in the use of the term *Falange*, or phalanx, by Spanish fascists).[12] Yet these scientific insights were, he believed, absent from the art of the period. Steinbeck therefore hoped to transmit them to the public, bringing literature into line with modern science: "No great poetry has evolved from our great dream of atoms and of interstellar space, of the quantum and the great snaky spirals of worlds— god in a winding sheet," he wrote in his journal. "Where can I find symbols dignified and simple enough to make it clean and lovely?"[13]

Steinbeck's representation of a strike in *In Dubious Battle* directly embodies this "scientific" understanding of mass behavior. From the initial encounter between the apple pickers and the Communist organizers through the impending defeat of the strike at the end of the novel, workers are portrayed as men driven to collective action by animal impulses and external pressures rather than by self-conscious political decisions. The Communists, meanwhile, disregard individual needs, human emotions, and concern for immediate gains. Instead they try to manipulate the mob to achieve their long-term goal of mass struggle. Finally, Steinbeck's own view of the phalanx is directly inserted into the novel through the character of Doc Burton, who comes to the aid of the strikers but continually questions party certitudes about the likely consequences of mob upheaval.

The novel opens with Jim Nolan joining the (implicitly Communist) Party so that he "might get alive again." Jim's deceased father was constantly harassed by antilabor police, his despondent mother has recently died, and Jim himself has only just been released from jail after being clubbed and arrested for vagrancy at a political rally he was merely observing on his way home from the movies. His life has soured, but the party activists he met in jail seemed to have real meaning in their lives. Now Jim, too, wants to "work toward something." He gets his chance when he accompanies the veteran organizer McLeod to the (fictional) Torgas Valley to foster a strike by apple pickers who have suffered a pay cut.[14]

When Jim and Mac arrive, they find the migrant laborers willing to accept the low wages. Mac, however, quickly befriends the pickers' natural leader, London, whose daughter-in-law is about to give birth. Mac lies about working in hospitals so he can oversee the delivery. By convincing the crop tramps to contribute their own clothes and labor to the delivery, he makes the men feel part of a movement. As Mac justifies his decision to Jim, "We've got to use whatever material comes to us. That was a lucky break. We simply had to take it. 'Course it was nice to help the girl, but hell, even if it killed her—we've got to use anything." "With one night's work," he continues, "we've got the confidence of the men and the confidence of London. And more than that, we made the men work for themselves, in their own defense, as a group."[15]

Mac reveals a fine sensitivity to the animal instincts that shape the behavior of the strikers. When an old picker, Dan, falls from a tree, Mac comments to Jim that "the old buzzard was worth something after all. . . . He tipped the thing off. We can use him now."[16] But he fears a directionless and violent reaction if the men are left to their own devices. "These guys'll go nuts if we don't take charge," says Mac, before telling London and his buddy Sam how to orchestrate the strike. "You go over, Sam, and tell 'em they ought to hold a meeting. And then you nominate London, here, for chairman. They'll put him in all right. They'll do almost anything." Mac then instructs London on how to manipulate the workers: "Here's the way you do it. If you want 'em to vote for something, you say, 'Do you want to do it?' and if you want to vote down somethin', just say, 'You don't want to do this, do you?' and they'll vote no. Make 'em vote on everythin', *everythin'*, see? They're all ready for it."[17] The farmworkers thus move from impulsive anger to organized action by way of engineered elections and remain manipulated objects throughout the strike.

Steinbeck's phalanx analysis becomes explicit in a passage involving the scab labor hired by the Growers' Association. Before the strikers meet a trainload of scabs, Mac expresses his fears to Jim: "This bunch of bums isn't keyed up. I hope to Christ something happens to make 'em mad before long. This's going to fizzle out if something don't happen."[18] He gets his wish when probusiness vigilantes fatally shoot a comrade, Joy, who has arrived with the scabs and is trying to win them over to the strike. Steinbeck describes the workers' response at the sight of Joy's blood: "A strange, heavy movement started among the men. London moved forward woodenly, and the men moved forward. They were stiff. The guards aimed with their guns, but the line moved on, unheeding, unseeing." The strikers have become an unthinking organism capable of challenging the police and the vigilantes: "The guards were frightened; riots they could stop, fighting they could stop; but this slow, silent movement of men with the wide eyes of sleep-walkers terrified them."[19] While the cops cower, Mac calls on another strike leader, Dakin, to take Joy's body back to the camp. Dakin wants to leave him for the police, stunned by Mac's willingness to exploit his dead friend. "Look at the cops," Mac tells him, "they're scared to death. We've got to take him, I tell you. We've got to use him to step our guys up, to keep 'em together. This'll stick 'em together, this'll make 'em fight."[20] The sheriff backs away as the mob growls, and Joy's body is later used in a public funeral and a march through town.

Mac understands that blood and violence stir the mob to action and that food sustains group man. These sources of stimulation dictate the mood swings that shape the strike. At one point, when food supplies are cut off and the strikers are questioning London's leadership, London revives the men's spirit by busting the jaw of an outspoken critic (and possible provocateur) who has falsely accused him of stashing canned goods. The violence inspires the crowd: "The eyes of the men and women were entranced. The bodies weaved slowly, in unison. No more lone cries came from lone men. They moved together, looked alike. The roar was one voice, coming from many throats."[21] Mac confides to Jim, "Didn't I tell you? They need blood. That works. That's what I told you."[22]

Lester Jay Marks notes the extent to which the narrative reflects Steinbeck's interpretation of the phalanx: "As the 'brain' of the group now transformed from nine hundred individual 'cells' into one 'big animal,' Mac senses its despair when the strike seems to be losing momentum. He knows just how to revive the animal: fill its belly and show it blood." Jackson Benson and Anne Loftis make a similar observation, that "with too much food, as with a satiated animal, [the strikers] tend to become apathetic."[23] Steinbeck reveals the biological and psychological drives behind the action, and this foreshadows the conclusion of the novel.

The strike begins to unravel. Anderson, a small farmer who initially allowed the strikers to camp on his land, files a trespass complaint after town vigilantes burn down his barn and beat his Communist-sympathizing son. Increasingly hungry and demoralized, the strikers are on the brink of abandoning the struggle. Mac concedes that the valley is too well organized by the farm owners for the strikers to triumph, but he explains to London that a final confrontation will contribute to the larger struggle. The men, however, have called for a vote to end the strike. This time they act on their own individual calculations about the pointlessness of getting killed. Mac directs London to endorse the meeting because an official "retreat" is at least better than simply "sneak[ing] off like dogs."[24] Jim's unexpected death then opens the way for Mac to reinvigorate the mob. Jim and Mac fall for a trap, and Jim is shot in the face with a shotgun. Mac carries him back to the camp and addresses the gathering. Propping Jim on the platform that previously held Joy's coffin, Mac uses the same words he used at Joy's funeral: "This guy didn't want nothing for himself. . . . Comrades! He didn't want nothing for himself."[25]

We are thus left with an endless and unresolved cycle of violence. "There is no ending in the life of Man," as Steinbeck wrote to Albee at the time. "The book is disorder," he continued, "but if it should ever come to you to read, listen to your own thoughts when you finish it and see if you don't find in it a terrible order, a frightful kind of movement."[26] This analysis is advanced in the novel through Doc, who makes scientific observations about the strike. Doc compares the struggle to the way germs battle within a body. When Mac asks, "You figure the strike is a wound?" Doc responds that "group-men are always getting some kind of infection." He adds, "I want to watch these group-men, for they seem to me to be a new individual, not at all like single men."[27] He then analyzes the menacing characteristic of the phalanx: "People have said, 'mobs are crazy, you can't tell what they'll do.' Why don't people look at mobs not as men, but as mobs? A mob nearly always seems to act reasonably, for a mob."[28]

When Mac discusses the long-term value of labor struggles, Doc offers his alternative theory. Mac declares that even doomed strikes can contribute to the political awakening of the workers. Doc says that this is just a rationalization. "When group-man wants to move," he observes, "he makes a standard. 'God wills that we recapture the Holy Land' or . . . 'We will wipe out social injustice with communism.' But the group doesn't care. . . . Maybe the group simply wants to move, to fight, and uses these words simply to reassure the brains of individual men."[29] Mac responds that organizers like himself, the conscious leaders of movements, refute the idea of group man. Doc has an answer for this, too. "You might be an effect as well as a cause, Mac. You might be an expression of group-man, a cell endowed with a special function, like an eye cell, drawing your force from group-man, and at the same time directing him, like an eye."[30] Similarly, in a later conversation, Jim optimistically opines, "Out of all this struggle a good thing is going to grow. That makes it worthwhile." "I wish I knew it," Doc replies, "but in my little experience the end is never very different in its nature from the means. Damn it, Jim, you can only build a violent thing with violence."[31]

In Dubious Battle therefore conveys a deep fear over the substance and consequences of mob behavior, including working-class struggles. To be sure, Steinbeck gives Mac and his comrades plenty of opportunities to denounce oppression by the owners and their own vigilante mob. Still, there is no suggestion that the collective acts of the farmworkers involve even the possibility of emancipation.[32] By definition, the real motives underlying phalanx action are outside of politics understood as a reasoned or deliberative process. Such upheaval entails no political awakening or, in this case, informed class consciousness. It is notable in this context that the only instance of thoughtful deliberation by the men occurs during the mob's dissolution, when they take steps to end the strike. Steinbeck's biologically inspired "science" of mass behavior accordingly minimizes the political potential of the working class, even as he portrays their plight in sympathetic terms.

This is not to say that the novel denies the attractiveness of selflessly serving a group. Jim's newfound feeling of belonging is explicitly contrasted with the loneliness and ineffectiveness felt by Doc. Both Jim and London also undergo a political education during the strike, even if what they learn are manipulative techniques and what Doc perceives as rationalizations. The fundamental conclusion, however, is that the phalanx is destructive. Surrendering to it, or even trying to give it direction, does not elevate an individual. Not surprisingly, Jim's one moment of assertiveness as a strike leader springs not from lucid political insights but from the fanatical delirium caused by a gunshot wound to his shoulder. Conversely, Mac and Jim seem far more human when they waver in their dedication to the cause, as when Jim expresses a desire to escape to an orchard where he can simply watch the apples grow. Ultimately, Mac's nonaggressive human emotions and his affection for Jim weaken his effectiveness as a party organizer, while Jim's desire to merge into the phalanx culminates with his physical destruction, not a longed-for new awakening.[33]

The Masses and the Individual in Steinbeck's Politics

What does the phalanx theory tell us about Steinbeck's response to the social realities around him? One clue lies in the ways Steinbeck reworked his knowledge of actual California strikes when composing the narrative of *In Dubious Battle*. Jackson Benson and Anne Loftis have documented how Steinbeck transformed the real organizers with whom he was familiar into the manipulative figures of the novel. While they reject any political judgments on that basis, the novel's interpretation of the facts is largely consistent with one characteristic of Steinbeck's subsequent writing on the major political issues of his day. However much Steinbeck embraced the cause of "the people," he never forgot the menace of mass man. This combination defined his New Deal liberalism.

In 1934 Steinbeck met and interviewed two young organizers from the Communist-led Cannery and Agricultural Workers' Industrial Union. Drawing on their firsthand knowledge of the 1933 peach and cotton strikes, Steinbeck incorporated various incidents from both conflicts into the fictional apple orchard strike. He also learned a great deal about leading

Communist organizers Pat Chambers and Caroline Decker, who seemed to function as models for Mac and Jim.[34] Yet, Benson and Loftis argue, "Chambers and Decker were much more caring, much more concerned about the workers and their needs" than were Mac and Jim. For example, Mac hopes for violence in the confrontation when the scabs arrive and "welcomes the shooting of Joy as useful." Benson and Loftis contend that this is "a serious deviation from the motivation and operation of the actual strike leaders." Under similar circumstances Chambers merely hoped to exhibit the strikers' "unity in the face of threats." "None of these organizers was so cynical," they write, "that he or she would deliberately design a 'blood sacrifice' to stir up the workers." Moreover, the strikers never marched against the police. "In truth, when they [the strikers], as unarmed men, were fired on, they wisely took to their heels. There is no indication in the reports on either the Peach or Cotton Strikes that unarmed strikers as a mob faced down the police."[35]

The organizers also believed that the cotton strike was made possible only by "the development of leadership from the ranks, from the bottom up."[36] Here again, Steinbeck's fiction distorts the actual roles of both Communists and workers. He displaces the political complexities of the strike to heighten our fear of the mob. Benson attributes the fabrications to Steinbeck's theory of the phalanx: "[Steinbeck's] mining of his sources for convincing detail was not an end in itself but a means by which he could construct a more powerful metaphor."[37] Most crucially, the novel's theme means any political judgment about *In Dubious Battle* is inherently off base: "We cannot fault Steinbeck for being convincing, nor can we blame him for having chosen from his sources what he wished for his own purposes. The trouble lies in our persistent tendency to view the novel on our own, usually political and journalistic, terms."[38]

Yet the phalanx theory was a political formulation. While Saxton and others assert that Steinbeck jettisoned the scientific "objectivity" of *In Dubious Battle* for overt political commitments in *The Grapes of Wrath*, this conclusion is too absolute.[39] Instead, the phalanx idea reappears in Steinbeck's assessment of California labor politics and in his broader response to communism and fascism. Richard H. Pells correctly locates *In Dubious Battle* within a literary tradition of the 1930s that moved from a "suspicion of the masses . . . into an attack on the very ideal of collectivism itself," complete with "a growing dread of men in groups."[40] By extending this assessment to an overall engagement with Steinbeck's politics, we get much closer to understanding his ambiguous relationship to the mob that might also be celebrated as "the people."

Both sides of Steinbeck's political ambivalence appear in *Their Blood Is Strong*, a 1938 pamphlet collecting and extending his 1936 journalistic essays on migrant farmworkers.[11] Many details in the pamphlet anticipate *The Grapes of Wrath*. In both publications Steinbeck celebrates the Okies and endorses unions and government intervention as solutions to exploitation. But *Their Blood Is Strong* also expresses Steinbeck's anxieties about mob behavior incited by acute poverty. For Steinbeck, the economic and political situation in California was a threat to American democracy. As he saw it, the growers' associations and farm speculators were creating subhuman peons who were excluded from political power. Describing three representative migrant families, Steinbeck discusses a progression of suffering until "dignity is all gone, and spirit has turned to sullen anger before it dies." "This," Steinbeck wrote, "is what the man in the tent will be in six months; what the man in the paper house with its peaked roof will be in a year, after his house has washed down and his children have sickened or died, after the loss of dignity and spirit have cut him down to a kind of sub-humanity." If the California economy requires such a "peon class," "then California must depart from the semblance of democratic government that remains here."[12]

At the root of the problem, corporate farming entailed a tightly knit political alliance that ran the state for its own benefit and controlled workers through repression. In Steinbeck's words, "Such organizations as Associated Farmers, Inc. have as members and board members officials of banks, publishers of newspapers, and politicians; and through close association with the state Chamber of Commerce they have interlocking associations with shipowners' associations, public utilities corporations, and transportation companies." The political consequences were devastating: "If the terrorism and reduction of human rights, the floggings, murder by deputies, kidnappings, and refusal of trial by jury are necessary to our economic security, it is further submitted that California democracy is rapidly dwindling away. Fascistic methods are more numerous, more powerfully applied, and more openly practiced in California than any other place in the United States." In turn, the repression will incite mob action. The "unrest, tension, and hatred" generated by the "policy of the large grower" will nurture a spirit of revolt, and therefore "constitutes a criminal endangering of the peace of the state."[13]

Steinbeck outlines a political economy of right-wing repression (and potential fascism) that goes beyond his concern with the irrational upheavals of the phalanx. Yet while workers were justified in opposing farm fascism, Steinbeck also worried about how their degraded condition would infect their politics. "The workers are herded about like animals," he observed, adding that "every possible method is used to make them feel inferior and insecure." As a result, "the attitude of the workers on the large ranch is much [like] that of the employer—hatred and suspicion." If for now the migrants have "taken refuge in a sullen, tense quiet," ultimately the situation can be resolved in only one of two ways: "They can be citizens of the highest type, or they can be an army driven by suffering and hatred to take what they need."[14] The themes of *In Dubious Battle* persist. Farm fascism degrades the workers, and the migrants in turn become a desperate mass without dignity, a volcano that will explode if conditions do not improve.

This dynamic, Steinbeck concludes, will ultimately destroy California's farm economy: "While California has been successful in its use of migrant labor, it is gradually building a human structure which will certainly change the state, and may, if handled with the inhumanity and stupidity that have characterized the past, destroy the present system of agricultural economics."[15] At stake, then, is an imminent transformation of society driven by the creation of the phalanx. Of course, this is not the whole story, and Steinbeck discusses possibilities for reform involving the efforts of the migrants themselves. But the fearful vision of *In Dubious Battle* remained in Steinbeck's mind and was connected to his views on communism and fascism.

When Steinbeck first formulated his phalanx theory, he cited Russia as a contemporary manifestation of the phenomenon. He wrote to Carlton Sheffield, "Russia is giving us a nice example of human units who are trying with a curious nostalgia to get away from their individuality and reestablish the group unit the race remembers and wishes."[16] In his view, communism ultimately derives from deep biological and psychological impulses rather than political beliefs or economic conflicts. This accords with Doc's position in *In Dubious Battle*. In a 1936 letter, Steinbeck described his personal distaste for Communists in California. "I don't like communists either, I mean I dislike them as people. I rather imagine the apostles had the same waspish qualities and the New Testament is proof that they had equally bad manners." Although he admired certain organizers for their dedication, he viewed them as fanatical and remote from human complexities. "Some of these communist field workers are strong, pure, inhumanly virtuous men," he wrote.[17] This insight did not prevent Steinbeck from participating in a variety of left-liberal Popular Front cultural activities that the party organized. But Steinbeck's observations nonetheless reveal the early point at which he associated communism and the party with his ideas about oppressive group behavior.

Steinbeck wrote a more complete and obviously critical statement about communism in *Sea of Cortez,* published in 1941. Collaborating with Ed Ricketts on this "leisurely journal of travel and research," Steinbeck describes the sources and ramifications of communism (and fascism) by means of his phalanx perspective:

> Ideas are not dangerous unless they find seeding place in some earth more profound than the mind. Leaders and would-be leaders are so afraid that the *idea* "communism" or the *idea* "Fascism" may lead to revolt, when actually they are ineffective without the black earth of discontent to grow in. The strike-raddled businessman may lean toward strikeless Fascism, forgetting that it also eliminates him. The rebel may yearn violently for the freedom from capitalist domination expected in a workers' state, and ignore the fact that such a state is free from rebels. In each case the idea is dangerous only when planted in unease and disquietude. But being so planted, growing in such earth, it ceases to be idea and becomes emotion and then religion.[18]

Confronted with the major political upheavals of the 1930s and early 1940s, Steinbeck worried about mass movements that obliterate the individual. Conformity and fanaticism define conflicts that fall outside liberal democratic politics, with mass movements relying on emotion, religion, and biological dynamics rather than rational political commitments. Thus the story in *In Dubious Battle* is not just a one-time application of a useful metaphor. The phalanx theory colored Steinbeck's political views throughout the thirties, and this would persist into the postwar period.

Steinbeck's analysis of communism and its repressive character ignores the actual political context, goals, and power struggles that determined Communist Party practices and that differentiated communism from other forms of radical politics and working-class insurgency. Instead, Steinbeck subsumed radical labor organization under Stalinism and understood Stalinism as an expression of the phalanx. He reduced radical politics to subpolitical, irrational upheavals defined by the qualities of group man and restricted legitimate politics to a kind of liberal individualism and pragmatic, group-based bargaining premised on acceptance of the basic social order. Morris Dickstein is therefore right when he argues that Steinbeck was concerned with "Communists as character types" but wrong to suggest that this removes him from theoretical or political debates regarding communism.[49]

Steinbeck's depictions of communism anticipate the postwar, liberal anticommunism embraced by the Truman administration. Portraying domestic communism as an alien conspiracy, "Truman and his anti-Communist, liberal supporters distinguished the Communist party from legitimate political oppositions."[50] As Michael Rogin emphasizes, political dissent was thus transformed into criminal disloyalty, with anticommunism "focus[ing] not on actual crimes but on memberships, beliefs, and associations." An oppressive political culture developed from the late 1940s onward: "Exaggerated responses to the domestic Communist menace narrowed the bounds of permissible political disagreement and generated a national-security state."[51] In this context, Steinbeck's argument—that communism allows no space for the single rebel or for any assertion of individuality—was precisely the rationale for repressing Communist and other radical politics within the labor movement and across American society as a whole. Since communism entailed the elimination of political (or other) dissent, Communists must be preemptively purged from the body politic in lieu of open political criticism of party objectives. As Rogin describes this countersubversive tradition in American politics, "Pluralists blame alleged extremists for intolerance, to read them out of legitimate political debate and thereby participate in the exclusionary impulse they attribute to their foes."[52]

Yet while Steinbeck's analysis anticipates the trajectory of liberalism from New Deal to Cold War, he did not participate in the domestic anticommunism of the postwar period. To be sure, he reiterated the same perspective on the Soviet Union and more generally denounced radical politics beyond the bounds of liberalism. Thus in 1954 he wrote in *Le Figaro* that "the bait of the Marxist movement was that once free of bourgeois control the masses would cease to be masses and would emerge as individuals. Authority and power would then melt away. This dream has long since been abandoned except in the baited areas. Far from disappearing, power and oppression have increased. The so-called masses are more lumpen than ever. Any semblance of the emergence of the individual is instantly crushed and the doctrine of party and state above everything has taken the place of the theory of liberated men."[53] Steinbeck's central concern was still the conflict between the oppressive group and the creative individual, offering no sense that human creativity and freedom might be contingent on the relationships that make up a community. Writing about the communist state, he concluded that "individuality must be destroyed because it is dangerous to all reactionary plans because the individual is creative. . . . The individual human brain working alone is the only creative organ in nature. The group creates nothing, although it sometimes carries out the creation of the individual." Accordingly, Steinbeck defined himself as the true revolutionary: "Herein is my revolt. I believe in and will fight for the right of the individual to function as an individual without pressure from any direction."[54] But this libertarian outlook led Steinbeck to reject abusive state power at home as well.

In 1957 Steinbeck, unlike other celebrities, came to his friend Arthur Miller's public defense when Miller was put on trial for contempt of Congress after refusing to answer questions before the House Un-American Activities Committee (HUAC). "If I were in Arthur Miller's shoes," Steinbeck wrote in *Esquire*, "I do not know what I would do, but I could wish, for myself and for my children, that I would be brave enough to fortify and defend my private morality as he has." In Steinbeck's view this sort of "individual courage and morals" served the country far more "than . . . the safe and public patriotism which Dr. Johnson called 'the last refuge of scoundrels.'"[55] Five years earlier Steinbeck had taken a similar position in support of another politically isolated friend, Elia Kazan. Kazan had appeared as a cooperative witness before HUAC. Expressing his deep respect for Kazan's decision to act according to his principles despite the inevitable condemnation from liberal intellectuals (what Steinbeck called "a kind of martyrdom"), Steinbeck wrote in a private letter that "I hope I could have had the courage to do what he did."[56] At stake here for Steinbeck in these cases was the integrity of the individual.

Steinbeck's views also departed from the repressive character of postwar liberalism in another context. Alongside his antipathy to communism, Steinbeck recognized the distortions and political danger of American anticommunism as early as the late 1930s. He denied that Communists were alien agitators who introduced conflict into an otherwise stable society. Instead, he treated political radicalism as the natural outcome of poverty and exploitation, and he frequently exposed anticommunism as a tool of business owners. As he wrote in *Their Blood Is Strong*, "The Associated Farmers . . . in the face of the crisis is conducting Americanism meetings and bawling about Reds and foreign agitators. It has been invariably true in the past that when such a close-knit financial group as the Associated Farmers becomes excited about our ancient liberties and foreign agitators, someone is about to lose something. A wage cut has invariably followed such a campaign of pure Americanism. And of course any resentment of such a wage cut is set down as the work of foreign agitators."[57] According to Steinbeck, a home-grown business class was accusing all opponents of communism. At the same time, this very class was creating the conditions for actual communist influence. The phalanx and its leaders would emerge only under particular material circumstances. If the repressive methods of corporate farms were pushing farmworkers toward mob behavior and thinking, then the struggle for human dignity must be directed first and foremost against the corporate interests, not the Communists.

It was in this context that Steinbeck wrote *The Grapes of Wrath* and embraced progressive political solutions to the exploitation of the farmworkers. Much of this—a vision of pragmatic government action in conjunction with the initiative of Okie families—can be seen as an extension of his liberal individualism. To borrow Benson's words, "A fairly accurate way of describing Steinbeck, perhaps even more accurately than a New Deal Democrat with middle-class values, is as an independent who valued individuality. . . . He wanted to be an individualist; he admired individualists; yet he also had a strong social conscience and a strong sense of right and wrong."[58] But Steinbeck also believed that the American order was evolving under crisis conditions. The mob remained a danger for Steinbeck, and this fear always shaped Steinbeck's engagement with radicalism. Yet he hoped that the same people who might descend to mob behavior might become a source of democratic resistance to corporate capitalism.

The New Deal and the People

The New Deal characteristics of Steinbeck's response to California's farm fascism are well known. The *San Francisco News* asked Steinbeck in 1936 to write about migrant workers, and his ensuing trip through the Central Valley resulted in a friendship with Tom Collins, the manager of the Arvin Sanitary Camp for migrant workers ("Weedpatch"). *Their Blood Is Strong* describes and commends Collins's projects to ameliorate migrant poverty and its dangerous political implications.[59] In Steinbeck's opinion, "The result has been more than could be expected. From the first, the intent of the management has been to restore the dignity and decency that had been kicked out of the migrants by their intolerable mode of life." Restoration of pride was, of course, essential to Steinbeck, since he "regard[ed] this destruction of dignity . . . as one of the most regrettable results of the migrant's life, since it does reduce his responsibility and does make him a sullen outcast who will strike at our government in any way that occurs to him." Instead, "the people in the camp are encouraged to govern themselves, and they have responded with simple and workable democracy."[60] Properly expanded, such camps could "allow the women and children to stay in one place, permitting the children to go to school and the women to maintain . . . [small maintenance] farms during the work times of the men." The overall result would be to "reduce the degenerating effect of the migrants' life . . . instill[ing] the sense of government and possession that has been lost by the migrants." "The success of these federal camps in making potential criminals into citizens," Steinbeck wrote, "makes the usual practice of expending money on tear gas seem a little silly."[61]

Steinbeck's analysis lies squarely within the American liberal tradition as it was evolving during the 1930s. In the words of Nelson Lichtenstein, Franklin Roosevelt's "reconceptualization of American liberalism was predicated on the belief that the greatest threat to the republican form of government now came from concentrated capital far more than from an overweening state."[62] The policies adopted under the New Deal may have been limited and contradictory, but the reformers recognized the danger posed by "economic royalists" to individual freedoms.[63] Steinbeck, fearing that the alternative to federal camps in California was corporate repression and mob violence, shared the New Dealers' faith in government as a mediator between conflicting interests and as a promoter of social stability, national unity, and economic recovery.[64] In addition, he advocated a political coalition along quintessentially New Deal lines. He argued that "it will require a militant and watchful organization of middle-class people, workers, teachers, craftsmen, and liberals to fight this encroaching [fascist] social philosophy, and to maintain this state in a democratic form of government."[65]

Lichtenstein asserts that a Jeffersonian philosophy underlies the New Deal attempt to restructure (without fundamentally challenging) American capitalism. A similar perspective underpinned Steinbeck's hopes for preserving democracy in California. The Okies were the perfect collaborators for camp managers like Collins because they embodied the best American traditions. In Steinbeck's opinion, "They are small farmers who have lost their farms, or farm hands who lived with the family in the old American way. They are men who have worked hard on their own farms and have felt the pride of possessing and living in close touch with the land."[66] From the perspective of Jeffersonian agrarian republicanism, such men were prepared to self-govern because of the independence, self-sufficiency, and virtue that arose from their relationship to the land.[67] They stood in stark contrast to the parasitic industrial interests that controlled California's farms. As Steinbeck put it,

> Having been brought up in the prairies where industrialization never penetrated, they have jumped with no transition from the old agrarian, self-containing farm, where nearly everything used was raised or manufactured, to a system of agriculture so industrialized that the man who plants a crop does not often see, let alone harvest, the fruit of his planting, where the migrant has no contact with the growing cycle.
>
> And there is another difference between their [old] life and the new. They have come from little farm districts where democracy was not only possible, but inevitable, where popular government, whether practiced in the Grange, in church organization, or in local government, was the responsibility of every man.[68]

All of this argument, of course, appears in *The Grapes of Wrath*, where the public migrant camp suggests the promise of government planning combined with the democratic orientation of the new class of Okie farmworkers. Weedpatch is managed by a thoughtful and sympathetic government official, Jim Rawley, while the migrants easily adapt to a committee system of self-government that quickly restores their dignity. The social basis for such democratic behavior is revealed earlier, when the Joads hold a traditional family council prior to leaving for California, although this familial self-sufficiency (and male dominance) will be eroded by migrant life outside the camp. Yet the novel does not end with the Joads in the federal camp, and its larger implication is that any return to family dignity will come through a collective movement that transcends the family or the mere revival on an individual basis of the qualities shared by the Okies.

It is possible to see Steinbeck's apparent shift in support for collective struggle as a reflection of Okie exceptionalism. Precisely because of their nature as a people, the Okies are capable as a *group* of restoring individual autonomy. "Their blood is strong," Steinbeck wrote in his newspaper account of the migrants. "And because of their tradition and their training, they are not migrants by nature." Accordingly, he argued, "it should be understood that with this new race the old methods of repression, of starvation wages, of jailing, beating, and intimidation are not going to work; these are American people."[69] Steinbeck's contrast between the Okies and other farmworkers in part reflects his awareness of the greater political vulnerability of Chinese, Japanese, Mexican, and Filipino immigrants. Nonetheless, this was also a racialized understanding of the cultural and biological capacities of the Okies, which, Steinbeck thought, equipped them to uphold democracy.[70] Perceiving the future of California farm labor as "white and American," Steinbeck ultimately concluded that "the new migrants to California from the dust bowl are here to stay. They are of the best American stock, intelligent, resourceful, and, if given a chance, socially responsible."[71]

As Michael Denning observes, "Steinbeck's racial populism deeply inflects *The Grapes of Wrath* as well."[72] The novel often stresses the Joads' status as true Americans, which allows them to participate in a class struggle that promises something other than the mob outcome explored in *In Dubious Battle*. To be sure, Steinbeck still warns of a "dead terror" that will arrive when "the armies of bitterness will all be going the same way."[73] But the threat of the self-destructive phalanx is balanced by the notion that individual (or family) well-being *requires* sustained participation in a larger community. The farm families spontaneously evolve into such a community, becoming "one family" in the roadside camps and through their common suffering and resilience as farmworkers.[74] Not just Tom but also Ma embraces Casy's social-gospel message of the need for group unity and collective struggle against the corporate order.[75] In hardship lies a potential for solidarity. Tom tells Ma his thoughts about "our people livin' like pigs, an' the good rich lan' layin' fallow" and about what would happen "if all our folks got together an' yelled, like them fellas yelled, only a few of 'em at Hooper ranch."[76] As Richard Astro notes, Ma likewise "shifts her reference orientation from the family unit to the larger migrant community as a whole."[77]

There is thus a substantial sense in which the Okies provide the bedrock for Steinbeck's populism. But it would be wrong to see his vision as bounded by race. Both Casy and Tom emphasize each individual's stake in the wider human community and proclaim a universal struggle for social justice. Enlightened by Casy's conclusion that "a fella ain't got a soul of his own, but on'y a piece of a big one," Tom adopts a universal perspective and tells Ma not to mourn his physical absence or fate because he will live spiritually in the struggles of the downtrodden.[78] As Warren French observes, "Tom has given up his concept of clan loyalty and has replaced it with the concept that one must help whoever needs help. Gradually, the rest of the family comes to share this concept."[79]

Astro links this transformation to the constructive possibilities of the phalanx. He writes that *The Grapes of Wrath* is fundamentally an account of how "the Joads, under Casy's guidance, realize that joint participation in a group movement (phalanx) aimed toward an agrarian ideal is necessary not only to ensure biological survival, but also to the moral end of affirming individual dignity." Astro explains that Steinbeck's phalanx theory presumes a subconscious "keying device which enables man to recognize his phalanx role and to discover how, through participation as a unit in the group, he fulfills himself as an individual." Collective action therefore provides room for conscious choice and political perspective, not just blind submission to subrational impulses: "[Steinbeck] surely realizes that there is more than one type of group-man; that there are creative and destructive phalanxes, and he maintains that man, as a 'thinking, figuring' being, must align himself with the group that will safeguard rather than devour his individuality."[80] (For further discussion of the potentially positive aspects of Steinbeck's theory of "group man," see chapter 12, by Mimi R. Gladstein and James H. Meredith.)

This is indeed a long way from the pessimism of *In Dubious Battle*. On one level it returns us to Saxton's account of Steinbeck's political evolution while clarifying the logic behind his endorsement of group struggle in *The Grapes of Wrath*. Yet it is precisely here that we need to see the ongoing significance of the phalanx analysis with regard to Steinbeck's support for collective political action. Steinbeck's recognition of positive collective struggle in *The Grapes of Wrath* is still bound by his individualism and enthusiasm for American political traditions. Mass struggle outside these traditions is interpreted as involving the loss of individuality, leading to a negative assessment of radical movements centered on the destructive power of irrational biological, emotional, and religious impulses. Both during and after the 1930s Steinbeck repeatedly depicted the interests of the individual *in conflict* with the group or phalanx. For Steinbeck, the individual was the only creative force in the world and was constantly threatened by communal pressures that Steinbeck opposed.

This tension between Steinbeck's willingness to embrace some forms of group struggle and his concern for the autonomy of the individual was never fully resolved, in part because his views on group man were ultimately contradictory. Nonetheless, a clear thread runs through his political analysis. Steinbeck saw the threat to individual dignity coming from powerful corporate interests in California during the late 1930s. Faced with this oppression and the possibility of violent reaction by impoverished migrants, he embraced not just government action and middle-class political intervention but also a movement of "the people." Except for this creative phalanx of former farmers, group man threatens the survival of the social order. In this sense the deeper fear of mass politics continued to shape Steinbeck's analysis even here, leaving American liberal individualism as the essence of his vision of freedom.

Finally, however, the underlying traditionalism of Steinbeck's politics need not obscure the significance of *The Grapes of Wrath* as a powerful expression of social reform and populist energies during the late 1930s. Steinbeck's political vision resembled the enthusiasm of New Dealers for the common people and reinforced the leftward trajectory of liberalism amid the rise of the CIO, corporate power, and fascism. Meanwhile, Communist support for a Popular Front against fascism meant that the party rejected Third Period class struggle in favor of appeals to "the people" and a cross-class coalition similar to the one endorsed by Steinbeck. Marshaling the slogan "Communism is twentieth-century Americanism," the party emphasized its native roots and affinity with American groups like the Okies. In these circumstances Steinbeck developed ties to the Popular Front milieu, including a (nominal) leadership role in the League of American

Writers.[81] More broadly, *The Grapes of Wrath* made Steinbeck an important and hugely successful figure in a left-aligned popular culture, combining criticism of contemporary business elites and a faith in the older democratic traditions of the society.[82]

Notes

1. William Rose Benét, "Apple Pickers' Strike," *Saturday Review*, February 1, 1936, 10; Fred T. Marsh, "*In Dubious Battle* and Other Recent Works of Fiction," *New York Times Book Review*, February 2, 1936, 7; see also Joseph Henry Jackson, "*Tortilla Flat* Author Produces Proletarian Novel of Sound Worth," *San Francisco Chronicle*, January 1, 1936, D4; all in Joseph R. McElrath Jr., Jesse S. Crisler, and Susan Shillinglaw, eds., *John Steinbeck: The Contemporary Reviews* (New York: Cambridge University Press, 1996), 51–61; this initial response to the novel is also discussed in Jackson J. Benson and Anne Loftis, "John Steinbeck and Farm Labor Unionization: The Background of *In Dubious Battle*," *American Literature* 52 (May 1980): 194.

2. Benson and Loftis, "John Steinbeck and Farm Labor Unionization," 197–98; Jackson J. Benson, *The True Adventures of John Steinbeck, Writer* (New York: Viking Press, 1984), 244–45, 270; Lester Jay Marks, *Thematic Design in the Novels of John Steinbeck* (The Hague: Mouton, 1969), 48; Louis Owens, *John Steinbeck's Re-vision of America* (Athens: University of Georgia Press, 1985), 92; Louis Owens, "Writing 'In Costume': The Missing Voices of *In Dubious Battle*," in *John Steinbeck: The Years of Greatness, 1936–1939*, ed. Tetsumaro Hayashi (Tuscaloosa: University of Alabama Press, 1993), 77–94; and see John Steinbeck, *Steinbeck: A Life in Letters*, ed. Elaine Steinbeck and Robert Wallsten (New York: Viking Press, 1975), 79–81, 98.

3. Benson and Loftis, "John Steinbeck and Farm Labor Unionization," 210, 221–23; Benson, *True Adventures*, 304; Owens, "Writing 'In Costume,'" 85–86.

4. Steinbeck to George Albee, January 15, 1935, in Steinbeck, *Life in Letters*, 98; and see Benson, *True Adventures*, 304.

5. Alexander Saxton, "*In Dubious Battle:* Looking Backward," *Pacific Historical Review* 73 (May 2004): 249–62, quotes from 256–58; see also David Wyatt, introduction to *New Essays on* The Grapes of Wrath, ed. David Wyatt (Cambridge: Cambridge University Press, 1990); Morris Dickstein, "Steinbeck and the Great Depression," *South Atlantic Quarterly* 103 (Winter 2004): 111–31.

6. Jay Parini, *John Steinbeck: A Biography* (London: Heinemann, 1994), 208–9; Owens, *John Steinbeck's Re-vision*, 90–91; Christopher Busch, "Overcome by Cain: Human Nature's Inner Battle in Steinbeck's 'Strike' Novel," in *The Be-*

trayal of Brotherhood in the Work of John Steinbeck: Cain Sign, ed. Michael J. Meyer (Lewiston, N.Y.: Edwin Mellen Press, 2000); Warren French, "Steinbeck's Use of Malory," in *Steinbeck and the Arthurian Theme*, Steinbeck Monograph Series 5, ed. Tetsumaro Hayashi (Muncie, Ind.: John Steinbeck Society of America, English Department, Ball State University, 1975).

7. Benson, *True Adventures*, 183–85, 191–93; on Steinbeck's earlier thought along related lines, see 240–46.

8. Benson, *True Adventures*, 268; see 265–70 for a summary of the sources and nature of Steinbeck's philosophy that heavily informs my discussion; for a further detailed analysis, see Richard Astro, *John Steinbeck and Edward F. Ricketts: The Shaping of a Novelist* (Minneapolis: University of Minnesota Press, 1973); see also Steinbeck, *Life in Letters*, 80, for Steinbeck on Jung.

9. Steinbeck to Carlton A. Sheffield, June 21, 1933, in Steinbeck, *Life in Letters*, 75–76; and see Benson, *True Adventures*, 267.

10. Steinbeck to Carlton A. Sheffield, June 21, 1933, and Steinbeck to George Albee, 1933, in Steinbeck, *Life in Letters*, 75–77, 80.

11. Steinbeck to George Albee, 1933, in Steinbeck, *Life in Letters*, 80.

12. On the antirationalist ideology of fascism as a mass movement, see Mark Neocleous, *Fascism* (Minneapolis: University of Minnesota Press, 1997); on fascist mass irrationalism from the perspective of the revolutionary Left, see Isaac Deutscher, *The Prophet Outcast: Trotsky, 1929–1940* (New York: Vintage Books, 1963).

13. Benson, *True Adventures*, 266–67.

14. John Steinbeck, *In Dubious Battle* (New York: Penguin Books, 1979), 7.

15. Ibid., 53–54.

16. Ibid., 90.

17. Ibid., 91.

18. Ibid., 145.

19. Ibid., 148.

20. Ibid., 149.

21. Ibid., 287.

22. Ibid., 288.

23. Marks, *Thematic Design*, 50; Benson and Loftis, "John Steinbeck and Farm Labor Unionization," 217.

24. Steinbeck, *In Dubious Battle*, 310.

25. Ibid., 313.

26. Steinbeck to George Albee, January 15, 1935, in Steinbeck, *Life in Letters*, 98–99.

27. Steinbeck, *In Dubious Battle*, 130–31.

28. Ibid., 131.

29. Ibid.

30. Ibid.

31. Ibid., 230.

32. For a similar conclusion about the novel's political pessimism that is less concerned with the nature of 1930s political upheaval, see Astro, *John Steinbeck and Edward F. Ricketts*, 122–23; on the novel's negative assessment of the consequences of labor conflict, see also Warren French, *John Steinbeck*, 2nd revised ed. (Boston: Twayne, 1975), 76; for the view that Steinbeck is sympathetic to Mac and the methods of the strike, see Jerry W. Wilson, "*In Dubious Battle:* Engagement in Collectivity," *Steinbeck Quarterly* 13, nos. 1–2 (1980): 31–42; Richard S. Pressman, "Individualists or Collectivists: Steinbeck's *In Dubious Battle* and Hemmingway's *To Have and Have Not*," *Steinbeck Quarterly* 25, nos. 3–4 (1992): 119–32.

33. For a similar analysis on this point, see Owens, *John Steinbeck's Revision*, 93, 96.

34. Benson and Loftis, "John Steinbeck and Farm Labor Unionization," 219–20; Benson, *True Adventures*, 296–306.

35. Benson and Loftis, "John Steinbeck and Farm Labor Unionization," 208, 216–17; see also Benson, *True Adventures*, 303.

36. Quoted in Benson, *True Adventures*, 302.

37. Ibid., 304; for related points, including Steinbeck's omission of Mexican workers from the ranks of the strikers, see also Benson and Loftis, "John Steinbeck and Farm Labor Unionization," 210; Owens, "Writing 'In Costume,'" 85–86.

38. Benson and Loftis, "John Steinbeck and Farm Labor Unionization," 223.

39. See, for example, Dickstein, "Steinbeck and the Great Depression," 116.

40. Richard H. Pells, *Radical Visions and American Dreams: Culture and Social Thought in the Depression Years* (Middletown, Conn.: Wesleyan University Press, 1973), 225.

41. See Warren French, ed., *A Companion to* The Grapes of Wrath (New York: Viking Press, 1963), 52.

42. John Steinbeck, *Their Blood Is Strong*, in French, *Companion*, 57, 62–64.

43. Ibid., 65, 69, 87.

44. Ibid., 68, 87.

45. Ibid., 59.

46. Steinbeck, *Life in Letters*, 76.

47. Steinbeck to Louis Paul, February 1936, in Steinbeck, *Life in Letters*, 120.

48. John Steinbeck and Edward F. Ricketts, *Sea of Cortez: A Leisurely Journal of Travel and Research* (New York: Viking Press, 1941), 258–59.

49. Dickstein, "Steinbeck and the Great Depression," 119.

50. Michael Rogin, *Ronald Reagan, the Movie, and Other Episodes in Political Demonology* (Berkeley: University of California Press, 1987), 72.

51. Ibid., 68, 73.

52. Ibid., 280.

53. John Steinbeck, "I Am a Revolutionary," in *Of Men and Their Making: The Selected Nonfiction of John Steinbeck*, ed. Susan Shillinglaw and Jackson J. Benson (London: Allen Lane, 2002), 89–90.

54. Ibid., 90; this same view is put forward using very similar language in *East of Eden*, chapter 13.

55. John Steinbeck, "The Trial of Arthur Miller," in *Of Men and Their Making*, 104; and see the discussion in Benson, *True Adventures*, 722, 811–13.

56. Steinbeck to Pat Covici, May 28, 1952, quoted in Benson, *True Adventures*, 722; and see the April 18 letter to Covici in Steinbeck, *Life in Letters*, 443.

57. Steinbeck, *Their Blood Is Strong*, 88–89.

58. Benson, *True Adventures*, 719–20.

59. Wyatt, introduction, 13; Benson, *True Adventures*, 332–33, 338–40.

60. Steinbeck, *Their Blood Is Strong*, 70–71.

61. Ibid., 73–74.

62. Nelson Lichtenstein, *State of the Union: A Century of American Labor* (Princeton, N.J.: Princeton University Press, 2002), 31.

63. Ibid., 31–32; Ellis W. Hawley, *The New Deal and the Problem of Monopoly: A Study in Economic Ambivalence* (Princeton, N.J.: Princeton University Press, 1966).

64. Frank Freidel, *Franklin D. Roosevelt: A Rendezvous with Destiny* (Boston: Back Bay Books, 1990), 98–100; William E. Leuchtenburg, *Franklin D. Roosevelt and the New Deal, 1932–1940* (New York: Harper and Row, 1963), 84–89, 109, 331–32; Steve Fraser, "The 'Labor Question,'" in *The Rise and Fall of the New Deal Order, 1930–1980*, ed. Steve Fraser and Gary Gerstle (Princeton, N.J.: Princeton University Press, 1989).

65. Steinbeck, *Their Blood Is Strong*, 87.

66. Ibid., 56.

67. Chester E. Eisinger, "Jeffersonian Agrarianism in *The Grapes of Wrath*," in *A Casebook on* The Grapes of Wrath, ed. Agnes McNeill Donohue (New York: Thomas Y. Crowell, 1968).

68. Steinbeck, *Their Blood Is Strong*, 57.

69. Ibid., 56–57.

70. On the political vulnerability of immigrant farmworkers, see ibid., 80–85; for an analysis of the same passages suggesting that Steinbeck was trying to appeal to the white readership of the *News*, see Dickstein, "Steinbeck and the Great

Depression," 124; see also Kevin Hearle, "These Are American People: The Spectre of Eugenics in *Their Blood Is Strong* and *The Grapes of Wrath*," in *Beyond Boundaries: Rereading John Steinbeck*, ed. Susan Shillinglaw and Kevin Hearle (Tuscaloosa: University of Alabama Press, 2002); for an analysis emphasizing Steinbeck's sympathetic engagement with racial "outsiders" in America, see Susan Shillinglaw, "Steinbeck and Ethnicity," in *After* The Grapes of Wrath: *Essays on John Steinbeck in Honor of Tetsumaro Hayashi*, ed. Donald V. Coers, Paul D. Ruffin, and Robert J. DeMott (Athens: Ohio University Press, 1995).

71. Steinbeck, *Their Blood Is Strong*, 85, 87; see also Michael Denning, *The Cultural Front: The Laboring of American Culture in the Twentieth Century* (New York: Verso, 1996), 267.

72. Denning, *Cultural Front*, 267.

73. Steinbeck, *The Grapes of Wrath* (New York: Viking, 1989), 119.

74. Ibid., 264.

75. On Casy's gospel of social reform, see Astro, *John Steinbeck and Edward F. Ricketts*, 134–35; see also the discussion of the Joads' "education of the heart" in French, *John Steinbeck*, 94–99.

76. Steinbeck, *Grapes of Wrath*, 571.

77. Astro, *John Steinbeck and Edward F. Ricketts*, 133.

78. Steinbeck, *Grapes of Wrath*, 572.

79. French, *John Steinbeck*, 98.

80. Astro, *John Steinbeck and Edward F. Ricketts*, 65–66, 68–70.

81. I am indebted to Alan Wald for emphasizing this side of Steinbeck's political activity. For a view of Steinbeck as more clearly (but complexly) aligned with the Left and proletarian fiction, see Alan Wald, "Steinbeck and the Proletarian Novel," in *The Cambridge History of the American Novel*, ed. Leonard Cassuto (New York: Cambridge University Press, 2011).

82. Dickstein, "Steinbeck and the Great Depression," 124, 127–28; Gary Gerstle, *American Crucible: Race and Nation in the Twentieth Century* (Princeton, N.J.: Princeton University Press, 2001), 146–54, 180; Harvey Klehr, *The Heyday of American Communism: The Depression Decade* (New York: Basic Books, 1984); for an analysis that explores the popular success of *The Grapes of Wrath* and that distinguishes Steinbeck's racial populism and sentimental politics from "authentic" Popular Front culture, see Denning, *Cultural Front*, 267–68.

CHAPTER 6

The Indifference of Nature and the Cruelty of Wealth

Michael T. Gibbons

THERE ARE FEW NOVELISTS in the history of American literature whose work has been the subject of as much disagreement as John Steinbeck's. For some critics, his work embodies a tradition of American thought that is indebted to Emerson, Whitman, and Dewey, and extends what is unique to that tradition (see chapter 2, by Zoe Trodd).[1] It is precisely the kind of literature that Emerson insisted Americans must develop for themselves. For others, Steinbeck's work reached its full aesthetic potential with *The Grapes of Wrath,* the book for which he won a Nobel Prize.[2] But the work following *The Grapes of Wrath,* beginning with the war novel *The Moon Is Down,* raises the question of whether the Nobel Prize should have been awarded on the basis of a single work. Steinbeck's harshest critics argue that even *The Grapes of Wrath* is flawed by naïve left-wing, if not outright Marxist, sentimentality.

Harold Bloom's assessment illustrates the ambivalence with which Steinbeck's work has been received.

> If Steinbeck is not an original or even an adequate stylist, if he lacks skill in plot and power in the mimesis of character, what then remains in his work, except its fairly constant popularity with an immense number of liberal middlebrows, both in his own country and abroad? Certainly he aspired beyond his aesthetic means. If the literary Sublime, or contest for the highest place, involves persuading the reader to yield up easier pleasures for more difficult pleasures, and it does, then Steinbeck should have avoided Emerson's American Sublime, but he did not. Desiring it both ways, he fell into bathos in everything he wrote, even in *Of Mice and Men* and *The Grapes of Wrath.*[3]

This seemingly harsh evaluation of Steinbeck—that he reached beyond his literary talents—is moderated by Bloom's account of why *The Grapes of Wrath,* and by implication literature like it, remains an important part of the American literary tradition: "Yet there are no canonical standards worthy of human respect that could exclude *The Grapes of Wrath* from a serious reader's esteem. Compassionate narrative that addresses itself so directly to the great social questions of its era is simply too substantial a human achievement to be dismissed. . . . One might desire *The Grapes of Wrath* to be composed differently, whether as plot or as characterization, but wisdom compels one to be grateful for the novel's continued existence."[1] Bloom's response raises a question: If one of the measures of great literature is that it addresses significant social questions in a compelling way, how are we to assess Steinbeck's work subsequent to *The Grapes of Wrath*—work that is often denigrated but that addresses the great social questions of not just a particular era but all eras in which similar social and economic conditions persist?

In this essay I examine Steinbeck's account of the relationships between nature, the human, and social and economic life. I argue that he saw the progressive refashioning of human life as rooted in a complex relation among individuals, nature, and the prevailing social and economic institutions. He viewed nature as a set of forces that is largely indifferent to and often obstructs the possibilities of human and social life. Still, modern social institutions pose the most serious threats to the human potential for creation and re-creation of social conditions consistent with the capacities that define the human. I draw not only on *The Grapes of Wrath* but also on some of Steinbeck's later works that amplify the ways in which people respond to social conditions that distort and undermine human existence. For if Bloom is right about what is of value in *The Grapes of Wrath*, then a reevaluation of Steinbeck's later works is in order, since they too address troubling aspects of modern society that Bloom finds in Steinbeck's most famous work.

The essay is divided into five sections. The first summarizes Steinbeck's core social and political beliefs. The second examines his views on the fragile relationship between human beings and the natural world. The third focuses on the ways that modern social institutions disrupt and disfigure human relationships and communities that provide dignity, security, and safety, none of which can be taken for granted (although many Americans in the late twentieth century did). The fourth section, drawing on the later work of Steinbeck, offers an interpretation of community and mutual interdependence in *Cannery Row*. That life is by no means idyllic. The individuals are neither heroic nor virtuous. All are flawed and exhibit characteristics that place them on the margins of society. But their social relationships enable them to be sufficiently decent to avoid the cruelties that characterize the broader political-economic system. The final section draws parallels between Steinbeck's work and the social and economic conditions of the contemporary American plutocracy. Steinbeck had worried about the ways in which modern capitalism, through commodification, corrupted social and political life. Moreover, he showed that new forms of wealth characteristic of modern capitalism are not, pace Joseph Schumpeter, forms of creative destruction but are simply destructive.[5] The havoc and hardships they impose on common citizens are not outweighed by their alleged benefits. In the end, the new forms of wealth prevent modern Americans from realizing authentic individual lives and social relationships.

Given that much in this essay turns on the idea of "authenticity," it is necessary to say something about what I mean by this term. I employ it in a relatively modest and open-ended fashion. I do not intend it to have grand philosophical significance. I simply mean a form of life in which relations are largely transparent, efforts to improve life are not doomed from the start, and the self-understanding of social actors is relatively consistent with the way society actually works. Insofar as injustice and inequality exist, the sources of those disfigurements are largely, if not completely, understood. Citizens reflect and embrace conditions that realize human potential. A certain degree of utopianism can be detected in my use of the term, yet it is neither utopia nor tragedy, though the recognition of tragic moment could be part of an authentic life.

By contrast, inauthentic life denotes social, political, and economic relations that are largely opaque. Attempts to reform those relations are hampered by forces poorly understood by social and political actors. Social and political actors routinely misunderstand sources of inequality and injustice. The self-understanding of social actors is greatly at odds with how the society actually functions. Human needs and potential are sacrificed for goals and purposes incompatible with human flourishing in the mundane world. All societies exhibit a degree of inauthenticity, but some more so than others.[6]

Politics and the Human

In chapter 14 of *The Grapes of Wrath*, Steinbeck presents a concise and clear statement of his social and political thought. The chapter begins with a comment about the "nervousness" that the western states and the large landowners of the region feel but do not understand. "The great owners, striking at the immediate thing, the widening of government, the growing labor unity; striking at new taxes and plans; not knowing that these things are results, not causes. Results, not causes; results not causes. The causes lie deep and simply—the causes are a hunger in the stomach, multiplied a million times; a hunger in a single soul, hunger for joy and some security, multiplied a million times; muscles and mind aching to grow, to work, to create, multiplied a million times."[7] Steinbeck reiterates "results, not causes" as if the large landowners are incapable of hearing the phrase the first or even the second time and are incapable of understanding it even if they do hear it. They see, hear, and understand neither the needs nor the wants of millions of Americans nor the most fundamental qualities of human beings:

> The last clear definite function of man—muscles aching to work, minds aching to create beyond the single need—this is man. To build a wall, to build a house, a dam, and in the wall and house and dam to put something of Manself, and to Manself take back something of the wall, the house, the dam; to take hard muscles from the lifting, to take clear lines and form from conceiving. For man, unlike any other thing organic or inorganic in the universe, grows beyond his work, walks up the stairs of his concepts, emerges ahead of his accomplishments. This you man say of men—when theories change and crash, when schools, philosophies, when narrow dark alleys of thought, national, religious, economic, grow and disintegrate, man reaches, stumbles forward, painfully, mistakenly sometimes.[8]

The definition of being human is active engagement, both physical and mental, with the world. To be sure, the story of humanity is not one of unmitigated progress. There are obstacles, false starts, threats, and dangers to be overcome. War, imprisonment, crushed labor strikes, and a perverse economic system assault a just, authentic life. But these are not reasons for despair. They are evidence of ongoing human engagement with the world. Every step forward, however small and however much resistance it meets, indelibly marks the world. Indeed, the absence of such struggle would signify the final domination of forces of injustice. "And fear the time when the strikes stop while the great owners live—for every little beaten strike is proof that the step has been taken. And this you can know—fear the time when Manself will not suffer and die for a concept, for this one quality is the foundation of Manself, and this one quality is man, distinctive in the universe."[9] Engagement entails a capacity to overcome and transform existence. The denial, corruption, or disfiguring of the capacities to transform—whether it comes from law, religion, the economic system, or disfigured forms of family life—negates distinctively human life.

Moreover, the conditions that threaten the success of human labor, thought, and activity provide opportunities for realizing the social aspects of human existence. Injustices might at first isolate human beings, yet they sow the seeds of solidarity. Steinbeck avers that "I lost my land" becomes "We lost our land" when one recognizes one's condition in others. "This is the beginning—from 'I' to 'we.'"[10] Lonely isolation quickly evolves into the movement of thousands, then millions. Factory owners and large landowners cannot understand this growing communal identity.[11]

Struggling with Nature

The opening of *The Grapes of Wrath* describes how nature made life so hard in Oklahoma during the early Dust Bowl era. Seasonal changes initially offered hope of a bountiful harvest early in the spring. Then the sun withered and wilted crops and weeds alike. A sprinkling of rain cannot moisten the ground or the leaves of the corn that promised economic subsistence. Then conditions worsened. Dust storms followed the drought and ended any hope of salvaging the crops: "During a night the wind raced faster over the land, dug cunningly among the rootlets of the corn, and the corn fought the wind with its weakened leaves until the roots were freed by the prying wind and then each stalk settled wearily sideways toward the earth and pointed the direction of the wind."[12] As anyone who has seen film footage of the period is aware, the storms were so overwhelming that residents had difficulty telling day from night. Nothing seemed to protect humans from bodily harm. Steinbeck reaches similar conclusions about human helplessness before the relentlessness of nature: "Now the dust was evenly mixed with the air, an emulsion of dust and air. Houses were shut tight, and cloth wedged around doors and windows, but the dust came in so thinly that it could not be seen in the air, and it settled like pollen on the chairs and tables, on the dishes.

The people brushed it from their shoulders. Little lines of dust lay at the door sills."[13] The forces of nature are too overwhelming to be neutralized by human action. This leads not to complete despair. Nature upends the routines of human beings and their quest for economic well-being and security. But calamities also renew determination.

> Men stood by their fences and looked at the ruined corn, drying fast now, only a little green showing through the film of dust. The men were silent and they did not move often. And the women came out of the houses to stand beside their men—to feel whether this time the men would break. The women studied the men's faces secretly, for the corn could go, as long as something else remained. . . . After a while the faces of the watching men lost their bemused perplexity and became hard and angry and resistant. Then the women knew that they were safe and that there was no break.[14]

The devastating windstorms that defeated every effort at human self-protection spurred new ideas and further physical effort.

The novel ends with a flood. It is another natural disaster that threatens human survival, yet it leads to group struggle and not to surrender. The rising water reinforces creativity, determination, and generosity as human beings come to the aid of one another, even in desperate times.

Steinbeck paints a remarkably similar picture in *East of Eden,* where seasonal changes in the Salinas Valley appear indifferent to the needs of human settlement. The winter rains portend a lush spring but the harsh summers could easily create a barren environment and disrupt human beings' ability to provide for themselves and realize their capacities.

> But there were dry years too, and they put a terror on the valley. The water came in a thirty-year cycle. There would be five or six wet and wonderful years. . . . Then would come six or seven pretty good years. . . . And then the dry years would come. . . . The land dried up and the grasses headed out miserably a few inches high and great bare scabby places appeared in the valley. The live oaks got a crusty look and the sagebrush was gray. The land cracked and the springs dried up and the cattle listlessly nibbled on dry twigs. Then the farmers and the ranchers would be filled with disgust for the Salinas Valley. The cows would grow thin and sometimes starve to death. People would have to haul water in barrels just for drinking. Some families would sell out for nearly nothing and move away.[15]

Steinbeck's message here is that the land, the environment, the seasons, the weather, and the cycles of fertility and drought are seldom hospitable to humans. Nature is indifferent to those eking out a living from their labor. Travel to California if you please, but it's a mistake, Steinbeck suggests, to presume that the wilderness provides sufficient resources to accommodate human life without struggle and determination.[16]

This stingy view of nature precludes two types of naturalism, each sometimes attributed to Steinbeck. The first is Romantic naturalism, found in the writings of authors such as James Fenimore Cooper. It presumes that human beings are more at home in the natural world than in cities. Cooper's Natty Bumppo appears more honest, more earnest, more transparent, and less self-interested, even if brutal at times, than citizens of London or the east coast of pre-Revolutionary America. This, however, is not Steinbeck's view. Steinbeck's nature neither is accommodating nor brings out the best in people, as the character of Pa Joad sometimes attests.

Nor does Steinbeck subscribe to a mechanical type of naturalism, according to which the lives and behavior of human beings are shaped, both psychologically and biologically, by laws of nature. His emphasis on human activity resembles Dewey's view of human thrownness in the world.[17] For both Dewey and Steinbeck, human beings inherit a world that they did not create. Nonetheless, human beings are not passive objects. They have the potential to change the conditions of their existence and to turn adversity into a new beginning. Steinbeck refuses to treat nature as irresistible or human beings as so many billiard balls that move only because of external forces.

Modern Society, Modern Institutions, and Disfiguring the Human

Whereas nature is indifferent to human needs, the social and economic institutions that constitute the modern world are not. Almost every major institution—religion, the law, the family, and most importantly, the modern economic system—distorts or disfigures human relations and imposes cruelty and vulnerability onto some of those who come into contact with it.

Religion and the Denial of the Human Spirit

Americans who were driven from the plains in the 1930s by drought and dust storms were committed to a religious fundamentalism that led to political quietism. People placed their hopes in God and the afterworld. But according to Steinbeck's stories, religious fervor only distorted the ability of individuals to realize their human potential. Religion did not perfect the human spirit but distorted and denied it. It limited their understanding of their social, political, and economic situation and thereby led them to tolerate injustice and the institutions that caused it.

The first indication of this problem in *The Grapes of Wrath* occurs during Tom Joad's encounter with Jim Casy. Casy is an unborn-again former preacher who has abandoned, or been abandoned by, his calling.[18] His crisis in faith occurs when he thinks for himself and questions why some things are deemed holy and others sinful. "I was a preacher. . . . But not no more. . . . Just Jim Casy now. Ain't got the call no more. Got a lot of sinful idears—but they seem kinda sensible."[19] Christian extremism, or at least the brand that Casy preaches, was too much at odds with the sensible "idears" of the common man of the 1930s. Casy's reconsideration is not the skepticism of elitist, eastern, university-educated intellectuals. Casy's doubts emerge from human striving and engagement with the world. Casy, speaking for Steinbeck, draws on the imagery of a turtle: "Every kid got a turtle some time or other. Nobody can't keep a turtle though. They work at it and work at it, and at least one day they get out and away they go—off somewheres. It's like me. I wouldn't take the good ol' gospel that was just layin' there to my hand. I got to be pickin' at it an' workin' at it until I got it all tore down. Here I got the sperit sometimes an' nothin' to preach about. I got the call to lead the people an' no place to lead 'em."[20]

Casy's doubts arise from analyzing and applying the Bible. These early doubts evolve into a full-blown rejection of redemptive religion that promises salvation from pain if one only follows the right religious principles. "Before I knowed it," Casy continues, "I was sayin' out loud, 'The hell with it! There ain't no sin and there ain't no virtue. There's just stuff people do. It's all part of the same thing. And some things folks do is nice, and some ain't nice, but that's as far as any man got a right to say.'"[21] Religion, or at least the Christian religion in the Bible Belt, distorts a proper appreciation of human life. It imposes a morality that is neither justifiable, nor consistent with social life, nor useful for encouraging an authentic life. To remain pious, Casy would have had to engage in self-deception that the sources of religious belief themselves seem to undermine. According to Steinbeck, the religious life cannot sustain itself. An examination even by an ordinary man reveals fundamentalist religion to be empty and ultimately directionless, incompatible with the needs of common men and women.

Casy's most damning indictment of religion is that it deceives people about their very nature, about their relationship to each other, and of course, about the existence of God. It is thereby partly responsible for the separation from one another that people feel. They are unable to recognize themselves in each other, in the way that Whitman describes.[22] "I figgered about the Holy Sperit and the Jesus road. I figgered, 'Why do we got to hang it on God or Jesus? Maybe,' I figgered, 'maybe it's all men an' women we love; maybe that's the Holy Sperit—the human sperit—the whole shebang. Maybe all men got one big soul ever'body's a part of.' Now I sat there thinking it, an' all of a sudden—I knew it. I knew it so deep down that it was true, and I still know it."[23] By thinking of themselves primarily in relation to God, human beings fail to see the common spiritual relations they share with each other. The religion of salvation, sin, and virtue directs people away from each other and toward an otherworldly realm of promises. It thus distorts the human soul. But Casy finds the truth of the human spirit within himself and in his relations to other men and women. He illustrates what might be called expressivism, the idea that the truth of the self can be found within oneself and without dependency on an otherworldly, divine being.

The Privatized Family

Family life, or at least the kind that Steinbeck portrays in his novels, also disfigures. The reader immediately senses that something is wrong with the Joad family when Tom describes his absence from the family to Jim Casy. Casy asks Tom about his father, and Tom responds,

> "I don't know how he is. I ain't been home in four years."
> "Didn't he write you?"
> Joad was embarrassed. "Well, Pa wasn't no hand to write for pretty, or to write for writin'. . . .
> "Then you ain't heard nothin' about your folks in four years?"
> "Oh, I heard. Ma sent me a card two years ago, an' las Christmus Gramma sent a card."[24]

The card contains a verse that mocks Tom for being in jail. His incarceration seems to have no serious effect on the Joad family. So little do they miss him that they cannot find the time, desire, or will to write a few lines, to visit, or even to send a proper card on birthdays, Christmas, or other holidays. The father's excuse, that he does not write letters, is as pathetic and as cold an excuse for ignoring one's incarcerated family member, particularly one's child, as one can imagine.

The theme of dysfunctional families continues in Steinbeck's later work. In *East of Eden* both the Trask and the Ames households offer a violent, stark picture of family life. Cyrus, the Trask patriarch, was wounded in the Civil War. After his leg is amputated, he contracts gonorrhea from a camp-following prostitute. He then transmits the disease to his wife. Mrs. Trask, convinced that her illness is punishment for the sexual dreams she experienced in her husband's absence, commits suicide, after which Trask marries a young and servile girl of seventeen. Although his battlefield experiences were minimal, he manages to fashion a lucrative career as a military expert, offering advice to an array of secretaries of war, vice presidents, and presidents. He urges his son Adam to join the army, and the boy resists.

> "I don't want to do it," said Adam.
>
> "After a while," said Cyrus, "you'll think no thought the others do not think. You'll know no word the others can't say. And you'll do things because others do them. You'll feel danger in any difference whatever—a danger to the whole crowd of like-thinking, like acting men."
>
> "What if I don't?" Adam demanded.
>
> "Yes," said Cyrus, "sometimes that happens. Once in a while there is a man who won't do what is demanded of him, and do you know what happens? The whole machine devotes itself coldly to the destruction of his difference. They'll beat your spirit and your nerves, your body and your mind with iron rods until the dangerous difference goes out of you. . . . A thing so triumphantly illogical, so beautifully senseless as an army can't allow a question to weaken it."[25]

Cyrus Trask's endorsement of military regimentation is the flip side of Jim Casy's repudiation of the regimentation of religion. Both require, in Steinbeck's view, an elimination of individuality. But most significant for our purposes are the dynamics of the Trask family. Cyrus orders Adam into the army, and though Adam protests, he complies as though he had no option. His one act of defiance comes when he reenlists, spiting his father, who expected him to run the family farm.

Meanwhile, Cathy Ames is a sexually precocious adolescent who eventually murders her own parents as revenge for their excessive discipline and to obtain her own freedom. Steinbeck suggests that Cathy's psychosis is caused by her parents, who seem to give her everything she wants without being emotionally engaged. She works as a prostitute before marrying Adam. The family spirals into dysfunction. After giving birth to their twin sons, she shoots and wounds Adam before abandoning the family.

The failures of Steinbeck's fictional families as institutions of mutual support and love challenge the prevailing understanding of the nuclear family during the late nineteenth and twentieth centuries. In a modern world driven by economic gain, status, and self-indulgence, Steinbeck's families produce individuals who are remote, indifferent, narcissistic, or openly dangerous to those with whom they live.

Capitalism and the Commodification of Life

In Steinbeck's stories the modern economic system and corresponding technology are the most fundamental sources of the corruption and disfigurement of human life. In chapter 5 of *The Grapes of Wrath* the spokesmen for the owners of the land inform the tenant farmers about the new realities of absentee ownership and the financial imperatives of corporate capitalism. The collapse of the cash crop means that the bank must find a new way to extract a profit from the land. It cannot wait another year for conditions to improve. "Well, it's too late. And the owner men explained the workings and the thinkings of the monster that was stronger than they were." A man borrowing money might be able to hold on for a year, but the bank cannot wait.

> They breathe profits; they eat the interest on money. If they don't get it, they die the way you die without air, without side-meat. . . .
> . . . The bank—the monster has to have profits all the time. It can't wait. It'll die. . . . It's not us, it's the bank. A bank isn't like a man. Or an owner with fifty thousand acres, he isn't like a man either. That's the monster.
> . . . The bank is something else than men. It happens that every man in a bank hates what the bank does, and yet the bank does it. The bank is something more than men, I tell you. It's the monster. Men made it, but they can't control it.[26]

Steinbeck provides two contrasting images of the land. First, banks view land as simply a commodity that either returns a profit or does not.

Modern capitalism changed farmers' relation to the land by turning them into tenant farmers who planted cotton that killed the land. In other words, modern capitalism completes the commodification of the land.

The emerging corporate economy of the late nineteenth and early twentieth centuries was driven by market imperatives outside the control of the people who formed its institutions. While some bankers in Steinbeck's novel sympathize with the tenant farmers, others detachedly accept their helplessness before the forces of capitalism.

> Some of the owner men were kind because they hated what they had to do, and some of them were angry because they hated to be cruel, and some of them were cold because they had long ago found that one could not be an owner unless one were cold. . . . Some of them hated the mathematics that drove them, and some were afraid, and some worshipped the mathematics because it provided a refuge from thought and feeling. . . . These last could take no responsibility for the banks or companies because they were men and slaves, while the banks were machines and masters all at the same time.[27]

The tenant farmers, the squatting men in Steinbeck's narrative, have a different relationship to the land: "It's our land. We measured it and broke it up. We were born on it, and we got killed on it, died on it. Even if it's no good it's still ours. That's what makes it ours—being born on it, working on it, dying on it. That makes ownership, not a paper with some numbers on it."[28] Mixing their labor with the land, feeling it with their fingers and working it with their hands, defines ownership, in a way that is suggestive of Locke's theory of ownership in state of nature. The farmers do not understand that this world no longer exists, if indeed it ever did. When land takes a commodity form, those with the legal title are its owners, even if they do not spend a moment laboring.

Significantly, the unaccountable financial monster changes relations within the family. When faced with only natural disaster, men could rely on their skill and determination. They could reassure the women and children that, as bad as things were, the families could always start over. But the new economy forces them to leave the only way of life and only home they have known.

> Where'll we go? the women asked.
> We don't know. We don't know.
> And the women went quickly, quietly back into the houses and herded the

children ahead of them. They knew that a man so hurt and so perplexed may turn in anger, even on people he loves. . . .

The children crowded about the women in the houses. What we going to do, Ma? Where we going to go?

The women said, We don't know yet. Go out and play. But don't go near your father. He might whale you if you go near him. And the women went on with the work, but all the time they watched the men squatting in the dust—perplexed and figuring.[29]

Uncertainty and despair injects violence—a previously unknown element—into the supposed security of the family.

Finally, rampant commodification generates forms of economic organization and technology that prevent human beings from recognizing themselves and others. After the owners leave, tractors arrive and reshape the landscape into a more useable and profitable commodity. The machines create their own pathways, ignoring "hills and gulches, water courses, fences, houses," and transform the natural world and the human life built on it.[30] More significantly, the new technology disfigures human beings: "The man sitting in the iron seat did not look like a man; gloved, goggled, rubber dusk mask over nose and mouth, he was part of the monster, a robot in the seat."[31] Like the owner men who have been assimilated by the bank monster, the driver has been assimilated by the tractor monster. The machine handler does not control this technology. He may be the driver, but he has no influence on the things the tractor does or the ways it does them.

When the driver pauses for lunch, the response of the tenant farmer conveys the theme of disfigurement and unrecognizability: "Why, you're Joe Davis's boy."[32] The goggles had masked the identity of a neighbor. The tenant farmer asks why someone would bulldoze his own people, and the driver says he needs the pay to put shoes on his children's feet and food on the table. The costs are great. Wages come with a loss of control over one's labor and separation from the community.[33]

But the driver is not the only helpless figure who lacks control. Corporate anonymity and absence of accountability bedevil the tenant farmer as well. When the farmer threatens to shoot the driver, the driver describes the futility of such an act: "It's not me. There's nothing I can do. I'll lose my job if I don't do it. And look—suppose you kill me? They'll just hang you, but long before you're hung there'll be another guy on the tractor, and he'll bump the house down. You're not killing the right guy." Nor would it do any good to kill the tractor driver's boss or the president of the bank or its board of directors. The farmer asks,

> "But where does it stop? Who can I shoot? I don't aim to starve to death before I kill the man that's starving me."
> "I don't know. Maybe there's nobody to shoot. Maybe the thing isn't men at all. Maybe like you said, the property's doing it. Anyway, I told you, I got my orders."[34]

Steinbeck depicts an economic system beyond the control of any individual. The absence of personal control and the control by anonymous, unidentifiable forces remystify a world that was supposedly disenchanted by the development of capitalism and the spread of technology. Steinbeck tells a tale of malevolent re-enchantment in which the forces that control one's life are difficult to locate and impossible to hold accountable. (For the influence of these passages on the work of Bruce Springsteen, see chapter 10, by Lauren Onkey.)

Nature may be hard and harsh and may make life a continuing struggle, but a political economy driven by commodification and profit creates cruelty.

Resistance and Late Capitalism

Although Steinbeck paints a grim picture of the prospects for a dignified life in the United States, he still hopes that people might create among themselves a life beyond narrow, immediate, private wants, a life in which the satisfaction of one's needs can be pursued with the support of and in support of others. One example of such generosity occurs when Ma Joad, asserting her authority within the Joad family, insists on including Jim Casy in the family's migration to California.

A second, more significant instance is when Tom Joad, in response to the killing of Jim Casy, decides to take up Casy's mission of working for the rights of working people and those whom some scholars today call the underclass. After a so-called sheriff kills Casy, Tom wrenches the pick handle used to crush Casy's skull from the sheriff and beats the murderer to death. After returning to the Joad camp, he confesses his act to his mother and concludes that it is best that he not stay with the family.

> Ma said, "How'm I gonna know 'bout you? They might kill ya an' I woldn' know. They might hurt ya. How'm I gonna know?"

> Tom laughed uneasily, "Well, maybe like Casy says, a fella ain't got a soul of his own, but on'y a piece of a big one—an' then—"
>
> "Then what, Tom?"
>
> "Then it don' matter. Then I'll be all aroun' in the dark. I'll be ever'where— wherever you look. Wherever they's a fight so hungry people can eat, I'll be there. Wherever they's a cop beatin' up a guy, I'll be there. If Casy knowed, why, I'll be in the way guys yell when they're mad an'—I'll be in the way kids laugh when they're hungry an' they know supper's ready. An' when folks eat the stuff they raise, an' live in the houses they build—why, I'll be there."[35]

Casy permanently alters Tom's thinking, his view of the world and his obligations to others. He is part of "we" as well as an "I" who struggles and who always meets with opposition and violence from the privileged few.

A similar transformation takes place within Ma Joad when she observes the kindness shown by Mrs. Wainwright after Rose of Sharon's baby is stillborn.

> Ma fanned the air slowly with her cardboard. "You been frien'ly," she said. "We thank you."
>
> The stout woman smiled. "No need to thank. Ever'body's in the same wagon. S'pose we was down. You'd a give us a han'."
>
> "Yes," Ma said, "we would."
>
> "Or anybody."
>
> "Or anybody. Use' ta be the fambly was fust. It ain't so now. It's anybody. Worse off we get, the more we got to do."[36]

For Steinbeck, natural catastrophes spawn two possible responses. One is to secure as much as one can for oneself and one's immediate family, as Joe Davis's son does. But that does not really change one's relation to the bank monster that oppresses because of its hunger and imperatives. The other response is to forge bonds of support, mutuality, and solidarity and collectively navigate the harsh world of organized irresponsibility.

Steinbeck believes the insular family cannot sustain its members without recognizing the mutual needs it shares with others. This lesson is driven home in the remarkable final scene of the novel. Rose of Sharon, exhausted by the long migration and still weak from having just given birth to a stillborn child, is comforted by a young boy who offers her a blanket. In the face of a system capable of turning the beauty of childbirth into the horror of human loss, the boy's kindness is doubly poignant. Steinbeck details the ways people rely on one another during the hardest of times, when they are pushed to the brink of survival by an economic system that imposes widespread misery for the comfort of a few.

> Suddenly the boy cried, "He's dying, I tell you! He's starvin' to death, I tell you."
>
> "Hush," said Ma. She looked at Pa and Uncle John, standing helplessly gaping at the sick man. She looked at Rose of Sharon huddled in the comfort. Ma's eyes passed Rose of Sharon's eyes, and then came back to them. And the two women looked deep into each other. The girl's breath came short and gasping.
>
> She said "Yes."[37]

Rose of Sharon coaxes the starving man into accepting the breast milk produced for her stillborn child. These last pages reiterate a number of Steinbeck's themes. One is that family bonds need not be insular. There are few greater symbols of family intimacy than the breast-feeding of mother and child. Moreover, the men of the family, to whom the women and children earlier looked for strength, can only gape helplessly at the starving man. Ma Joad and Rose of Sharon, in their maternal roles, provide the strength needed both to sustain the family and to save a dying man. Finally, the scene emphasizes that human beings, even after they have experienced something as profoundly horrifying as the death of a child, have sufficient resources to overcome, though not forget, the most serious of tragedies.

If the closing pages of *The Grapes of Wrath* provide us with an image of life-affirming resistance to the life-denying, endangering practices of the unaccountable economy, *Cannery Row* provides us with an image of a subculture that is not driven by economic gain, social status, commodification, or assimilation into unaccountable economic institutions. The book does not propose a practical alternative to mainstream American culture, but it does juxtapose values Americans claim to embrace with values the economic system actually rewards. This contrast is made explicit in Doc's commentary on Mack and the boys who live at the Palace Flophouse: "'It has always seemed strange to me,' said Doc. 'The things we admire in men, kindness and generosity, openness, honesty, understanding and feeling are the concomitants of failure in our system. And those traits we detest, sharpness, greed, acquisitiveness, meanness and self-interest are the traits of success. And while men admire the quality of the first they love the produce of the second.'"[38] This tradeoff is not inevitable, says Doc: "Everywhere in the world there are Mack and the boys."[39] Some refuse to enter into a Faustian bargain with the economic system, while others sell their souls. But even though the inhabitants of Cannery Row are in many ways atypical Americans, they are not unique.[40]

To be sure, Steinbeck is not creating saintly heroes. Many characters— Dora, the madam of the local brothel; Lee Chong, who owns the grocery; the boys from the Palace Flophouse; and even the main character, Doc—have foibles. But this, I think, is part of the message. For Steinbeck, a life worth living is a life that embraces certain virtues in spite of other character flaws. This message is clearly expressed in the opening lines of the novel. The residents of the neighborhood "are, as the man once said, 'whores, pimps, gamblers, and sons of bitches,' by which he meant Everybody. Had the man looked through another peephole he might have said, 'Saints and angels and martyrs and holy men' and he would have meant the same thing."[41] There is no simple, uniform order that makes life easy and comfort an entitlement. In many respects this community of marginalized "drop-outs" from society resembles the Great Tide Pool located on the tip of Monterey Peninsula, where Doc collects marine animals for research laboratories. The tide pool "is a fabulous place; when the tide is in, a wave-churned basin, creamy with foam, whipped by the combers that roll in from the whistling buoy on the reef. But when the tide goes out the little water world becomes quiet and lovely. The sea is very clear and the bottom becomes fantastic with hurrying, fighting, feeding, breeding animals. . . . The smells of life and richness, death and digestion, of decay and birth burden the air."[42] Both Cannery Row and the Great Tide Pool are defined by a diversity of life. Both can be harsh and violent as well as beautiful because both contain life and death.

Steinbeck does not offer sentimentalism about dropouts and incompetents. He contrasts those whose lives are tyrannized by institutions that have lulled them into a comfortable, insulated, even affluent, sheep-like existence and those who have no—or at least fewer—illusions because they are not completely assimilated into economic institutions beyond their control.

Steinbeck discerns an authenticity among the marginalized. For example, the main character of the novel, Doc, is a graduate of the University of Chicago and the proprietor and owner of Western Biological Laboratory. He is, despite his unassuming demeanor, the most educated man on Cannery Row. "He wears a beard and his face is half Christ and half satyr, and his face tells the truth. It is said that he has helped many a girl out of one trouble and into another. . . . He can kill anything for need but could not hurt a feeling for pleasure."[43] If it were not for the kindness he shows to most everyone he meets, Doc's status as half Christ, half satyr would suggest two equally strong sets of passions. "Doc would listen to any kind of nonsense and change it for you to a kind of wisdom. . . . He could talk to children, telling them very profound things so that they understood. . . . He was concupiscent as a rabbit and gentle as hell. Everyone who knew him was indebted to him."[44]

Aside from his powerful sexual desires, Doc has another weakness: beer. There is little he does that is not preceded, accompanied, or followed by the consumption of beer. Whatever his foibles, the people of Cannery Row turn to Doc for personal advice, loans, work, and despite his lack of medical credentials, medical advice.

His presence in Cannery Row can best be explained by overwork and a response to the failure of an early romantic relationship. Doc decided to get away from it all by walking from Chicago to Florida. "He walked among farmers and mountain people, among the swamp people and fisherman": the people of the heartland. "He said he was nervous and besides he wanted to see the country, smell the ground and look at grass and birds and trees, to savor the country, and there was no other way than to do it save on foot."[45] But those he meets in his travels often view him with suspicion. The world outside of Cannery Row is not amenable to those who either tell the truth or do not fit preconceived notions of the normal. The combination of truth and deviance become threatening. "A man with a beard was a little suspect."[46]

Similarly, "Mack and the boys" reside in the Palace Flophouse, a dilapidated building that they "rent" from Lee Chong. They could be described as vagrants, dropouts, or homeless. But Steinbeck portrays them as decent men, even if sometimes incompetent, whose situation is partly a consequence of their virtues. Mack and the boys "are the Virtues, the Graces, the Beauties of the hurried mangled craziness of Monterey and the cosmic Monterey where men in fear and hunger destroy their stomachs in the fight to secure certain food, where men hunger for love but destroy everything lovable about them."[47]

As if anticipating criticisms of the story line, Steinbeck intimates that the boys' situation in some respects arises from conscious decisions: "What can it profit a man to gain the whole world and to come to his property with a gastric ulcer, a blown prostate, and bifocals? Mack and the boys avoid the trap, walk around the poison, step over the noose while a generation of trapped, poisoned, trussed-up men scream at them and call them no-goods, come-to-bad-ends, blots-on-the-town, thieves, rascals, bums."[18] Steinbeck adds that their way of life is more compatible with the natural order of things, in which biological survival counts more than either social status or the hoarding of wealth. He compares the boys to "the coyote, the common brown rat, the English sparrow, the horse fly, and the moth," despised animals that live off the refuse of society and that, in the case of the coyote and the rat, are tricksters who make the best of nondomesticated existence. But each is provided for by "Our Father who art in nature."[19]

The Palace Flophouse boys are immune to the pressures of conventional society. They are unimpressed with ceremonies and public demonstrations of civic pride. Instead, they observe the hypocritical patrons of Dora's brothel, "the city officials and prominent business men who came in the rear entrance back by the tracks and who had little chintz sitting rooms assigned to them."[50] When the Fourth of July parade is about to begin, Doc bets that the boys will ignore it completely, even though during the Red Scare displays of patriotism and civic pride were at their peak. Doc rightly believes that the boys will be unimpressed with the thoroughly choreographed public display. "And not a head turned, not a neck straightened up. The parade filed past and they did not move. And the parade was gone."[51] Again, Steinbeck is not painting an idyllic or romanticized image of the boys' life or of life on Cannery Row. But he is suggesting that the good life promised by post–World War II America was not what it was cracked up to be: it came at the cost of one's safety, one's health, control over one's life. Moreover, the more polite residents of Cannery Row proclaim certain values while really desiring their opposites.[52] Even if Mac and the boys, Doc, or Dora do not present us with a viable alternative to postwar American society, they juxtapose the ideals that our society mouths with those it actually embraces and thus challenges us to be honest with ourselves.

Steinbeck and Contemporary Crises

How, then, do we assess Steinbeck's criticism of work in late capitalism? Are there insights to be had, or are his novels period pieces, as some critics claimed in the 1950s and 1960s?[53] Are they geographically narrow and regionally confined?

One response is found in the thoughts of the tenant farmer in *The Grapes of Wrath* as the tractor driver is about to plow under the farmer's house and yard.

> The tenant pondered. "Funny thing how it is. If a man owns a little property, that property is him, it's part of him, an it's like him. If he owns property only so he can walk on it and handle it and be sad when it isn't doing well, and feel fine when the rain falls on it, that property is him, and some way he's bigger because he owns it. Even if he isn't successful he's big with his property. That is so."
>
> And the tenant pondered more. "But let a man get property he doesn't see, or can't take time to get his fingers in, or can't be there to walk on it—why, then the property is the man. He can't do what he wants, he can't think what he wants. The property is the man, stronger than he is. And he is very small, not big. . . . Only his possessions are big—and he's the servant of his property. That is so too."[54]

It is not just that the growth of capitalism changes human beings' relations to the land, the bank, or any other corporation. Steinbeck narrates for us the effects of this economic system of organized irresponsibility on the larger society. If one looks at the early defenses of capitalism found in the works of Adam Smith, Sir James Steuart, and David Hume, one sees that the typical defense of a market is that transactions make everyone better off without any, or with very few, substantial costs—that is, negative externalities—being imposed on the rest of society.[55] Insofar as there are adverse developments associated with the rise of capitalism, these are outweighed by the benefits to be had by the new efficiencies. About a hundred years later, Andrew Carnegie would argue that everyone engaged in market transactions is still better off. Carnegie argues that although the process of accumulation of monopoly capital causes serious harm, in the long run the advantages outweigh the disadvantages for society and the human race.[56] Most defenders of the market make this argument. The idea that the market might destroy some or even all of those involved directly in market transactions or that wealth might actually be economically destructive is not, as Alan Greenspan's 2008 testimony before the Senate showed, seriously considered.[57] Greenspan admitted that the possibility that unregulated financial markets would result in behaviors destructive of wealth and the well-being of large numbers of citizens never had occurred to him.[58]

However, we should have known long ago, and we certainly must know by now, the flaws in such thinking. As the recent real estate, automobile industry, and monopoly banking crises have shown, not only do some un-regulated market transactions result in massive negative externalities, but the very purpose of some transactions is to create and bet on such externalities. Moreover, it has become clear that the effects of disaster in the unaccountable system are not confined to bystanders. Those directly involved in speculation, for example, in the real estate bubble, also are adversely affected. If we learn nothing from the economic crises of the early twenty-first century, we should learn that some forms of market transactions have disastrous consequences for everyone, those who voluntarily seek economic gain and those who are forced to pay for the externalities, be it pollution, bankruptcy, or other problems. Moreover, we should finally recognize what the Puritans recognized: that not all forms of wealth are beneficial and that some forms of wealth are destructive of whole communities, as the permanent residents of the coast of Maine, the island of Nantucket, and other communities to which the Aspen effect has spread are beginning to realize.[59] And if we learn Steinbeck's lesson, we will have caught up to the tenant farmer who knows the difference between owning something and being owned by it.

Notes

1. The classic statement of this position is Frederic I. Carpenter, "The Philosophical Joads," *College English* 2, no. 4 (1941), reprinted in *John Steinbeck's* The Grapes of Wrath, ed. Harold Bloom (New York: Chelsea House, 1988), 7–15. For a slightly different account, see Charles Shively, "John Steinbeck: From the Tide Pool to the Loyal Community," in *Steinbeck: The Man and His Work*, ed. Richard Astro and Tetsumaro Hayashi (Corvallis: Oregon State University Press, 1971), 25–34.

2. See, for example, Edmund Wilson, *The Boys in the Back Room: Notes on California Novelists* (San Francisco: Colt Press, 1941), 42, 49; Harold Bloom, introduction to Bloom, *John Steinbeck's* The Grapes of Wrath; Warren French, *John Steinbeck* (New York: Twayne, 1961), 113–19; and especially Bernard Bowron, "*The Grapes of Wrath:* A 'Wagons West' Romance," in *A Companion to* The

Grapes of Wrath, ed. Warren French (Clifton, N.J.: Augustus M. Kelley Publishers, 1972), 208–16.

3. Bloom, introduction, 4.

4. Ibid., 5.

5. Joseph Schumpeter, *Capitalism, Socialism and Democracy* (New York: Harper, 1975), 82–85.

6. Here I am drawing on Charles Taylor, *The Ethics of Authenticity* (Cambridge: Harvard University Press, 1992); and Charles Guignon, *On Being Authentic* (London: Routledge, 2004).

7. John Steinbeck, *The Grapes of Wrath* (New York: Penguin Books, 1997), 150.

8. Ibid.

9. Ibid., 151.

10. Ibid., 152.

11. Shively sees Steinbeck as endorsing the idea that human beings are part of one great whole: "Reality is, in fact, a whole or an Absolute, composed and unified by the presence and actions of the individual parts to Steinbeck." Shively, "John Steinbeck," 29. I think this a serious overstatement of the relation of human beings to the world and trivializes the significance of struggle that Steinbeck emphasizes. Here it is perhaps worth pointing to the similarities between Steinbeck's view of human nature, Manself as he refers to it, and Marx's notion of species-being in Karl Marx, *Economic and Philosophic Manuscripts of 1844*, trans. Michael Milligan (Buffalo, N.Y.: Prometheus Books, 1988). Steinbeck, of course, could not have been familiar with the latter, as the manuscripts did not emerge until the post–World War II period and were not translated into English until the sixties. All this makes the similarities all the more interesting.

12. Steinbeck, *Grapes of Wrath*, 2.

13. Ibid., 3.

14. Ibid., 3–4.

15. John Steinbeck, *East of Eden*, in *Novels, 1942–1952* (New York: Library of America, 2001), 311–12.

16. Perhaps the most obvious indication of this indifference to human existence is the symbol of the turtle, which serves as an exemplar for the relationship between human beings and their environment.

17. For example, see John Dewey, *Reconstruction in Philosophy* (Boston: Beacon Press, 1967).

18. This is the first of several notable allusions to Emerson, who abandoned his ministry after confessing to his congregation that he no longer had a calling nor could sincerely preach the divine origins of the Bible.

19. Steinbeck, *Grapes of Wrath*, 20.

20. Ibid., 21.

21. Ibid., 23.

22. See Walt Whitman, *Leaves of Grass: The Complete 1855 and 1881–92 Editions* (New York: Library of America Classics, 2011).

23. Steinbeck, *Grapes of Wrath*, 24.

24. Ibid., 26.

25. Steinbeck, *East of Eden*, 333–34.

26. Steinbeck, *Grapes of Wrath*, 32, 33. It is interesting to compare these comments to those of Woodrow Wilson in his speech "The New Freedom": "You know what happens when you are the servant of a corporation. You have in no instance access to the men who are really determining the policy of the corporation. If the corporation is doing the things that it ought not to do, you really have no voice in the matter and must obey the orders, and you have oftentimes with deep mortification to co-operate in the doing of things which you know are against the public interest. Your individuality is swallowed up in the individuality and purpose of a great organization." Available at Project Gutenberg, http://www.gutenberg.org/catalog/world/readfile?fk_files=165486&pageno=4.

27. Steinbeck, *Grapes of Wrath*, 31–32.

28. Ibid.

29. Ibid., 34–35.

30. Ibid., 35.

31. Ibid.

32. Ibid., 36.

33. There is another very telling image. At the end of his lunch the driver finishes a "branded pie and threw away the crust" (37). His action captures the new economic inequality, in which some enjoy lunch, including dessert, and throw away food, while the unassimilated and the marginalized struggle for survival.

34. Steinbeck, *Grapes of Wrath*, 38.

35. Ibid., 419.

36. Ibid., 445.

37. Ibid., 455.

38. Steinbeck, *Cannery Row*, in *Novels, 1942–1952*, 192–93.

39. Ibid., 193.

40. None of the main characters, with the exception of Lee Chong, have any family members dependent upon them and for whose well-being they are responsible. And Lee Chong's family is largely absent from the narrative. Parents, wives, husbands, partners, or children are simply not present.

41. Steinbeck, *Cannery Row*, 101.

42. Ibid., 118, 119.

43. Ibid., 117.

44. Ibid.

45. Ibid., 166–67.

46. Ibid., 166.

47. Ibid., 108–9.

48. Ibid., 109. The response of the trussed-up men could just as easily be used to describe the response of some of the critics of Steinbeck's novel. See Bloom, introduction.

49. This passage is followed by, "Our Father who art in nature who has given the gift of survival to the coyote, the common brown rat, the English sparrow, the house fly and the moth, must have a great and overwhelming love for no-goods and blots-on-the-town and bums, and Mack and the boys. Virtues and graces and laziness and zest. Our Father who art in nature." The suggestion here is that if there is a God, he looks after those who are on the margins and outskirts of society as much as those whose lives are more conventional. Each of the animals mentioned relies for its well-being in part on the activity of human civilization.

50. Steinbeck, *Cannery Row*, 162.

51. Ibid., 193.

52. It is no coincidence that when any of their group travel very far outside of their enclave, they encounter problems with the law. This could be interpreted as the characters being misfits. But it is more likely that Steinbeck is stressing the extent to which participation in the system of organized irresponsibility comes with costs that people do not recognize.

53. See, for example, Howard Levant, *The Novels of John Steinbeck: A Critical Study* (Colombia: University of Missouri Press, 1974).

54. Steinbeck, *Grapes of Wrath*, 37.

55. See Albert O. Hirshmann, *The Passions and the Interests: Political Argument for Capitalism before Its Triumph* (Princeton, N.J.: Princeton University Press, 1977). Adam Smith's case is more complicated than that of Steuart and Hume. But all three did see commercial society counteracting the less desirable human passions and improving the political order.

56. Andrew Carnegie, "The Gospel of Wealth," 1889, http:// xroads.virginia .edu/~drbr/wealth.html.

57. Greenspan is the former chairman of the U.S. Federal Reserve Bank. His influence, on many accounts, made him the most influential political actor in the U. S. economy from 1987 to 2006.

58. For Greenspan's testimony before Congress, see Edmund L. Andrews, "Greenspan Concedes Error on Regulation," *New York Times*, October 23, 2008, http://www.nytimes.com/2008/10/24/business/economy/24panel.html.

59. The Aspen effect refers to the extreme rise of housing prices in a commu-

nity, sufficient to make it economically impossible for average citizens and workers to live in that community. For example, the average home on Nantucket now sells for over $600,000. Needless to say, firemen, police, schoolteachers, grocery clerks, small business owners, and similar workers are unable to afford such prices. On the coast of Maine, real estate prices have been driven up by those seeking vacation homes. The increase in real estate prices has driven real estate taxes on the coast so high that fishing and lobstering families, some tracing their family businesses back several generations, are unable to make enough to meet the cost of living.

CHAPTER 7

"The Technique of Building Worlds": Exodian Nation Formation in John Steinbeck's *The Grapes of Wrath*

Roxanne Harde

PUBLISHED IN 1939, *The Grapes of Wrath* is a creative cultural product with its roots in Steinbeck's journalistic training, his radical worldview, and the Bible. On the one hand, the novel makes explicit the veracity of its textual representation of migrant workers during the Depression. On the other hand, like John Winthrop and William Bradford before him, Steinbeck draws on biblical typology to add resonance to a text based on historical events and to clarify the processes that change loosely knit groups of oppressed and marginalized peoples into a new nation with its own political codes. In this way Steinbeck draws together key aspects of American political tradition and its cultural roots, particularly those embedded in the Old Testament. For the Puritans immigrating to the New World, the Old Testament Exodus served as a model and a divine guarantee; once again a divinely chosen group had escaped from oppression across a body of water to a new promised land. Like the Hebrews and the Puritans before them, the Okies construct a national identity that garners authority through claims to status as a redeemer nation. While critics have paid attention to Steinbeck's use of biblical imagery, especially in *The Grapes of Wrath* and *East of Eden,* his appropriation and revision of both the book of Exodus and the Mosaic prophet in the formation of a new Okie nation have yet to receive a sustained reading. This chapter addresses this lacuna by arguing that Steinbeck broadly patterns the narrative of the Oklahoma migrants on Exodus, in order to "build" a world that offers them national identity and the possibility of justice and liberty even as it reinstates national myths of manifest destiny and the redeemer nation. In tracing the ways in which Exodus influences *The Grapes of Wrath*, it shows how Exodus foreshadows the novel, shapes the formation of the Okie nation, and offers a model of prophecy. It concludes by tracing Exodian typology into contemporary revisions of Steinbeck's American Exodus.

"There Are No New Stories and I Wouldn't Like Them If There Were": Correlation and Influence

Aside from the fact of an exodus and heroes who cannot find peace in the Promised Land with their people, there is little direct correlation between the details of Exodus and *The Grapes of Wrath*. Rather, they mainly are connected through narrative strategies and the grand sweep of their plots. The similarities between their basic narratives are clear. It is no coincidence that Dorothea Lange and Paul Taylor titled their journalistic record of the Okie migration *An American Exodus* (1939).[1] The influence of Exodus on *The Grapes of Wrath* (1939) is as evident as that of Genesis on Steinbeck's *East of Eden* (1954), although he took liberties with both the details and the broad sweep of these narratives. At one point in *The Grapes of Wrath*, Ma Joad notes that her father-in-law "quoted Scripture all the time. He got it all roiled up."[2] Like Grandpa Joad, Steinbeck "roils up" biblical stories to suit his ends. "There are no new stories," Steinbeck noted to his publisher Pascal Covici in 1939, "and I wouldn't like them if there were."[3] *The Grapes of Wrath*, then, is Steinbeck's retelling of an old story in order to comment on the national changes that he, like Lange and Taylor, was observing.

The formal and stylistic aspects of Exodus echo through Steinbeck's narrative and intercalary chapters. *The Grapes of Wrath* is divided into two interspersed narratives: the specifics of the Joad family's exodus told by an omniscient narrator and the westerly migration told by a third-person prophet-narrator. Steinbeck gave the name "intercalary" to these general chapters. The term means a day or a month inserted in the calendar to harmonize it with the solar year; an intercalation is an interposition out of the ordinary course, but one meant to make things come out right. Intercalary is also defined as a refrain, those portions that hold a song together and give the whole its shape. As Steinbeck's choice of terms suggests, the intercalary chapters, in their "we" narrative told in the rhythms of the Old Testament, are essential to understanding the book. In Exodus a group of runaway slaves shapes a national identity, and Steinbeck's intercalary narrative suggests that a nameless, faceless group of migrant workers, held together by a growing national identity and given its voice by the prophet-balladeer, may do the same.

Michael Coogan argues that because the event of the Hebrew exodus was magnified in the story and song that contribute to the written, polyvocal narrative in the book, it understandably became a dominant theme of later writers, who saw in the events of their times a kind of reenactment of the original exodus. Novels such as Robert A. Heinlein's *Stranger in a Strange Land* (1961) and Denis Johnson's *Tree of Smoke* (2007) draw on Exodian politics, and *Exodus!* (2000), by Eddie Glaude Jr., follows the tropes of Exodus to examine race and nation in nineteenth-century America. *The Grapes of Wrath* keeps the tropes of migrant politics and nation formation at its forefront, true, but it also follows Exodus in interweaving story lines that are specific and open-ended.

Exodus traces the steps of political change: oppression, liberation, social contract, political struggle, and finally, a new society. Ostensibly, it relates a specific narrative of the Hebrew descendants of Abraham through the Isaac-Jacob-Joseph line. The Hebrews are referred to as "the people" some eighty times over the forty chapters of Exodus, and the plethora of detail—names, directions, directives—in the Exodian narrative works to hide its lack of specificity.[1] As biblical scholars like Coogan point out, the book disrupts attempts to pin down its historical specifics. Its opening line, "And these are the names," shows the intent to disclose, but at no point does Exodus name a ruler, a place, or an event that would allow it to be placed in history. The unnamed king, "who did not know Joseph," feared the strength of his slaves and dealt with them harshly, "but," as Exodus 1:12 notes, "the more they were oppressed, the more they multiplied and the more they spread abroad." God sends Moses to deliver the sons of Israel, and the intervention of supernatural divinity culminates in the Passover, the release of the slaves, and the defeat of Pharaoh and his forces at the Red Sea. The remaining two-thirds of the book glorifies God, details the law Moses brings to the people, and describes the building of the tabernacle. Exodus ends with the glory of the Lord filling the tabernacle as the "house of Israel" continues its journey to the Promised Land. The book concerns itself with the promise of Yahweh to Abraham, but that promise, of land and progeny, is left unfulfilled in the entire Pentateuch and only reaches its conclusion in Joshua, at the beginning of the Deuteronomic history. This open-ended aspect of Exodus figures in *The Grapes of Wrath* and in the tendency of American culture to look continually ahead.

Just as Exodus invokes a sense of timelessness through specific non-specificity, the prophet-narrator of *The Grapes of Wrath*'s intercalary chapters gains authority from an encompassing general view, from a refusal to focus on details, and from a narrative voice that, in its broad sweep, invokes the stately rhythms of the Old Testament. As in Exodus, Steinbeck calls his migrants "the people," and he consistently refers to them as such in his letters and writing journal. Steinbeck's journal, published as *Working Days* (1989), shows how "the people," the Dust Bowl migrants, had captured his imagination. Early in the writing of *The Grapes of Wrath*, he describes how the Joads are taking shape: "Yesterday it seemed to me that the people were coming to life."[5] Nevertheless, as Michele Landis points out, the novel lacks the contexts of identity, detailed emotions, and personalities in the main characters. She argues that Steinbeck had to make the Joads "sufficiently generic" that his "readers' attachment to the Joads never overwhelmed their status as representatives of a type."[6] Steinbeck's intercalaries focus on generic people and are told, like Exodus, in declarative sentences shaped out of the common language. Steinbeck, for example, matches sentences like this: "The whole congregation of the Israelites journeyed by stages" with "The families moved westward, and the technique of building worlds improved," or "The people thirsted there for water" with "The people in flight from the terror behind."[7]

While the Joad narrative focuses on a group tied together by blood and follows the details of its trek from the American Dust Bowl of the 1930s to the promised land of California, the intercalary chapters form a nation from disparate groups of people who share common oppressions and misfortunes.[8] Although Steinbeck's Okies hold varying Christian traditions and political allegiances, they are all white, of Anglo-European origin, and they identify themselves as American: "We ain't foreign. Seven generations back Americans, and beyond that Irish, Scotch, English."[9]

Arguing that Steinbeck's "Okies are the latter-day carriers of the national origin myth, a matrix of stories that justify conquest and settlement, transforming the white settlers into an indigenous people who believe they are the true natives of the continent," Roxanne Dunbar-Ortiz identifies the ways in which Steinbeck both unites the migrant groups and reinstates colonial ideologies.[10] However, Exodus 33:2 makes clear that its chosen people are not multiracial, as God promises to send an angel ahead of the Israelites to "drive out the Canaanites, the Amorites and the Hittites and the Perizzites, the Hivites and the Jebusites." Exodus 33:10 adumbrates the whites-only migrant Okie nation as God warns the people "not to make a covenant with the natives of the land against which you are going, or they will provide a snare in your midst." Dunbar-Ortiz rightly points out the narrowness of Steinbeck's vision, but that narrowness accurately reflects the Hebrew exodus and the Mosaic authority that united thousands of migrants into a nation unified by one desire.

Like the Old Testament, Steinbeck is preoccupied with the fate of one group of people: "I have set down what a large section of our people are doing and wanting, and symbolically what all people of all time are doing and wanting. . . . This migration is the outward sign of the want."[11] The object of desire is land, and the struggle is to reenter an uninhabited and fecund garden from which they are separated by space and time. As both Exodus and *The Grapes of Wrath* make clear, the first fall was more than a fall away from God and into sin; it was a fall away from the land that fed and nurtured humanity. In this novel and in *East of Eden* Steinbeck articulates the quest with overwhelming westward motion, the beginnings where home is not a place but an idea, where humans are positioned east of Eden, and where the "westering" is as present as it is in Exodus.

Reading Exodus as a political text that has influenced modern forms of political action, particularly revolution, Michael Walzer argues that political radicals find in the text a pattern to reenact: "Within the sacred history of the Exodus, they discovered a vivid and realistic secular history that helped them to understand their own political activity."[12] H. Mark Roelofs similarly argues that "the Moses narratives . . . may be regarded as the purest expression of Biblical nationalism." Roelofs particularly looks to the defining characteristics—Moses as the charismatic hero who congregates the people, who become a nation—that are both "historical fact, and experience to be met and understood in a narrative structure."[13] Suggesting Exodus is not so much a theory as a paradigm of revolutionary politics, Walzer argues that Exodus is "part of the cultural consciousness of the West—so that a range of political events . . . have been located and understood within the narrative frame that it provides."[14] Walzer points out that important motifs of the story—the covenant, moral regeneration, aggression against internal and external enemies of the nation, murmurings against the prophet-leader, unification and movement of a people, and divine interventions—may be crucial in modern Exodian politics.

Walzer focuses on the march and finds it more important than divine intervention. He describes it as "an event set within the larger process of the deliverance, a crucial feature of the Exodus Pattern. Like the pattern as a whole, it is self-consciously reenacted by later generations of Bible readers."[15] Steinbeck took the title of his manuscript from "The Battle Hymn of the Republic" noting that he liked both the title and the song "because it is a march and this book is a kind of march—because it is in our own revolutionary tradition."[16] Walzer concludes his study of revolutionary politics in Exodus by pointing out that the way to the better place, the promised land, is always through an exodus: "There is no way to get from here to there except by joining together and marching."[17] Like America's Founding Fathers, Steinbeck finds in Exodus a narrative paradigm proclaiming a vision that is still valid. In writing the history of the Okie migration, Steinbeck was inspired both by the Hebrew migration that powers the book of Exodus and by its formation of a new nation through revolutionary politics.

"This Is the Beginning—From 'I' to 'We'": Influence and Confluence

Steinbeck's Okie nation is unified by more than the quest for a new promised land. The stages of nation formation in *The Grapes of Wrath* follow the Exodian narrative and show the same kinds of temporal lapses. The story moves in fits and starts, usually just out of pace with the story of the Joads. Exodus offers the astonishing narrative of slaves who rebelled, won freedom, created their own laws, and established themselves as a nation. Like the story of the Hebrew nation, Steinbeck's intercalary chapters oscillate between unification of the people and growing national power. Thus, as the people take to the road, the narrative describes the Okies' growing anger about the hardened hearts of their oppressors: the landowners as latter-day pharaohs. The anger foreshadows violence that will follow: "When the owner men told us to go, that's us; and when the tractor hit the house, that's us until we're dead. To California or any place—every one a drum major leading a parade of hurts, marching with our bitterness. And some day—the armies of bitterness will all be going the same way. And they'll all walk together, and there'll be a dead terror from it."[18] This is not, however, the first hint of an army. The famously symbolic turtle of the third chapter gestures first toward migration, the moving of house and home, and then toward military maneuvers. As he began the novel, Steinbeck returned often to the word *phalanx* to refer to the unification and action of the Okies. Originally describing a line of soldiers with shields joined and long spears overlapping, the word came to mean a number of persons banded together in support of or opposition to some cause.[19] Later, Charles Fourier used the term to describe a group of people living communally. Steinbeck himself came across the idea in Edward F. Ricketts's group-man theory of the eco-logical phalanx. As a great lover of dictionaries, Steinbeck likely also knew that the Romans referred to their own phalanx formation as a *testudo,* or tortoise, and he thus conflates all meanings in the turtle as a representative feisty survivor figure tied to the land. (For further discussion of Steinbeck's phalanx theory, see chapter 5, by Charles Williams.)

The narrative voice in the intercalary chapters of *The Grapes of Wrath* also offers the language of organic growth and thereby insists that the growth and unification of the Okie nation are both natural and good:

> One man, one family driven from the land; this rusty car creaking along the highway to the west. I lost my land. A single tractor took my land. I am alone and I am bewildered. And in the night one family camps in a ditch and another family pulls in and the tents come out. The two men squat on their hams and the women and children listen. Here is the node, you who hate change and fear revolution. Keep these two squatting men apart; make them hate, fear, suspect each other. Here is the anlage of the thing you fear. This is the zygote. For here "I lost my land" is changed; a cell is split and from its splitting grow the thing you hate—"we lost our land." . . . And from this first "we" there grows a still more dangerous thing: "I have a little food" plus "I have none." If from this problem the sum is "we have a little food," the thing is on its way, the movement has directions. Only a little multiplication now, and this land, this tractor are ours. . . . This is the thing to bomb. This is the beginning—from "I" to "we."[20]

The prophecy rests on words such as *node, zygote,* and *anlage* that indicate an organic, even foreordained, joining and growth for humans and plants. That the people can join together and grow in fertile soil suggests they have the right to do so. The inherent right of these migrants to claim land and become a nation forms the crux of the conflict and the prophecy, in both

Steinbeck's novel and the book of Exodus. That the prophecy of *The Grapes of Wrath* includes violence and fear further connects the novel to Exodus and its elimination of all groups who oppose the tribe of Israel. Exodian influence, as the multitude of Hebrews streams toward its new nation, becomes a confluence as more and more migrants enlarge and enliven the growing Okie nation that becomes a "we."

Chapter 17 retraces the steps of nation formation, repeating the stages of the lone family growing with others into a world:

> Because they were lonely and perplexed, because they had all come from a place of sadness and worry and defeat, and because they were all going to a new mysterious place, they huddled together; they talked together; they shared their lives, their food, and the things they hoped for in the new country. Thus it might be that one family camped near a spring, and another camped for the spring and the company, and a third because two families had pioneered the place and found it good. And when the sun went down, perhaps twenty families were there. In the evening a strange thing happened: the twenty families became one family. . . . Every night a world created.[21]

United, like the disparate tribes of Hebrews, by common oppressions, fears, and dreams, the migrant families begin to form "worlds," in Steinbeck's terms. However, just as the narrator suggests that something great and terrible will come as the people change "from 'I' to 'we,'" the seemingly innocuous worlds of chapter 17 promise more than migrant families merely spending the night in each other's company.

As the narrative progresses, the ever-forming worlds solidify into nations, groups of people united by a national identity as they, again like the tribes of Israel, develop codes and laws. Following Moses, the prophetic intercalary voice brings those laws to light and develops their wider meaning. *The Grapes of Wrath* was far from the first text that noticed the separation and codification of the Okie nation. The May 1933 *New Republic* reported on migrant tent villages and semipermanent shanty towns called Hoovervilles after food commissioner Herbert Hoover: "Hoovervilles are in a separate nation, with separate codes." Tellingly, the intercalary narrator introduces the term *Hooverville* in chapter 19, making clear that it is a tag of shame imposed by outsiders, long after delineating the codes of the developing Okie nation in chapter 17:

> At first the families were timid in the building and tumbling worlds, but

gradually the technique of building worlds became their technique. Then leaders emerged, then laws were made, then codes came into being. And as the worlds moved westward they were more complete and better furnished, for their builders were more experienced in building them.

The families learned what rights must be observed—the right of privacy in the tent; the right to keep the past black hidden in the heart; the right to talk and to listen; the right to refuse help or to accept, to offer help or to decline it; the right of the hungry to be fed; the rights of the pregnant and the sick to transcend all other rights.

And the families learned, although no one told them, what rights are monstrous and must be destroyed: the right to intrude upon privacy, the right to be noisy while the camp slept, the right of seduction or rape, the right of adultery and theft and murder. These rights were crushed, because the little worlds could not exist for even a night with such rights alive.

And as the worlds moved westward, rules became laws, although no one told the families. . . .

The families moved westward, and the technique of building the worlds improved so that the people could be safe in their worlds.[22]

This central chapter describes nation formation as a largely tacit process that resembles natural evolution as the people, through their codes, make loose-knit communities into a single nation. The language of myth is at play here, the elision of the specific events that instigated these laws and their codification. More complex, however, is the focus of prophetic voice on the word *rights* as the descriptor for all human action. The contraposition of laws and codes against egotistical rights that are "monstrous and must be destroyed" suggests the building of a national mythology along the lines of Exodus. Instead, however, of a nation formed from the top down, through God's law given to Moses on Sinai, Steinbeck's nation forms from the bottom up as the Okies agree on and codify the laws they need to make their nation work. Further, this kind of rhetoric could be used to justify the migrant nation moving on the legal holders of the Californian garden. A right can be defined as a legal or moral recognition of choices or interests to which a particular political community attaches weight; the assertion of a right makes the demand that the law recognize that right. Given Steinbeck's agenda, his intent "to put a tag of shame on the greedy bastards who are responsible for this," neutralizing certain capitalistic or egotistical "rights," lays the foundation for seeing the hungry fed and the migrant landed.[23] If rape and theft and murder, actions that normally breach civil and moral codes, are defined as rights that should be seen as monstrous and destroyed, then the right of landholders to destroy food or to allow land to lie fallow in the face of mass starvation must also be seen as monstrous, another right that should be destroyed. By defining both acts of violence and acts of capitalism as rights, chapter 19 argues for recognition that "a fallow field is a sin and the unused land a crime against the thin children" and thus turns the narrative's claim that the Okies "changed their social life" into the prophecy that they might change all social life.[21]

"If We Was All Mad the Same Way": Confluence and Prophecy

In its move to prophesy, to speak the truth about injustice and envision change, *The Grapes of Wrath* follows Exodus. Both works narrate through the use of distinct and often prophetic voices. Scholarship on Exodus tends to focus on the disparity between its various sections: differences in vocabulary, style, and interest of the Pentateuchal Yahwistic, Elohistic, and Priestly sources. And while the book, woven together by multiple editors from the oral tradition, has literary and thematic unity, several chapters and groups of verses are often regarded as intrusive, disruptive, thematically or chronologically. Among these are the Book of the Covenant, the Priestly sections detailing the media of Israel's worship, and all of chapter 18, in which Jethro reunites Moses with his wife and family and instructs his son-in-law on how to govern efficiently through small groups and via tacit leadership. These disruptions parallel Steinbeck's intercalary chapters. Composed over seven centuries, the literary structure of Exodus is composite in all its meanings as the joining of traditions, the weaving of sources, and the exposition of themes. The prophetic narrators of Exodus blur the distinguishing features of history with inflated numbers, shifting chronology, and divine interventions. Steinbeck structures his specific and intercalary narratives in the same way. In Exodus there are narratives about Moses alongside narratives of Israel's oppression and narratives of the intransigence of the ruler alongside narratives of the rescue and provision by Yahweh. There are instructions appropriate to an urban life alongside instructions for an agricultural one. In *The Grapes of Wrath* there are symbol-laden narratives of the sun and the turtle alongside the specifics of Tom Joad's life and narratives about the crimes of the wealthy alongside narratives about the feeding of symbolic and specific children.

In a discussion about fictionalizing the historical, Steinbeck wrote his agent, Elizabeth Otis, "I'm trying to write history while it is happening and I don't want to be wrong." He wanted his history to have far wider implications than the historical reality of the Okies he knew and championed.[25] While prophecy is meant to be specific, it is often also meant to hold an enduring relevance, as it speaks with symbol against cultural trends or constrictions. Like the Old Testament prophet, Steinbeck's intercalary narrator imbues his message with a sense of timelessness through an utter lack of detail and through universal symbols, such as the turtle. From the first chapter to the penultimate, he shoulders a Mosaic authority as he simultaneously looks backward and forward in descriptions of the migration, the growing nation, and the codification of the law. Further, Steinbeck's intercalary narrative is as composite in structure as the narrative of Exodus. While the intercalations are by one omniscient narrator, that voice pauses in several places over an embedded and authoritative prophet, the nameless guitar man of the camps who welds the people "to one thing, one unit" in chapter 17.[26] As in Exodus, the narrative voice of the intercalary chapters stands outside the story, weaving together sources and themes, emphasizing the group above the individual, and describing how groups of itinerant workers form a national identity.

However, the intercalary voice is not alone in prophesying. The novel shifts the prophet's mantle from one character to the next, drawing links between each and multiple biblical prophets, especially Moses and Jesus. Andrew Dix notes that in Steinbeck's work "Christianity is not so easily got rid of; it remains as a ghostly presence." In particular, Dix points out Steinbeck's blurring of Old and New Testament: "The number of the Joads recalls Christ's disciples as well as the tribes of Israel."[27] Relying on the syntax and symbol of the intercalary chapters, the shifting Joad prophetic voice envisions the future, from Casy's declaration that a change is coming, to Ma's claim for the endurance of the people, to Tom's vision of a national soul. The Joad narrative is laden with prophecy, in the sense of the word as the utterance of a prophet and in its obscure meaning as a group of prophets. Jim Casy is, fittingly, the first of this group. "I went off alone an' I sat and figured," he tells Tom. "The sperit's strong in me, on'y it ain't the same. I ain't so sure of a lot of things."[28] Casy's quest to speak the truth, to respond to massive human suffering with a new vision, is quickly echoed by Ma Joad. "I got to thinkin' an' dreamin' an' wonderin'. They say there's a hun'erd thousand of us shoved out. If we was all mad the same way," she says to Tom, "they wouldn't hunt nobody down."[29] When Tom asks her if those tens of thousands feel the same way, she describes them as "kinda stunned. Walk aroun' like they was half asleep."[30] All the same, Ma cautions Tom not to fight the authorities. Walzer argues that "the Exodus is not a lucky escape from misfortune. Rather, the misfortune has a moral character, and the escape has a world-historical meaning. Egypt is not just left behind; it is rejected; it is judged and condemned."[31] Similarly, Ma judges and condemns the sociopolitical structures that privilege banks over families. Her prophesy is a full, if suspicious, endorsement of the westward migration, the movement that will eventually shape the disparate groups and families into a new nation. She inspires Tom to help people get "mad the same way."

Characterizing Exodus as the story of a people rather than of individuals who populate Genesis, Walzer describes Moses as a prototype of Christ, who works to a spiritual end that he cannot reveal even as he makes this-worldly political changes: "The people see and want; Moses has a vision and a program."[32] However, for as often as Steinbeck invokes both Mosaic and apostolic prophecy—Ma as Miriam, Casy as Moses/Jesus, Tom as Jesus/Moses, and all as revolutionary political leaders—he blurs their voices into one stream of prophesy. They form a confluence with the intercalary narrator and the guitar man, conjoined voices that speak for transformative justice as they continually evaluate political leadership and economic inequalities and their responses to both. In arguing that the Bible offers a hermeneutic tool through which to interpret leadership, Aaron Wildavsky notes that "Moses was a leader who taught his people to do without him by learning how to lead themselves."[33] Steinbeck's various prophet-leaders shift the mantle of leadership throughout; they form a people able to lead themselves. Wildavsky concludes that in rejecting the old order, Moses "transforms preferences, thus generating different demands. Once the people choose a way of life, their preferences follow from their regime. But they do not choose forever. Like Moses, they continuously evaluate their institutions."[34] The Joad prophecies culminate in radical action: Rose of Sharon sending her dead baby down the water like Moses to tell the truth and giving of her breast to a starving man.

Ultimately, like Exodus, the prophetic narrative in *The Grapes of Wrath*—as it relies on symbol and nonspecificity, offers a vision of truth and justice, and codifies a people into a nation—becomes part of the culture's mythology. Frederic Carpenter sees the novel as combining three great skeins of American thought: Emerson's transcendental oversoul, his faith in the common man, and Protestant self-reliance; Whitman's religion of the love of all men and his mass democracy; and a Christianity that is active and earthly rather than passive and otherworldly.[35] Carpenter correctly points out the liberation theology offered by the novel, which, like Exodus, is a text rooted in monotheism. However, Carpenter's claim that the novel sets forth "great" trends in American thought offers insight into the novel's status as American cultural capital. Like Exodus, the novel's westward quest, its attention to the plight of the individual, its notion of the formation of all oppressed into a nation, and its wide, symbol-laden vision offer a uniquely lasting and influential American myth.

Coogan notes that the Exodus narrative tends to mythologize as it historicizes. The history is out of joint, and the mythology arises as historical claims shade into the supernatural. Events like the parting of the Red Sea combine existing mythology with the geographical reality of a vast swamp (the sea of reeds that likely mired Pharaoh's mounted army) into the mythic warning not to mess with God's people. Having described rotting food and filthy migrant camps, the mytho-prophetic narrative of *The Grapes of Wrath* juxtaposes a child dying from pellagra against the waste of food when the market bottoms out. The sorrow and anger take on mythic proportions as the narrative voice focuses outward on those who hold the monstrous rights. The account of the child ends with praying to God but also preying upon the owners' fears:

> Pray God some day kind people won't all be poor. Pray God some day
> a kid can eat.
> And the associations of owners knew that some day the praying would stop.
> And there's the end.[36]

The account of the wasted food and the dead child initiates the beginnings of the fulfillment of prophecy: "And children dying of pellagra must die because a profit cannot be taken from an orange. And coroners must fill in the certificates—died of malnutrition—because the food must rot. In the eyes of the people there is failure; and in the eyes of the hungry there is a growing wrath. In the souls of the people the grapes of wrath are filling and growing heavy, growing heavy for the vintage."[37] Arguing that Exodus teaches readers that revolutionary politics always begin with suffering— *"the beginning of liberation lies in man's capacity to suffer"*—Erich Fromm suggests that "because God is revealed in history, the prophet cannot help being a political leader; as long as man takes the wrong way in his political action, the prophet cannot help being a dissenter and a revolutionary."[38] Individual misery depicted in general terms by the prophet takes on the proportion of myth. The prophetic vision sows, as much as it sees, the grapes of wrath.

"I'll Be Ever'where—Wherever You Look": American Exodus

Amid the formation of a people the American dream of individuality must be left behind, and Steinbeck posits a redefinition of human instincts, boundaries, laws, and desires. He begins this redefinition with Casy's quest for new meaning, develops it with the figure of the nameless, faceless guitar man, and concludes it with an American earth mother feeding a man in need. In aligning the intercalary chapters with the mythology of the Hebrew exodus, Steinbeck offers an economic, legal, and political reading of the American power structures that caused the Depression and oppressed the ensuing migrant populations. For as much as he relied on Exodus for his framework, Steinbeck defined this novel as his "truly American book."[39]

However, even as the novel undertakes a reformation of human rights and their role in American national identity, its mythology is ultimately, and very much like Exodus, an exclusionary myth. It leaves out the Mexican, Asian, and African Americans who worked side by side in the fields with the Dust Bowl migrants and who stayed in those fields long after the Dust Bowlers had been assimilated into middle America. Just as the Hebrews were God's chosen people, *The Grapes of Wrath* makes clear that being white and of Anglo-European origin is a prerequisite to inclusion in the growing nation: "And then the dispossessed were drawn west—from Kansas, Oklahoma, Texas, New Mexico; from Nevada and Arkansas families, tribes, dusted out, tractored out. . . . We ain't foreign. Seven generations back American and beyond that Irish, Scotch, English, German. One of our folks was in the Revolution, an' they was lots of our folks in the Civil War—both sides. Americans."[10]

Steinbeck makes clear what *American* means in a letter about *The Grapes of Wrath*, as he reinforces the culture's idea of itself as a democratic, Christian, redeemer nation: "The fascist crowd will try to sabotage this book because it is revolutionary. They try to give it a communist angle. However, The Battle Hymn is American and intensely so. . . . So if both words and music are there the book is keyed into the American scene from the beginning."[11] Some commentators believe that the book is subversive. Noting that the novel is "politically unstable to a degree not matched by Steinbeck's other texts," Dix finds it "readable in terms of orthodox Marxist observance, Communist heresy and even downright apostasy from the cause of the Left."[12] Steinbeck, however, refuses to have his Okies follow any particular party line. This choice suggests that the novel's prophetic politics rest in revision and change.

In his analysis of Exodus's prophetic politics, David Gutterman focuses on the themes of enslavement, liberation, the creation of a polity, political leadership, and principles of social and economic justice.[13] Israel cannot transcend the realm of politics, Gutterman argues: "The Exodus narrative is fundamentally a political story; it is an ideological telling of a people's history—a story that in the telling not only engages in rhetoric in order to define and raise the political stakes, but also defines the identity of a people."[14] *The Grapes of Wrath* ends, as does Exodus, with a unified nation of people still lost in the wilderness, their identity and political vision a retelling of the Exodus narrative. "Narratives," Gutterman argues, "are the tools humans use to define themselves (individually and collectively) and their world—tools that organize and enable life."[15] When John Winthrop began the formation of the American nation with his "City upon a Hill" sermon, he pointed out that as the eyes of the world were upon them, they "shall be made a story and a by-word through the world."[16] Steinbeck's determination to leave this novel open-ended and apart from any particular political doctrine reinforces its revolutionary vision; his story is a narrative tool made for forging social change. Tom's final and pivotal speech, embedded in the American consciousness by Henry Fonda in John Ford's 1940 movie, offers that same vision: "I'll be ever'where—wherever you look. Wherever they's a fight so hungry people can eat, I'll be there. Wherever they's a cop beatin' up a guy, I'll be there. . . . I'll be in the way guys yell when they're mad an'—I'll be in the way kids laugh when they're hungry and they know supper's ready. An' when our folks eat the stuff they raise an' live in the houses they build—why, I'll be there."[47]

Even though it was and is an ethnically narrow vision, Steinbeck's revision of the Exodian national identity and the prophet figure continues to be a matrix of cultural production. Just as Exodus functions as a foundation for the entire Bible, as it first offers the continuing themes of coming and presence, relationship and responsibility, Steinbeck's fictional and prophetic reporting provided a reference point for political and cultural trends. In terms of conventional politics, for example, the novel forced Washington to reevaluate national water policies and subsidies. In terms of popular art, Steinbeck's guitar man continues to inform the culture as the chosen prophetic voice. Based loosely on Steinbeck's friend Woody Guthrie, these singers become entwined, in the novel and after it, with the Guthrie myth in a mode of cultural production that continues today. Just as Guthrie inspired Steinbeck, he was in turn moved by Ford's film version of *The Grapes of Wrath* to include Casy and his theory of the "one big soul" in the song "Vigilante Man" and to repeat almost verbatim Tom's prophecy in the ballad "Tom Joad." Profoundly influenced by the mythology of Tom Joad, as set forth by Steinbeck then reified by the film and Guthrie, Bruce Springsteen has returned again and again to it for inspiration. As early as *Nebraska* (1982) he made oblique references to the Joad narrative. (For further discussion of Steinbeck's influence on Springsteen, see chapter 10, by Lauren Onkey.) Like Guthrie's "Tom Joad," Springsteen's "The Ghost of Tom Joad," from the 1995 album of the same name, repeats Tom's prophecy verbatim, but where Guthrie wrote a recap of events, Springsteen opens the narrative up to the same kind of yearning that Steinbeck describes as he brings his audience into the hunger and displacement of the present. The song, like the novel and like the exodus, ends with the prophet looking forward, looking ahead into the Promised Land and envisioning political change. But Springsteen looks to Steinbeck for the technique of building worlds, singing about oppression that brings together disparate peoples then offering them a latter-day vision of the Promised Land:

> You got a hole in your belly and a gun in your hand
> The highway is alive tonight

Where it's headed everybody knows
I'm sittin' down here in the campfire light
Waitin' on the ghost of Tom Joad[48]

Notes

1. Dorothea Lange and Paul Taylor, *An American Exodus: A Record of Human Erosion* (New York: Reynal and Hitchcock, 1939).

2. John Steinbeck, *The Grapes of Wrath* (New York: Penguin, 1992), 123.

3. John Steinbeck, *Steinbeck: A Life in Letters*, ed. Elaine Steinbeck and Robert Wallsten (New York: Penguin, 1975), 178.

4. All biblical quotations come from the New Revised Standard Version.

5. John Steinbeck, *Working Days: The Journal of* The Grapes of Wrath, *1938–1941*, ed. Robert DeMott (New York: Viking, 1989), 40.

6. Michele L. Landis, "Fate, Responsibility, and 'Natural' Disaster Relief: Narrating the American Welfare State," *Law and Society Review* 33, no. 2 (1999): 297–98.

7. Exodus 17:1, 17:3; Steinbeck, *Grapes of Wrath*, 266, 166.

8. Steinbeck, *Grapes of Wrath*, 318.

9. Ibid., 318.

10. Roxanne Dunbar-Ortiz, "One or Two Things I Know about Us—Rethinking the Image and Role of the Okies," *Queen's Quarterly* 102 (1995): 574–75.

11. Steinbeck, *Life in Letters*, 859.

12. Michael Walzer, *Exodus and Revolution* (New York: Basic Books, 1984), x.

13. H. Mark Roelofs, "Hebraic-Biblical Political Thinking," *Polity* 20, no. 4 (1988): 575.

14. Walzer, *Exodus and Revolution*, 7.

15. Ibid., 96.

16. Steinbeck, *Life in Letters*, 171.

17. Walzer, *Exodus and Revolution*, 149.

18. Steinbeck, *Grapes of Wrath*, 119.

19. *Oxford English Dictionary*, s.v. "phalanx."

20. Steinbeck, *Grapes of Wrath*, 206.

21. Ibid., 264–65.

22. Ibid., 265–66.

23. Steinbeck, *Life in Letters*, 151.

24. Steinbeck, *Grapes of Wrath*, 319, 257.

25. Steinbeck, *Life in Letters*, 162.

26. Steinbeck, *Grapes of Wrath*, 272.

27. Andrew Dix, "'Curiousest grace I ever heerd': Christian and Marxist Heresies in *The Grapes of Wrath*," in *Figures of Heresy: Radical Theology in English and American Writing, 1800–2000*, ed. Andrew Dix and Jonathan Taylor (Brighton, UK: Sussex Academic Press, 2006), 122.

28. Steinbeck, *Grapes of Wrath*, 28.

29. Ibid., 104.

30. Ibid.

31. Walzer, *Exodus and Revolution*, 21.

32. Ibid., 103.

33. Aaron Wildavsky, *The Nursing Father: Moses as Political Leader* (Tuscaloosa: University of Alabama Press, 1984), 1.

34. Ibid., 216.

35. Frederic I. Carpenter, "The Philosophical Joads," in *John Steinbeck's* The Grapes of Wrath, ed. Harold Bloom (New York: Chelsea, 1988), 15.

36. Steinbeck, *Grapes of Wrath*, 326.

37. Ibid., 477.

38. Erich Fromm, *You Shall Be as Gods: A Radical Interpretation of the Old Testament and Its Tradition* (New York: Holt, Rinehart and Winston, 1966), 92, 118; emphasis in original.

39. Steinbeck, *Life in Letters*, 174.

40. Steinbeck, *Grapes of Wrath*, 317–18.

41. Steinbeck, *Life in Letters*, 174

42. Dix, "Curiousest grace I ever heerd," 128.

43. David S. Gutterman, *Prophetic Politics: Christian Social Movements and American Democracy* (Ithaca, N.Y.: Cornell University Press, 2005), 10.

44. Ibid., 11.

45. Ibid., 28.

46. John Winthrop, "A Model of Christian Charity," in *The Heath Anthology of American Literature*, 5th ed., ed. Paul Lauter et al., vol. A (Boston: Houghton Mifflin, 2006), 317.

47. Steinbeck, *Grapes of Wrath*, 572.

48. Bruce Springsteen, "Ghost of Tom Joad." Copyright © 1995 Bruce Springsteen (ASCAP). Reprinted by permission. International copyright secured. All rights reserved.

PART III

Steinbeck in American Political Culture

CHAPTER 8

Focusing on the Migrant: The Contextualization of Dorothea Lange's Photographs of the John Steinbeck Committee

James R. Swensen

FOR MORE THAN HALF a century, John Steinbeck's 1930s writings—
The Grapes of Wrath in particular—and the photography created under the
auspices of the Farm Security Administration (FSA) have been synonymous
with the Great Depression.[1] Americans use these works of art, rightfully
or not, as lenses through which to view the conditions and the challenges
of America in the latter half of the 1930s.[2] More recently, in the wake of
the devastation caused by hurricanes Katrina and Rita and the economic
meltdown known as the Great Recession, Americans have used Steinbeck's
writings, coupled with the images of the FSA, to contextualize the deprivation and calamity before our eyes. In many ways the "Okies" and "Arkies,"
the migration of which Steinbeck and FSA photographer Dorothea Lange
(1895–1965) so vividly represented in the 1930s, became the forerunners of
the modern refugee fleeing the destruction and chaos of New Orleans and
of the middle-class family facing eminent foreclosure.

Despite the obvious parallels in subject matter and style between
Steinbeck's writings and the FSA photographs, the collection of more than
two hundred thousand images amassed by the FSA contains only six references to Steinbeck.[3] This omission is not surprising, considering that FSA
photographers were instructed to focus not on Washington politicians, Hollywood starlets, or famous literary figures but on the faces and problems of
rural America. According to Roy Stryker, director of the Historical Section,
"Our job was to educate the city-dweller to the needs of the rural population."[4] All six allusions to Steinbeck appear in captions to photographs shot

by Dorothea Lange in October 1938. The allusions refer not to the author himself but to the John Steinbeck Committee to Aid Agricultural Organization and its attempts to support migrants during the cotton strike of 1938.[5]

This essay analyzes Lange's images and thereby the context of the John Steinbeck Committee at a critical moment in its history. The analysis of the committee and Lange's work in turn will shed further light on Steinbeck and his politics during this important period of his career.

Steinbeck's Name

The Committee to Aid Agricultural Organization was formed in the summer of 1938 in San Francisco and soon thereafter split into divisions in Northern and Southern California. Shortly after its inception, Steinbeck was named its state chairman, and the committee adopted his name to increase its profile. The Southern Division of the Steinbeck Committee to Aid Agricultural Organization, headquartered in Los Angeles, was led by author and attorney Carey McWilliams, who had never met Steinbeck despite their shared interest in California's rural working classes.[6] Both divisions attracted individuals who wanted to raise public awareness about the plight of thousands of migrants entering the state in pursuit of a better life.[7] The rosters of concerned citizens included Hollywood actors and actresses, local lawyers, secretaries, doctors, and housewives.[8]

The organization's stated purpose was "to provide the necessary support, financial and moral, to help agricultural workers in California build a strong union."[9] In fact, the Steinbeck Committee saw the formation of unions—a foreign concept for many former Oklahoma and Arkansas farmers—as a key to alleviating California's mounting migrant problem. To achieve this end, the Steinbeck Committee published pamphlets; solicited money through fund-raisers, parties, and signed-book auctions; and promoted labor laws and social security reform.[10]

The Steinbeck Committee also worked with various labor groups, including the United Cannery, Agricultural, Packing, and Allied Workers of America (UCAPAWA), a new and avowedly left-wing CIO charter.[11] Created in 1937, the UCAPAWA sought to unionize agricultural labor, which previously had been seen as a nonskilled trade.[12] The Steinbeck Committee wished to help the UCAPAWA become stronger and more self-supporting and therefore worked closely with the UCAPAWA executive committee, provided financial aid, and did anything else it could do to further their joint cause.[13]

Although Steinbeck's role within the Steinbeck Committee was largely titular, his name carried weight. One pamphlet asked, "Will you join my committee to aid agricultural organization?"[14] Even before the publication of *The Grapes of Wrath*, Steinbeck's reputation was growing. *Tortilla Flat* (1935), *In Dubious Battle* (1936), and *Of Mice and Men* (1937) made Steinbeck a rising star in the literary world. His politics, sympathies, and notoriety made him a perfect figurehead for the group. Photographer Horace Bristol remembers that Steinbeck was still relatively accessible and popular but not yet a celebrity.[15] His emphasis on plebian subjects engaged in heroic (or mock-heroic) struggles contributed to his reputation as a defender of the common man. In the words of one critic, Steinbeck's work featured "warm powerful portraits of common men, [with] each book showing some advance over the one preceding, each book showing great power moving toward maturity."[16]

In addition, Steinbeck had become recognized as an expert on agricultural affairs. As a youth and young man he had firsthand experience with agricultural labor, but his deeper knowledge of the subject derived from the extensive research he undertook for his books. His research for *In Dubious Battle,* for example, exposed him to the world of clandestine labor organizing.[17] Not long afterward Steinbeck wrote a series of exposés in the *San Francisco News* in 1936 on the conditions and challenges faced by California's new migrant laborers. Travelling incognito through the picking fields, he heard the stories of the Dust Bowl refugees and saw, firsthand, the frightening conditions they faced and the callousness of the large growers. By 1938 these experiences allowed him to speak authoritatively about labor conditions in the California countryside.

Although some critics argue that Steinbeck was not interested in politics and hid his ideological commitments, his actions and ideas were clearly left of center.[18] Like many on the Steinbeck Committee, Steinbeck was a New Deal Democrat and held what Jackson Benson calls "generalized, liberal sympathies."[19] These sympathies contributed to an appearance of political ambiguity. Conservatives knew he was somewhere on the left, but radicals thought he was too far to the right.[20] According to his former neighbor, the reformer Ella Winter, "He did not want to be connected with any one side lest people thought he was writing propaganda."[21] Even his experiences among union organizers and the poor did not radicalize him.[22] (For more on Steinbeck's political experiences and thinking prior to *The Grapes of Wrath,* see chapter 1, by Cyrus Ernesto Zirakzadeh.)

Despite ideological hesitations, Steinbeck supported organizing labor to ameliorate economic woes.[23] He was not alone. "Organize" was the one-word battle cry sweeping through California, McWilliams remembered.[24] Even Florence Thompson, Lange's famous "Migrant Madonna," was active in a union, organized meetings, and negotiated wages.[25] Steinbeck saw organization as the best political response to starvation and saw the legal opportunity to form unions as an essential right.[26] In 1936 he wrote, "It is understood that [migratory laborers] are being attacked not because they want higher wages, not because they are Communists, but simply because they want to organize. And to the men, since this defines the thing not to be allowed, it also defines the thing that is completely necessary to the safety of the workers."[27] His ardor for labor organizing grew after he visited the fields. On the pages of the *San Francisco News* he reported, "Agricultural workers should be encouraged and helped to organize, both for their own protection, for the intelligent distribution of labor and for their self-government through the consideration of their own problems."[28]

Steinbeck's sympathy for labor aligned the interests of progressive groups and causes. In May 1937 he wrote Cicil McKiddy, a labor organizer from Oklahoma and an important source for *In Dubious Battle,* "Look you know that I'll do anything for this movement that makes sense." Still, he had some reservations about committing himself politically. "It isn't going to do a goddamn bit of good to put my name over a bunch of crap," Steinbeck cautioned. "Too many people do that."[29]

Steinbeck may not have been on the front lines of the Steinbeck Committee to Aid Agricultural Organization, but by allowing the group to use his name he was assisting its cause. His dedication to the underprivileged and the downtrodden and his opposition to oppression and exploitation made his name a perfect banner for the Steinbeck Committee's crusade. *San Francisco News* columnist John D. Barry proclaimed that Steinbeck "has come forward at a time when revolutionary changes are going on in the world. He will be a factor in those changes and a significant factor, too. His sympathies are not with the special people, but with those at a disadvantage, sorely in need of a gifted and valiant literary champion."[30]

United Cause

Steinbeck and the Steinbeck Committee maintained close connections with another liberal organization, the Simon J. Lubin Society of California.[31] Founded on November 6, 1936, by the intrepid reformer Helen Hosmer and others, the society sought to "educate public opinion to an understanding of the problems of the working farmer and the condition of agricultural laborers."[32] The society was named in honor of Simon J. Lubin, an ardent defender of farm labor in California who had died earlier that year.[33] Like the Steinbeck Committee, it was composed of a small group of individuals whom McWilliams called "liberal professional people."[34] Both organizations endorsed progressive Democrat Culbert Olson's bid for governor and opposed the Associated Farmers of California, which many reformers, including Steinbeck, Hosmer, and McWilliams, considered culpable for many of the migrants' woes.[35] If Lubin symbolized past efforts to organize farm laborers in California, Steinbeck was the current face of the fight.[36]

The two organizations differed, however. In contrast to the Lubin Society, which concentrated broadly on farm-labor issues in California, the Steinbeck Committee focused on recent white migrants who were arriving from Oklahoma, Arkansas, and surrounding states at a rate of nearly six thousand a month.[37] For Steinbeck, these refugees represented something different from what he called the former "peon class" of Californian farm labor—Chinese, Mexicans, and Filipinos.[38] Steinbeck saw the families pushed out of middle America by drought and other forces beyond their control as a "new race" of American people.[39] Believing them to be of pure American stock, he attributed to them atypical intelligence, resourcefulness, and courage.[40] (For more on Steinbeck's mixture of culturalist and racialist thinking, see chapter 1, by Cyrus Ernesto Zirakzadeh.)

These same virtues, however, posed an obstacle to the organizing of migrant laborers.[41] As former farmers, they saw themselves as "rugged individualists" who could solve their problems alone. In addition, the new migrant workers were isolated and widely dispersed on farms throughout California, which made attempts to unionize them extremely difficult.[42] Their ceaseless movement across the state and across state lines in pursuit of the next crop to harvest also undermined efforts to maintain a local union chapter. Furthermore, they had minimal experience with labor organizations and were often unable to meet a union's financial obligations. They were also hampered by a chronic labor surplus that was growing every day and that kept wages down and made strikebreakers plentiful.[43] Confronting penury, they were reluctant to jeopardize their limited income by participating in a strike.[44] In all, organizing the "new race" would be a challenge for any group, regardless of resources or drive.

There were also formidable external challenges. Organized in 1934 to combat a growing wave of perceived "Red activities," the growers' group known as Associated Farmers of California employed various tactics to prevent field hands from organizing. "We have an excellent formula for getting rid of cockroaches, grasshoppers and CIO agitators," wrote one member of the Associated Farmers.[45] This formula included intimidation, blacklists, espionage, strikebreaking, pressure for antipicketing legislation, and vigilante attacks.[46] The activities of the Associated Farmers were so brutal that the LaFollette Committee later labeled it "local fascism."[47] Not surprisingly, it was the bête noire of Steinbeck, Hosmer, and many within the New Deal.[48]

Despite all of these challenges, the Steinbeck Committee remained. "Our interests are one with our fellows," one pamphlet proclaimed. "The workers in the field cannot lift themselves by their bootstraps. Speed is essential. Those now engaged in the work of organizing are too few, too handicapped by poverty, to do the work that must be done in the time required."[49]

Their Blood Is Strong

Early in 1938 Steinbeck gave the Lubin Society permission to reprint the articles on migrant workers that he had written for the *San Francisco News* in 1936.[50] The Lubin Society used profits from the sale of the subsequent pamphlet, titled *Their Blood Is Strong*, to fund its activities.[51] The pamphlet included four photographs by Dorothea Lange that detailed the misery of newly arrived migrant workers living in ramshackle squatter camps.[52]

Although Steinbeck and Lange did not meet until 1939, they were alike in important ways. Both were products of a liberal climate in Northern California, both were active in progressive causes, and both turned to federal and local governments for support.[53] They were also alike in that they witnessed firsthand the deprivations of California's migrants, and both used their talents to mollify the suffering of those around them.

Lange, like Steinbeck, did not advertise her politics. Her husband, Dr. Paul S. Taylor, denied that she belonged to any organized groups. "No, no, not political or otherwise. No she didn't belong to any, she didn't even belong to the f/64 photographers club. . . . She didn't belong to any thing."[54] Clark Kerr believed that she was one the most "nonideological persons" he had ever known.[55] Still, she attended political gatherings and arguably some of her best work was made in moments of political tension.[56] Tagged a "liberal sentimental," not a radical, Lange supported progressive causes that helped the underprivileged.[57] However, biographer Linda Gordon noted, "[Lange] was politically an individualist. Enraged by social injustice and admiring resistance to it, she conceived of resistance and the heroic primarily in individual terms."[58]

Lange's most important photograph in *Their Blood Is Strong* is of a steely-eyed young migrant mother nursing her young son, which graced the cover of the twenty-five-cent pamphlet (figure 1). This woman was a symbol of Steinbeck's "new race." In spite of hardship, she was beautiful and determined, healthy, and still able to succor her child.[59] She stood in sharp contrast to another mother figure in Steinbeck's text who was struggling for survival in California's "land of plenty": "The mother, usually suffering from malnutrition, is not able to produce breast milk. Sometimes the baby is nourished on canned milk until it can eat fried dough and cornmeal. This being the case, the infant mortality is very great."[60] These two images of motherhood jointly created a powerful portrait of the migrant experience. Lange's mother exhibited the strength of character of these new pioneers. Steinbeck's mother, hard and thin, revealed the toll of poor housing and ill treatment, which could be prevented.

Steinbeck's strongly worded and candid denouncements were enhanced and made more accessible by Lange's sympathetic images. As Susan Sontag has observed, "Photography is designed potentially for all. All can read it."[61] The pamphlet was carefully crafted to convince its readership that *"Your help is needed."*[62] It worked. *Their Blood Is Strong* was reportedly read "far and wide," and its four printings kept the society solvent.[63]

The Cotton Strike of 1938

Both the Lubin Society and the Steinbeck Committee argued that in places like the San Joaquin Valley absentee owners with tremendous capital were

Figure 1. Dorothea Lange, "Drought refugees from Oklahoma camping by
the roadside. They hope to work in the cotton fields. The official at the border
(California-Arizona) inspection service said that on this day, August 17, 1936,
twenty-three car loads and truck loads of migrant families out of the drought
counties of Oklahoma and Arkansas had passed through that station entering
California up to 3 o'clock in the afternoon." LC-USF34-009665-E. Library of
Congress.

transforming California agriculture. California's rural landscape was being
industrialized. Farms grew larger, profits soared, and the demand for cheap
labor increased. Corporate agriculture produced more than profits, however. It also produced unrest. As labor congresses struggled to make inroads
into rural communities, fieldworkers began to assert their power. From 1930
to 1939 there were more than 140 farm strikes across California.[64]

Like other crops in California, cotton was big business in the 1930s.

In 1938 the state boasted a record 618,000 acres of cotton, yielding more than seven hundred thousand bales and netting California growers nearly $40 million in revenue.[65] Early in the decade, migrant laborers were paid reasonably well. As late as 1937 many farm laborers received ninety cents per hundred pounds of cotton picked, and many hoped the rate might soon reach a dollar. Yet by 1938, in spite of record yields, wages dropped to seventy-five cents per hundred pounds due to decreased demand for cotton and an increase in the supply of labor.[66] Understandably, tension mounted. Two years earlier Steinbeck had correctly forecast the upcoming turmoil in the fields: "The men will organize and the large growers will meet organization with force. It is easy to prophesy this. In Kern County the grange has voted $1 a hundred pounds for cotton pickers for the first picking. The Associated Farmers have not yielded from seventy-five cents. There is tension in the valley, and fear for the future."[67]

Unlike the larger, better organized, and far more successful cotton strike of 1933, the 1938 strike was spontaneous and local.[68] It began on October 1 when three hundred pickers, protesting low wages, walked off a job at Camp West Lowe near Shafter, California.[69] The organizational center of the nascent strike lay at the nearby FSA labor camp, which allowed the CIO to conduct meetings in the camp's halls and featured CIO-written articles in the camp's newspaper.[70] When growers began blacklisting the workers who lived in the Shafter camp, the strike intensified.[71] By the middle of the month, nearly four thousand workers reportedly were on strike, bringing cotton production to a standstill.[72] Bowing to the workers' pressure, many smaller growers began offering ninety cents to a dollar per hundredweight. Soon, however, the Associated Farmers and the Farm Bureau stepped in and set wages of seventy-five cents across the board.

Initially caught off guard, the UCAPAWA sent organizers from San Francisco to the San Joaquin Valley to assist the strikers.[73] The leadership of the UCAPAWA proposed raising wages by 25 percent for the backbreaking labor.[74] In ideal conditions with good cotton and fair weather, a strong picker could pick two hundred pounds in one day and, at seventy-five cents per hundredweight, earn $1.50—a subsistence wage in McWilliams's estimation. "I can't feed these five children of mine on 75-cent cotton," one migrant reported to Lange, "so I'm pullin out of here but I don't know where I'm goin."[75]

Fred Soule, the regional information leader of the FSA in San

Figure 2. Dorothea Lange, "Migratory field worker picking cotton in San Joaquin Valley, California. These cotton pickers are being paid seventy-five cents per one hundred pounds. Strikers organizing under the Congress of Industrial Organizations union (CIO) demand one dollar. A good male picker, in good cotton, under favorable weather conditions, can pick about two hundred pounds in a day's work." LC-USF34-018588-C. Library of Congress.

Francisco, sent Lange to cover the situation in Kern County.[76] Once she arrived she used her camera, as she often did, to probe the situation and understand its breadth. She began by photographing anonymous pickers, possibly strikebreakers, in empty fields full of cotton where once black, Mexican, and "refugee whites" picked together (figure 2).[77] She found tensions running high and strikers at a breaking point. At some point she photographed four squatting migrants "talking it over" (figure 3). "I don't care: let them throw me in jail," they told her. "There's somebody will take my place."

At the Shafter camp she documented the camp bulletin board, complete with notices of migrants returning home to Missouri and Oklahoma. Prominent on the board was the short essay "Definition of a Scab," purport-

Figure 3. Dorothea Lange, "Striking cotton pickers talk it over. The strike is failing. Kern County, California. 'I don't care: Let them throw me in jail. There's somebody will take my place.'" LC-USF34-018464-E. Library of Congress.

edly by Jack London, which the UCAPAWA had posted.[78] "Esau sold his birthright for a mess of potage," it declared. "Judas Iscariot sold his Saviour for thirty pieces of silver. Benedict Arnold sold his Country for a promise of a commission in the British Army. The modern strike-breaker sells his birthright, his country, his wife, his children, and his fellow man for an unfulfilled promise from his employer, trust or corporation. . . . Esau was a traitor to himself. Judas Iscariot was a traitor to his God. Benedict Arnold was a traitor to his country. A strike-breaker, to his God, his country, his family, and his class."[79] The union knew that migrants willing to work at any wage just to feed their family would undermine its efforts. So the union played on workers' pride to keep them from crossing the picket line. "A Real man never becomes a Strike-Breaker," the posting concluded.

Lange's portrait of the strike also included images of those who tried to help the strikers and their families. She photographed members of International Labor Defense delivering clothing and shoes, and representatives from the FSA, Lange's own agency, distributing relief commodities and food from an old warehouse in Bakersfield.[80] Despite protests from the Associated Farmers, the only requirement for FSA aid was, "Are you an agricultural worker and are you hungry?"[81] Some of the more poignant scenes that Lange captured were small symbols of defiance, like a campaign sticker for Democrat Culbert Olson on a striker's windshield and a hand-painted sign in front of an independently owned gas station bolstering the strikers: "This is your Country don't let the big men take it away from YOU."[82]

One of the most important aspects of her assignment was the coverage of the John Steinbeck Committee's Bakersfield Conference on October 29, 1938. By the time Lange photographed the proceedings, the strike was already in its fourth week and its participants were growing weary and increasingly less hopeful. The Steinbeck Committee had less than two weeks to organize the all-day meeting, which was called at the urging of the UCAPAWA.[83] The purported reason for the gathering was to address the issues of "wretched housing, inadequate relief and a truly dangerous health problem" that were plaguing the migrants.[84] Discussion of the strike and wage increases nearly overshadowed these concerns. As one desperate speaker pleaded, "Nobody can go out in the field and pick cotton and have what the body needs to live on at 75¢ a hundred."[85]

The meeting began at 1:20 p.m. in the crowded confines of the Kern County Labor Temple. It was packed to capacity, with a few people lingering outside (figure 5). The more than 350 participants included strikers, union officials, lawyers, physicians, social workers, and delegates from the FSA and other governmental agencies.[86] The growers were not invited.[87] A predominately white crowd, old and young, male and female, filled every seat and every open space of the hall, including the stairs and the landing. Some even held on to the plumbing along the rafters of the ceiling to gain

Figure 4. Dorothea Lange, "Gas station. Kern County, California." LC-USF34-018401-E. Library of Congress.

a view of the speakers (figure 6). Most of the crowd watched the speaker, who stood in front of an American flag, while a few followed the activities of the photographer. Lange's juxtaposition of the intent faces and crowded hall suggest that these individuals could take strength and hope from their numbers. Her photos emphasize the collective spirit of these people and refute the notion that these newcomers to California were unable or unwilling to organize.[88]

Figure 5. Dorothea Lange, "Conference called by the Steinbeck Committee to Aid Agricultural Organization during the cotton strike. Bakersfield, California." LC-USF34-018413-E. Library of Congress.

In Steinbeck's absence, the meeting was called to order by Alice Orans, executive secretary of the Southern Division of the Steinbeck Committee, and featured speakers from the UCAPAWA and FSA as well as from the strikers themselves. They spoke passionately about the effects of poor working conditions and meager wages. This was particularly true of the session's third speaker, a former farmer L. R. Duncan. In what one report called a "painfully graphic" manner, Duncan described his family's flight from Texas

Figure 6. Dorothea Lange, "Listening to the speaker at the Conference to Aid Agricultural Organization during the cotton strike (Steinbeck Committee). Bakersfield, Kern County, California." LC-USF34-018411-E. Library of Congress.

to the picking fields of California. Once they arrived Duncan and his family experienced a variety of degradations that eventually led to a "typhoid-malarial fever" that laid him up in the Madera County Hospital for five weeks. As with others, Duncan and his family found respite at the federal camp in Shafter but were unable to find work. At some point Duncan became a leader in the strike, and he made the most of his opportunity at the conference to energize his audience. During his cathartic sermon he moved from tears one moment to a "smile like a burst of sunlight [that] spread across his features." The minute-taker also noted that "his whole personality gave the impression of true strength of character and manliness, without bitterness or rancour [*sic*] because of his experiences. A truly remarkable personality."[89] Rondal Partridge, Lange's young assistant, remembered Duncan as a fiery speaker full of conviction.[90] He resembled a rogue preacher, Partridge recalled, in the way "he ignited his crowd."[91] Duncan concluded his remarks by proclaiming,

> You know there are hundreds and thousands of workers in the fields today who don't even know you are considering them. They don't even know anybody's interested in their conditions and they're not to blame. Many of them have said, "Brother, it's pick 75¢ cotton, or STARVE." They're to be pitied because they think the only thing they can do is to pick the 75¢ cotton. It's a shame and a disgrace—because we can't live on it. I am proud there are higher officials with greater influence than our politicians that are really thinking about us. And I thank every one of you. God Bless you.[92]

Lange focused her lens on Duncan as he addressed his audience (figure 7). From this angle the once-conspicuous American flag seen behind the speaker in earlier photographs is now barely visible. Lange captured the speaker working his audience with his entire body, accentuated by the harsh light of her strobe.[93] He leans into the crowd as if he is ready to pounce, imploring them to act. In the intensity of his eyes one sees a desire—bordering on desperation—to sway, push, and inspire his audience, to make them embrace his cause in a seemingly impossible terrain.

In her typical fashion, Lange not only caught the image but also recorded what her subjects said through detailed captions. Paul Taylor, in fact, posited that her ear was as good as her eye.[94] She recorded in a "folk-speak" manner that approximated Duncan's accent: "Brother, 'Hits pick seventy-five cent cotton or starve. Brother, 'hits pick seventy-five cent cotton or else." She thus retained and embellished his most dramatic catchphrase.

Lange's images capture several features of the Steinbeck Committee. The photographs show that it was not composed of Hollywood celebrities or government administrators. Steinbeck is conspicuously absent. Instead, numerous migrants capture center stage. To the members of the Associated Farmers and its supporters these images might have appeared menacing: L. R. Duncan might have looked more threatening and crazed than in-

Figure 7. Dorothea Lange, "Speaker, migratory worker,
leader in the cotton strike, at Conference to Aid Agricultural
Organization (Steinbeck Committee), Bakersfield, California.
Saying: 'Brother, 'Hits pick seventy-five cent cotton or starve.
Brother, 'hits pick seventy-five cent cotton or else.'" LC-USF34-
018774-D. Library of Congress.

spired. For the Steinbeck Committee, however, the camera's focus was
precisely where it belonged.

Before closing at 6:00 p.m. the Bakersfield Conference drafted several
resolutions dealing with housing and health initiatives, the scarcity of fed-

eral camps, the need for increases in education, and the need for relief and work programs.[95] It also organized tours of the area and of federal camps for those interested. After several hours of speeches, debate, and resolutions, the migrants who attended the conference probably did not know who Steinbeck was, but they knew that the committee bearing his name was eager to help.

Despite the hopefulness conveyed by Lange's images, the strike was not going well. In spite of the workers' initial exuberance, the stoppage was failing. Lange wrote upon arrival that she was witnessing the "tail end of a long heart-breaking strike, unsuccessful."[96] As the strike lingered, conditions in the camps worsened. "Families of five and six persons are crowded into shacks scarcely no bigger than outhouses, and no cleaner," reporter Marc Stone detailed. "About 90 per cent of the workers are sick; children suffer from rickets, influenza is common; many adults wear crude bandages over open sores."[97] In these dire conditions, many were anxious to return to work. Armed escorts brought in strikebreakers, which allowed cotton gins to maintain production less than a week after the strike began.[98] Even though the strike was disorganized and even quixotic, the organizers continued to establish pickets and hold meetings in an effort to galvanize support.

During the waning days of the strike Lange photographed a night street rally in the Mexican colonies outside Shafter. Working behind the speaker, Lange photographed a crowd that was far more diverse than the one she had documented only a few days earlier at the Bakersfield Conference. In the picture Mexican farm laborers listen intently alongside their white counterparts (figure 8). In attendance (and in Lange's image) was L. R. Duncan—still intense and possibly waiting for his turn to speak. Lange also found among the crowd a young girl with light hair and soiled arms squatting on the ground in an undersized, fur-trimmed coat (figure 9). The child, identified by Lange as an "undernourished cotton picker's child," was photographed as she listened closely to the speaker.

In another image of the rally Lange captured a second strike leader standing outside the crowd watching the photographer. According to Lange's caption, this man had arrived from Oklahoma earlier that spring and become a migratory worker. He was one of the first to join the strike, was active in the UCAPAWA, and became a member of the "flying squadron," which rushed picketers to the fields in an automobile caravan.[99] He drove the first car, which, Lange pointed out, was a risky and dangerous

Figure 8. Dorothea Lange, "Kern County, California. Night street meeting of cotton strikers near end of defeated strike. Strikers received seventy-five cents per 100 pounds; demanded one dollar. In 1910 cotton growers in Imperial County advertised for pickers in the Southwest to come to Imperial Valley to pick for one dollar per 100 pounds." LC-USF34-019285-D. Library of Congress.

activity when the legality of picketing in California was in limbo and local law officials were arresting members of the caravans for inciting riots.[100] That fall Lange photographed this man, who remained safely anonymous, several times.[101] In one image he smiles sheepishly at the camera; in another shot he proudly displays his small union membership book. A CIO pin on his lapel indicates his affiliation, and a second pin urges a no vote on proposition number 1—an antipicketing ordinance.[102]

Her most well-known image of this leader, however, is far more menacing (figure 10). Gruff and pugnacious, he stands at a distance, looking suspiciously at Lange's camera through the corner of his eye. Richard Steven Street contends that he has the "look and stance of an assassin."[103] The implied violence of this photograph suggests the lengths to which some

Figure 9. Dorothea Lange, "Kern County, California. Undernourished cotton picker's child listening to speeches of organizer at strike meeting to raise wages from seventy-five cents to ninety cents a hundred pounds. Strike unsuccessful." LC-USF34-018732-E. Library of Congress.

organizers were willing to go as well as the limits of Lange's coverage. According to Linda Gordon, Lange was uncomfortable with social conflict and organized activism.[104] She wanted to do more but admitted to Stryker that "it was too dangerous to go."[105] Gordon explained further, "Lange could not get close enough—it was too dangerous to do so, neither side trusted her, and

Figure 10. Dorothea Lange, "Migratory field worker, leader of the cotton strike of October 1938, which took place just before the election. Kern County, California." LC-USF34-018614-C. Library of Congress.

she did not move quickly. For strikers, the very existence of photographs was dangerous and could lead, at the least, to being blacklisted out of work."[106]

Her final image of the strike leader was not void of hope, however. The composition is complex. In a strong foil to the brooding squadron leader is a campaign poster with the beaming face of Culbert Olson, the Democratic candidate for governor. Lange, Taylor, Steinbeck, and their ilk put their faith in the progressive Olson and hoped that his election might lead to a better defense of civil liberties and assist a far broader demographic than that of his predecessor, Republican governor Frank Merriam.[107]

Fallout

By November 4 the cotton strike in Kern County had ended. The growers routed the strikers and their union. The Associated Farmers won through intimidation and by refusing to acknowledge the union's existence. They also ignored mediation efforts by the federal government.[108] As for the strikers, wages remained fixed at seventy-five cents, and their resolve faded.[109] Leaders were arrested, and the caravans of picketers were disrupted. Still, some saw the work stoppage as a building experience. One striker wrote to Sanora Babb the day after the strike ended,

> We didn't get the dollar that we asked for, but I am proud to say that we didn't loose all together either. . . . There was so many that lost self confidence because we didn't win in 2 or three weeks and went back to the end. I really think that we gained an awful lot . . . if nothing else but experience and will get together and work harder to organize in a way that we stick together like brothers and sisters should in a union that is as good as the one which we belong to, the CIO who fought so hard to better labor conditions.[110]

The failed strike demoralized the UCAPAWA, which limped into 1939 with losses in membership and momentum.[111] Making matters worse, another cotton strike in 1939 near Madera was also unsuccessful and turned violent.

Despite these setbacks, all was not lost for labor and the Steinbeck Committee. The election of Culbert Olson initially shook up California's political landscape and helped reshape the Steinbeck Committee. Olson appointed Carey McWilliams head of the Division of Immigration and Housing. McWilliams relinquished his duties with the committee on January 30, 1939, and actress Helen Gahagan Douglas assumed the leadership and became an ardent supporter of migrants' rights. This would be another stage in the political education of Gahagan, who, before her affiliation with the Steinbeck Committee, was only marginally involved with politics.[112] (Later Gahagan would become a congresswoman from California.) Sometime in the fall of 1938 she offered the patio of her home, known as "The Outpost," for a Steinbeck Committee meeting. From her room she overheard tales of horror and indifference and soon joined the discussion. As she later recalled, "I could not know it then [but] that afternoon I took my first step into politics."[113] She toured the Hoovervilles and federal camps and later followed migrants back to Oklahoma.[114] The glamorous Gahagan and her husband, the actor Melvin Douglas, were well connected politically and enjoyed access to powerful people in California as well as in Washington.[115] They were invited to the White House, met members of Roosevelt's administration, and could, if compelled, telegram First Lady Eleanor Roosevelt directly for support.[116] With Gahagan at its helm, the Steinbeck Committee enjoyed greater public visibility and political access.

Under Gahagan and Douglas's leadership, the Steinbeck Committee organized a Christmas banquet for the denizens of the Shafter FSA camp—known as a "Christmas for One-Third of the Nation."[117] During the 1938 strike the Shafter camp had suffered numerous deprivations. Now, a month after the end of the strike, it would become the host site for a party for workers (and growers) from all over Kern County. It was a tremendous undertaking. The Steinbeck Committee ultimately fed and entertained more than twelve thousand people. Promising "one bright day in their otherwise drab lives," the group collected donations from all across California.[118] It also brought an impressive cadre of actors to Shafter, including Henry Fonda, Gene Autry, and Eddie Cantor.[119] The Steinbeck Committee organized a live program and a nationally broadcast radio program that featured the talents of Edward G. Robinson, Gale Sondergaard, Virginia Bruce, and Bob Hope. Toys and Christmas stockings filled with fruit, nuts, and candy were distributed to the five thousand children in attendance (possibly even the young girl Lange had photographed weeks earlier). According to Alice Orans's final report, "From the smiling faces of children and parents we sensed that these people not only had had a wonderful Christmas, but felt that the forces back of our committee were going forward with the fight to bring the good life to them."[120]

Many members of the Steinbeck Committee realized that this fight required more than a party and seasonal goodwill; it required sustained drive and energy.[121] This was not lost on Steinbeck, who showed his support by writing a short article, "The Stars Point to Shafter." "Candy and food today—and starvation tomorrow," he wrote. "The children will be unhappy tomorrow. The gifts will only serve to emphasize the poverty of the re-cipients. . . . This can make for hatred unless one thing—if the gifts can be symbols of support, not of charity, if the meaning of this party can be 'We are working with you, not for you, to the end that the good life which is your right will not be longer withheld. These gifts and food are a promise that you are not alone.'"[122]

After *The Grapes of Wrath* was published in 1939, much changed. Steinbeck became truly famous—much to his chagrin. (For more on Steinbeck's struggles with fame, see chapter 10, by Lauren Onkey.) The novel made the issue of the overland migration, once primarily a regional concern, a national and even international issue. At the same time, the book worsened relations between the migrants and their supporters, on the one hand, and the well-organized and powerful farm contingents in California, on the other. Uncomfortably in the middle of the tempest, Steinbeck was both praised and demonized. Supporters lauded the author for his verity and his ability to bring to the fore a pressing, contemporary issue. Members of the UCAPAWA were emboldened by the novel and used its findings to garner support.[123] Others, however, thought the book was not radical enough, and many considered it sensational, vulgar, and inflammatory. Steinbeck wanted to withdraw from the public eye and was leery of putting his name on anything lest he suffer further attention.[124] (See Rick Wartz-man's prologue, this volume, for more on the complex political responses to Steinbeck's historical fiction.)

Not surprisingly the backlash also affected the Steinbeck Commit-tee. Where once it had benefited from its association with the author and his rising fame, it was now forced to reconsider its affiliation in order to maintain effectiveness. Steinbeck's name generated scorn from outside and strife within. Critics of the Steinbeck Committee scrutinized the members' politics and reported alleged (and real) affiliations with the Communist Party.[125] In September 1939 the committee decided to drop Steinbeck's name and adopt a far more impersonal moniker, the Committee to Aid Agricultural Organization.[126] By 1940 many Steinbeck Committee members had joined the larger, renamed committee. Carey McWilliams, now a well-known crusader for migrant rights following the publication of *Factories in the Field,* became the national chairman of the organization, which had branches in the San Francisco Bay Area, Kern County, Colorado, Philadelphia, Washington, D.C., and New York City.

Before this name change took place, the Steinbeck Committee experienced a final florescence. During the summer of 1939 Woody Guthrie, the young Okie folk singer, worked for the committee among the "old junk heap jalopies" and cotton strikers from Brawley in the Imperial Valley to Bakersfield. He met Steinbeck earlier that year and was soon on the road "around to forum halls, rallies, picnics, meetings and all kinds of public places," spreading the Steinbeck Committee's cause.[127] Guthrie was also present on March 3, 1940, for the "Grapes of Wrath Evening," a benefit concert with proceeds going to the committee. Organized by Will Greer and held at the Forrest Theater in New York City, the midnight concert featured Guthrie and singers Leadbelly, Aunt Molly Jackson, and Pete Seeger.[128] Even at this date the committee benefited from Steinbeck's fame, which extended beyond the West Coast.[129] In many ways it is fitting that Guthrie, "The Dust Bowl Balladeer," would be associated with the committee. Like Steinbeck and Lange, he staunchly defended the migrants and used his talents and fame to influence public opinion on their behalf. He, too, would come to symbolize this tumultuous period of American history.[130]

By the time the United States entered World War II in the final month of 1941, California's migrant problem was surpassed by other issues. Eventually *The Grapes of Wrath* fell from the best-seller list, and Steinbeck regained the composure that he momentarily had lost. Having been let go by the FSA for the final time, Lange documented the forced evacuation of Japanese Americans under Executive Order 9066. Meanwhile, the Okies and Arkies participated in both the war effort and the industrial boom and began the process of assimilation.[131] In this changed political climate organizations like the Steinbeck Committee lost momentum and eventually disbanded.

For a brief moment, however, the Steinbeck Committee fulfilled its mandate. It had pooled its resources and talents to help California's struggling migrants. From the cotton strike of 1938 through the committee's lavish Christmas party, it defended the dignity of a maligned people. Active when Steinbeck was writing *The Grapes of Wrath*, the Steinbeck Committee was a reflection of its namesake and should be seen as a proactive, public response to a world that the author believed needed to be changed.

Notes

I would like to thank the following individuals for their assistance with this project: Catherine Powell and Ben Blake at the Labor Archives and Research Center, San Francisco State University; Meg and Rondal Partridge; Carolyn Haneman at the Carl Albert Center for Congressional Research and Studies, University of Oklahoma; Sstoz Tez at the Martha Heasley Cox Center for Steinbeck Studies, San Jose State University; Jan Grenci at the Library of Congress; Lori Wear, curator of collections, at the Kern County Museum, Bakersfield, California.

1. It is important to note that what is typically referred to as FSA photography was actually created under the direction of three different Roosevelt "Alphabet Agencies." The photography division, or Historical Section, as it was known, was originally created for the benefit of Rexford Tugwell's Resettlement Administration in 1935. The Historical Section was transferred to the Department of Agriculture's Farm Security Administration by the fall of 1937 and later, in 1942, to the Office of War Information (OWI). In spite of these bureaucratic changes and internal and external challenges, Roy Stryker, director of the Historical Section, maintained a relatively constant vision of how photography could serve the Roosevelt administration and the nation. For more information on Stryker and the Historical Section, see F. Jack Hurley, *A Portrait of a Decade: Roy Stryker and the Development of Documentary Photography in the Thirties* (Baton Rouge: Louisiana State University Press, 1972); Carl Fleischhauer and Beverly W. Brannan, eds. *Documenting America: 1935–1943* (Berkeley: University of California Press in association with the Library of Congress, 1988); Stu Cohen, *The Like of Us: America in the Eyes of the Farm Security Administration*, ed. Peter Bacon Hales (Boston: David R. Godine, 2009).

2. Anne Loftis claims that "*The Grapes of Wrath* and Dorothea Lange's photograph *Migrant Mother* are frequently paired as symbols of an era." This sentiment could also include Lange's broader work in the late 1930s. Loftis, *Witnesses to the Struggle: Imaging the 1930s California Labor Movement* (Reno: University of Nevada Press, 1998), 189.

3. For more information on the ways in which the FSA and Steinbeck worked synergistically, see Jackson Benson, *The True Adventures of John Steinbeck, Writer* (New York: Viking Press, 1984); Hurley, *Portrait of a Decade*, 140; Roy Stryker and Nancy Wood, *In This Proud Land: America, 1935–1943, as Seen in FSA Photographs* (Boston: New York Graphic Society, 1975), 14; Therese Thau Heyman, *Celebrating a Collection: The Work of Dorothea Lange* (Oakland, Calif.: Oakland Museum, 1978), 77–78. The FSA archives are stored in the Library of Congress with the work of the

closely related OWI. For more, visit the extensive FSA-OWI online collection at the Library of Congress website, www.memory.loc.gov.

4. Roger T. Hammarlund, "Portrait of an Era," *US Camera* 25, no. 11 (November 1962): 71.

5. The official name of the committee was the John Steinbeck Committee to Aid Agricultural Organization. At the time it was also referred to as the "John Steinbeck Committee" or simply the "Steinbeck Committee." It is sometimes erroneously referred to as the John Steinbeck Committee to Aid Agricultural Workers. See Benson, *True Adventures*, 424; Ingrid Winther Scobie, *Center Stage: Helen Gahagan Douglas, A Life* (New York: Oxford University Press, 1992), 106.

6. Rick Wartzman, *Obscene in the Extreme: The Burning and Banning of John Steinbeck's* The Grapes of Wrath (New York: PublicAffairs, 2008), 36; Carey McWilliams, *The Education of Carey McWilliams* (New York: Simon and Schuster, 1978), 78.

7. Loftis finds significance in McWilliams and Steinbeck's differing levels of activity within the committee. Whereas Steinbeck lent his name and not much else, McWilliams, the original chairman of the southern group, proffered far more of his talents and time to the committee's success. See Loftis, *Witnesses to the Struggle*, 166, 175. Despite his high level of involvement, mention of the Steinbeck Committee is conspicuously absent from McWilliams's biography. See Peter Richardson, *American Prophet: The Life and Work of Carey McWilliams* (Ann Arbor: University of Michigan Press, 2005).

8. Despite friendships with Pare Lorentz and Charlie Chaplin, Steinbeck had a complicated relationship with Hollywood. He was enamored of the industry and simultaneously repulsed by its pretenses. The makeup of the committee reflected Steinbeck's ambivalence. The conversion of his work into film only increased his contact with the star-filled city to the south. See Kevin Starr, *Endangered Dreams: The Great Depression in California* (New York: Oxford University Press, 1996), 255–56; Benson, *True Adventures*, 372ff.

9. Wartzman, *Obscene in the Extreme*, 97–98; John Steinbeck et al., "Will You Join My Committee to Aid Agricultural Organization," pamphlet, Leonard Collection, San Francisco State University Archives, box 266, folder 10. See also Alice Barnard Thomsen, "Erich H. Thomsen and John Steinbeck," *Steinbeck Newsletter*, Summer 1990, 3.

10. Scobie, *Center Stage*, 106–7; Benson, *True Adventures*, 424; Loftis, *Witnesses to the Struggle*, 171.

11. Jerold S. Auerbach, *Labor and Liberty: The La Follette Committee and the New Deal* (Indianapolis: Bobbs-Merrill, 1966), 183–84.

12. For more on the UCAPAWA, see U.S. Department of Labor, *Labor*

Unionism in American Agriculture, Bulletin no. 836 (1945; reprint, New York: Arno Press, 1975), 27–29.

13. See "Statement of Plan of Work," Leonard Collection.

14. Steinbeck et al., "Will You Join."

15. Horace Bristol, "Documenting *The Grapes of Wrath,*" *Californians,* January–February, 1988, 40.

16. Wilbur L. Schramm, "Careers at Crossroads" [1939], in *Critical Essays on Steinbeck's* The Grapes of Wrath, ed. John Ditsky (Boston: G. K. Hall, 1989), 42.

17. Jackson J. Benson, "The Background to the Composition of *The Grapes of Wrath,*" in Ditsky, *Critical Essays,* 53.

18. Cliff Lewis, "Art for Politics: John Steinbeck and FDR," in *After* The Grapes of Wrath: *Essays on John Steinbeck in Honor of Tetsumaro Hayashi,* ed. Robert de Mott et al. (Athens: Ohio University Press, 1995), 23–24. See also Peter Lisca, "*The Grapes of Wrath:* An Achievement of Genius," in The Grapes of Wrath: *A Collection of Critical Essays,* ed. Robert Con Davis (Englewood, Calif.: Prentice Hall, 1982), 49; Benson, "Background to the Composition," 52.

19. Benson possibly summed up Steinbeck's politics best when he concluded, "[Steinbeck] cared deeply about the poor, but his commitment was to writing, not to political solutions." Benson, "Background to the Composition," 52, 68; Benson, *True Adventures,* 371.

20. Steinbeck's support of liberal causes and unionization made it possible for many to label him, as Keith Windschuttle recently did, a "non-conformist Marxist." Windschuttle, "Steinbeck's Myth of the Okies," *New Criterion* 20, no. 10 (June 2002): 24.

21. Quoted in Wartzman, *Obscene in the Extreme,* 76.

22. Benson, "Background to the Composition," 53.

23. Steinbeck wrote his friend George Albee that the real subject of *In Dubious Battle* was "the symbol of man's eternal, bitter warfare with himself." "I'm not interested in strike as means of raising men's wages," he continued, "and I'm not interested in ranting about justice and oppression, mere outcroppings which indicate the condition. But man hates something in himself. He has been able to defeat every natural obstacle but himself he cannot win over unless he kills every individual. And this self-hate which goes so closely in hand with self-love is what I wrote about." Jackson J. Benson and Anne Loftis, "John Steinbeck and Farm Labor Unionization: The Background of 'In Dubious Battle,'" *American Literature* 25 no. 2 (May 1980): 197.

24. McWilliams, *Education of Carey McWilliams,* 81–85; Carey McWilliams et al., "What Should America Do for the Joads?," *Town Meeting: Bulletin of America's Town Meeting of the Air,* 5, no. 22 (March 11, 1940): 15; Kevin Starr, "Carey McWilliams's California: The Light and the Dark," in *Reading California: Art,*

Image, and Identity, 1900–2000, ed. Seeplan Buran et al. (Berkeley: University of California Press, 2000), 23–25.

25. Wartzman, *Obscene in the Extreme*, 153.

26. John Steinbeck, "Dubious Battle in California," *Nation*, September 12, 1936, 304; Walter Rundell, "Steinbeck's Image of the West," *American West* 1 (1964): 10.

27. Steinbeck, "Dubious Battle in California," 304.

28. John Steinbeck, *The Harvest Gypsies: On the Road to* The Grapes of Wrath (Berkeley, Calif.: Heyday Books, 1988), 60.

29. John Steinbeck to Cecil [*sic*] McKiddy, May 3, 1937, Martha Heasley Cox Center for Steinbeck Studies, San Jose State University. At the time McKiddy was involved with the longshoremen's union and may have been working for the newsletter *Black Gang News* or *Western Worker.* He was apparently pestering Steinbeck for articles or other assistance.

30. John Steinbeck, *Their Blood Is Strong* (San Francisco: Simon J. Lubin Society of California, 1938), n.p.

31. The Simon J. Lubin Society of California was formed by Dr. Russell Rypins, Leigh and Hope Athern, the actor Chester Conklin, Carey McWilliams, the politician Samuel Yorty, the columnist John D. Barry, Father Charles Phillips, and Helen Hosmer. Hosmer, a former secretary to Fred Soule in the Resettlement Administration's Division of Information (Region IX), was the key figure of this group and the catalyst of the society's success. In addition to producing pamphlets like *Their Blood Is Strong* and another directly attacking Associated Farmers, Hosmer also oversaw the publication of the bimonthly newsletter the *Rural Observer.* The society faded from view in the early 1940s when Hosmer began a family and moved on. Walter J. Stein, *California and the Dust Bowl Migration* (Westport, Conn.: Greenwood Press, 1973), 261; Starr, *Endangered Dreams*, 232; "Helen Hosmer: A Radical Critic of California Agribusiness in the 1930s," oral history interview by Randall Jarrell, University of California, Santa Cruz, University Library, Regional History Project, 1992, available at http://www.oac.cdlib.org/ark:/13030/hb4b69n74p/?brand=oac4.

32. Steinbeck, *Their Blood Is Strong.*

33. A lifelong supporter of progressive causes, Simon J. Lubin was responsible for the creation of the California Immigration and Housing Commission and was, according to McWilliams, "a distinguished California liberal." Carey McWilliams, *Factories in the Field: The Story of Migratory Farm Labor in California* (Boston: Little, Brown, 1939), 281.

34. The organizations also shared a number of members, including McWilliams and Helen Gahagan Douglas. McWilliams, *Factories in the Field*, 281; McWilliams, *Education of Carey McWilliams*, 78.

35. Stein, *California and the Dust Bowl Migration*, 244–45. "Helen Hosmer: A Radical Critic," 79–85.

36. See Starr, *Endangered Dreams*, 231.

37. Stein, *California and the Dust Bowl Migration*, 245; Wartzman, *Obscene in the Extreme*, 89; Jan Goggans, *California on the Breadlines: Dorothea Lange, Paul Taylor, and the Making of a New Deal Narrative* (Berkeley: University of California Press, 2010), 251.

38. Steinbeck, "Dubious Battle in California," 303.

39. Steinbeck, *Harvest Gypsies*, 22–23.

40 Ibid., 22, 62; Steinbeck, "Dubious Battle in California," 303.

41. Frank J. Taylor, "California's Grapes of Wrath," *Forum*, November 1939, 236.

42. Edith E. Lowry, *They Starve That We May Eat* (New York: Council of Women for Home Missions and Missionary Education Movement, 1938), 30.

43. See Auerbach, *Labor and Liberty*, 181.

44. U.S. Department of Labor, *Labor Unionism in American Agriculture*, Bulletin no. 836 (1945; reprint, New York: Arno Press, 1975).

45. Quoted in Auerbach, *Labor and Liberty*, 189.

46. Ibid., 181, 187.

47. The LaFollette Civil Liberties Committee was formed in 1936 to investigate the abuse of civil liberties in the U.S. labor force. It was chaired by Senators Robert M. LaFollette Jr. of Wisconsin and Elbert D. Thomas of Utah. In December 1939 it began hearings in San Francisco—much to the delight of Lange, Taylor, and others—and later in Los Angeles. Auerbach, *Labor and Liberty*, 181–85.

48. See Richard Steven Street, *Everyone Had Cameras: Photography and Farmworkers in California, 1850–2000* (Minneapolis: University of Minnesota Press, 2008), 260; Steinbeck, *Harvest Gypsies*, 33–37. From his vantage point in D.C., Stryker considered the Associated Farmers "one of America's greatest menaces." Roy Stryker to Dorothea Lange, February 2, 1939, Roy Stryker Papers, University of Louisville, Louisville, Ky.

49. Steinbeck et al., "Will You Join."

50. *Their Blood Is Strong* featured Steinbeck's original seven essays (collectively known as *The Harvest Gypsies*) along with an eighth, "Starvation under the Orange Trees," that originally appeared in the *Monterey Trader* on April 15, 1938.

51. Steinbeck, *Their Blood Is Strong*. See also Benson, *True Adventures*, 373. From May 1938 to July 1939 Steinbeck repeatedly insisted to his literary agent, Elizabeth Otis, that all proceeds were to go to the society. For further details, see Steinbeck's correspondence with Otis in the John Steinbeck Collection, Stanford University Special Collections.

52. Steinbeck, *Their Blood Is Strong.* Lange's images also appeared alongside Steinbeck's prose in the original *San Francisco News* stories in 1936.

53. Pare Lorentz, the documentary filmmaker and friend to both Lange and Steinbeck, wrote that despite the thematic similarities in their work, "there was no correspondence or even conversation among any of the three of us in those first years of work." The repeated collisions of their work, however, strongly suggest that they were aware of one another and what the others were doing. Quoted in Milton Meltzer, *Dorothea Lange: A Photographer's Life* (New York: Farrar Straus and Giroux, 1978), 202. In 1939 relations between Lange and Steinbeck became strained when the author refused to write a preface for *American Exodus*, Lange and Paul S. Taylor's powerful documentary text on the overland migration. "She is awful mad at me," he wrote to his agent, Elizabeth Otis. "All this off the record. I'm pretty sore at her too." Steinbeck to Otis, July 30, 1939, John Steinbeck Collection, Stanford University Special Collections.

54. Paul S. Taylor, *Paul Schuster Taylor: California Social Scientist* (Berkeley: Regional Oral History Office, Bancroft Library, University of California, 1973), 222; see also Heyman, *Celebrating a Collection,* 47.

55. Clark Kerr, "Paul and Dorothea," in *Dorothea Lange: A Visual Life,* ed. Elizabeth Partridge (Washington, D.C.: Smithsonian Institution Press, 1994), 41.

56. As soon as she began venturing from the studio to the streets in 1933, Lange was drawn to turbulent and dramatic events such as May Day gatherings, street demonstrations, strikes, and the internment of Japanese Americans in 1942. However, as Sandra Phillips points out, even in these moments of political tension Lange chose to make personal observations rather than overt political statements. Sandra S. Phillips, "Dorothea Lange: An American Photographer," in *Dorothea Lange: American Photographs* (San Francisco: Chronicle Books and the San Francisco Museum of Art, 1994), 18; Linda Gordon and Gary Y. Okihiro, *Dorothea Lange and the Censored Images of Japanese American Internment* (New York: W. W. Norton, 2006), 19–25.

57. Gordon and Okihiro, *Dorothea Lange and the Censored Images,* 187.

58. Ibid., 136.

59. Steinbeck, *Harvest Gypsies,* 22.

60. The mother had already lost four children to malnutrition or sickness before meeting Steinbeck. Steinbeck, *Harvest Gypsies,* 50–51.

61. Susan Sontag, *Regarding the Pain of Others* (New York: Picador, 2003), 20.

62. Steinbeck, *Their Blood Is Strong;* emphasis in the original. For more on the nature of documentary photography, see William Stott, *Documentary Expression and Thirties America* (Chicago: University of Chicago Press, 1973).

63. McWilliams, *Factories in the Field*, 281; Meltzer, *Dorothea Lange*, 182.

64. David F. Selvin, *Sky Full of Storm: A Brief History of California Labor* (San Francisco: California Historical Society, 1975), 61.

65. The actual value of the 1938 cotton crop was $31,928,000 in lint and close to $7,000,000 in seed. Raymond P. Barry, ed., "Labor in California Cotton Fields," unpublished monograph, Federal Writers Project, Oakland, Calif., 1938, available at Calisphere, University of California, California Digital Library, http://content .cdlib.org/view?docId=hb88700929;NAAN=13030&doc.view=frames&chunk .id=div00042&toc.id=0&brand=calisphere.

66. The decrease in demand was due to the Agricultural Adjustment Act restrictive program. For more on the state of California's cotton fields, see U.S. Department of Labor, *Labor Unionism in American Agriculture*, 176.

67. Steinbeck, "Dubious Battle in California," 304.

68. For more on the 1933 cotton strike, see Derva Weber, *Dark Sweat, White Gold: California Farm Workers, Cotton, and the New Deal* (Berkeley: University of California Press, 1994), 79–111; Selvin, *Sky Full of Storm*, 62; U.S. Department of Labor, *Labor Unionism in American Agriculture*, 427.

69. Sol Camp, a member of the Camp family—some of the Associated Farmers' staunchest supporters—owned Camp West Lowe. Weber, *Dark Sweat, White Gold*, 181–82; Wartzman, *Obscene in the Extreme*, 99.

70. Weber, *Dark Sweat, White Gold*, 182–84.

71. Ibid., 182.

72. An internal report by the Steinbeck Committee estimated that six thousand workers were involved in the strike. "Cotton Striker's Woes Increase," *L.A. Times*, undated clipping in Carey McWilliams Papers, Special Collections, Charles E. Young Research Library, University of California, Los Angeles. For more on the strike see "Report of the Bakersfield Conference on Agricultural Labor—Health, Housing and Relief—Held October 29, 1938, Bakersfield," Leonard Collection.

73. U.S. Department of Labor, *Labor Unionism in American Agriculture*, 171.

74. Additional demands included testing weighing machines, job stewards, and drinking water near the fields. U.S. Department of Labor, *Labor Unionism in American Agriculture*, 171–72.

75. Meltzer, *Dorothea Lange*, 190.

76. Ibid., 191.

77. Dorothea Lange, caption to FSA photograph LC-USF34-018598-C, Library of Congress, Washington, D.C.

78. Although it is sometimes credited to London and similar to his speech "The Scab" (1903), his authorship of "Definition of a Scab" is questionable.

79. See Dorothea Lange, "Shafter, Calif. Nov. 1938. The Farm Security Administration camp for migratory workers, Close-up of campers bulletin board,

during cotton strike," FSA photograph LC 34-18574-D, Library of Congress, Washington, D.C.

80. The FSA provided $4.41 worth of flour, shortening, evaporated milk, beans, cornmeal, sugar, and coffee per family. Wartzman, *Obscene in the Extreme*, 100. See Dorothea Lange, captions to FSA photographs LC-USF34-018475-E and LC-USF34-018632-C, Library of Congress, Washington, D.C.

81. Wartzman, *Obscene in the Extreme*, 100.

82. See Dorothea Lange and Paul S. Taylor, *American Exodus: A Record of Human Erosion in the Thirties* (New Haven, Conn.: Yale University Press, 1969), 106.

83. Edward R. Mares, district secretary UCAPAWA, to Sara Chance, October 18, 1938, Maritime Federation of the Pacific, San Francisco State University, Labor Archives [hereafter Maritime Federation Archives], box 65, folder 1.

84. "Report of the Bakersfield Conference," Leonard Collection.

85. Testimony of Louise Cantrell, "Minutes of the Conference of the John Steinbeck Committee for Aid in Agricultural Organization, held at Bakersfield, California, Saturday, October 29th, 1938," Maritime Federation Archives.

86. For a more complete list of prominent participants and representatives from the various organizations at the Bakersfield Conference, see "Report of the Bakersfield Conference," Leonard Collection, 7. One of the attendees was Ella Winter, the journalist, activist, and widow of Lincoln Steffens, the prominent social critic and Russophile who died in 1936. The Steffenses were friends and former neighbors of Steinbeck. Winter later married actor Donald Ogden Stewart, who, along with John D. Barry, conducted tours of the strike area on behalf of the Steinbeck Committee.

87. Dorothy Foster to Alice Orans, secretary of the Southern Committee, [October] 1938, Maritime Federation Archives. One grower from Fresno, a Mr. R. F. Schmeiser (also recorded as Schmitzer), attended but declined to address the audience when given an opportunity.

88. Gordon and Okihiro, *Dorothea Lange and the Censored Images*, 255.

89. "Minutes of the Conference," Maritime Federation Archives, 14.

90. Rondal Partridge, conversation with the author, June 22, 2010.

91. Ibid. Because she was Lange's assistant, not an independent photographer, Partridge's work was often included with and credited to Lange. Since, according to Partridge, Lange had little experience with flash photography, it is possible that some of her coverage on this occasion must also be credited to her twenty-year-old assistant as well. See Street, *Everyone Had Cameras*, 287. For more on Partridge and her career, see Elizabeth Partridge and Sally Stein, *Quizzical Eye: The Photography of Rondal Partridge* (San Francisco: California Historical Society Press, 2003).

92. "Minutes of the Conference," Maritime Federation Archives, 16–17.

93. Lange had mastered the use of natural lighting as a studio photographer, but she was not proficient with artificial lighting. On this occasion and with the assistance of Rondal Partridge she probably employed a Mendelson flashgun, a heavy piece of equipment that can be seen off to the left of the speaker in Lange's photograph from the back of the conference hall, and a Kalart speed gun. Partridge also recorded Duncan's intense gesticulations from the opposite side of the rostrum without the use of Lange's flash. Street, *Everyone Had Cameras*, 285–87; Partridge, conversation with the author, June 22, 2010.

94. Taylor, *California Social Scientist*, 240. Despite their statements to the contrary, it is clear that Lange and Taylor sometimes edited their captions, but never to the extent done in Margaret Bourke-White and Erskine Caldwell's *You Have Seen Their Faces*. According to Linda Gordon, their editing "aimed to produce more beautiful and more respectful images, never to fabricate or sensationalize." As the conference minutes attest, Lange's caption was largely accurate. See Gordon and Okihiro, *Dorothea Lange and the Censored Images*, 280–81.

95. For more on the conference's list of recommendations, see "Program of the John Steinbeck Committee to Aid Agricultural Organization on Housing, Health and Relief for Agricultural Workers, Adopted by the Bakersfield Conference, October 29, 1838," Leonard Collection.

96. Dorothea Lange to Roy Stryker, quoted in Meltzer, *Dorothea Lange*, 190.

97. Marc Stone, "Utter Squalor as 6000 Fight Associated Farmers," newspaper clipping, McWilliams Papers.

98. On October 9, a little more than a week after the strike began, the United Press reported that cotton operations were running at 50 percent of capacity. Newspaper clipping, McWilliams Papers.

99. Dorothea Lange, caption to FSA photograph LC-USF34-018613-C, Library of Congress, Washington, D.C. For more on the "Flying Squadron," see U.S. Department of Labor, *Labor Unionism in American Agriculture*, 167.

100. Wartzman, *Obscene in the Extreme*, 100–101.

101. In addition to photographing this man at the night rally and in four portraits of him standing near an Olson campaign poster, Lange photographed the strike leader dancing at the Shafter Halloween party. See Dorothea Lange, *Halloween Party at Shafter Migrant Camp, California*, LC-USF34-018551-D, Library of Congress, Washington, D.C.

102. See Weber, *Dark Sweat, White Gold*, 136.

103. Street, *Everyone Had Cameras*, 306. Street may have been borrowing from William Stott, who noted that he had "the eye of a hired killer." Stott, *Documentary Expression*, 229.

104. Gordon and Okihiro, *Dorothea Lange and the Censored Images*, 136. See also Phillips, "Dorothea Lange," 18–20.

105. Gordon and Okihiro, *Dorothea Lange and the Censored Images*, 234.

106. Ibid., 233.

107. Incumbent Republican governor Frank Merriam was notoriously anti-labor and an ardent supporter of large agriculture. His opponent, Olson, favored unionization and attacked corporate farms. In his narrow victory Olson received 53.36 percent of the vote in the formerly conservative San Joaquin Valley, due in large part to the support of migrant labor. Gordon and Okihiro, *Dorothea Lange and the Censored Images*, 232; Weber, *Dark Sweat, White Gold*, 173–77.

108. U.S. Department of Labor, *Labor Unionism in American Agriculture*, 171.

109. Wartzman, *Obscene in the Extreme*, 101.

110. Sanora Babb, *On the Dirty Plate Trail: Remembering the Dust Bowl Refugee Camps*, ed. Douglas Wixom (Austin: University of Texas Press, 2007), 158.

111. U.S. Department of Labor, *Labor Unionism in American Agriculture*, 169–73.

112. Ingrid Winther Scobie, "Helen Gahagan Douglas and the Roosevelt Connection," in *Without Precedent: The Life and Career of Eleanor Roosevelt*, ed. Joan Hoff-Wilson and Marjorie Lightman (Bloomington: Indiana University Press, 1984), 155.

113. Helen Gahagan Douglas, *Full Life* (Garden City, N.Y.: Doubleday, 1982), 142; Scobie, "Helen Gahagan Douglas," 156.

114. Gahagan Douglas, *Full Life*, 143; For more on Helen Gahagan Douglas's activities with the Steinbeck Committee, see her untitled presentation in box 189, folder 6, Helen Gahagan Douglas Archives, Carl Albert Center, Congressional Research and Studies, University of Oklahoma, Norman, Okla.

115. Scobie, "Helen Gahagan Douglas," 158–60.

116. In February 1939 the Steinbeck Committee telegrammed the first lady on at least two occasions to protest the curtailment of FSA camps and to request the extension of the LaFollette Civil Liberties Committee to California. See Lewis, "Art for Politics," 24.

117. Stein, *California and the Dust Bowl Migration*, 245. The Christmas party was originally a joint venture between the Steinbeck Committee and the Citizen News Unit of the American Newspaper Guild. See Alice Orans, "Summary Report of Christmas for One-Third of the Nation Project," Gahagan Douglas Archives, box 189, folder 6; "[Christmas for One-Third of a Nation Press] Release," McWilliams Papers.

118. "[Press] Release on Receipt," McWilliams Papers; Gahagan Douglas secured the support of nearly 50 organizations, more than 60 California businesses, and 120 individual donors, including Bob Hope, Shirley Temple, and John Steinbeck, who donated his talents and money to the event. For more on those who lent their support, see Orans, "Summary Report," 4–6.

119. Scobie, "Helen Gahagan Douglas," 158; Wartzman, *Obscene in the Extreme*, 97–98.

120. Orans, "Summary Report," 3.

121. In 1939 the Steinbeck Committee organized a second Christmas party for camp denizens in the San Joaquin Valley. Unfortunately, less is known about this event, and it is possible that it has become conflated with the party of the previous year.

122. John Steinbeck, "The Stars Point to Shafter," *People's World*, December 24, 1938, newspaper clipping in McWilliams Papers; Wartzman, *Obscene in the Extreme*, 98.

123. Wartzman, *Obscene in the Extreme*, 11. For more on the UCAPAWA and its continued fight against the Associated Farmers, see "After the Battle," *Fortune* 31, no. 2 (February 1945): 233.

124. The aftermath of publication of *The Grapes of Wrath* and its reception were particularly difficult for Steinbeck, who suffered emotionally and physically. At one point he even considered giving up writing. Benson notes that in this period Steinbeck became increasing careful about putting his name out in public, "feeling that if he could withdraw his name from circulation, he might be able to escape." Benson, *True Adventures*, 423–24.

125. According to Gahagan Douglas, critics of the committee and its efforts "were convinced . . . that we were coming down with a red flag in one hand, a bomb in the other, with the film 'Grapes of Wrath' under our arms, for the express purpose of stirring up discontent." For more, see Scobie, "Helen Gahagan Douglas," 161–62; Scobie, *Center Stage*, 110; Gahagan Douglas, *Full Life*, 145–46.

126. Stein, *California and the Dust Bowl Migration*, 245, 261. The change was actually a return to the committee's original name before its ties to Steinbeck.

127. Ed Cray, *Ramblin Man: The Life and Times of Woody Guthrie* (New York: W. W. Norton, 2004), 155. See also Sara Halprin, *Seema's Show: A Life on the Left* (Albuquerque: University of New Mexico Press, 2005), 130–32.

128. See Cray, *Ramblin Man*, 167–68.

129. Even though the committee had dropped Steinbeck's name by this time, it still lingered. It is not uncommon, therefore, to see this event associated with the "John Steinbeck Committee."

130. For more on the combined importance and interconnectedness of these three artists, see Charles Shindo, *Dust Bowl Migrants in the American Imagination* (Lawrence: University Press of Kansas, 1997).

131. For more on the assimilation of the Okies and their culture, see James N. Gregory, *American Exodus: The Dust Bowl Migration and Okie Culture in California* (New York: Oxford University Press, 1989).

CHAPTER 9

Participatory Parables: Cinema, Social Action, and Steinbeck's Mexican Dilemma

Marijane Osborn

AT THE END OF 1939 Steinbeck found himself exhausted by his work over the spring and summer on the medical documentary *The Fight for Life* (about care in maternity hospitals), by the publicity surrounding the publication of *The Grapes of Wrath* in April of that year, and by the mixed public reactions to the book, some of which—in circles of privilege and power—were quite violent.[1] On October 16 he wrote, "I have to go to new sources and find new roots."[2] Then on November 13 he wrote, with a somewhat panicky humor, "There are things in the tide pools easier to understand than Stalinist, Hitlerite, Democrat, capitalist confusion, and voodoo. So I'm going to those things that are relatively more lasting to find a new basic picture."[3] On February 28, 1940, he was exuberant: "We'll be off to Mexico within a week. I'm terribly excited, as I guess my handwriting shows."[4] He was about to leave with Ed Ricketts for a voyage around the Gulf of California. On that trip, and in relation to it, he found the new source, the new basic picture that he sought. The sequence of novels, screenplays, and travel accounts set in Mexico constitutes what might be considered the single most neglected aspect of John Steinbeck's writing.[5]

That Steinbeck would find Mexico and its people congenial to his imagination will not surprise readers of "Flight," *Tortilla Flat*, and Steinbeck's other *paisano* stories, set in or near Monterey and the Salinas Valley. In these stories he drew on his experience as a young man working side by side with Mexican laborers (*paisanos*) in the fields and visiting them in their homes. "Flight," especially, published in *The Long Valley* in 1938, is essentially a Mexican story set on the central coast of California. With the exception of that more serious tale, a major difference between the lively *paisano* stories and Steinbeck's three major fictions set in Mexico—*The Forgotten Village, The Pearl,* and *Zapata*—is that the latter writings are overtly political in nature. They are political in that they are concerned not only with displaying the lives of interesting subaltern populations but also with revealing how the power structures in which such people exist oppress them with poverty, powerlessness, or ignorance (each of these conditions, of course, contributing to the others). They also bring attention to and examine the success of particular efforts to take action to redress this injustice and ameliorate unjust social conditions, and readers familiar with Steinbeck's fiction will correctly anticipate the usual outcome of such efforts to be ambiguous and fraught with unintended consequences. These stories are parables of injustice because in them Steinbeck creates "real people," individuals with great strength of character with whom we identify and whose difficult lives we want to see improved, as a stand-in for larger populations and their problems. He says this himself in his brief introduction to *The Forgotten Village* (the book of the film): "We wished our audience to know this family very well, and incidentally to like it, as we did. Then, from association with this little personalized group, the larger conclusion concerning the racial group could be drawn with something like participation."[6]

This essay examines how these three stories set in Mexico unveil a particular aspect of Steinbeck's concern for distressed peoples, a concern that is well known and relatively uncomplicated when the subject is Caucasian agricultural workers, like the Joads of *The Grapes of Wrath,* who are exploited by other Caucasians within a culture familiar to them and to the writer. In the case of Mexico, however, that same concern enters both the colonialist realm, where complacent assumptions about race are a factor, and the vexed arena of "humanitarian intervention," in this case non-military engagement that is intended to minimize the suffering of peoples in a state (or a culture within a state) foreign to the persons intervening. In other words, here Steinbeck is entering territory far more complex and ethically problematic than in his novels and stories about people mainly of his own race and culture. As for the Californian *paisanos,* he typically evades serious engagement with their lives by representing them as colorful rather than oppressed. His deep involvement with underprivileged Chicago women giving birth in *The Fight for Life* made him aware of the potential of film to engage the spectator in the sufferings of others, film having a visual impact quite different from the power of words alone to express. He drew on his recently developed awareness of the immersive nature of cinema, together with a long-standing (to date insufficiently explored) sympathetic relationship with the Chicanos of the Salinas area, when he went with camera and a partly American crew to explore and "translate" the medical theme of the Chicago film in a native Mexican village. It took his friend Ed Ricketts to make him aware of the ethically problematic issues raised by this imposition of one culture on another.

Steinbeck's main writings set in Mexico, both fiction and nonfiction, were all published in the 1940s. First came *The Forgotten Village*, a pseudo-documentary film released in 1940, with the book version published in May 1941.[7] This was followed by the nonfiction *Sea of Cortez* (1941), in which Steinbeck and Ricketts report on their 1940 voyage along the coast of Baja California. During that trip Steinbeck first heard the folktale that would become the basis for the most famous of his Mexican stories, *The Pearl*. Conceived in 1940 as a movie and containing scenes lifted directly from *The Forgotten Village*, it first appeared as a long short story titled "The Pearl of the World" in the *Woman's Home Companion* in December 1945. In July of that year Steinbeck also made notes—in Spanish—for another Mexican story titled "El camión vacilador." This generously conceived novel was to be a picaresque epic, "a Don Quixote of Mexico," in which a busload of tourists travel haphazardly (*vacilando*) around the country.[8] Later Steinbeck retitled the novel *The Wayward Bus* and relocated it to an imaginary area of central California, ultimately giving it only a tangential connection to his Mexican writings.

In 1945, while working on the screenplay for *The Pearl* in Cuernavaca, Steinbeck was approached about writing a screenplay on the remarkable revolutionary hero Emiliano Zapata. Despite expressing anxiety about whether, "with men living who helped to trick and murder Zapata," the Mexican government would let him "make it straight. I would only make it straight," he found the idea of the project attractive.[9] (In fact, he had been thinking about it for many years, and his interest had been reawakened in 1939 when the villagers acting roles in *The Forgotten Village* told him of the legend of the living Zapata.) In September 1947 Steinbeck and the Mexican director Emilio Fernandez released the American-Mexican film *La perla/The Pearl*. The book, illustrated with sketches by the celebrated Mexican political muralist José Clemente Orozco, appeared at the same time. The next year Steinbeck spent the summer collecting further material about Zapata, and late in 1949 he sent his account of Zapata's life to the producer Darryl F. Zanuck, who appreciated its completeness but observed that it was not a screenplay. Steinbeck titled this version, a long essay containing valuable oral history not found elsewhere, "Zapata, the Little Tiger." Zanuck assigned Steinbeck an assistant to help him turn this document into a screenplay, and in 1950 he finally turned in his "little double-action jewel of a script," as he described it.[10] The essay and screenplay are gathered in a book, edited with supporting material by Robert E. Morsberger, titled *Zapata. Viva Zapata!: The Screenplay* was Steinbeck's most significant political statement since *The Grapes of Wrath*, written a decade earlier.

When Steinbeck began this "Mexican decade" in 1940 with the Sea of Cortez voyage with Ed Ricketts, the two men engaged in long conversations, portions of which are recorded in *The Log from the Sea of Cortez*. These conversations appear to have consolidated many of Steinbeck's political and philosophical leanings into a form and attitude that today we might call postcolonialism (a vexed term that I adopt here to refer to an awareness of and dismay about colonial exploitation and degradation of indigenous populations). When, however, this passionate concern for the oppressed was combined with ideas transferred from ecology and Ricketts's philosophy of non-teleological thought (and Ricketts's corollary ethos of nonintervention), Steinbeck's postcolonialism became fraught with internal contradictions. The trip also brought Steinbeck into contact with Mexican versions of poverty, ignorance, and racism that form the political basis of both *The Forgotten Village* and *The Pearl*. Later, when Steinbeck researched the history of Zapata, he found that the theft of hereditary village farmlands was the main inspiration for Zapata's fervor and the chief motivating force behind the revolution itself.

Where Cultures Collide: *The Forgotten Village* and *The Pearl*

The protagonist of *The Forgotten Village* is an Indian boy named Juan Diego. The name is significant because a much earlier Chichimec Indian of that name is said to have borne the cloak on which the famous Virgin of Guadalupe was miraculously displayed; Steinbeck tells the story in "The

Miracle of Tepeyac" (1948). Possibly he named the young protagonist of *The Forgotten Village* Juan Diego because of the acculturation implicit in the miracle story. On the other hand, perhaps the naming is ironic, since the film values Western science over supernatural intervention.

Village life is established by a sequence of scenes where Juan Diego's mother goes to the village *curandera* (wise woman and healer) to find out the gender of the baby she is about to bear, Juan Diego is shown working in the cornfields with his father, his young brother later becomes ill and dies despite the *curandera*'s efforts, and the new baby is born with the *curandera*'s aid. Then Juan Diego's sister also falls ill. Juan Diego learns from doctors visiting the village that she is apparently dying of cholera (an intestinal infection usually acquired, as in this case, by drinking water contaminated with the cholera bacterium) and that a simple vaccination might save her life. The *curandera* prefers the application of a snakeskin to the belly of the victim as a remedy. Fearing for both her personal livelihood and the traditional village way of life, she accuses the doctors of practicing a sort of evil urban witchcraft and planning to inject the sick children of the village with, as she exclaims, "horses' blood!" Juan Diego kidnaps the girl by night and obtains the vaccination that will save her; as a result, he is exiled from his family and the village. At the end of the film, with help from outsiders, the boy makes the long journey to the city, where he will attend school to become a doctor himself. This film about birth, children at risk, and the benefits of modern medical intervention obviously owes much to Steinbeck's previous involvement with *The Fight for Life*.

Steinbeck's involvement with a film advocating cultural intervention provoked a serious rift and philosophical debate with Ed Ricketts about the legitimacy of interfering with indigenous cultures. Although many might agree with Steinbeck (in *The Forgotten Village*) that saving a few children from death by cholera by poking them with a needle is worth the intrusion into native custom, this debate remains a quandary for most well-intentioned persons today: at what point does such intervention cross a boundary between acceptable aid and cultural aggression?[11] Firmly maintaining that crossing that boundary is always aggressive, in the summer of 1940 Ricketts wrote an "anti-script" titled "Thesis and Materials for a Script on Mexico" that was to "stand in opposition" to Steinbeck's *The Forgotten Village*. After several pages differentiating between "outer or intellectual-material things" and the "inward things" that promote serenity, Ricketts wrote, "The chief character in John's script is the Indian boy who becomes so imbued with the spirit of modern medical progress that he leaves the traditional way of his people to associate himself with the new thing. The working out of a script for the 'other side' might correspondingly be achieved through the figure of some wise and mellow old man. . . . A wise old man, present during the time of building a high speed road through a primitive community, appropriately might point out the evils of the encroaching mechanistic civilization to a young person."[12] Ricketts's scenario, unpromising in terms of cinematic drama, offers anecdotes intended to demonstrate that rural Mexicans are in many ways better people, and more honest, than city folk anywhere. Ricketts attributes this superiority to their contentment with "inward things." The essay is not really a script at all but instead a further declaration of Ricketts's philosophy of nonintervention, which Steinbeck parodies with humor, sadness, and sympathy in his 1945 novel *Cannery Row.*

In fact Steinbeck himself wrote a much better antiscript for *The Forgotten Village.* During its filming in Mexico he encountered the flamboyant Mexican filmmaker Emilio Fernandez and his brilliant cinematographer Gabriel Figueroa, and the three of them discussed making a film. Soon engaged in this project, Steinbeck expanded the mild and minor plot of the folktale about a pearl diver that he had encountered in La Paz and retells in *The Log from the Sea of Cortez* into a concern with some of the same issues he had explored in *The Forgotten Village.*[13] These issues are absent in the original, one-paragraph folktale in which the boy diver who finds the giant pearl recognizes that the buyers are trying to cheat him and, in a grand gesture, hurls the pearl back into the sea. In his rewriting of the tale Steinbeck makes the young man an Indian named Kino who lives in a native village near La Paz in Baja California with a wife and baby; in other words, unlike the boy in the folktale, this man has a life.[14] Among other things, the new plot interrogates the basic moral premise in *The Forgotten Village:* that Western medicine has more value than native traditions. When Kino's baby is stung by a scorpion, the parents take him to the doctor—another addition to the story—and that callous practitioner exclaims to his servant, "Have I nothing better to do than cure insect bites for 'little Indians'? I am a doctor, not a veterinary."[15] But as soon as he hears that Kino has found a magnificent pearl, the doctor readily changes tactics. Hoping to obtain the pearl as his fee, he goes to the village and surreptitiously poisons the baby, who has now nearly been cured of the scorpion sting by the native medicine of his mother, Juana. Returning an hour or so later with an antidote, the doctor claims that *he* has cured the baby: "I have won the fight."[16] Steinbeck portrays this doctor with his false "medicine" as the antithesis of the concerned city doctors in *The Forgotten Village,* whose goal is to cure children and to bring the benefits of modern medicine to the rural Indians.

In *The Pearl* Steinbeck speaks for the "other side," as Ed Ricketts calls it. The phrase refers to those oppressed by "the evils of the encroaching . . . civilization," the modern urban culture that they are helpless to resist. This oppression is seen most clearly when Kino first takes his baby to the doctor for help and we understand the rejection from his point of view:

> This doctor was not of his people. This doctor was of a race which for nearly four hundred years had beaten and starved and robbed and despised Kino's race, and frightened it too, so that the indigene came humbly to the door. And as always when he came near to one of this race, Kino felt weak and afraid and angry at the same time. Rage and terror went together. He could kill the doctor more easily than he could talk to him, for all of the doctor's race spoke to all of Kino's race as though they were simple animals.[17]

Zapata: "Land and Liberty!"

A similar type of condescension occurs in the opening scene of Steinbeck's screenplay *Viva Zapata!* A group of villagers, Zapata among them, approaches President Porfirio Díaz for help, and Díaz, enthroned in his audience room, looks down on them "kindly." "Now, then, my children," he says, "what's the problem you have brought me?" When they reply that a big hacienda near their homes is taking over their land—the subsistence farms that are the source of their independence—Díaz blandly insists that they take the matter to the courts. Before casually dismissing them, he cautions them to find the boundary stones in the fields that mark precisely where their territory begins and ends. With that, the group obediently retreats, leaving one man standing alone. The man points out that the boundary stones are on land that is "fenced, guarded by armed men. At this moment they are planting sugar cane in our corn fields." Díaz asks whether his own land has been taken, and the man replies, "My father's land, my President, was taken long ago." Díaz looks at him for a moment, then he speaks past him to the other villagers: "My children. I am your father, your protector, I am of your blood. Believe me these things take time, you must have patience."[18]

The man, not yet named in the script, persists: "To do as you suggest—
to verify those boundaries—we need your authority to cross that fence."
When Díaz replies, "I can only advise," the other says, "Then naturally, my
President, we will do as you advise. Thank you, my President. (He bows)
With your permission?" As the group of country folk begins to depart, Díaz
calls out suddenly, "You!" He asks the man his name, and the man purpose-
fully replies, "Emiliano Zapata." Then, according to the screenplay (followed closely in the movie) we see "Diaz's Hand, circling the name 'Zapata'
on the card which the Attendant gave him when he entered the room."[19]
This politely antagonistic scene sets up the film, and the revolution, as a
conflict between those in power and the native farmers. For the politicians
and owners of the huge haciendas, time is a card they can afford to wait to
play in their game, but the Indians need to tend their fields *now* in order to
grow food and enable them and their families to survive.

It is a significant scene. From the moment his name is circled, the
audience knows that Zapata is "destined," probably in one of two ways: to
attain a position of authority from which he will circle the names of others
or to die for the cause. As it turns out, both scenarios come true, and Steinbeck's political interest in Mexico is most strongly and vividly expressed in
his screenplay about this leader of the Mexican Revolution. The political
element is much more explicit here than in Steinbeck's longer essay that
preceded it; as Morsberger tells us, "For the final shooting script, he added
[among other items] much of the film's political philosophy."[20] Zapata's favor-
ing of agrarian reform implemented as peacefully as possible is made clear
by his disagreements with the ruthless Fernando, an imaginary Communist
character that Steinbeck added to Zapata's history to provide the voice of
a murderous revolutionary. "A composite of all those who have betrayed
democratic revolutions and replaced them with repression," Fernando is
furious when Zapata renounces power in which he anticipated having a
share and the revolutionary violence Fernando longs for, and in the end it is
he whose machinations lead to Zapata's death.[21]

Film is one of the most immersive of all art forms: most of us will actually flinch when the bullets hit Zapata's body. As we relax in the darkened
cinema and compliantly project ourselves into the field of action, the images
of the "moving picture" that surrounds us become a potent instrument of
indoctrination. Steinbeck, wishing wholeheartedly to improve the lives of

the oppressed—those mistreated and ill, uneducated, without land, without agency—grasped this compelling aspect of film, though at first he missed the more unsavory implications of its allure.

The Three Stories as Movies

Steinbeck initially conceived of each of his three Mexican stories as films. Although the 1940 film *The Grapes of Wrath* considerably toned down the message of the novel, the Mexican stories became, or remained, quite political in their film versions. First released was *The Forgotten Village* in 1941, then *La perla/The Pearl* in 1947, then *Viva Zapata!* in 1952. *The Pearl* was remade in 2001.

Unlike *The Pearl*, *The Forgotten Village* was never conceived as anything but a film (the book version being genuinely a "book of the film," complete with a lavish set of stills), and Steinbeck guided it through its entire production. Its political message is that education in modern science can only ever be beneficial. This message becomes most overt in the last few minutes, where the director, Herbert Kline, intercuts a montage of classroom scenes with Juan Diego's intent and hopeful face.[22] The accompanying voice-over says, "Changes in people are never quick. But the boys from the villages are being given a chance by a nation that believes in them. From the government schools, the boys and girls from the villages will carry knowledge back to their own people, Juan Diego."[23] Ricketts wrote his anti-script in response to this optimistic message.

In *The Pearl* Kino also believes that his son's formal education will lead to the benefits of progress. As he gazes into the crystal ball of the huge pearl, he sees his son, grown older, "sitting at a little desk at a school. . . . He will know, and through him we will learn."[24] Here Kino sees education as the way to freedom from oppression—a message identical to that offered by *The Forgotten Village*. Whether ending the traditional way of life of his village actually would be a good thing is never clearly established, however, for the baby dies and the pearl that would buy his all-healing education is discarded. The pearl offers Kino a final vision in which he sees his son lying dead as the indirect result of his reformist efforts. Readers of *The Pearl* respond differently to this discrepancy: does Steinbeck mean that Indians should not aspire to formal education? Does he now agree with Ricketts that no one should interfere with a traditional indigenous way of life? Perhaps Steinbeck, with his longing to improve people's lives, was simply questioning the *ease* of the move that Kino dreams for his son.

From the first, Steinbeck imagined *The Pearl*—a tale of inequality, exploitation, and retribution for defying exploitation—as a film. At first the book was an accessory to the movie, its 1947 publication timed to coincide with release of the film. The movie was filmed in Mexico, the earliest example of American-Mexican cooperation on such an enterprise. It won a Golden Globe award for Gabriel Figueroa's cinematography and is still ranked among the one hundred all-time top films in Mexico.[25] But it never gained such approval in the United States. *New York Times* reviewer Bosley Crowther claimed that "the one philosophical weakness in the story as told on the screen is the evident irresolution in the symbolism of the pearl."[26] However, as the thematic music (that Steinbeck himself wrote into the text of the story) indicates, the meaning of the pearl changes as events progress, and Steinbeck clearly intended the symbolic "irresolution." As John H. Timmerman explains, using the "participating reader" idea central to this essay: "Into a narrative the author provides conflicts and choices that the reader works through, thereby placing his or her own personhood into the resolution and effects of those conflicts and choices. The reader participates in the story. While symbolism may guide possible choices, it is not structured in an exclusively determinative way to admit one choice only; for example, consider the conflicting meanings and choices provided by the symbolic gem in *The Pearl*."[27]

Even though the symbolism of the pearl shifts and glimmers as it offers Kino insubstantial visions, perhaps influenced by Ed Ricketts's concept of "non-teleological thinking," the story does have a telos, a mutating direction toward an end that can be described, using Timmerman's words again, as one "that is ongoing and draws the reader into possibilities the author holds forth."[28] In the story, that shifting of the pearl always points to and draws us ever more deeply into the perils and injustices of indigenous life when surrounded by an exploitive, "civilized" modern culture. Much of that message of concern is lost in the prettiness of the film, as it combines elegant scenic shots with the effects of Greek drama. For example, the "chorus" of white-gowned women who comment and mourn and the village festivities that unconvincingly resemble the polished Ballet Folklórico seem to have little function other than to provide local "Mexican" color.

However, the movie also contains some effective dramatic additions to Steinbeck's story as it expands the narrative into a feature-length film. In one added scene the blubbery doctor is sent by the *patrón*—the man behind the pearl dealers—to kill Kino and obtain the pearl or else forfeit his own life. The doctor, accompanied by his black dog, is seen paddling a boat through a misty swamp. Despite the doctor's murderous purpose, the scene is peaceful and lovely. But later a second man, also stalking Kino, decides to rid himself of his clumsy rival, shooting first the doctor, who overturns the boat in his death throes, and then the black dog, still struggling in the water. The scene's cruelty reveals much about the attitudes of the stalker and his *patrón*. It also foreshadows Kino's later aquatic struggles, leading the viewer to expect a similar outcome for him. Yet in aligning the now-victimized doctor with Kino, the scene also confuses the viewer about where his or her allegiance to the characters should lie. Some of these changes and additions obscure the political point of the film. Oppression is hidden first by the beauty of the cinematography and then by the cinematic excitement of the hunt, with its successive victims.

Whereas *La perla* became a Mexican classic, *Viva Zapata!* became an American one, with Marlon Brando giving an electrifying performance as Zapata and Anthony Quinn winning an Oscar for his role as Zapata's problematic brother. Unlike Nunnally Johnson's screenplay for *The Grapes of Wrath,* in which the political tone is muted compared with Steinbeck's novel, the essentially political nature of Zapata's story is preserved. Even though "memories of the striking visual style of *Viva Zapata!* may well be the most concrete element viewers take away from a screening of the film," the political statements are more overt in Steinbeck's screenplay than in his "original" story of the "Little Tiger."[29] As previously noted, Steinbeck adds to the screenplay a spokesman for the political opposition in the person of Fernando. But the film also adds, or enhances, the racial nuance that the white Marlon Brando achieves with his brilliant portrayal of the half-Indian Zapata *as Indian*. Even though Steinbeck references race throughout his essay—for example, "The Indians were treated like animals, they were driven like animals" is emphasized in his screenplay when the villagers are attacked by the government police, the *rurales*—the theme is amplified in the film's visual representation of the issue.[30] We see inequality in the opening scene where the Indian farmers, bent and holding their hats as they meekly seek his help to reclaim their farmlands, approach the president of

Mexico. But soon afterward this suppression of the poor by those in power erupts into violent action.

Director Elia Kazan appears to have looked to filmmaker Sergei Eisenstein for much of his inspiration. Perhaps the most Eisensteinian moment in the film is an extraordinarily political procession scene, now regarded as a classic of cinema. The exultant spirit of the sequence is set up against the pathos of the preceding scene, and matching motifs in these two scenes are of the sort that make Steinbeck's writing so rhythmic. The first scene is touching and sad and reveals the main reason for the revolution. Two mounted *rurales* drag along a gentle old man who had previously been noted in the opening scenes and significantly named Innocente. Zapata appears on horseback and asks what Innocente has done, while his brother Eufemio tries to give the thirsty old man a drink from his flask. In response the *rurales* spur their horses and jerk Innocente off his feet, dragging him to his death. Eventually Zapata manages to catch up and slash the rope, and the man's body rolls to the side. When his wife and others gather to mourn him, it is revealed that Innocente's heinous crime was to break through the new fence into his ancestral field. His wife, weeping over the body, scolds him for being "stubborn," but another Indian squatting nearby defends him gently: "No . . . not stubborn . . . the field is like a wife . . . live with it all your life, it's hard to learn that she isn't yours. (gesturing toward Emiliano) *He* understands."[31]

Subsequent events lead to a dramatic transference of power. First, because of his interference in the Innocente incident and other similar actions, Zapata is taken into custody by the *rurales*. When Eufemio sees his brother taken, he hunkers down and, in an apparent act of idleness, picks up two stones from the plaza and begins to click them together rhythmically. He is sending a message. The women working in the plaza join in. They click stones and bang their ollas (water jugs), increasing the power of the rhythmic call.[32] Over this music of the stones, Kazan cuts to show men, singly and in groups, moving silently from the fields and hillsides to join the procession where, echoing the fate of Innocente, Zapata is now being pulled along a road by a rope around his neck. The country folk gradually flow together as Eufemio and others of the band show up on horseback with rifles. Outnumbered, the captain of the *rurales* is forced, without overt violence, to let Zapata go. Power has shifted and now lies with the Indians.

Noting that this scene is "reminiscent of the funeral in Eisenstein's *Battleship Potemkin*," Butler argues that it is "one of the few in which the power of the people is rendered *visually*, where Zapata's rebellion begins to look like a *people's* revolution."[33] This powerful scene also projects two elements of Steinbeck's own philosophy. It dramatizes his "ecological" idea of a community as a living organism ("a thing like a colonial animal") where "how news travels . . . is a mystery not easily to be solved."[34] If the clicking of the stones was a prearranged signal for the peasants to assemble, this is not evident in the film. The scene also provides a perfect illustration of Steinbeck's famous statement in chapter 14 of *The Log from the Sea of Cortez* that "the people we call leaders are simply those who, at the given moment, are moving in the direction behind which will be found the greatest weight, and which represents a future mass movement."[35] The film clearly suggests that Zapata never wished to lead. He is thrust by circumstance to the forefront of the revolution, becoming a focus for the mass movement of peasants sympathetic to his situation and concerned with the unjust appropriation of their legally sanctioned ancestral lands.

Rather oddly, in view of his inclusion of musical themes in *The Pearl* and *Cannery Row,* Steinbeck completely neglects any mention in his screenplay of a score for this dramatic moment. Instead he emphasizes the mysterious emergence of the "country people" as they come "casually walking along . . . moving secretly through the cane . . . following, very casually . . . moving down a hill."[36] In addition to adding the rhythmic call of the stones, Kazan has the white-clad figures spring up as if from the land itself, emerging from trees and cane fields like will-o'-the-wisps. In Steinbeck's screenplay the crowd vanishes as mysteriously as it appeared: "The country people suddenly and silently melt away. The twelve Rurales are on a deserted road. They look at each other . . . and then around at the deserted country."[37] Instead of depicting this vanishing magic, Kazan plays the mysterious Indian telegraph of the stones against the white man's telegraph line at the end of the scene. The cutting of that line, cutting off the *rurales'* ability to report what has just taken place, is a dramatic show of defiance.

These scenes reveal what Steinbeck believed the revolution to be about: "Tierra y Libertad," as the slogan says (Land and Liberty). Toward the end of the film the newly appointed president Madero offers Zapata "tierra" in the form of a large estate, "a fine old custom," he explains, "to reward victorious generals." Madero fully expects Zapata to accept that traditional bribe and to cease his revolutionary activities, as Pancho Villa did before him. Zapata replies, "I did not fight for a ranch! . . . The land I fought for was not for myself!"[38] Unlike Villa, "Zapata, with his simple plan and his simple war cry of 'Land and Liberty,' never changed."[39] His uncompromising altruism makes Zapata a hero to the dispossessed. It is why, for example, modern insurgents in the southern part of Mexico who have formed a "peaceful revolutionary" group that seeks control over their local resources, especially land, call themselves "Zapatistas" and claim that their movement is proof of the legend that "Zapata lives."[40] As Morsberger emphasizes in his essay "Steinbeck's Zapata" and as the film itself makes clear, Steinbeck was interested in democratic reform (in particular, the return to the Indians of their expropriated land), not violent revolution, and accordingly he presents Zapata in the role "of agrarian reformer, not a revolutionary remolder of society."[41] The screenplay pits Zapata's agenda against that of the Communist Fernando. The Mexican Communists who wanted to appropriate Zapata to their cause were infuriated by Steinbeck's nonrevolutionary message as well as his focus on Zapata's renunciation of power, a historical event that they claim never occurred.[42]

Whereas the film *Viva Zapata!* stays close to Steinbeck's original script, the 2001 remake of *The Pearl,* written and directed by Alfredo Zacarías, does not.[43] Above all, the role of the doctor is expanded, possibly to accommodate the film's only big-name actor. Richard Harris gleefully plays the part of the evil doctor, who is accompanied by a black dog (one of several themes borrowed from *La perla* and added to Steinbeck's original story), and in this version, instead of being a middle-class Hispanic, the doctor is extremely "white," with a pallid face and white hair and clothing. Harris portrays him as both suave and disgusting as he mistreats his dark-skinned servant and molests the servant's pretty daughter; Zacarías thus picks up and elaborates on a hint from the meeting between Kino and the servant in Steinbeck's story.[44] He also expands on a later conversation in Steinbeck's novel about two Indians who long ago set off, first one, then the other, to take pearls to the mainland city to get a fair price for them and who, each in turn, disappear.[45] Whereas some commentators think that the Indians absconded with the pearls, this is not made clear in the book; they are simply "never heard of again."[46] Out of this brief and ambiguous passage in the original Zacarías develops a new ending to the story.

It begins with Kino making two discoveries. He discovers the skeletons of the Vanished Ones in the cave where he and Juana take shelter and realizes that they were murdered for their pearls, and he also finds out that the urban doctor is "the one pearl buyer with many hands" behind the pearl buyers trying to cheat him.[47] Another white man, a close-cropped militaristic gringo whom the doctor sends out to murder the little family for their priceless pearl, takes the place of the "dark ones" who hunt the family in the novella.[48] Such shifts from the original tale, greatly emphasizing the story's theme of racial oppression, allow Zacarías to build to his triumphant conclusion. Although Steinbeck leaves Kino's fate hanging, with the least reflection it is obvious: as an Indian who has killed several people—including, in the film, a white man—his crimes would soon be discovered and claims to self-defense would be ignored. Juana says to Kino after he is first driven to kill: "Do you remember the men of the city? Do you think your explanation will help?"[49] At the end of the book, after Kino discards the giant pearl that draws violence upon him, Steinbeck has "the people say" that the couple has "come out on the other side" and that there seems "a magical protection about them."[50] But the optimism of this conclusion is unconvincing, so Zacarías adds a further scene, solving the problem of Kino's fate and allowing the Indians a final, defiant gesture.

In an argument resting on Steinbeck's employment of "structural and stylistic innovations to effect our involvement," Robert DeMott says that in *Cannery Row* Steinbeck has "figuratively and subtly made us accomplices, co-conspirators in his eco-textual and language project, and has allowed us to enter the frame with him."[51] Although DeMott is discussing Steinbeck's written work, from *The Grapes of Wrath* onward it appears that Steinbeck was also thinking cinematically, running the stories as movies in his mind. In the summer of 1949 Steinbeck wrote that "man is born with a built in mechanism of illusion, closely tied to his glands and his cortex" and that his "preoccupation with illusion" can be "trapped, isolated, measured and forecast."[52] As I understand this, Steinbeck is suggesting that illusory techniques, such as those in both language and cinema, may be used to lure us into his texts, to cause us as engaged readers to "participate" in his stories, that is, to accept and endorse their theses as we occupy the world he creates. Although this potentially hypnotic approach might be considered exploitive, as it can seduce an unwary reader into acquiescing to concepts controlled by the writer, into participating by reading uncritically, Steinbeck claims that the purpose of all his writing is for one end: to make us "try to understand each other."[53]

Since Steinbeck was committed to reform rather than violent revolution, some leftist activists have rejected claims that he was essentially on their side. But he sought actively to alert his audience to social injustice through stories that serve as parables.[54] In his three stories of Mexico Steinbeck demands the participation of readers and viewers as he situates them in the ambiguous, and in Ed Ricketts's view untenable, position of the humanitarian intervening in an alien culture's problems. In this, Steinbeck's depiction of these ambiguities anticipates and foreshadows the ongoing dilemmas of our time, demanding that we consider these complexities for ourselves.

Notes

1. This film about the dangers of childbirth was made by the celebrated film critic and documentary filmmaker Pare Lorentz at the request of President Franklin D. Roosevelt. Steinbeck was hired as writer and researcher and spent much time in the Chicago Maternity Hospital from April 25, 1939, until late in May. Afterward he reported to his friend and publisher Pat Covici that "Chicago was horrible" and "I never worked such long hours in my life." The Chicago work was followed by "several periods of two or three weeks each" in Hollywood for the shooting of "some difficult interior scenes" in which Steinbeck was involved. Jackson J. Benson observes that "Steinbeck's experience with *The Fight for Life* and a developing friendship with its author also played an important part in turning his interest back toward science"—an important element in Steinbeck's writing throughout the following decade, as is often acknowledged. Benson further suggests that Steinbeck's own film *The Forgotten Village* "seems to have sprung directly from his work on *The Fight for Life.*" Benson, *John Steinbeck, Writer: A Biography* (New York: Penguin, 1990), 397–401. Lorentz's documentary is in the National Archives; see the archival description at http://arcweb.archives.gov/arc/action/ExternalIdSearch?id=1234&jScript=true.

2. John Steinbeck, *Working Days: The Journals of* The Grapes of Wrath, *1938–1941*, ed. Robert DeMott (New York: Viking, 1989), 106.

3. John Steinbeck, *Steinbeck: A Life in Letters*, ed. Elaine Steinbeck and Robert Wallsten (New York: Penguin, 1976), 193–94.

4. This was not Steinbeck's first trip to Mexico; he had previously enjoyed three and a half months at the end of 1935 based in Mexico City, from which he and his first wife, Carol, ventured to nearby destinations. She also went along as

cook on the Sea of Cortez voyage, but by then the marriage was in trouble, and she is hardly mentioned in the account of that voyage. (Carol filed for divorce in 1942.) Ibid., 200.

5. I make this general claim despite good work on *Zapata*. For a recent example of neglect, see Susan Shillinglaw and Kevin Hearle, eds., *Beyond Boundaries: Rereading John Steinbeck* (Tuscaloosa: University of Alabama Press, 2002). The index to this book contains multiple references to the worldviews of India and Japan, but astonishingly considering its title, no entry for Mexico and very few entries referring to stories set in Mexico or even to those concerning persons of Mexican and Indian descent in Central California. For example, there are no entries for *The Pearl* (published in 1945) or the celebrated earlier story "Flight" (1938). Nor are any of these Mexican-interest stories mentioned in the even more recent brief entry "Politics and Steinbeck's Fiction," in *A Critical Companion to John Steinbeck: A Literary Reference to His Life and Work*, ed. Jeffrey Schultz and Luchen Li (New York: Checkmark Books, 2005), 308–10. Susan Shillinglaw's useful and generous account "Steinbeck and Ethnicity," in *After* The Grapes of Wrath: *Essays on John Steinbeck in Honor of Tetsumaro Hayashi*, ed. Donald V. Coers, Paul D. Ruffin, and Robert J. DeMott (Athens: Ohio University Press, 1995), 40–57, is a notable exception to this neglect.

6. John Steinbeck, *The Forgotten Village* (New York: Viking, 1941), 5.

7. A pseudodocumentary is a film that looks like a documentary but is, to some degree, acted. Benson calls the form "semi-documentary" and describes it as having "real people acting out familiar roles." Benson, *John Steinbeck*, 453.

8. Steinbeck, *Life in Letters*, 284.

9. Ibid., 282.

10. Ibid., 407.

11. According to the World Health Organization webpage (www.who.int), preventive vaccination is no longer considered as effective against cholera as the film suggests and is therefore no longer advocated. Treatment of contaminated water (as in the film), among other hygienic precautions, continues to be urged.

Regarding intervention, see, for example, Helen Cobban, "Having an Effect on Vulnerable Others: Two Aspects of the Present U.S. Actions toward Afghanistan," October 9, 2001, http://helenacobban.org/teach-in.html. Ed Ricketts was ahead of his time in his awareness and concern about well-meaning intrusions into traditional cultures. The issue was raised by a number of anthropologists in the 1980s. See, for example, Jay Ruby, ed., *A Crack in the Mirror: Reflexive Perspectives in Anthropology* (Philadelphia: University of Pennsylvania Press, 1982); and James Clifford and George F. Marcus, eds., *Writing Culture: The Poetics and Politics of Ethnography* (Berkeley: University of California Press, 1986).

12. Edward F. Ricketts, *Breaking Through: Essays, Journals, and Travelogues of Edward F. Ricketts*, ed. Katherine A. Rodger (Berkeley: University of California Press, 2006), 207.

13. John Steinbeck, *The Log from the Sea of Cortez* (New York: Penguin, 1995), 85–86.

14. During this period in his writing, most of Steinbeck's names are symbolic. The priest in *The Pearl* explains to Kino, "Thou are named after a great man—and a great Father of the Church. . . . Thy namesake tamed the desert and sweetened the minds of the people." John Steinbeck, *The Pearl* (New York: Penguin, 1992), 27. Father Eusebio Kino (1644–1711) was a dedicated Jesuit priest who cared about and helped Indians, mainly from tribes in Sonora and Baja California, among whom he labored. He founded twenty-two missions in western Mexico.

15. Steinbeck, *Pearl*, 11.

16. Ibid., 35.

17. Ibid., 9.

18. John Steinbeck, *Zapata* (New York: Penguin, 1993), 226–28.

19. Ibid., 228–29.

20. Robert E. Morsberger, "Emiliano Zapata: The Man, the Myth, and the Mexican Revolution," in Steinbeck, *Zapata*, 6.

21. Steinbeck, *Zapata*, 12.

22. Steinbeck, *Forgotten Village*, 138–42.

23. Ibid., 140.

24. Steinbeck, *Pearl*, 31.

25. The list was published in the one hundredth issue of the Mexican magazine *Somos* (July 16, 1994).

26. Bosley Crowther, review of *The Pearl* (film), *New York Times*, February 18, 1948.

27. John H. Timmerman, "John Steinbeck: An Ethics of Fiction," in *The Moral Philosophy of John Steinbeck*, ed. Stephen K. George (Lanham, Md.: Scarecrow Press, 2005), 38.

28. Timmerman, "John Steinbeck," 38. On Ricketts's concept, see Ricketts, "Essay on Non-Teleological Thinking," in *Breaking Through*, chapter 5.

29. Jeremy G. Butler, "*Viva Zapata!:* HUAC and the Mexican Revolution," in *The Steinbeck Question: New Essays in Criticism*, ed. Donald R. Noble (Troy, N.Y.: Whitston, 1993), 248.

30. Steinbeck, *Zapata*, 28, 230–31. Compare with the "veterinary" comment in *The Pearl.*

31. Ibid., 253; emphasis in the original.

32. The music at this point, a score by Alex North, is brilliant. Morsberger describes the way it works with the scene: "Seeing his brother taken prisoner,

Eufemio Zapata [Quinn] begins pounding a message with two stones, and the message is relayed telegraphically by others pounding stones, until a vast number of peasants congregate from all directions upon the procession of rurales and force them to release their prisoner. North begins his music for this episode by picking up the rhythm of the stones with a bolero-type theme with timbals and bongos, to which he adds a marimba and then flutes, guitars, and plucked strings." He explains that the music reflects the peasants' purpose as well as acting as a defiant rallying cry. Robert E. Morsberger, "Of Mice and Men: Scoring Steinbeck Movies," in Coers, Ruffin, and DeMott, *After* The Grapes of Wrath, 69.

33. Butler, "*Viva Zapata!*," 247; emphasis in the original.

34. Steinbeck, *Pearl*, 27.

35. Steinbeck, *Log from the Sea of Cortez*, 115.

36. Steinbeck, *Zapata*, 257.

37. Ibid., 260.

38. Ibid., 282–83.

39. Ibid., 158.

40. The *Encyclopedia Britannica* article on the leader of the Zapatistas, Subcomandante Marcos, is under the title "Rafael Giullén Vicente, Mexican Leader." The full version, giving a brief account of the movement, is available at http://www.britannica.com/hispanic_heritage/article-9475884.

In the final scene of the film Zapata's white stallion appears magically on a hilltop, dramatizing a legend among the peoples of the state of Morelos. Steinbeck changes Zapata's bay horse to a symbolically white one, matching the famous painting of Zapata by Diego Rivera. See Morsberger's discussion in Steinbeck, *Zapata*, 5, 218. This glimpse of the horse implies that, like England's legendary King Arthur ("the once and future king"), who fascinated Steinbeck all his life, Zapata never "really" died, hence the screenplay's title, *Viva Zapata!*—Zapata lives.

41. Morsberger, "Steinbeck's Zapata: Rebel versus Revolutionary," in Steinbeck, *Zapata*, 207.

42. Ibid., 220.

43. Not all the changes from the book were Zacarías's idea. The Steinbeck heirs were incensed when they saw the screenplay, in which Zacarías planned to include nudity in the film. Their objections were successful. So, for the scene where Steinbeck has Kino shed his clothing in order to make his dark body less visible when he climbs down the cliff at night, the film shows him wearing an absurd white loincloth, bright as a searchlight, but luckily he is unobserved by his enemies below. For an account of the controversy, see Burhan Wazir, "Steinbeck Son Rages at Sex Travesty," *Sunday Observer* (London), June 15, 2000.

44. Steinbeck, *Pearl*, 10.

45. Ibid., 46.

46. Sydney J. Krause, "*The Pearl* and 'Hadleyburg': From Desire to Renunciation," in *Steinbeck's Literary Dimension: A Guide to Comparative Studies*, series 2, ed. Tetsumaro Hayashi (Metuchen, N.J.: Scarecrow, 1991), 146, 160.

47. Steinbeck, *Pearl*, 42.

48. Ibid., 63.

49. Ibid., 61.

50. Ibid., 88.

51. Robert DeMott, "The Place We Have Arrived: Writing/Reading toward *Cannery Row*," in Shillinglaw and Hearle, *Beyond Boundaries*, 305.

52. Benson, *John Steinbeck*, 649.

53. Quoted in Shillinglaw, "Steinbeck and Ethnicity," 55.

54. Ibid., 40–41.

CHAPTER 10

"Not Afraid of Being Heroic": Bruce Springsteen's John Steinbeck

Lauren Onkey

IT IS NOT HARD TO FIND connections between John Steinbeck and Bruce Springsteen. Most obviously, Springsteen recorded an album titled *The Ghost of Tom Joad* in 1995, and during the subsequent tour he received the first John Steinbeck In the Souls of the People Award from the Center for Steinbeck Studies. The *New York Times* dubbed him "Steinbeck in Leather" in 1997. But more importantly, both artists sought to effect social change with their work, although they shied away from radical or revolutionary political organizations. Both were also embraced by a large audience, a fact that was sometimes used to undermine the significance of their political work.[1]

Springsteen did not learn his songwriting craft from John Steinbeck—he is, as he put it, a child of Bob Dylan and Elvis Presley. But he has been inspired by Steinbeck's vision of collective responsibility in *The Grapes of Wrath*, the vision of Preacher Casy's "one big soul." At a benefit concert for the Steinbeck Research Center at San Jose State University in October 1996, Springsteen described Steinbeck's work as an antidote to isolation and a model of "useful" art:

> As a writer you try to increase understanding, and . . . compassion . . . in order to combat that fear . . . the seed of all that hate and prejudice; that's sort of what art can do. . . . You get a chance to sort of fight some of that isolation, you feel it's part of the American character in some fashion. In *The Grapes of Wrath*, Preacher Casy calls that isolation "the wilderness," and that's what it is. . . . I think that Steinbeck's work, particularly *The Grapes of Wrath*, it was there to reach in and pull you out of that wilderness, out into the world. . . .

It's a work that's resonated for me throughout my whole life. . . . And for me, that particular novel always showed the usefulness of beauty. . . . I know that it was always something that I aspired to, to do work that meant something. What I always loved about Steinbeck's work was that it wasn't afraid of being heroic and that he risked, he hung his ass out there . . . for you, for me.[2]

This essay explores what Springsteen means by the risk of "being heroic" and how that phrase can help us understand Steinbeck's popular legacy. I suggest that the heroism Springsteen speaks of is the risk of trying to communicate big ideas (writing "the big book," as Steinbeck called *The Grapes of Wrath*) to a broad audience, to risk *popularity.* Springsteen has used Steinbeck's example to extol the value of speaking to and thereby creating a large community of listeners rather than to an insider, elite, or avant-garde audience. But to speak to a broad audience can signify a lack of depth or artistic vision. Steinbeck's reputation has suffered in academic literary studies in part because he was popular, both in his lifetime and later on, among teenage readers. Most overtly political studies of Springsteen's work ignore the singer's obvious passion for pop music traditions and his belief in the political power of popular music.[3] In this essay I will show how Bruce Springsteen's John Steinbeck, which he has created and circulated through an extended "gospel response" to *The Grapes of Wrath,* advocates communal consciousness and the political usefulness of popular art.

As Morris Dickstein has said, many readers "leave Steinbeck behind as an enthusiasm to be outgrown."[4] The academy has certainly left Steinbeck behind; few articles of literary analysis are published on Steinbeck other than those published in the specialized journal *Steinbeck Studies.* Only 66 dissertations on his work have been written in the United States since 1954, as compared to 675 dissertations on his contemporary William Faulkner.[5]

When Steinbeck was awarded the Nobel Prize for Literature in 1962, critics famously derided the decision, complaining that Steinbeck's best days were behind him and that such a popular, sentimental writer should not be rewarded. This battle was the culmination of a war that Steinbeck had waged with literary critics since the early days of his career.[6] On the eve of the acceptance ceremony Arthur Mizener wrote a scathing article in the *New York Times* titled "Does a Moral Vision of the Thirties Deserve a Noble Prize?" that dismissed Steinbeck for sentimentality and didacticism. He attributed Steinbeck's reputation to the "trendiness" of his subject matter in *The Grapes of Wrath.* According to Mizener, after the 1930s most "serious" readers stopped reading Steinbeck. He argued that Steinbeck's "moral dis-torts the story" and that he was "an incurable amateur philosopher" whose work was a "mere illustration" of his ideas, which Mizener mocks as "pro-found" abstractions and "dazzling profundities." In *The Grapes of Wrath*, Mizener argues, "the characters are constantly being forced to display in an implausible way Steinbeck's theory about them." His final criticism was for the European judges, revealing a Cold War anticommunism in rejecting the values of social democracies: "Perhaps those Europeans who influence the awarding of the prize are simply behind the times and in all sincerity believe that the judgments of the thirties are still the established judgments. This attitude would be reinforced, from one direction, by the European social democrat's inclination to place a very high value on sentimental humani-tarianism, especially when it is displayed about the poor, especially when these poor exist in a society that is supposed by many of them to be the last stronghold of uncontrolled capitalist exploitation."[7]

In his Nobel acceptance speech Steinbeck defended himself by at-tacking the critics as elitist: "Literature was not promulgated by a pale and emasculated critical priesthood singing their litanies in empty churches. . . . Literature is as old as speech. It grew out of human need for it, and it has not changed except to become more needed. The skalds, the bards, the writers are not separate and exclusive."[8] Steinbeck's defenders have created what Dickstein calls a "counter myth" about these attacks, portraying the author as an embattled "man of the people." The image is not quite ac-curate. Steinbeck embraced and made a fetish out of the critics' rejection, as is evidenced by his attack on critics in his Nobel acceptance speech. Yet it is clear that this rejection, and the embrace of it by Steinbeck and his sup-porters, has been influential in keeping Steinbeck out of university study. Springsteen, by contrast, embraces Steinbeck for the very reasons critics have derided him. (For further discussion of the uproar over the awarding of the Nobel Prize to Steinbeck, see chapter 4, by Adrienne Akins Warfield.)

Springsteen's version of John Steinbeck can be read as a form of gos-pel response to the writer's work. As Craig Werner argues, the "call and response" principle of African American culture constitutes gospel politics. The pattern of call and response is well known: "An individual voice, fre-quently a preacher or singer, calls out in a way that asks for a response. The response can be verbal, musical, physical—anything that communicates with the leader or the rest of the group. The response can affirm, argue, redirect the dialogue, raise a new question. Any response that gains attention and elicits a response of its own becomes a new call."[9] Springsteen responds to Steinbeck's call—both as an artist and as a citizen who feels responsible for the social conditions that Steinbeck depicts. What is especially useful about reading Springsteen's Steinbeck as a gospel response is that it emphasizes community. Such community can be seen as a version of Casy's "one big soul": "Both in its political contexts and its more strictly musical settings, call and response moves the emphasis from the individual to the group. . . . Call and response is the African American form of critical analysis, a process that draws on the experience and insights of the entire community. The individual maintains a crucial role; a carefully crafted call can lead to the best, most useful insights."[10] Springsteen's response to Steinbeck both affirms Steinbeck's ideas and raises new questions about them, namely, whether people of color, especially immigrants, are part of the "one big soul" and whether rock and roll music can achieve the social impact that Springsteen believes *The Grapes of Wrath* did.

Like many Americans, Bruce Springsteen first read John Steinbeck's *The Grapes of Wrath* and *Of Mice and Men* in high school in the 1960s; he told Will Percy, "I came by the film [*The Grapes of Wrath*] before I really came by the book. I'd read the book in high school, along with *Of Mice and Men* and a few others, and then I read it again after I saw the movie."[11] But Springsteen did not reveal any Steinbeckian influence on his songwriting (or any explicit literary or cinematic influences at all) until his 1978 album *Darkness on the Edge of Town*, a stark, guitar-driven collection of rock songs that directly confront the multifaceted aspects of American class politics. The album was his first sustained exploration of the everyday lives of his characters; they grappled with work ("Factory"), fading relationships ("Racing in the Street"), and psychological isolation ("Streets of Fire"). The album also includes "Adam Raised a Cain," a song about father-son conflict seemingly inspired by the film version of *East of Eden*. In *Songs* Springsteen writes, "I intentionally steered away from any hint of escapism and set my characters down in the middle of a community under siege."[12] Springsteen began to explore the individual *in community*, the "one big soul ever'body's a part of."

But it was John Ford's *The Grapes of Wrath* that influenced how Springsteen thought about how art could represent familial and class conflict on *Darkness on the Edge of Town*, not Steinbeck's. He told Paul Nelson in 1978,

"I'd gotten into seeing movies. I saw *The Grapes of Wrath* on TV, which I used to turn off. . . . That's a terrible thing to say, but I always remember turning it off and turning on something that was in color. Then I realized it was a stupid thing to do because one night Jon [Landau, his producer and subsequent manager] and I watched it, and it opened up a whole particular world to me."[13] He told *CREEM*'s Robert Duncan that same year that the film made him think about how capitalism made economic changes seem inevitable or natural rather than the product of decisions by the powerful:

> The movie affected me a lot. It brought up a lot of questions I didn't think about before. There's the great part where [Tom Joad's] coming back from prison and he finds that little guy [Muley Graves] hiding in the closet. Little guy says, "They're coming." "Well, who's coming?" "They're coming. Taking away all the land." And then the guy comes on the tractor and it's their friend. They ask him, "Who's doing this?" And the tractor guy just says, "Well, I got my orders from this guy and it goes back to him." To me, it's like, Where do you point the gun? There's no place to take aim. There's nobody to blame. It's just things, just the way. Whose fault is it? It's a little bit of this guy, a little bit of that guy, a little bit of this other guy. That was real interesting to me. . . . And it was great that when that movie came out it was a very popular movie.[14]

These comments not only show Springsteen's interest in the power-lessness of farmers and industrial workers, which permeates songs like "Factory," "The River," "Born in the U.S.A.," "Sugarland," "Johnny 99," and "Youngstown," but also his interest in the potential popularity and usability of art that gives voice to such powerlessness. During this same period Springsteen talked often about the importance of finding a community where an interest in art could be cultivated for people on the margins of American society: "If you grow up in a particular house where the concept of art is twenty minutes in school that you *hate,* and there's no books, no music, there's nothing. . . . That's a problem for a lot of people—a lot of my friends. . . . That's why the importance of rock & roll was just incredible. It reached *down* into all those homes where there was no music or books or any kind of creative sense, and it infiltrated the whole thing."[15] Ford's *The Grapes of Wrath* inspired Springsteen to consider how his audience could use his work in the same way that he used pop music as a kid. Springsteen built on this idea to construct Steinbeck's work as a place where high and low culture converge, where the high culture of novels can live up to the power of rock and roll music and where a critical appreciation of rock and roll records is on par with critical appreciation of film and literature. Springsteen promotes Steinbeck as a model for populist, accessible social consciousness, one that can be accessed through film, pop singles, or Steinbeck novels.

Although Springsteen has drawn on these ideas throughout his subsequent career, he explicitly evoked Steinbeck twice: in 1978 and on the *Ghost of Tom Joad* album and world tour in the mid-1990s. In both periods when Springsteen was explicitly inspired by Steinbeck he was in the throes of an artistic crisis brought on by a new level of fame, the kind of crisis that Steinbeck would have recognized. After the success of *Of Mice and Men* (1937), Steinbeck wrote, "I was not made for success. I find myself now with a growing reputation. In many ways it is a terrible thing."[16] His wife Elaine told biographer Jay Parini, "Publicity always depressed him."[17] Springsteen had a similar response to his initial burst of success with *Born to Run* in 1975, which went platinum and landed him on the covers of *Time* and *Newsweek* in the same week. This success quickly gave way to charges of hype that affected Springsteen deeply.[18] He subsequently underwent a protracted legal battle with his manager over control of the rights to his songs and the direction of his career. The legal problems prevented him from recording until 1977. When he returned, his songwriting reflected a desire to understand the community out of which he came rather than just to escape it. Fame and stardom frightened Springsteen into feeling that his life and image were out of control, and he responded by trying to account for society's losers:

> I think when I got in that spot, I really did feel . . . attacked on the essence of who I felt that I was. So at that point I realized that, unattached from community, it was impossible to find any meaning. . . . *Darkness on the Edge of Town* was basically saying, you get out there and you turn around and you come back because that's just the beginning. . . . I got out there—hey, the wind's whipping through your hair, you feel real good, you're the guy with the gold guitar . . . and all of a sudden you feel that sense of *dread* that is overwhelming everything you do. . . . The *Darkness* record was a confrontation record . . . all those people, all those faces, you gotta look at 'em all.[19]

Springsteen used Ford's *The Grapes of Wrath* to help avoid the potential amnesia of fame, as a way to write about the lives of people who didn't make hit records and travel around the country. The album and subsequent tour were successful, but album and concert reviews suggested that Springsteen's "confrontations" were not always welcome to an audience looking for escape.[20]

After *Darkness on the Edge of Town* Springsteen continued to explore, with increasing complexity, ways to represent the class structures that surrounded his characters' lives. Introducing "Independence Day" in 1981, Springsteen explained how reading Henry Steele Commager and Allan Nevin's *Pocket History of the United States* helped him to understand his father's disenfranchisement: "They helped me understand how when I was a kid all I remember was my father worked in a factory, his father worked in a factory. . . . . And the main reason was because . . . . they didn't know enough about themselves . . . and they didn't know enough about the forces . . . that controlled their lives."[21] For a decade, Springsteen wrote many songs about characters who become victims of that ignorance and songs that expose the economic, social, and political forces that shape their lives. The songs on *Darkness on the Edge of Town* and *The River* (1980) explore the nature and consequences of that lack of knowledge ("Jackson Cage," "Independence Day," "Factory," "The Price You Pay," "The Promise," "Darkness on the Edge of Town"); the songs on *Nebraska* (1982) and *Born in the U.S.A.* (1984) begin to fill in the details about those "forces," with references to conditions for Vietnam veterans and the effect of deindustrialization on communities and families ("Johnny 99," "Highway Patrolman," "Born in the U.S.A.," "My Hometown"). His targets remain generally vague—"layoff," "the economy," an unnamed force that sends people to war—which seems to reflect his characters' inability to understand why they remain disempowered.

While Springsteen did not mention Steinbeck in interviews or from the stage during this period, he was carrying out the idea he originally found in *The Grapes of Wrath,* of making music that could help people make political and social connections to each other. In August 1981, for example, Springsteen performed a benefit concert for the Vietnam Veterans of America (VVA). Introducing Bobby Muller, the president of the VVA, Springsteen talked about the importance of facing the legacy of the war:

> It's like when you feel like you're walking down a dark street at night and out
> of the corner of your eye you see somebody getting hurt or somebody getting

hit in the dark alley but you keep walking on because you think it don't have
nothing to do with you and you just want to get home. . . . Well, Vietnam
turned this whole country into that dark street and unless we're able to walk
down those dark alleys and look into the eyes of the men and the women that
are down there and the things that happened, we're never gonna be able to
get home and then it's only a chance. You guys out there, you're 18 or 19 years
old. . . . It happened once and it can happen again.[22]

This phase of Springsteen's career peaked with the massive *Born in
the U.S.A.* tour in 1984–1985, where he reached the largest audience of
his career, regularly selling out football stadiums. His use of patriotic ico-
nography—including an enormous American flag that he employed as his
stage backdrop—led Ronald Reagan and George Will to declare his music
a "grand, cheerful affirmation" of America. Springsteen responded to this
Republican embrace by supporting various community organizations, especially food banks, at each stop on the tour, a practice that he's continued
ever since. He would make a personal donation to the organization; describe
its work from the stage before singing "This Land Is Your Land" (including
its more radical verses, which he did not include on *The River* tour when
he first began to perform the song); and encourage fans to donate time and
money as well, telling the crowd, "nobody wins unless everybody wins."[23]

At the end of the tour, at the peak of his popularity, he performed
one of his darkest songs, "Seeds," about workers displaced from northern
industrial towns to the oil fields of Texas, now living homeless:

Well big limousine long shiny and black
You don't look ahead you don't look back
Well I swear if I could spare the spit
I'd lay one on your shiny chrome
And send you on your way back home
So if you're gonna leave your town where the north wind blow
To go on down where that sweet soda river flow
Well you better think twice on it Jack
You're better off buyin' a shotgun dead off the rack
You ain't gonna find nothin' down here friend
Except seeds blowin' up the highway in the south wind.[24]

Springsteen attempted to use the celebrity fest that was the *Born in the
U.S.A.* tour to say that these "seeds," these displaced workers, were born

in the U.S.A., too, and they may be the seeds of the grapes of wrath. It was his and his audience's responsibility to help those who had been left behind during late capitalism. However, because these social messages were offered against a backdrop of massive popular success and plenty of songs that had no overt political implications (for example, "Cadillac Ranch," "Glory Days," "Pink Cadillac," "I'm on Fire"), they could easily be ignored or written off as ways for Springsteen to assuage his guilt over his success or to gain critical credibility. Springsteen was trying to walk the high wire between massive public attention and social responsibility, and it didn't always work. As Springsteen said to Will Percy in 1998, "If your work is involved in trying to show where the country is hurting and where people are hurting, your own success is used to knock down or undercut the questions you ask of your audience. It's tricky, because American society has a very strict idea of what success is and what failure is. . . . It's ironic if 'celebrity' is used to reassure lots of people, barely making it, that 'Look, someone's really making it, making it big, so everything is all right, just lose yourself and all your troubles in that big-time success!'"[25] Springsteen backed away from the glare.

Beginning with 1987's *Tunnel of Love,* Springsteen spent a decade writing songs focusing on relationships between men and women, which resulted, by accident or design, in a scaling back of his popularity. While not a complete break from what he'd done before—all of his albums have relationship songs—there was a shift from the kind of writing he did from *Darkness on the Edge of Town* through *Born in the U.S.A.,* where characters were placed in social conditions. It can be read as a retreat from the "we" to the "I." Songs like "Brilliant Disguise," "Human Touch," and "Better Days" explore marriage, love, fidelity, and sex largely without social or class context. Later Springsteen described it as a deliberate decision: "I drew a lot of my earlier material from my experience growing up, my father's experience, the experience of my immediate family and town. But there was a point in the mid-eighties when I felt like I'd said pretty much all I knew how to say about all that. I couldn't continue writing about those same things without . . . becoming a stereotype of myself."[26]

In 1992–1993 he toured behind two of his least critically successful albums, *Human Touch* and *Lucky Town,* following his break from his longstanding and popular E Street Band. Springsteen has attributed the lukewarm response to those records in part to their break from his earlier, more serious songs: "We didn't go out just to make music, we went out to make *essential* music. It was fun and entertaining and hopefully enjoyable, but at the core there was something serious and essential that tied into the experience of living in America. I think the criticism of some records I made in the late '80s or '90s centered around that idea."²⁷ As he did after *Born to Run*, Springsteen described mass popularity and commercialization as risky. They had turned him into what Steinbeck once called a "trade mark." In 1935 Steinbeck declined an invitation to accept an award from the Commonwealth Club for best novel for *Tortilla Flat*. In a letter to Joseph Henry Jackson, he expressed fear that his writing would suffer if he became famous: "In the last few books I have felt a curious richness as though my life had been multiplied through having become identified in a most real way with people who were not me. And I am afraid, terribly afraid, that if the bars ever go down, if I become a trade mark, I shall lose the ability to do that. . . . I am very glad that the book got the prize, but I want it to be the book, not me."²⁸

In 1995 Springsteen sought new ways to connect his work to social issues, to represent "people who were not me," and recorded *The Ghost of Tom Joad*. At the beginning of the tour he told Bob Costas, "The bottom line is that America will always be judged against the American idea, which was some concept of a shared burden. I guess what I was trying to do for myself was to put myself back in touch with those ideas, those values."²⁹ He returned to *The Grapes of Wrath* as a way to articulate the idea of a shared burden. He said that the new characters "felt like an extension of the characters I've written about in the past, the Steinbeckian influences in my work. I brought them into the present."³⁰ *The Ghost of Tom Joad*, released in November 1995, was a collection of softly sung, acoustic songs with a cast of characters far from Springsteen's own experience, although some resembled the industrial and postindustrial American men he'd written about previously. The grim songs are about immigrants, ex-cons, child prostitutes, Gulf Coast fishermen, and steelworkers thrown out of their jobs, "the new world order." Confronted with this landscape, the singer of the title track "searches for the ghost of Tom Joad," the spirit that would connect these characters and provide them a sense of community. In the middle of the song the speaker is "waiting" for the ghost, and at the end he is "with" the ghost. The ghost of Tom Joad is present not in the songs themselves but in the speaker and listener. The listener must acknowledge the presence of these Americans because they are part of the same soul—that is, our shared burden. Springsteen sang the songs quietly, accompanied usually by just his guitar or with the muted sounds of a small band. The album challenges listeners not just with its relentless subject matter but also because it does not offer Springsteen's usual rousing rock and roll sound as a way to face the picture that he paints. There are no illusions of escape or transcendence: "The highway is alive tonight / but nobody's kiddin' nobody about where it goes."[31] (See chapter 11, by Cyrus Zirakzadeh, for further discussion of the political ideas expressed in Springsteen's "The Ghost of Tom Joad.")

The Grapes of Wrath became a touchstone on the tour supporting *The Ghost of Tom Joad.* "Red River Valley," the song employed by Ford throughout his movie version of *The Grapes of Wrath*, was played over the PA every night just before Springsteen came on stage, where he opened the show with either "The Ghost of Tom Joad" or Woody Guthrie's song about the film, "Tom Joad."[32] Springsteen made several references on stage and in interviews to the final scene of the novel, where Rose of Sharon offers her breast to a starving man. Most importantly, he delivered a nightly monologue before "Across the Border" in which he talked about the impact of John Ford's film and Steinbeck's novel on his ideas about art and his social vision. That story developed over the course of the tour, from an evocation of Ma Joad's line that "we're the people who just keep going" to a long discussion of the film's dance scene and Tom's farewell to his mother, a far less optimistic scene than that offered by Steinbeck's novel (see chapter 11, by Cyrus Ernesto Zirakzadeh, for a discussion of the different political orientations of the novel and the movie). The monologue linked the comments he made in 1978 about growing up in a house "without culture" to his embrace of the film while asserting that rock and roll could be as life changing as Steinbeck.

The transformation of Bruce Springsteen on the *Ghost of Tom Joad* tour was not simply that he was talking about John Steinbeck. Everything about the tour was a departure from what Springsteen had previously done on stage. He played solo; he asked for quiet; he dressed in the kind of work clothes his father wore rather than his usual raggedy rock-star chic. With his moustache and slicked-back hair he sometimes even looked like Steinbeck. Although he had always told stories from the stage, the stories on the *Joad* tour were more explicitly and consistently political than anything he had done before. He talked about conditions for migrant workers; he attacked welfare reform and made references to "the Gingrich mob" that had just taken control of Congress; he described the abandonment of northern industrial cities like Youngstown, Ohio, and its effects on an entire community, reminding us that steelworkers "build the bridges we cross." All of his stories and political speeches circled around conditions for the working class, songs that seemed to be inspired by Tom Joad's ghost.[33] The *Ghost of Tom Joad* album and tour were about as far from gospel music as one could imagine in both musical style and Springsteen's demand for quiet from the audience. But his performance can be seen as a gospel response to Steinbeck's call. Americans' shared burden means acknowledging immigrant migrant workers and "criminals" who fill the prisons that replaced steel mills as the major employer in cities like Youngstown.

Springsteen explicitly called for his audience to do something about what they heard. In this sense the *Ghost of Tom Joad* tour was much more of a response to Steinbeck's novel than Ford's film. As George Bluestone points out in his analysis of Ford's adaptation of Steinbeck, "The film scrupulously steers clear of the book's specific accusations," especially about legal authority. Tom's farewell speech, which Springsteen is so enamored of, "is pruned until little remains but its mystical affirmation." Bluestone concludes that in the film "the politico-economic tendency is merely an urge in search of a name it is never allowed to find."[34] On tour Springsteen was willing to make specific accusations and asked that his audience make personal and political decisions as a result of seeing his show.

In the past twenty years *The Grapes of Wrath* has come under criticism for its implicit racism. As Charles Cunningham points out, "The novel scarcely mentions the Mexican and Filipino migrant workers who dominated the California fields and orchards into the late thirties, instead implying that Anglo-Saxon whites were the only subjects worthy of treatment."[35] The same could be said about many of Springsteen's songs about white working-class displacement such as "Born in the U.S.A." or "Seeds." As his music turned more overtly political, it lost some of the diverse characters and sense of a broad racial community that permeate early albums like *The Wild, The Innocent & the E Street Shuffle*. Indeed, the E Street Band itself became far more racially homogenous during this period. Perhaps that is why Springsteen appealed to conservatives after the success of *Born in the U.S.A.* His work suggested that white men suffered most in postindustrial America.[36] But on *The Ghost of Tom Joad*, Mexican and Vietnamese immigrants share the stage with white workers in "Youngstown," "Straight Time," and "The New Timer." Immigration became the central political issue of the show. (For a discussion of Steinbeck's concern with the exploitation of nonwhites, see chapter 9, by Marijane Osborn.)

Every night of the tour Springsteen ended the show with a set of songs about Mexican immigrants: "Sinaloa Cowboys," "The Line," "Balboa Park," and "Across the Border." The performance demanded attention: Springsteen sat on a stool and sang quietly. Before each song he told a story that set up the song: conditions for migrant workers before "The Line," a song about a border guard; the value of children and the "grace" they bring to the world before "Balboa Park," a story of young immigrant boys who work as prostitutes; and the value of family before "Sinaloa Cowboys," a song about the lure of the methamphetamine trade for immigrants, who could make half a year's farm labor pay in a day preparing the drug. The set and the show culminated in the story about *The Grapes of Wrath* preceding "Across the Border," which proposed the usefulness of art and beauty in the face of despair, because art could pose what Springsteen called "the fundamental question": "Are we all individual souls, and is there such a thing as independent salvation? Can you really in the end just save yourself, or are we connected in some fashion? And do we sort of rise and fall—at least in spirit—as one?"[37] Springsteen's identification with Casy suggests that he is more optimistic than Steinbeck's narrator.

Casy's optimism also provides context for "Galveston Bay," the story of a conflict between Vietnamese immigrants and Texas fisherman on Texas's Gulf Coast in the 1970s. Springsteen told an interviewer that the song was inspired in part by rereading *The Grapes of Wrath* (he repeated versions of this story on stage):

> The book ends on a singular act of human kindness or compassion—the entire book leads to that point. That had a lot of meaning for me at the moment I re-read it because I was searching for a way to go beyond broad platitudes or whatever you want to call them. I was looking for a way to make whatever light there is in the world feel real now. So I found myself turning at the end of my record to one person making one decision. I think the things I use to bring some light into the show are those types of things, that's why I play "Spare Parts" and "Galveston Bay." To me, those things are possible, those are things that . . . any individual at your show can walk out of the building and can lead the next day with that idea or that possibility.[38]

Le Bing Son and Billy Sutter, both Vietnam war veterans, although in different armies, work on fishing boats in the gulf. The white fishermen become
increasingly hostile to the presence of the refugees and claim "America for
Americans." Two white men attack Le, who kills them in self-defense. After
he is acquitted, Billy threatens to kill him. But as he heads out to murder
Le, he changes his mind, slips the knife back in his pocket, returns home,
kisses his wife, and then goes back out to work. The song ends as abruptly
as *The Grapes of Wrath:*

> In the early darkness Billy rose up
> Went into the kitchen for a drink of water
> Kissed his sleeping wife
> Headed into the channel
> And cast his nets into the water
> Of Galveston Bay.[39]

Billy plays against type; he retreats from excluding Le and asserting the pri-
macy of whiteness in America. Bryan Garman argues that although Springsteen links the song to Steinbeck's ending "the two events are significantly
different: her breast-feeding is an act of human kindness that saves a life
and establishes close bonds between people, whereas Sutter simply decides
not to take a life and ultimately fails to reach out to his intended victim.
. . . Before collective movements can be formed, people have to recognize
that the world can be changed and then assume a sense of responsibility for
transforming it."[40] I think that the distinctions that Garman sees are accurate, but Springsteen used the song to inspire a sense of responsibility in his
audience. The point for Springsteen seems to be not only what Billy Sutter
does—although his decision not to be consumed by fear and resentment is
significant in a set of songs where characters are motivated by fear and isolation—but also what the audience will now do about that story. He assumes
that his audience members are not economically displaced and knows that
they are overwhelmingly white; Springsteen therefore points them toward
community action designed to alleviate economic injustice against people
of color and the working class.

Springsteen's shows in the southwest in late October 1996 exemplify
the connections he drew between his music, Steinbeck, and political action.
He performed in Albuquerque; Tempe, Arizona; San Diego; Fresno; Santa
Barbara; and San Jose, where he played a benefit for the John Steinbeck

Research Center.[41] The shows opened with Woody Guthrie's "Tom Joad," and the show in Fresno included Guthrie's song about a group of Mexican immigrants who died in a plane crash after being deported in 1948, "Deportee (Plane Wreck at Los Gatos)." At the Steinbeck benefit in San Jose, he actually read two passages from the novel during his long introduction to "Across the Border": excerpts from chapter 28, when Tom says goodbye to Ma, the speech that he draws from in "The Ghost of Tom Joad," and the final chapter, where Rose of Sharon saves the starving man.

He concluded that string of dates by playing at a rally in Los Angeles against Proposition 209, which proposed to amend the California constitution to prohibit public institutions from discriminating on the basis of race, sex, or ethnicity—essentially outlawing affirmative action (it was passed with 54 percent of the vote that November). He spoke against Prop 209 at all the California shows. By helping the campaign against Prop 209, Springsteen was challenging his overwhelmingly white audience to account for its own position of privilege. At the concert in San Diego Springsteen said, "Republicans Bob Dole and Governor Wilson are cynically using this issue to play to our fears and to divide Californians along lines of race and gender. They need to be sent a message that we will not stand for it. There have been too many people who have sacrificed too much to go back now. If you believe in an America that provides justice and opportunity for all of its citizens, it is important for all Californians to stand together and vote no on Prop 209."[42]

In Fresno he urged the audience to support California Rural Legal Assistance, an organization that defended the rights of farmworkers and the rural poor and attempted to educate them about their rights: "I think it's ironic that so many of the people that work so hard to put food on our tables can't afford to have food themselves or who have kids that go to bed hungry. . . . Fifty years after Steinbeck wrote *Grapes of Wrath,* there's still people working under conditions in the Central Valley that as Americans, we really shouldn't tolerate. . . . Only language and the skin color is different. . . . They need your help and they deserve your support."[43] When Springsteen took music into the areas where much of it was set, he urged his audience to act on its emotional response to the songs.

Finally, Springsteen used Steinbeck to advocate for the value of popular culture that seeks to reach the mainstream. In San Jose Springsteen did not shy away from the connections he saw between Steinbeck and rock and roll; he said that Steinbeck's work became "as important to me as all the beautiful voices I heard on those records I loved as a kid. It had the same kind of musical power, just the beauty in the writing."[14] He expanded on this idea that rock and roll was legitimate culture in the introduction to "Across the Border" at other points on the tour. In a show in Asbury Park, New Jersey, in November 1996, he said,

> I grew up . . . in a house where you weren't exposed to a lot of culture or any-thing, there wasn't a lot of talk about what novels you read or films you saw or art. . . . Everybody was pretty busy keeping their heads above water. . . . The first thing I really remember was . . . the radio on in the kitchen in the morn-ing . . . just the sound of the singers' voices . . . an excitement that I couldn't imagine. . . . It was just some feeling of all the happiness and the pain that the world could hold coming . . . out of those little records. . . . Stuff that people thought was junk ended up being really subversive because it made you think, made you dream, made you imagine a world bigger than the one you knew and a life that was worth risking things for. . . . It was a real connection to the beauty and vitality of life. . . . When I was twenty-six, a friend of mine showed me John Ford's *Grapes of Wrath* and . . . I got something from that film that I got from all those records. I remember sitting there at the end of it watching the credits roll, thinking that that was what I wanted to do, I wanted to do work that would mean something. . . . I would try to inspire people. . . . There was something . . . in the film and in . . . the Steinbeck novel, and it . . . really was in those records too, I always found something heroic in them, . . . in a sense that people trying to make a connection, instead of hiding, coming out, showing themselves.[15]

Those "little records" are the benchmark for artistic value; *The Grapes of Wrath* earns its stripes by measuring up to the radio, not the other way around. Unlike some of his critics, Springsteen does not frame his interest in Steinbeck as a sign that he now understood "real" art and had outgrown rock and roll.[16] Springsteen's rock and roll is too often seen as the opposite of, or even irreconcilable with, his songs about the Vietnam War or his charitable work with food banks or his interest in Steinbeck or John Ford. When Springsteen discusses Steinbeck, he repudiates this idea. At the same time, though, Springsteen sees Steinbeck as enriched because he is acces-sible to a wide audience. As he said in 1995, "A lot of the things I really liked were things that were very mainstream records, they were from people who came from the outside of the mainstream but changed the mainstream to accommodate who they were by the force of their ideas and their talent and their presence. . . . I didn't live in an environment where there was a lot of cultural education, you weren't exposed to things that were outside of the mainstream. . . . The mainstream was what you had and what came across the radio I found liberating and meaningful."[17]

Ironically, Springsteen felt the need to scale back the popular trappings when he reengaged with Steinbeck. The *Ghost of Tom Joad* tour did not play in stadiums, and the album was not a massive hit. But the tour did continue for more than a year, playing in the United States, Canada, Australia, Japan, and many European countries (including Poland and the Czech Republic). Springsteen received a great deal of publicity. Newspapers reviewed his shows, and periodicals interviewed him. Writers discussed many of the ideas about class, race, poverty, and powerlessness that Springsteen raised. When he returned to playing with a rock band in 1999, he continued to work with community-support groups and to talk about political and social issues from the stage. Engaging with Steinbeck seemed to give Springsteen a way to reconceive the latter part of his career, again to mix mass success with political writing. His 2012 album *Wrecking Ball* is probably his most successful in this regard.

There is perhaps an unconscious desire to legitimate the "serious" study of Springsteen and other rock musicians by connecting them with literary authors. But Springsteen used Steinbeck in part to say that we need to take rock and roll songs as seriously as we do *The Grapes of Wrath*, that the artist's embrace of popularity can be a step toward claiming "one big soul." Springsteen's Steinbeck shows us the political and artistic value of Steinbeck's popular reach. Steinbeck's availability and accessibility invited Springsteen to respond, creating, we hope, an ever-widening community.

Notes

Thanks to David Bottimore, Charlie Board, Glenn Heath, and Flynn McLean for sharing their Springsteen materials.

1. See Arthur Mizener, "Does a Moral Vision of the Thirties Deserve a Nobel Prize?," *New York Times Book Review*, December 9, 1962, 43–45. For a similar approach to Springsteen, see John Lombardi, "St. Boss: The Sanctification of Bruce Springsteen and the Rise of Mass Hip," *Esquire*, December 1988, 139–53.

2. Bruce Springsteen, San Jose Event Center, San Jose, Calif., October 26, 1996, audience recording.

3. See, for example, Bryan Garman, *A Race of Singers: Whitman's Working-Class Hero from Guthrie to Springsteen* (Chapel Hill: University of North Carolina Press, 2000); Robert Coles, *Bruce Springsteen's America: The People Listening, a Poet Singing* (New York: Random House, 2003); Jim Cullen, *Born in the U.S.A.: Bruce Springsteen and the American Tradition* (New York: Harper Collins, 1997); and David Masciotra, *Working on a Dream: The Progressive Political Vision of Bruce Springsteen* (New York: Continuum, 2010).

4. Morris Dickstein, "Steinbeck and the Great Depression," *South Atlantic Quarterly* 103, no. 1 (Winter 2004): 111.

5. See the *MLA International Bibliography* for an index of literary scholarship.

6. Jay Parini traces the roots of this negative critical response to Malcolm Cowley's review of *The Grapes of Wrath* in the *New Republic*: "I can't agree with those critics who say that *The Grapes of Wrath* is the greatest novel of the last ten years; for example, it doesn't rank with the best of Hemingway or Dos Passos. But it belongs very high in the category of the great angry books like *Uncle Tom's Cabin* that have roused a people to fight against intolerable wrongs." Parini writes, "In Cowley's implicit refusal to take the novel seriously as a work of art one sees the origins of a critical response that would dog Steinbeck to the end." Parini, *John Steinbeck: A Biography* (New York: Henry Holt, 2005), 220.

7. Mizener, "Moral Vision," 44.

8. John Steinbeck, "Acceptance Speech for the Nobel Prize for Literature in 1962," in *A Casebook on* The Grapes of Wrath, ed. Agnes McNeill Donohue (New York: Thomas Crowell), 293.

9. Craig Werner, *A Change Is Gonna Come: Music, Race and the Soul of America* (Ann Arbor: University of Michigan Press, 2006), 11.

10. Ibid., 14.

11. Will Percy, "Rock and Read: Will Percy Interviews Bruce Springsteen," *Doubletake*, Spring 1998, 37.

12. Bruce Springsteen, *Songs* (New York: Avon, 1998), 68.

13. Paul Nelson, "Springsteen Fever," *Rolling Stone*, July 13, 1978, 12. Springsteen also became more interested in film in this period, especially film noir and the work of John Ford. This was possibly as a result of his deepening friendship with his producer, Jon Landau, who had worked as a film critic for *Rolling Stone* in the early 1970s. Springsteen told Percy that "films and novels and books, more so than music, are what really have been driving me since [the late seventies]." Percy, "Rock and Read," 37.

14. Robert Duncan, "Lawdamercy, Springsteen Saves!" *CREEM*, October 1978, 42.

15. Nelson, "Springsteen Fever," 12–13.

16. John Steinbeck, *Working Days: The Journals of* The Grapes of Wrath, *1938–1941*, ed. Robert DeMott (New York: Viking, 1989), 1.

17. Parini, *John Steinbeck*, 187.

18. In the fall of 1975, when Springsteen first played London, he was so unnerved by seeing the hall plastered with posters saying, "At Last London Is Ready for Bruce Springsteen!" that he ran around the theater and tore them all down. Dave Marsh, *Bruce Springsteen: Two Hearts, The Definitive Biography, 1972–2003* (New York: Routledge, 2004), 631. In preparing the release of *Darkness on the Edge of Town* he first proposed that the record be put out with no promotion at all: "I was so blown away by what happened last time, I initially thought of doing *no* ads. Just put it out, literally just put it out." Dave Marsh, "Bruce Springsteen Raises Cain," *Rolling Stone*, August 24, 1978, 40.

19. Bruce Springsteen cited in Marsh, *Two Hearts*, 631.

20. For example, Peter Knobler wrote in *Crawdaddy*, "On *Born to Run*, Bruce was flying down streets he knew, a flawless escape. On *Darkness*, he's being chased. It's not an easy album to listen to." Knobler, "Wounded in the Badlands," *Crawdaddy*, August 1978, 67. In the *New York Times* John Rockwell described the characters on the album as "lost and desperate, trying to retain their idealism and excitement of their youth but surrounded by the ghosts of former friends who have disappeared, sold out or settled down." Rockwell, "Jagger, Springsteen and the New Angst," *New York Times*, June 11, 1978, 30.

21. Bryan Garman summarizes the book this way: "*Pocket History* celebrates the mythic land of freedom and opportunity, asserting that the United States is an 'interesting' country 'because its people have been conscious of a peculiar destiny, because upon it have been fastened the hopes and aspirations of the human race.'" Garman, *Race of Singers*, 197.

22. Bruce Springsteen, introduction of Bobby Muller, Los Angeles Sports Arena, Los Angeles, Calif., August 20, 1981, audience recording.

23. This version of "This Land Is Your Land" is the one included on *Bruce Springsteen and the E Street Band Live 1975–1985*, Columbia, 1986. For a discussion of how Springsteen began to work with charities on tours, see Marsh, *Bruce Springsteen*, 492–502.

24. "Seeds," by Bruce Springsteen. Copyright © 1986 Bruce Springsteen (ASCAP). Reprinted by permission. International copyright secured. All rights reserved.

25. Percy, "Rock and Read," 41.

26. Ibid., 39.

27. Karen Schoemer, "Heart of Darkness," *Newsweek*, April 1, 1996, 67.

28. John Steinbeck, *Steinbeck: A Life in Letters*, ed. Elaine Steinbeck and Robert Wallsten (New York: Viking, 1975), 119.

29. Bruce Springsteen, interview by Bob Costas, *Columbia Records Radio Hour*, CBS Radio, November 21, 1995.

30. Edna Gunderson, "In 'Joad' Springsteen Answers the Ghosts of His Past," *USA Today*, December 1, 1995.

31. "The Ghost of Tom Joad," by Bruce Springsteen. Copyright © 1995 Bruce Springsteen (ASCAP). Reprinted by permission. International copyright secured. All rights reserved.

32. In 1940 Guthrie was asked by Victor Records to record a song about Ford's *The Grapes of Wrath;* the seventeen-verse song managed to summarize the entire film. Guthrie biographer Joe Klein writes that "Woody was tremendously— uncharacteristically—proud of the song, and when the *Daily Worker* gave much of its entertainment page one day to printing the words, he wrote, 'I think the ballad of the Joads is the best thing I've done so far.'" Klein, *Woody Guthrie: A Life* (New York: Alfred A. Knopf, 1980), 159.

33. On the liner notes to the album, Springsteen thanks the following "sources": Dale Maharidge and Michael Williamson, *Journey to Nowhere;* Morris Dees, *A Season for Justice;* Sebastian Rotella, "Children of the Border," *Los Angeles Times*, April 3, 1993; Mark Arax and Tom Gordon, "California's Illicit Farm Belt Export," *Los Angeles Times*, March 13, 1995; and John Ford's *The Grapes of Wrath*, which is listed as "based on the novel by John Steinbeck." Although not credited, "The Line" appears to be inspired in part by the film *The Border* (1982, directed by Tony Richardson), and "Galveston Bay" by *Alamo Bay* (1985, directed by Louis Malle). In concert Springsteen credited Jim Thompson's crime novel *The Killer Inside Me* (1952) as inspiration for "My Best Was Never Good Enough."

34. George Bluestone, *Novels into Film* (Baltimore: John Hopkins University Press, 1957), 159, 161.

35. Charles Cunningham, "Rethinking the Politics of *The Grapes of Wrath*," *Cultural Logic: A Journal of Marxist Theory and Practice* 5 (2002), paragraph 1. See also Michael Denning's reading of *The Grapes of Wrath* in *The Cultural Front: The Laboring of American Culture in the Twentieth Century* (New York: Verso, 1996).

36. Springsteen has written few songs from a woman's point of view; he seems to have difficulty imagining women as psychologically and emotionally disempowered in the way that he does men. The women in his songs are strong sufferers, not unlike Ma Joad in *The Grapes of Wrath*. For more on the political outlook of Steinbeck's fictional character Ma Joad, see Cyrus Zirakzadeh, chapter 1, this volume.

37. Bruce Springsteen, introduction to "Across the Border," San Jose Event Center, San Jose, Calif., October 26, 1996, audience recording.

38. Gavin Martin, "Hey Joad, Don't Make It Sad . . . (Oh, Go on Then)," *New Musical Express*, March 9, 1996, 30, 32.

39. "Galveston Bay," by Bruce Springsteen. Copyright © 1995 Bruce Springsteen (ASCAP). Reprinted by permission. International copyright secured. All rights reserved.

40. Garman, *Race of Singers*, 244.

41. The benefit was the result of meeting Elaine Steinbeck in December 1995 at the New York City show, where Springsteen inquired about the most appropriate organization for a donation to honor Steinbeck. In addition to the benefit concert, he made a personal donation of $50,000. See Claudia Perry, "A Voice for the Voiceless," *San Jose Mercury News*, October 25, 1996.

42. Springsteen, introduction to "Across the Border," San Diego, Calif., October 22, 1996, audience recording.

43. Springsteen, introduction to "Across the Border," Saroyan Theater, Fresno, Calif., October 23, 1996, audience recording.

44. Springsteen, introduction to "Across the Border," San Jose.

45. Springsteen, introduction to "Across the Border," Paramount Theater, Asbury Park, N.J., November 26, 1996, audience recording.

46. In an otherwise useful article about Steinbeck and Springsteen, Gavin Cologne-Brookes describes Springsteen's approach on *The Ghost of Tom Joad* as "mature" in contrast to a "youthful solipsism." Cologne-Brookes, "The Ghost of Tom Joad: Steinbeck's Legacy in the Songs of Bruce Springsteen" in *Beyond Boundaries: Rereading John Steinbeck*, ed. Susan Shillinglaw and Kevin Hearle (Tuscaloosa: University of Alabama Press, 2002), 34–46.

47. Springsteen, interview.

CHAPTER 11

Retelling an American Political Tale: A Comparison of Literary, Cinematic, and Musical Versions of *The Grapes of Wrath*

Cyrus Ernesto Zirakzadeh

AT THE TWENTY-FIFTH anniversary concert for the Rock and Roll Hall of Fame, at Madison Square Garden in 2009, Bruce Springsteen and the E Street Band with guest performer Tom Morello (the lead guitarist of the recently disbanded rock group Rage Against the Machine) performed a loud, electrified version of Springsteen's song "The Ghost of Tom Joad." Films of the performance record fans cheering wildly. To make sure that the listeners understood the importance of the song's message, Springsteen prefaced the performance with comments about being part of a long American musical tradition—stretching back to early folk, blues, and rock artists—that recognized the divergence in interests and values of "Main Street" and "Wall Street." The problems of American society are not new, Springsteen was intimating through his commentary, and recalling how past Americans responded can give twenty-first-century Americans clues about how to see and respond to their current crises.

The performance illustrates the continued use of *The Grapes of Wrath* to discuss often-ignored aspects of America—in particular, the personal suffering caused by deep downswings in the national economy, the tyranny of corporate capitalism, and the role of the state in protecting private property. Producers and consumers of popular culture in 2009 found meaning and relevance in a piece of literary fiction written decades before they were born. Steinbeck's tale is a cultural artifact that many Americans, living in different parts of the country and raised in different social circumstances, share.

Yet Steinbeck's story was not merely repeated at the concert. The story was modified. This is not surprising. When artists draw on public myths to discuss current conditions, they often move some of the original characters, fictitious events, and philosophic claims into the background and bring new elements to the foreground.

The constant remaking of a tale is evident when we juxtapose the narratives told in three periods by three sets of artists: the original *Grapes of Wrath* story, researched and composed by John Steinbeck during the Great Depression; the cinematic version of *The Grapes of Wrath*, which was written, directed, and produced during the Second World War and amid the New Deal recovery; and Springsteen's 2009 rendering of the tale during the so-called Great Recession of the early twenty-first century, when new forms of poverty were bubbling in cities and suburbs.[1] In each version the need and possibilities for progressive political action are depicted differently. Steinbeck highlights the failure of the current capitalist state and predicts a new social order arising from local initiatives by displaced small-scale farmers. The three filmmakers celebrate the effectiveness of New Deal experiments and hail the emergence of a new state-regulated form of capitalism. Springsteen's rockers express distrust toward the state yet, unlike Steinbeck, explore the creative anger of atomized victims instead of the resiliency and moxie of families.

The Fambly

As I have argued in chapter 1, the political message of Steinbeck's novel is simultaneously radical and conservative.[2] He denounces the evolution of American capitalism both through the story of the Joads and through the roughly one-dozen philosophic declarations, sociological essays, and human interest sketches that pepper the book and describe American life in general (as opposed to describing the fate of the Joads). Paradoxically, despite Steinbeck's relentless criticism of capitalism, the book's proposed solution is, in terms of culture, remarkably conservative. One should trust both the self-sacrificing maternal values found among older women in modest, middle-class families and the set of manly virtues, such as tenacity, curiosity, inventiveness, and self-reliance, found in many owners of small-scale family farms. According to the book, economic salvation cannot occur through normal political channels. Government officials too often side with the rich and, consequently, regulate the poor with loitering laws, antiunion laws, and other legislation that intimidates the homeless and punishes those without property. Because of the acute class bias in American politics, poor people must rely on themselves. And they will, the narrator assures readers. The men and women who formerly owned and labored on small farms, out of an instinctual drive for physical survival, will adjust and modify their frontier habits and will adopt appropriate collective values in the makeshift communities that they form along highways and in abandoned railcars. From these humble social seedlings a new society will emerge while the contemporary capitalist order inevitably declines and departs.

From the outset, the book contends that modern capitalism induces people in all walks of life—the desperately poor, the property-owning middle classes, and the extremely wealthy—to do some stupid, self-destructive things. Unlike literary romances about western expansion, such as Jack Schaefer's *Shane*, Steinbeck's tale is not one of conquering wilderness and transforming it into a home for civilized, virtuous people. The story of a westward trek springs from a series of materially motivated, shortsighted gambles by owners of both large and modest commercial properties.

In the book small-scale farmers in the southwest and the south-central United States decide to raise cotton in hopes of striking it big in the world economy. At the time, geopolitical conditions (the development of large standing armies, in particular, which needed uniforms and other forms of cloth) had made cotton a widely sought-after commodity.[3] Dreaming of increased revenue, the small farmers in Steinbeck's novel actually cheer for battles and death: "Get enough wars and cotton'll hit the ceiling."[4] This style of get-rich-quick calculation, according to the book's anonymous narrator, is the outcome of decades of social evolution, as the increasingly secure offspring of the first generation of settlers think less about physical survival amid critters, outlaws, and Indians and more and more about money. As the narrator puts it, over time "crops were reckoned in dollars, and land was valued by principal plus interest, and crops were bought and sold before they were planted. . . . And all their love was thinned with money, and all their fierceness dribbled away in interest until they were no longer farmers at all, but little shopkeepers of crops, little manufacturers who must sell before they can make."[5]

The book reports that specialization in cotton, while arguably sensible from a commercial point of view, inadvertently exhausted the soil and destroyed its natural cohesion. The barren topsoil became powdery. Winds then stirred enormous dust storms, which made the air unbreathable and the farmland unusable. As a result, family farmers, who once had hoped to master the puzzling ups and downs of commercial markets and make a killing, could no longer grow enough saleable crops to pay outstanding loans and to keep their mortgages afloat.

Finding themselves deeply in debt, a group of small farmers in the story leave for California, abandoning their farmsteads to equally shortsighted and narrowly money-oriented bankers and realtors who themselves can stay afloat only by generating revenues and profits. Even the bankers and realtors are, according to the narrator, "caught in something larger than themselves."[6] Pressured constantly to increase profit margins, the bankers and realtors tear down the former residents' hovels and resell the now-exhausted land to absentee owners in the East. Aggressive profit seeking from all quarters thus eviscerates once-healthy communities of self-sufficient yeoman farmers. Because of a complex yet traceable set of market pressures, the distinctively egalitarian social order, which allegedly had contributed to making everyday people in America nobler, tougher, and freer than the common people in other nations, was rapidly disappearing. Capitalist development and the egalitarian and self-sufficient culture of the western pioneers had proven, in practice, to be incompatible. In the real world the American dreams of a free-market economy and a free-and-equal social order are not complementary but discordant (or so the book argues).

What should a marginalized person do in such circumstances? Many of the book's fictional scenes and events assail the Horatio Alger myth that an individual can succeed through effort, honesty, and persistence. The half-dozen male members of the Joad family hope to obtain gainful employment in California and then, after prudently saving wages, purchase new farmland. (The women, whose beliefs and values are more communal and nurturing, are less optimistic about salvation through the labor market.) The men's dream of salvation through hard work proves unrealizable despite their dogged efforts. According to the book, the problem is structural. Gigantic incorporated farms already monopolize all potential farmland in California (even land that is not yet being cultivated). Meanwhile, the abundance of dispossessed farmers makes it easy for agribusinesses to pay below-subsistence wages for temporary, backbreaking work. When the migrants manage to find potentially gainful work, the agribusinesses further exploit the wage earners through company stores that charge artificially high prices and through the manipulation of the scales when pickers present their boxes of fruit. All the while private security forces and local vigilante groups terrorize the economically vulnerable peons. Local police officers, enforcing taxpayers' health and safety and antiunion laws, function not to promote justice but to buttress the stratified social order. Sheriffs and deputized civilians identify, harass, arrest, and oftentimes even expel from towns rebellious individuals among the migrant farmworkers who might try to organize collective resistance.

The book's thesis is that the situation is untenable. The country's economic order and its political supports are causing an increasing number of hardworking and normally law-abiding citizens to die from hunger and exposure. As a result, the newest class of American poor (that is, eager wage laborers from middle-class, property-owning backgrounds) angrily ask why they should starve while others live in opulence. In the book, righteous rage has reached a boiling point. As the narrator puts it toward the end of the story, "In the eyes of the people there is the failure; and in the eyes of the hungry there is a growing wrath. In the souls of the people the grapes of wrath are filling and growing heavy, growing heavy for the vintage."[7]

What political outcome might these heavy grapes produce? Many American readers in the 1930s would, of course, fear a proletarian revolution led by a professional vanguard party. Steinbeck, who defended individualism against proponents of state socialism throughout his life and who resisted the romantic view of the Soviet Union that some of his friends and neighbors held, predicted a different sort of revolution brewing in the United States.[8] The novel forecasts a rural anarcho-syndicalist movement in which the state plays a minimal role in economic matters and small teams of workers organize production and make decisions about distribution.

In the novel there is no obvious escape from poverty for the thousands of formerly property-owning families, such as the Joads, Wilsons, and other travelers on Highway 66, *except* to band together and draw on dual traditions of maternal self-sacrifice and manly courage, defiance, and inventiveness. As Alfred Kazin points out, the hungry and homeless characters in Steinbeck's books are not simply victims to be pitied. They are, in Kazin's phrase, "primitive, with a little cunning."[9] According to the unnamed narrator of Steinbeck's novel, the newly dispossessed laborers experiment daily with economic arrangements along the highways. On the fly, they construct new cultural habits, laws, and beliefs.[10] "At first the families were timid," the narrator informs the reader, "but gradually the technique of building worlds became their technique. Then leaders emerged, then laws were made, then codes came into being."[11] Allegedly, former owners of small farms and failed businesses, out of necessity, finally jettison previous notions of private property, develop a more collective understanding of fate, and experiment with owning and using property (including tools and machinery) in common.[12] Worried about physical survival, these strangers who meet on the roadside are compelled to talk to their overnight neighbors about their sufferings and to swap conjectures about new ways of owning property and working the land.

Among men, in particular, the initially competitive sense of "I" morphs into a more inclusive sense of "we."[13] Through repeated defeats in their attempts to succeed, they swallow their pride and confess publicly that they are bewildered. Their prior experience as self-employed producers has fostered dignity and creativity. Their highly developed sense of self-reliance and initiative allows them to question conventional understandings of property and ownership and to explore the sharing of labor and tools in a decentralized, democratic manner.

Meanwhile, the women, having been responsible in the past for the feeding, clothing, and healing of men and children, extend their sense of duty to strangers and expand their collectivist outlook to poor people outside their immediate biological families. It is not an accident that Ma Joad is the first person in the Joad family to wonder aloud what might happen if all the poor in the country acted as a unified political actor. She confides to her firstborn, "Tommy, I got to thinkin' an' dreamin' an' wonderin'. They say there's a hun'erd thousand of us shoved out. If we was all mad the same way, Tommy—they wouldn't hunt nobody down."[14] Nor is it by accident that the book ends with an initially selfish teenager, Rose of Sharon, discarding fantasies of the "good life" that she had acquired from movie magazines. Instead, she begins to feel, think, and even act like her mother and ministers to others in need. In the book's closing scene Rose has completely shed her narrowly individualistic worldview and altruistically breast-feeds a starving and unknown man in an abandoned barn. The Joads have learned to treat their fellow losers in the capitalist system as part of a universal family.

The book contends that the character traits and social habits fostered on family farms in the United States will lead to a new type of postcapitalist order. The future is not some sort of state-controlled system akin to the Soviet Union. Instead, America's healthy frontier culture will be preserved and enhanced. Free, self-directing individuals will prevail without the problems of large-scale private corporations and far-flung, unpredictable markets.

The State

The tone of Steinbeck's novel is apocalyptic. The book opens with the violent lyrics of "The Battle Hymn of the Republic" and closes with a description of a great flood engulfing all in sight but a small cluster of poor folk stranded on a hill. While it discusses a family's misfortunes, the book is not primarily a maudlin tale of a single family's struggles. It first and foremost tells of the impending death of an evil economic order and the triumph of a culturally superior way of life still found on America's rural frontier.

The tone of the movie, released only a year after the publication of the book, is very different. "The Battle Hymn of the Republic" is never heard by moviegoers. Instead, the filmmakers use different tempos of "Red River Valley" in their soundtrack (a nostalgic version at the beginning of the film and a jaunty version at the end). In addition, the great flood scene and the image of Rose of Sharon breast-feeding a stranger are expunged. The film instead closes with Ma Joad proclaiming that "the people" will never be defeated by temporary economic setbacks. Then the screen is filled with a long shot of a seemingly endless line of jalopies chugging up a gentle hillock, followed by screen credits and the upbeat, full orchestral rendering of "Red River Valley" as the final piece of background music. Peace, hope, and gratitude replace the book's sense of anger and desperation and its predictions of a radical transformation of the economy.[15]

The difference in tone in part reflects the different political beliefs of the author and the filmmakers. John Ford directed the film, Darryl F. Zanuck produced it and played a large role in the final editing, and Nunnally Johnson wrote the screenplay. Although these filmmakers differed somewhat as to Roosevelt's New Deal (Nunnally was an avid advocate and defender of the government's new economic initiatives; Zanuck was more guarded), all three believed in the general efficiency of capitalism and distrusted collectivist experiments in communist countries. As Zanuck put it, "I guess what I detest more than anything is any form of regimentation or any type of suppression of the individual. So far as I can see, or far as history will let me see, the Democratic system is the only chance for survival, and the free enterprise system (call it Capitalistic if you like) is the only form of commerce that results in general prosperity."[16] The three also were advocates of conventional family life. Ford, in fact, believed that the film version of *The Grapes of Wrath* was "before all else the story of a family, the way it reacts, how it is shaken by a serious problem, which overwhelms it. It is not a social film on this problem; it's a study of a family."[17] Ford, of course, was not manufacturing an entirely new story. Steinbeck indeed gave former frontier families a valued role in his narrative. But he saw these families as a counterweight to America's capitalist practices. Steinbeck's family therefore had a socioeconomic significance that Ford, who differentiated social questions from domestic life, missed.

Given the filmmakers' ideological predispositions, it is not surprising that capitalism appears far less ruthless and shady in the film than it does in the novel. The filmmakers left out of the movie several incidents in the book in which used-car salespersons, foremen in the fields, and store clerks try to hoodwink impoverished Americans. These daily problems that (according to the book) capitalism poses for everyday Americans are not represented on screen. In addition, the filmmakers do not use the voice of an unseen speaker to echo the anticapitalist commentary that the anonymous narrator makes in Steinbeck's book. Moviegoers consequently hear no explication of the logic of capitalism and no prediction of the inevitable growth of "grapes of wrath." Finally, the artists omitted from their film several incidents in the book in which midlevel government functionaries, police officers in particular, badger the homeless migrant workers and, conversely, aid rural big businesses.[18]

According to the film, the problems facing the farmers are natural (the inexplicable dust storms that render the land useless for agriculture) and mechanical (the faceless army of tractors that level the farmsteads and that no one seems to control). The film links neither terror to the farmers' get-rich-quick schemes. The family is depicted as a collection of innocent victims unmotivated by greed, not as eager participants in market transactions who are partly responsible for their own straits.

There are several mean characters in the film: insensitive landowners, greedy sales clerks, and vicious vigilantes. Their unkind behavior appears as reflections of unkind personalities, not the byproduct of day-to-day market

forces that compel such behavior. There are, conversely, some unexpectedly kind characters in the film, such as a police officer in California who
had emigrated from Oklahoma, who never appeared in the book. The film
seems to say that good and bad folks appear throughout society and thereby
implies that the levers of power are not entirely in the hands of the wealthy
and cruel.

The movie, in fact, suggests that governments are effective in helping
poor families to survive momentarily tough times. This becomes evident
when the Joads visit a federal government camp for migrant workers. Lasting twenty-five minutes, the camp sequence is by far the longest of the film's
fifteen visual series.[19] A similar camp appears in Steinbeck's novel, but it
plays a smaller role in the arc of the story and has different characteristics
and consequences.

Steinbeck, when researching poor people's lives for his novel, had visited a newly established federal camp for migrant workers. The residents
and local administrators nicknamed their humble center Weedpatch, which
is the name that Steinbeck chose for the fictional camp in the novel. According to some scholars, the lanky manager of the fictional Weedpatch
camp is modeled after Tom Collins, a person Steinbeck interviewed while
conducting research.[20] Collins was hardly a typical government functionary.
Although on the government's payroll, Collins was by instinct a participatory
democrat (if not an anarchist) who distrusted state officials and believed in
people running their own affairs. Having been born out of wedlock and
abandoned as a child, he had been misused and abused by government
officials. He therefore treated his camp as a utopian experiment in which
residents, with only minimal direction from state professionals, determine
and enforce their own rules.[21] This political outlook appears in the novel, as
the Collins character intentionally avoids meddling in the residents' affairs
and instead urges them to make their own policies and organize their own
events.

In the book the federal camp plays an important role in that it offers the migrants a respite from the grind of seeking gainful employment.
Although the Joads live in relative comfort at the camp (which includes
systems of indoor plumbing that befuddle the former farmers), the camp's
promise is in many ways illusory. The Joad men, unable to find work but able
to secure food and shelter, become despondent and lethargic. The lassitude

alarms Ma Joad, who reasons that the government camp, while providing a short-term salve, cannot save the family from its broader, chronic economic problems.[22] She badgers the passive menfolk into packing the jalopy and resuming their search for stable, gainful employment. The job search after the layover at Weedpatch camp proves futile, however, and leads to ever more dreadful consequences and new forms of suffering, including the malnutrition of Rose of Sharon and the stillbirth delivery of her child. Like Circe's island in Homer's *Odyssey,* Weedpatch camp offers the visitors merely a temporary escape from real-world responsibility. It does not provide a serious solution to the family's dire economic situation.[23]

In the movie the camp appears almost at the end of the story. Its modest name is transformed into the more impressive sounding "Wheat Patch Camp," which, among other things, evokes images of food, nutrition, and maybe even prosperity. On the screen, the camp administrator, who encourages residents' self-rule, does not resemble the long and lanky Collins. Instead, the camp overseer (played by the actor Grant Mitchell) bears an uncanny physical resemblance to President Franklin Delano Roosevelt, whose administration had temporarily funded such camps for migrant farmworkers. This image evokes a sympathetic awareness of this real-world New Deal initiative for fending off the worst consequences of market downswings and signals to the viewer the federal government's commitment to helping the country's less fortunate. Moreover, in the film version the camp fulfills its promise. It successfully revives the will of the Joad family (rather than making its members lethargic), and they leave the camp with high hopes. At the movie's conclusion, the clan, hearing rumors of twenty days' work north of the camp, eagerly leaves for the nearby job prospects. Pa Joad says that life has dealt the family some hard blows. Ma Joad chuckles, gives a short speech, and then, squinting with determination, proclaims, "We're the people that live. They can't wipe us out. They can't lick us. We'll go on forever, Pa, 'cause we're the people." A few minutes later, the screen credits appear.

Visually and sonically, the closing conveys to the audiences that with proper government aid, the hardworking poor in America will enjoy success in America's capitalist economy. The family, the state, and the increasingly corporate system of production and property ownership can harmoniously coexist, and they can do so to one another's advantage.

The Lonely Individual

On a superficial level, the literary and cinematic versions of *The Grapes of Wrath* tell the same tale about a dispossessed Oklahoma farming family struggling against odds to survive. A thoughtful observer, however, will notice that different messages about capitalism, the state, and interfamilial relationships are told. Steinbeck's novel contends that a radical reconstruction of the American economic system is needed and that this is most likely to occur through spontaneous collective action and makeshift alliances among nonelites. Notions of anarchism, local-level experiments with socialism, and rule from below complement the book's relentless critique of America's capitalist economy. In the Ford-Zanuck-Johnson movie the problems of capitalism seem transitory and correctable, the New Deal state seems willing and able to help the Depression-era poor survive (and even prosper in the end), and populist experiments in local economic self-governance appear unneeded. As the literary critic Warren French points out, even though the novel and the film employ similar characters, settings, and experiences, "they are very different works, expounding different philosophies and presenting the same basic social situation, the plight of migrant farm workers in California in the late 1930s, in quite different ways."[24]

Springsteen's song "The Ghost of Tom Joad" departs both from Steinbeck's vision of daring economic experiments among dispossessed families and from the Ford-Zanuck-Johnson upbeat tale of a capitalist economy that is workable when supplemented by moderate government intervention.[25] Springsteen instead describes the struggles of a lonely man who one night at dusk hears the voice of Tom Joad.

Tom Joad is a peculiar character in both the book and the movie. In the book Tom is impetuous, obstinate, moody, and violent and somehow repeatedly finds himself in situations in which killing seems the right thing to do. After impulsively killing one of the vigilantes who murdered his friend Jim Casy, a labor-organizing former preacher from Oklahoma, Tom hides in a cave near a thicket. His mother visits him and gives him some money and food with which to survive. They talk briefly. Ma asks a few questions, while Tom rambles incoherently, jumping among topics and using short, staccato sentences. Among other things, he contemplates becoming an "outlaw," fantasizes about anarchistic collectives ("Throw out the cops that ain't our people. All work together for our own thing—all farm our own lan'."), and admits in frustration that many of his friend's words about an overarching collective fate and the value of helping others are easier to parrot than to understand.[26] Some of Jim's sayings, however, intuitively make sense to Tom. They involve the importance of not battling alone and seeing one's fate as intertwined with the fates of other sufferers. Implications of these beliefs are that whatever physically happens to a person is secondary. One's spirit continues to live in people's angry denouncements of unfairness and in their fights to change the world so that hungry children can eat and once again laugh, so that police brutality ends, and so that everyday people can live in their own homes and directly consume the products of their labor. Tom confesses that he does not fully understand what Jim was driving at but he is becoming obsessed with Jim's statements and at times he even feels as if he can see his deceased friend.[27]

Ma Joad fears what might later happen to her obviously confused son. As she leaves the cave, she fights back her tears. This is the last that the reader sees or hears of Tom. He appears as a temperamentally hotheaded adult left alone in a cave where he is valiantly wrestling with difficult social, personal, and religious questions. He possibly is doomed to a life of further violence and tragic run-ins with the law; he is also possibly on the verge of conversion into an altruistic human being who wishes to help the poor and the powerless.

In the movie Tom is a different sort of creature, more pensive and better able to express his gentler side. In his final speaking scenes he is not hiding underground "like a rabbit" (the words used in the novel).[28] He meets with and gives parting kisses to Ma Joad near the dance floor and parking lot of Wheat Patch camp. As in the book, Tom has recently killed a local vigilante in retaliation for the death of his labor-organizing friend Jim Casy. Now, observing investigators looking at the license plates of the camp's vehicles, Tom infers that the police are onto him and that his presence poses a threat to his family. He therefore decides to leave the family.

When saying goodbye to Ma Joad, Tom repeats many of the statements in the book, but his monologue is shorter, less rambling, and more logically coherent. It is also slightly less edgy. Tom's dream about common people seizing land and then expelling the police is absent in the movie. In the film (but not in the book) Ma Joad earnestly asks Tom if he will kill again, and Tom assures her that he will not. But the heart of Tom's original speech remains. He tells his mother that even if they do not meet again, she will see the significance of his life wherever the poor and hungry struggle for better lives, wherever police beatings are challenged, wherever common people fight for the right to own their homes, and wherever men passionately yell about injustices and children laugh. Then he leaves his mother (rather than his mother leaving him). He ascends a hill against the backdrop of a rising sun.

The series of images stirs the viewer's hopes, partly because the actor playing Tom is Henry Fonda, whom many moviegoers in 1940 would have associated with his performance as Abraham Lincoln in John Ford's 1939 film *Young Mr. Lincoln*. In that film the male character also climbs a hill at the end of the movie and moves toward his destiny. Are we seeing another strong-willed western leader (with a clear moral compass) in the making?[29]

In Springsteen's song Tom never physically appears, and there is no retelling of his prison days, his evolving friendship with Jim Casy, his travels in California with his dispossessed family, his two killings, or his final flight from the law. The song only paraphrases key passages from Tom's farewell to his mother.

The song comprises three verses, each with its own topic that provides background for the next part of the song. The first verse describes the legal vulnerability, economic insecurity, and physical suffering of common people in America at the end of the twentieth century. The lyrics are filled with images of restless people seeking food and shelter. The second verse focuses on the behavior of a solitary, unnamed individual preparing to sleep in a cardboard box. The person might be a preacher, as he carries a prayer book with him, but the individual might not be a clergyman, as he also carries a gun. In the final verse the ghost of Tom Joad appears and makes comments that might provide succor to this apparently unemployed and homeless man who cannot find answers in typical American sources of inspiration: the highway and the Bible. The down-on-his-luck male knows that America's vaunted highway system does not lead to adventure and individual liberation ("nobody's kiddin' nobody about where it goes"). The Bible's promise that in Heaven "the last shall be first and the first shall be last" likewise proves frustrating when (according to the song's lyrics) you "got a hole in your belly and gun in your hand" and are "sleeping on a pillow of solid rock."[30]

The theme of unfulfilled dreams leading individual men to confusion and despair is common in Springsteen's work. In his lyrics, men who have labored in good faith in either the military or a large company suddenly find themselves unemployed and unemployable as factories unexpectedly close down and the surrounding communities go bankrupt without the infusion of wages.[31] Working men's friendships and domestic lives suffer accordingly. Relationships with coworkers end, marriages break up, homes are lost, couples separate. There is no local community—no friendship or partner-ship—that can help individuals cope, that can repair broken hearts, or that can spawn new, energizing dreams. Men, as they age, find themselves alone, poor, and stunned about what went wrong. To borrow some of Springsteen's most common metaphors, the United States is filled with innumerable eco-nomic lost souls who feel as if they are burning and dying inside and who are seeking protective cover in backstreets and alleys.[32] These are all com-mon images in the history of rock and roll, and Springsteen freely borrows from the genre's storehouse of images and employs them in his stories about heartbreak and hard luck in post–World War II America.[33]

Springsteen never dissects the large-scale market forces that cause such human disaster. His lyrics contain nothing as systematic as the narra-tor's musings in Steinbeck's novel—and this is true of all of his songs, not just "The Ghost of Tom Joad." Springsteen, however, continuously insists that such suffering is the result not of personal failings but of an unfair economic system that abuses those born without wealth. Those common-ers who cannot achieve upward mobility become despondent, scared, and withdrawn. He unflinchingly refuses to concede that America's promise of a land of plenty and opportunity for all has been realized. As he declared from the stage during his 1990s Tom Joad tour, "If you believe that America has metamorphosized into a race-and-gender-blind society, you also believe in Santa Claus."[34]

In "The Ghost of Tom Joad" Springsteen's frank and unsentimental per-spective is extended to conventional politics. Springsteen's song shares with Steinbeck's novel the presumption that government in America favors the wealthy and often is an oppressor of, not a friend to, the poor. According to the lyrics, police helicopters survey cityscapes in search of unruly transients (this point is made aurally in a cover version of Springsteen's song by Rage Against the Machine in which screaming guitars convey the mechanized surveillance that poor people daily confront). The first verse sardonically contrasts President George H. W. Bush's grandiloquent proclamations of a "new world order" with the reality of extensive poverty, families sleeping in their cars in the Southwest with "no home no job no peace no rest."[35]

Local overnight shelters for the homeless cannot handle the number of people seeking help. Unemployed Americans find no Weedpatch, much less a Wheat Patch, offering even temporary respite from hunger, disease, and exposure to the elements. According to the song's anonymous narrator, the government has cruelly left the country's poorer inhabitants to their own devices. The government is too corrupt to trust.[36]

The second verse adopts a more psychological orientation to America's situation and describes a murderous anger brewing within those individuals who are socially isolated. The homeless man, losing patience with biblical promises of a rosier afterlife for those who are meek and peaceful, carries a gun and contemplates its use.

This again is a recurrent motif in Springsteen's music. Everyday people, when repeatedly denied opportunities to find dignified and steady work, become enraged. Not knowing where to direct the anger, they tend to resort to violence, commit petty and serious crimes, and harm either others or themselves. Sometimes in his songs people direct the anger inward, feel ashamed and unable, become emotionally burnt out, and give up fighting for a better life.[37]

Thus far Springsteen's song is depressing. The first two verses contend that America is falling apart socially and that, because of economic deprivation and social disintegration, Americans are becoming psychologically weak and unstable. In the final verse and chorus the man, having smoked a discarded cigarette and vainly looked for comfort in a Bible, sits with and overhears statements by a phantom who is speaking to his mother, Ma Joad.

This scene can be challenging for a listener to envision, and for some listeners it may even seem wildly implausible. But there are ways to make sense of Springsteen's ghost. Could it be that the economically marginalized and socially disconnected man (possibly a former preacher) is now hallucinating? Or alternatively, is it possible that the man is obsessed by something he once heard or perhaps something he once read in the more radical passages of the Bible—similar to the experience of Tom, who, in Steinbeck's novel, has heard some challenging ideas about solidarity and thereafter thinks that he can see his dead friend Jim Casy?

Whatever the cause of the apparition, the homeless man eavesdrops and learns of a new option for dealing with his dire circumstances. The ghost declares to his invisible mother that he will be present wherever poor folk fight back against hunger, joblessness, police brutality, and hatred. "Fightin" and "strugglin'" are the dominant motifs in the semi-soliloquy, which is in keeping both with Tom's obstinate personality in Steinbeck's book and with the statements by Henry Fonda in the movie. The ghost neither expands on a transcendentalist theory of an oversoul that all people share (the doctrine that Jim Casy vainly had tried to teach Tom in the novel) nor defends labor unions (an implied vocation in the film's version of Tom's farewell speech).[38] The ghost also does not advocate the people seizing property and collectively ruling themselves, which Tom mentions in passing in the book. The apparition simply calls for an individual's militant resistance to all forms of oppression and solidarity with others on the margin of society. In the Madison Square Garden performance the song then morphed into an incendiary instrumental solo featuring Morello that was both loud and blisteringly fast, with tapping, scratching, sweep picking, thick distortion, and whammy-bar screams and crashes.

Springsteen and his fellow musicians announce through the song's lyrics, electrified sound, and pyrotechnic solo that a political powder keg exists in America. Unlike the various pundits who recently have predicted a decline in working-class politics in America, the band insists that chronically unemployed Americans are not simply giving up.[39] They are becoming embittered, enraged, and emboldened by their sufferings. They have ceased to be soothed by politicians' promises of boundless economic opportunity for all and by biblical injunctions to be patient. A willingness to react like the impertinent Tom Joad is spreading. Fury is increasingly common among America's socially decimated poor, alongside a newly discovered feeling of solidarity.

But if the musicians' assessment of the poor is accurate, what is to be done politically? What collective projects should be undertaken? How can the economy be redesigned? How can the bias in America's political process be corrected? Springsteen's songs never address these topics. At concerts he sometimes sings of leaping on a metaphysical train to a better world and helping others jump aboard (a common image in soul, blues, and R&B music), and he sometimes mimics a gospel revival show (see chapter 10, by Lauren Onkey, for more on these concert rituals). But he offers no practical, tactical advice on how to organize and channel the anger of lonely, disconnected people beyond urging people to be active in local social service organizations.[40]

Moreover, Springsteen's lyrics in "The Ghost of Tom Joad" are ultimately ambiguous. He does not imitate Steinbeck and claim to be seeing a new society already evolving on the edges of highways. He never predicts that the poor will embrace the ghost's call for solidarity, and we do not learn if the hobo will follow the ghost. Indeed, the song's second verse suggests a troubling possibility: that the frustration of chronic and inescapable poverty can easily lead to understandable yet counterproductive violence, whenever a person finds "a hole in your belly and a gun in your hand."[41]

Springsteen's version of the Joad saga thus diverges both from Ford, Zanuck, and Johnson's faith in New Deal liberalism and from Steinbeck's optimistic forecast of a spontaneous, decentralized socialism led by former family farmers. Springsteen's rendition of the tale defends no specific political program or economic policy. It is instead a paean to social activism by individuals. The musical composition calls on listeners to face the extent of injustice in America and, more concretely, to recognize a troubling social psychology that is emerging from the closing of rust-belt companies, from the globalization of manufacturing and heavy industry, from the migration of capital to nonunionized regions of the world, and from the overall collapse of domestic employment opportunities since the Vietnam War. A solution, the song suggests, may be for individuals to try to reach out to those in need and behave more altruistically. The allusion to the Depression-era story, in addition, might prompt listeners to recall that during the 1930s famished Americans formed unions that crossed racial lines, called general strikes in San Francisco and other major cities, supported avowed socialist candidates who ran for public office, and descended en masse on Washington.

Whether Springsteen's antistate, voluntarist ideas can satisfactorily address the complex economic problems, psychological pain, and enormous governmental structures that are represented in the various versions of *The Grapes of Wrath* is an open question. Steinbeck and the three filmmakers, trusting in farming families and the state, do not broach the question of how unattached individuals might constructively respond to economic dislocation. In times of chronic unemployment and social breakdown, it is a question worth asking.

Notes

Arguments in this chapter were first presented at the 2004 American Political Science Association meeting and the 2005 Western Political Science Association meeting. The author thanks Michael McCann, Laurie Naranche, and Simon Stow for their reflections on those conference papers and thanks the two anonymous reviewers for the University Press of Kentucky for their useful comments on an earlier draft of the chapter.

1. The phrase *Great Recession* is useful insofar as it helps readers imagine both the stock market crash that began at the end of George W. Bush's second term and the sudden halt to macroeconomic growth in the United States during the first two decades of the twenty-first century. The phrase is also potentially misleading, however, for at least two reasons. First, because the phrase is so historically specific, *Great Recession* can imply that the widespread economic doldrums of the early twenty-first century were largely, if not solely, a consequence of irresponsible banking practices. That is, that the Great Recession was due to human error and greed among a few plutocrats and not to a structural problem endemic to capitalism itself. Second, the term *recession* tends to be used euphemistically, to suggest that the multiyear recession during the early twenty-first century is a normal pause (or what defenders of the economic order call a momentary "market correction") in the story of American capitalism's otherwise endless growth. The phrase thus obscures the possibility that (1) the broad market downturn of the Great Recession is an example of what many Marxist historians and economists call a "crisis of overproduction and underconsumption" that is common in capitalist societies and (2) the so-called Great Recession therefore has striking similarities to the Great Depression of the 1930s and could be a harbinger of tough times ahead.

As I will elaborate later in this chapter, the explanation for the Great Depression in *The Grapes of Wrath* is based on the notion that the dynamics of capitalist competition, in the long run, undermine economic security and prosperity. The book's extended critique of the entire logic of capitalism is therefore radical. In fact, it has some similarities to a common Marxist view of capitalism being inevitably unworkable and unsalvageable. Of course, this does not mean that Steinbeck's politics and political vision were in a serious sense Marxist. While his critique resembles the type of arguments about the destructive power of market competition in human affairs that Marxists sometimes make (although they also recognize the creative capacity of capitalism), his view of the industrial working class and his thoughts about the state's roles in economic development are quite different from what Marx and his intellectual descendants (regardless of whether they are communist or social democratic) have advanced. For an explication of how some Marxist economists and historians make sense of the underlying logic of capitalist slides and slumps, see Paul M. Sweezy, *The Theory of Capitalist Development: Principles of Marxian Political Economy* (New York: Monthly Review Press, 1942).

2. For more on these two sides of Steinbeck's political thinking, see Cyrus

Ernesto Zirakzadeh, "John Steinbeck on the Political Capacities of Everyday Folk: Moms, Reds, and Ma Joad's Revolt," *Polity* 36, no.4 (2004): 595–618; and chapter 1, this volume.

3. John Steinbeck, The Grapes of Wrath *and Other Writings, 1936–1941* (New York: Library of America, 1996), 243. All *Grapes of Wrath* page citations refer to this edition of the novel.

4. Ibid.

5. Ibid., 456.

6. Ibid., 242.

7. Ibid., 581.

8. Rick Wartzman, *Obscene in the Extreme: The Burning and Banning of John Steinbeck's* The Grapes of Wrath (New York: PublicAffairs, 2008), 75–76; Jackson J. Benson, *The True Adventures of John Steinbeck, Writer* (New York: Viking Press, 1984), 295, 315–16, 424–25; John Steinbeck, *Steinbeck: A Life in Letters*, ed. Elaine Steinbeck and Robert Wallsten (New York: Viking Press, 1975), 120; John Steinbeck, *Log from the Sea of Cortez*, in Grapes of Wrath *and Other Writings*, 729–31, 927; John Steinbeck, America and Americans *and Selected Nonfiction*, ed. Susan Shillinglaw and Jackson J. Benson (New York: Viking, 2002), 25–27, 89–90.

9. Alfred Kazin, *On Native Grounds: An Interpretation of Modern American Prose Literature* (New York: Harcourt Brace, 1942), 399.

10. Steinbeck, *Grapes of Wrath*, 416–23.

11. Ibid., 419.

12. Ibid., 369–71, 416–23, 456–64.

13. Ibid., 370–71.

14. Ibid., 291.

15. Several superb analyses of the film have been published, including George Bluestone, *Novels into Film: The Metamorphosis of Fiction into Cinema* (Baltimore, Md.: Johns Hopkins Press, 1957), 147–69; Warren French, *Filmguide to* The Grapes of Wrath (Bloomington: Indiana University Press, 1973); Russell Campbell, "Trampling Out the Vintage: Sour Grapes," in *The Modern American Novel and the Movies*, ed. Gerald Peary and Roger Shatzk (New York: Frederick Unger, 1978), 107–18; Vivian C. Sobchack, "*The Grapes of Wrath* (1940): Thematic Emphasis through Visual Style," *American Quarterly* 31, no. 5 (1979): 596–615; Joseph R. Millichap, *Steinbeck and Film* (New York: Frederick Ungar, 1983), 26–50; Louis Owens, The Grapes of Wrath: *Trouble in the Promised Land* (Boston: Twayne, 1989), 96–105; Leslie Gossage, "The Artful Propaganda of Ford's *The Grapes of Wrath*," in *New Essays on* The Grapes of Wrath, ed. David Wyatt (Cambridge: Cambridge University Press, 1990), 101–25; and Michael Denning, *The Cultural Front: The Laboring of American Culture in the Twentieth Century*

(London: Verso, 1997), 260–72. All of these works have influenced both my current appreciation of the film and my understanding of its parallels and divergences from the novel.

16. Quoted in Wartzman, *Obscene in the Extreme*, 204. See also Campbell, "Trampling Out the Vintage," 110–13.

17. Quoted in Tag Gallagher, *John Ford: The Man and His Films* (Berkeley: University of California Press, 1986), 177. See also Campbell, "Trampling Out the Vintage," 115–16. For a comparison of Ford's political orientation and those of his fellow filmmakers, see Richard H. Pells, *Radical Visions and American Dreams: Culture and Social Thought in the Depression Years* (Middletown, Conn.: Wesleyan University Press, 1973), 279–81.

18. While many scholars have argued that the movie and the novel differ in these ways, they disagree about the reasons for the filmmakers' revisions of Steinbeck's original story. Millichap believes Ford's deeply rooted views about family and about America's bountifulness influenced how he filmed and, in effect, told the story. Millichap, *Steinbeck and Film*, 32–36. Bluestone contends that differences between the media of literature and film affect the types of stories that can and cannot be told: "An art whose limits depend on a moving image, mass audience, and industrial production is bound to differ from an art whose limits depend on language, a limited audience and individual creations. In short, the filmed novel, in spite of certain resemblances, will inevitably become a different artistic entity from the novel on which it is based." Bluestone, *Novels into Film*, 63–64. Wartzman offers a more standard political explanation. He argues that myriad pressures, from Wall Street anger to the investigations by the Hayes Office to condemnation by the Catholic Church, caused the filmmakers to mute the more radical aspects of the novel. Wartzman, *Obscene in the Extreme*, 199–209. Gossage is fairly unique among scholars. He contends that the film *retains* the book's radical message and that the revisions in the story line are superficial and reflect Zanuck's "meddling" out of fears of a backlash from the authorities. Gossage, "Artful Propaganda," 104–7, 120–23.

19. French, *Filmguide*, 6.

20. Anne Loftis, *Witnesses to the Struggle: Imaging the 1930s California Labor Movement* (Reno: University of Nevada Press, 1998), 134; Owens, Grapes of Wrath: *Trouble in the Promised Land*, 5; Robert DeMott, introduction to John Steinbeck, *The Grapes of Wrath* (New York: Penguin Books, 1992), xix.

21. Jackson J. Benson, *Looking for Steinbeck's Ghost* (Reno: University of Nevada Press, 2002), 79–94.

22. Steinbeck, *Grapes of Wrath*, 582–83.

23. My interpretation of the fictional Weedpatch camp is not entirely new. Decades ago John H. Timmerman offered a similar reading: "Ironically Weedpatch

has its own psychological nettles. For example, it robs the people of their will. At ease with their heaven-sent manna, the migrants do not want to risk the struggle into Canaan. In the camp, the migrants find themselves becoming more and more dependent, depleted in will and direction." Timmerman, *John Steinbeck's Fiction: The Aesthetics of the Road Taken* (Norman: University of Oklahoma Press, 1986), 123.

24. French, *Filmguide*, 21.

25. For other reflections on Bruce Springsteen's music as a form of political commentary and theorizing, see Lauren Onkey, chapter 10, this volume; Gavin Cologne-Brookes, "The Ghost of Tom Joad: Steinbeck's Legacy in the Songs of Bruce Springsteen," in *Beyond Boundaries: Rereading John Steinbeck*, ed. Susan Shillinglaw and Kevin Hearle (Tuscaloosa: University of Alabama Press, 2002), 34–46; Jefferson Cowie, *Stayin' Alive: The 1970s and the Last Days of the Working Class* (New York: New Press, 2010), 17–18, 207–9, 337–42, 357–62; Bryan K. Garman, *A Race of Singers: Whitman's Working-Class Hero from Guthrie to Springsteen* (Chapel Hill: University of North Carolina Press, 2000); David Masciotra, *Working on a Dream: The Progressive Political Vision of Bruce Springsteen* (New York: Continuum, 2010); and Marc Dolan, *Bruce Springsteen and the Promise of Rock 'n' Roll* (New York: W. W. Norton, 2012). Most of these studies (such as the essay by Cologne-Brookes) discuss Springsteen's song "The Ghost of Tom Joad" in relation either to Springsteen's entire album of the same name or to his evolving musical corpus as a whole. In this chapter I am interpreting only a particular performance of the song and am attempting to unpack the internal logic of the song's argument.

26. Steinbeck, *Grapes of Wrath*, 654–56.

27. Ibid., 656.

28. Ibid., 653.

29. For further reflections on Ford's decision to have Henry Fonda play Tom Joad and on the implications of the shot of Tom climbing a hill, see Gallagher, *John Ford*, 166, 172–74, 178–79.

30. "The Ghost of Tom Joad," by Bruce Springsteen. Copyright © 1995 Bruce Springsteen (ASCAP). Reprinted by permission. International copyright secured. All rights reserved.

31. Springsteen has periodically written songs about different forms of gender-based oppression, but they are not as common as his songs about men suffering economic defeat. The evolution of sexual themes in his art (both live performances and recorded music) is a complicated topic that exceeds this study. Readers curious about Springsteen's evolving male persona probably should explore biographical treatments of his career, such as Dave Marsh, *Bruce Springsteen: Two Hearts, the Definitive Biography, 1972–2003* (New York: Routledge, 2004). For an insightful

and provocative analysis of the types of manliness that Springsteen has projected over the years, see Garman, *Race of Singers*, 214–26, 230–35.

32. Readers who are unfamiliar with Springsteen's music may wish to listen to the albums *Born to Run* (1975), *Darkness on the Edge of Town* (1978), *Nebraska* (1982), *Born in the U.S.A.* (1984), and *The Rising* (2002). These albums contain some of his most popular songs, many of his favorite images, and some of his most widely quoted lyrics. The album *The Ghost of Tom Joad* (1995) was critically acclaimed but did not include many hits.

33. Readers who are unfamiliar with 1950s and 1960s rock and roll may find this hard-luck understanding of the genre puzzling. After all, there are streams of rock and roll, such as instrumental surf music, that do not focus on loneliness, social inequality, and undeserved poverty. If readers listen closely to the lyrics of the following non–British Invasion rockabilly, soul, and blues songs, they will have a better sense of the musical tradition that Springsteen builds on: "Heartbreak Hotel," "Mystery Train," "Down in the Boondocks," "Chain Gang," "Folsom Prison Blues," "The Dark End of the Street," "I'd Rather Go Blind," "Killing Floor," "One Bourbon, One Scotch, One Beer," and "Five Long Years." In terms of the British Invasion, Springsteen was especially drawn to the Animals, whose hits include "House of the Rising Sun," "We Gotta Get Out of This Place," and "Please Don't Let Me Be Misunderstood."

34. Quoted in Masciotra, *Working on a Dream*, 13.

35. "The Ghost of Tom Joad," by Bruce Springsteen. Copyright © 1995 Bruce Springsteen (ASCAP). Reprinted by permission. International copyright secured. All rights reserved.

36. As historian Bryan Garman and journalist Marc Dolan have noted, Springsteen's long-standing distrust of formal government (because of its moral corruptness and inefficiencies) and his celebration of voluntary groups and charitable work sometimes superficially resemble the views of the late neoconservative politician Ronald Reagan. Garman, *Race of Singers*, 228; Dolan, *Bruce Springsteen and the Promise of Rock 'n' Roll*, 221–22, 430. As Springsteen pithily puts it, "I want to try to work more directly with people; try to find some way that my band can tie into the communities that we come into. I guess that's a political action, a way to just bypass that whole electoral thing. Human politics. People on their own can do a lot." Quoted in Masciotra, *Working on a Dream*, 9–10. Part of what differentiates Reagan's and Springsteen's visions of citizens voluntarily working together without government intervention (besides their clashing opinions on whether markets in America work fairly) is Springsteen's celebration of public-spiritedness and his criticisms of greed and selfishness.

37. These problems are explored primarily after Springsteen's *Born to Run* album, which focused on the dilemmas and dreams of young adults. In later al-

bums he says much more about the challenges facing older people who have lost their jobs, whose social networks have disintegrated, and whose self-respect has dissolved.

38. On first glance Springsteen's compressed version of Tom's goodbye speech resembles Tom's phrases in the lyrics of Woody Guthrie's ballad "Tom Joad." However, in the context of Guthrie's entire *Dust Bowl Ballads* album, which includes "Pretty Boy Floyd" and "Vigilante Man," it is conceivable that in Guthrie's imagination Tom will pursue the role of a populist outlaw, akin to Pretty Boy Floyd. This is compatible with Steinbeck's presentation of Tom's rambling remarks in the final meeting with his mother (the film version, as one would expect, is silent about Tom's outlaw leanings). Like Guthrie, Springsteen leaves the political program implied by Tom's ghost unstated and ambiguous. For more on Guthrie's political beliefs and on Guthrie's and Springsteen's sometimes parallel and sometimes divergent visions, see Denning, *Cultural Front*, 270–71, 518n22; and Garman, *Race of Singers*, 177–92, 235–45.

39. For a survey and critique of recent theories about the disappearance of working-class politics in the United States, see Cowie, *Stayin' Alive*.

40. In the words of Garman, Springsteen "leaves it to the listener to put his moral advice into practice." *Race of Singers*, 251.

41. "The Ghost of Tom Joad" by Bruce Springsteen. Copyright © 1995 Bruce Springsteen (ASCAP). Reprinted by permission. International copyright secured. All rights reserved.

PART IV

John Steinbeck: Ambivalent American?

CHAPTER 12

Patriotic Ironies: John Steinbeck's Wartime Service to His Country

Mimi R. Gladstein and James H. Meredith

IRONIES ABOUND IN THE story of Steinbeck's service to his country during World War II. Although his biographers generally acknowledge that Steinbeck was not, beyond his novels and journalism, particularly politically active until the war, others' perceptions of his political leanings created considerable barriers for his attempts to serve his country. While many of his countrymen and peers sought deferments, cushy assignments, or other ways to escape military service, Steinbeck paradoxically had to fight his government in order to serve his nation.

During the 1930s Steinbeck published a number of novels that sympathetically portrayed laborers, particularly migrant workers, while simultaneously criticizing a capitalist economy that ignored the plight of the common man, such as the Okie in *The Grapes of Wrath* or the migrant worker in *In Dubious Battle*. Despite such criticisms of his country, we argue, throughout his life Steinbeck acted like a bedrock American patriot. His was a complex kind of patriotism, not easily pigeonholed, as it contained a critical streak and existed alongside a more universal and ecological view of humankind than is traditionally associated with the potentially parochial characterization of patriotism. After his country was attacked, he became concerned with the evils that fascism posed not only to his country but also to the world. In this his patriotism converged with his larger cosmopolitan perspective.[1] In addition, Steinbeck, anticipating later environmental thinkers, adopted an ecological view of humankind, a view that saw human communities or groups as part of a symbiotic whole, operating similarly to a tide pool. In *The Log from the Sea of Cortez,* published in 1941, he insists on the interconnectedness of the most minute and the largest components of the universe. His observation about the tide pool and the stars leads him to the conclusion that "ecology has a synonym which is ALL."[2]

Unlike many of his literary contemporaries, Steinbeck was too young to participate in World War I, or what Dos Passos called the "Big Show." The writers who were adults during the Great War were, in one way or another, deeply affected by it. F. Scott Fitzgerald, one of the few writers who actually served in the U.S. military, did not see combat, his most significant regret in a life that was full of them. Hemingway was hit by a mortar while serving with the Red Cross Ambulance Service on the Italian Front and for the rest of his life his limp reminded all, especially his friend Fitzgerald, that he had seen action at the front. Although William Faulkner's "war wounds" occurred during a drunken escapade on Armistice Day, this did not stop him from returning home with a jaunty cane and a feigned limp. By contrast, e.e. cummings's experience of being held in a detention camp provided material for one of his first major works, *The Enormous Room*. While the list of who's who in modernism and the military is extensive, the closest Steinbeck came to military service in the Great War was as a cadet in an early version of what would later become high school ROTC. He participated in marching drills and target practice and helped local farmers whose laborers had gone to war.[3] Although he missed the Big Show, Steinbeck would not miss the next opportunity to serve his country. This he did with some distinction during World War II.

At the outbreak of the Second World War John Steinbeck was middle-aged and famous, the latter due to the publication of *The Grapes of Wrath* in 1939. The hysteria and acclaim that followed that novel's success did not blind Steinbeck to the world outside. While preparing for a trip to the Sea of Cortez—a momentary escape from his new status as a popular writer—Steinbeck was mindful of an impending political storm. In a letter to his friend Carlton Sheffield Steinbeck writes, "The world is sick now. There are things in the tide pool easier to understand than Stalinist, Hitlerite, Democrat, capitalist confusion and voodoo." Though he says that he wishes to "escape the general picture," he acknowledges "the waves of nerves from Europe."[4] Mexico did not prove to be an "escape." What he saw there prompted Steinbeck to write to Joseph Hamilton, an uncle working in Washington, "The Germans have absolutely outclassed the Allies in propaganda. If it continues, they will completely win Central and South America away from the United States."[5]

By June 1940 Steinbeck was so concerned about what he perceived to be an imminent "crisis in the Western Hemisphere" that he wrote directly to President Franklin D. Roosevelt and offered his services.[6] On the advice of Archibald MacLeish, then chief librarian of the Library of Congress, the president met with Steinbeck. The author proposed the creation of a propaganda office that would employ his contacts in Hollywood. Nothing came of the meeting, and later, when he perceived that nothing was being done to address his concerns, Steinbeck had the temerity to write again. This time he proposed a more imaginative method for countering the "growing Nazi power."[7] The idea, not original to Steinbeck, was to scatter large amounts of counterfeit German money over Germany and Italy.[8]

Although neither idea found favor with the federal government, Steinbeck persevered in his efforts to help his country in its time of need, a struggle all the more commendable given the turmoil in his personal life. His first marriage, to Carol Henning, was unraveling, and he began an affair with Gwen—later Gwyn—Conger. The conflict and intrigues that attended his divorce and remarriage generated considerable emotional upheaval and occasioned mental, physical, and geographic uncertainty. Steinbeck and Gwyn crisscrossed the country: when Carol was in New York, they stayed in California; and when Carol came back to California, they moved to New York.

Roy Simmonds suggests, however, that one of the eastward moves was "not altogether self-motivated" but a result of Steinbeck's communications with Roosevelt.[9] Steinbeck attended talks in Washington about plans for a comprehensive American propaganda machine.[10] Subsequently, the Foreign Information Service was established, with playwright Robert Sherwood at its helm. Steinbeck's writing skills were seen as an asset for the agency's "most famous outlet . . . the 'Voice of America' broadcasts."[11] Steinbeck noted, however, that when his voice was tested for possible broadcasting duties his enunciation and the boom in his voice made him difficult to understand.[12] Other agencies and departments, including the Writers' War Board and the Air Force, valued Steinbeck's gratis work. Here he felt that he was contributing to the war effort.[13]

The path to service, however, did not run smoothly. Steinbeck's writings about migrant workers and Communist organizers had made him a controversial figure. The establishment in Washington and in his home county, Monterey, viewed him with suspicion. Indeed, Steinbeck would have to fight the perception that he was a Communist for the rest of his life. In *Travels with Charley*, for example, written during the last decade of his life, he writes of earlier arguments with his sisters in which they accused him of talking like a Communist.[14] Though he wanted to serve and others wanted his assistance, Steinbeck had difficulty obtaining security clearance both from government agencies and from the local draft board. Indeed, Roy Simmonds identifies what he calls a "covert crucifixion [of Steinbeck] by government and army officials."[15] Simmonds's conclusions are corroborated by documents presented by Thomas Fensch in his 2002 volume *Top Secret: The FBI Files on John Steinbeck*. Steinbeck had an inkling of the conspiracy against him. In a 1942 letter to Attorney General Francis Biddle, Steinbeck inquires, "Do you suppose you could ask Edgar's boys to stop stepping on my heels? They think I'm an enemy alien. It's getting tiresome."[16] Adding to the irony of Steinbeck's battle to counter perceptions that he was a Communist is that it occurred at a time when the United States was allied with Soviet Russia.[17]

In 1942 Steinbeck finished writing *The Moon Is Down* and *Bombs Away: The Story of a Bomber Team*. The books emphasize the importance of the individual sacrificing for the good of the larger group during times of crisis. (For further discussion of the ambiguities of this aspect of Steinbeck's thought, see chapter 5, by Charles Williams.) Written as a modern fable, *The Moon Is Down* treats one small community as emblematic of the strivings of all democratic peoples. The reduction in scope paradoxically enlarges the moral lessons of the story: that sacrifices for the cause of freedom will, in the end, overwhelm fascism and that a united people led by self-sacrificing leaders will ultimately triumph over evil.[18] Steinbeck wrote that the purpose of the novel/play was to celebrate the "durability of democracy." He had initially set the story in an unnamed American town whose citizens resist Nazi-like invaders by refusing to cooperate and engaging in sabotage. Steinbeck, however, ran into resistance from the Foreign Information Service. They argued that public morale would be hurt by the suggestion that America could be conquered. Steinbeck was ready to put the project aside when Norwegian, Danish, French, and Czech friends suggested that he circumvent criticism by not specifying the occupied country.

In *John Steinbeck as Propagandist:* The Moon Is Down *Goes to War,* Donald Coers writes that Steinbeck placed the story in an unnamed country. Steinbeck calls it "cold and stern like Norway" and made the names of the characters as international as he could.[19] Even the German conquerors are simply called invaders. Coers comments, "Steinbeck had been eager to lend his talents to the Allied war effort, and he had hoped that *The Moon Is Down* would boost morale both in his own country and in occupied Europe by proclaiming that free people are inherently stronger than the 'herd people' controlled by totalitarian leaders, and that, despite the initial advantage of the military mighty dictators, the democracies would eventually win the war."[20]

At the end of the story the town's only elected official, Mayor Ogden, is executed by the leader of the conquering forces, Colonel Lanser, who, Nazi-like, insists he is just following orders. However, instead of quelling the town's rebellion, Ogden's martyrdom fuels the burgeoning insurrection. Before dying the mayor tells Colonel Lanser, "You don't understand. When I become a hindrance to the people, they'll do without me." In other words, making the mayor a hostage, a "hindrance," will not serve the invaders. The death of the mayor dramatically illustrates Steinbeck's overarching viewpoint during the war years: that, if kept alive long enough to regain its momentum, the inert power of a democratic people will, in the end, overcome totalitarianism. Despite evil's temporary success in Europe and the Pacific, good will eventually triumph.

Reviews of the novel were mixed. The influential commentator Clifton Fadiman dismissed it as "melodramatic" and "bad propaganda." John Gunther expressed dismay because Steinbeck was "almost maddeningly fair-minded to the Germans." James Thurber joined in criticizing the depiction of the "German" officers as unrealistic.[21] The book was very popular in Europe, however. Resistance leaders credited it with bolstering confidence at a crucial point during the war. In November 1946 the king of Norway presented Steinbeck with the Haakon VII Cross in recognition of the role of *The Moon Is Down* in shoring up morale in his occupied country. *The Moon Is Down* was also translated and circulated, at considerable risk, in Denmark, Holland, and France. Donald Coers argues that "few books have demonstrated more triumphantly the power of ideas against brute military strength, and few books in recent times have spoken with such reassurance to so many people of different countries and cultures."[22] Thus Steinbeck served not only the American war effort but also that of its allies.

Bombs Away approaches the theme of how democracies mobilize for war in an entirely different way. James H. Meredith places the book "in the tradition of Walt Whitman during the American Civil War," noting that it was "written in the vernacular, to appeal to the mothers and fathers throughout the country." *Bombs Away,* he argues, is "a contribution to American literature because it cogently conveys, in mythopoeic simplicity, the vital democratic regeneration of the United States in the face of a real and grave danger."[23]

Rodney P. Rice, however, sees the book quite differently. *Bombs Away,* he writes, is "a noteworthy piece of propaganda that exhibits thoughtful manipulation of that technique in service of a worthy cause," albeit one "justified as a reasonable response to an unreasonable threat, and through its pragmatic focus on how the practical results of human activity can improve the human condition." As such, Rice explains, "it represents a significant, directed, and responsible action designed to protect the democratic phalanx against an ominous threat, the cancerous growth of fascism, which in 1942 threatened to infect and destroy common humanity with a false vision of ultimate causes, absolute origins, and infallible truths."[24] Nevertheless, Meredith argues that the book "should under no circumstances be equated with other propaganda during that period, such as Leni Riefenstahl's *Triumph of the Will.*" Steinbeck was not writing propaganda in the strictest sense of the word. He was not "intentionally biased or misleading" in this book but sought to encourage Americans "to accept this new war machine, the bomber" because "the US government needed large numbers of its citizens to fight in it to defeat the evils of fascism." "Even democracies sometimes need a push by their governments to do the right thing," Meredith observes.[25]

In his highly successful earlier writings, such as *The Grapes of Wrath,* Steinbeck emphasizes that the primary way to combat the large-scale problems of modernity, including a worldwide economic depression and global fascism, is through collective effort, in other words, teamwork. For Steinbeck, teamwork was a simple concept. Just as it takes a village to educate a child and fight poverty, it takes a united nation to fight a war. Recognizing the costs of freedom, Steinbeck realized that it is sometimes necessary to forgo unfettered individualism. And although Steinbeck remained a critic of capitalism's capacity to provide for all its citizens, his wartime position was straightforward: the American form of government was superior to fascism and should be defended. In this he resolved to his own satisfaction a key democratic paradox: that sometimes a democracy's citizens must work within undemocratic institutions and become a part of a hierarchical team, such as the military, in order to defeat an evil such as fascism. This recognition was suggested by the subtitle of the book, "The Story of a Bomber Team." During the war Steinbeck worked as a faithful literary "soldier" of the government instead of as an individual writer. He temporarily exchanged his writing plow for the sword.

Bombs Away is a remarkable achievement. Steinbeck foresaw the importance of strategic bombing in the fight against global fascism.[26] Moreover, he communicated the representative nature of the individual bomber team. In 1942 America was coalescing into one large team to defeat fascism. Steinbeck writes in the introduction that it is "the intention of this book to set down in simple terms the nature and mission of a bomber crew and the technique and training of each member of it. For the bomber crew will have a great part in defending this country and in attacking its enemies. It is the greatest team in the world."[27] Steinbeck describes the bomber team as "truly a democratic organization" because each member of the crew has an equally important and contributive role.[28] Still, by emphasizing the team, Steinbeck subverts the romantic tradition of the individual pilot established during World War I: "The pilot is still in the public mind the darling of the Air Force. To the Air Force, however, he is only one of a number of specialists highly trained to carry out a military mission. But the public, led on by fiction and newspapers, still considers the pilot the overshadowing officer in an airplane. . . . It was after the war that the complicated tactics of air warfare were developed. Then the mission became more important than the game. Then air forces became integrated groups waging warfare of attacks on ground objectives."[29] Steinbeck further argues that the new style of warfare will defeat global fascism. Targets and instruments of violence have changed; they now include "the destruction plants, shipyards, docks, ships, and transportation systems, and these have become the new targets for the bombers, just as the bombers have become the main weapons of the Air Force." The pilot, he asserts, is "no longer individually the most important man in the Air Force"; his identity has been subsumed into a unit, a team.[30]

Hemingway once said he "would rather have cut three fingers off his throwing hand" than to have written such a book as *Bombs Away*.[31] It is little wonder that Hemingway disparaged Steinbeck's story of a bomber team: it deemphasized the individual and emphasized collective effort, running directly counter to Hemingway's approach to war writing. Steinbeck developed a more individualistic view after the war in such works as *East of Eden*. But in the 1940s, when his country and democracy were being threatened by wholly undemocratic forces, he still believed, as he had during the Great Depression, that collective effort was the only path to victory. He consistently believed that an unfettered individualism must be downplayed in times of social crisis.

Steinbeck's depiction of the suppression of the traditional individualistic identity of the pilot in modern war is analogous to the individualistic writer sublimating his identity to write propaganda for the national team in time of war. Although in hindsight the disparaging comments made by Hemingway—and more recently Simmonds, who called *Bombs Away* the "equivalent of a recruiting poster"—may seem aesthetically justified, the book clearly demonstrates that Steinbeck understood the emerging importance of strategic bombing to the final outcome of World War II.[32] In 1942 the eventual Allied victory over global fascism was anything but assured. Granted, Steinbeck's propagandistic book does not foretell the horrific casualty rates these bomber teams would cause—rates that far outstripped anyone's best estimations. Still, Steinbeck should be lauded for his willingness to make personal and literary sacrifices, both for his country and for humanity.

Steinbeck constantly searched for new ways to contribute to the war effort. Arguably, many of his ideas did not receive the serious attention they merited. One grew out of his interest in marine biology. Steinbeck believed that information he and Ed Ricketts had accumulated during their collecting trip to the Sea of Cortez might prove to be valuable to the military. Years later, in "About Ed Rickets"—which was published as an appendix to *The Log from the Sea of Cortez*—Steinbeck described the fiasco that resulted from their attempt to alert the government to information in Japanese zoological studies. As he relates it, Japan had drawn a "bamboo curtain over these islands and over the whole area."[33] Nonetheless, when he and Ricketts requested information about marine life from Japanese universities, the Japanese zoologists, being good scientists, sent them studies of not only the distribution of species but also the conditions and environment of their habitat, including wave shock, tidal range, currents, reefs, winds, and the characteristics of the coast and sea bottom.[34] Steinbeck practically chortles in print as he notes that when the surveys began to arrive, he and Ricketts excitedly realized that "here was all the information needed if we were to make beach landings."[35] In the "comic opera" that followed, their attempts to alert the government to this information were met first by a mimeographed form letter and second by the arrival of a dense lieutenant commander of naval intelligence who refused to accept that the reports were written in English, which was the scientific language of the world. Steinbeck speculates, "I have always wondered whether some of the soldiers whose landing craft grounded a quarter of a mile from the beach and who had to wade ashore under fire had the feeling that bottom and tidal range either were not known or were ignored."[36]

Steinbeck remained undeterred. By mid-July 1942 he had been appointed special consultant to the secretary of war and was assigned to headquarters of the Army Air Force. He expected to be called to service at any time. Unbeknownst to him, the FBI file on him was growing. In December 1942 one letter attempts to alert J. Edgar Hoover to the possibility that Steinbeck would agitate for better conditions at Japanese relocation centers and claims that his books were being used as "examples of the immoral life of the U.S. in foreign countries opposed to us." The writer also suggests that Steinbeck's books should not be allowed to "go through the U.S. mails because of their scurrilous and obscene passages."[37]

Although Steinbeck hoped to be drafted, the Monterey County Draft Board obstructed his efforts. Jay Parini writes, "Despite all indications to the contrary, he continued to nurse the hope that he might secure a commission in the armed forces as an intelligence officer."[38] Martin Frankel, the Counter Intelligence Corps special agent who investigated Steinbeck in California, concluded that he was loyal and patriotic and would make a good officer because of his considerable writing skills. In spite of the agent's favorable reports, the War Department decided that Steinbeck should "not be considered favorably for a commission in the Army of the United States."[39] Among the adverse information in his file was the statement "Subject has associated with individuals who are known to have a radical political and economic philosophy, and with some members of the Community Party."[40] A report from the American Legion Radical Research Bureau claimed that Steinbeck contributed to the *Pacific Weekly*, a "Red publication at Carmel";

that he was chairman of the Committee to Aid Agricultural Organization, a "Very Red outfit"; and that his former wife, Carol, was a "registered communist."[11] Agent Charles O. Shields countered such claims by citing people who actually knew Steinbeck. Barbara Burke, who bought Steinbeck's first house in Los Gatos, considered him "unquestionably loyal." She recounted hearing him say that he had never voted the Communist ticket and that he was opposed to his wife's registration.[12] Martin Ray also declared Steinbeck to be "absolutely loyal."[13] Some of the notes in the file would be amusing if the subject were not so serious. One Hugh Porter, who did not know Steinbeck personally, observed that the second-class mail delivered to Steinbeck was often of a communist or radical bent. He also observed that Steinbeck was "impulsive, eccentric and unreliable socially."[14] The cashier at the Los Gatos bank reported that Steinbeck was usually "very poorly dressed."[15]

For much of 1942 Steinbeck was left in limbo. Monterey Draft Board 119 would neither defer Steinbeck, which he reluctantly requested at the insistence of General "Hap" Arnold, nor draft him, even though he was called before the board and passed his physical. Ricketts, five years his senior, was drafted. Max Wagner, another close friend, was also drafted. Steinbeck did not want a deferment. He wrote his friend Toby Street, "These Washington sons of bitches are putting me in the position of a draft dodger and I don't like it."[16]

Eventually Steinbeck received clearance to go overseas. The experience was not without its disenchantments. In a March 1943 letter he complains that he can no longer put up with the "jealousies, ambitions, and red tape in Washington."[17] When it became clear that he would not be commissioned, Steinbeck tried to obtain accreditation as a correspondent from the *Herald Tribune, Collier's*, the Associated Press, or any other news outlet. He wanted very much to participate in the war. He wrote, "I think a big push is starting soon and I would like to see it. That is why I am trying to go as war correspondent."[18] The *Herald Tribune* hired him on the condition that he could obtain clearance from the War and State Departments. After the expected petty harassments from the authorities, Steinbeck finally left for Europe in June 1943.

Steinbeck spent less than half a year overseas as a war correspondent. Lacking military experience, he nonetheless participated in his country's war effort firsthand. Given the obstacles he had to overcome, his tenacity warrants admiration; Steinbeck could easily have skipped such a dangerous assignment. He had also recently married, and his new wife, Gwyn, opposed his departure.[49] He was, in turn, worried about her fidelity. In his letters he begs her to "keep this thing we have inviolate and waiting."[50] Gwyn did not make it easy for him. Her letters describe the number of men who flirted with her, some of his friends among them.

Steinbeck adopted an egalitarian style of reportage. Rather than flying, he arrived in England on a troopship because he wanted to share the experience of ordinary soldiers. Like his friend Ernie Pyle, who was also covering the Western Front, Steinbeck focused on privates and other low-ranking soldiers. His first communiqué describes the helmeted men on the ship as looking like "long rows of mushrooms."[51] He writes about the characteristic odor that fatigue, gun oil, and leather emit. And he affectionately details their naïveté, reporting, without comment, the first experience some mountain boys had of the sea. One claims that he heard that the sea is salty "clear down to the bottom." Steinbeck continues:

> "Now you know that ain't so," the other says.
> "What do you mean, it ain't so? Why ain't it so?"
> "Now, son," he says, "you know there ain't that much salt in the world. Just figure it out for yourself."[52]

In England Steinbeck reported from a bomber station, observing that "Britain drafts its women and they are really in the Army, driver-mechanics, dispatch riders, trim and hard in their uniforms."[53] He writes of the steadfast character of the people of Dover, the city closest to the enemy, and of the coastal batteries that defend against the German bombers heading for London and Canterbury. Steinbeck's dispatches reflect a novelist's perspective.[54] Much of his work, rather than being hard news, examines the common soldier's viewpoint, detailing, for example, the way the men talk before going out on a mission. As a writer and a fellow participant, Steinbeck was sensitive to the strain they were under, describing it as "a bubble that grows bigger and bigger in your mid-section. It puffs up against your lungs so that your breathing becomes short. Sitting around is bad."[55]

Although the overall tone of his dispatches from this period has a positive bent, his cold, hard, and skeptical side is also present. Steinbeck's patriotism did not preclude criticism of his country. Perhaps the clearest articulation of his understanding of the writer's role came in his 1962 Nobel Prize acceptance speech, when he explained that while a writer might expose "grievous faults and failures," he did so for the "purpose of improvement."[56] John Schaar concurs that "it is possible to treasure our own, even while criticizing it, and to judge others even while respecting them."[57] In a July 16, 1943, piece written from London, Steinbeck reminds his readers that as a result of World War I and its disappointing aftermath "ours is not a naïve Army. Common people have learned a great deal in the last twenty-five years, and the old magical words do not fool them any more." As he did in in his worker-sympathetic prewar novels, Steinbeck warns against a country "taken over by special interests through the medium of special pleaders." He expresses the worry that fortunes will be made by war profiteers while the soldiers "get $50.00 a month," asking, "Will they go home to a country destroyed by greed?"[58] (For further discussion of the critical aspects of Steinbeck's patriotism, see chapter 13, by Robert S. Hughes, and chapter 14, by Simon Stow.)

In late August 1943 Steinbeck, after once again battling for permission, arrived in North Africa. His August 28 communiqué from Algiers describes the polyglot of languages, the heat, and the tourist traffic in collectables. After about a month of preparation, during which the "American troops trained on the beaches of North Africa for the beaches of Italy," Steinbeck finally became a part of what he had wanted to experience—what he had called "a big push."[59] In early October he was part of the assault on Salerno beach.[60]

When Steinbeck selected the dispatches to be part of his compilation *Once There Was a War,* he included only one reference to his time with a secret U.S. Navy commando-like group prior to the Salerno invasion. Its mission was to confuse and deceive the enemy by landing a small craft, making a commotion that belied its size, and then withdrawing. The purpose was to trick the Axis forces into moving their troops north of Naples. These forays took place almost nightly, and Steinbeck went along on many of them. One resulted in the capture of the island of Ventotene, where the Italian soldiers surrendered but the Germans held out. In a stranger-than-fiction turn, the officer in charge of the attack was Douglas Fairbanks Jr., whose swashbuckling Hollywood image was obviously matched by his real-life actions. Fairbanks formed a high opinion of Steinbeck: "John, to his everlasting glory and our everlasting respect, would take his foreign correspondent badge off his arm and join in the raid. If you are caught in a belligerent action without a badge and carrying a weapon, and you are a foreign correspondent, you are shot. You don't get any of the privileges of an ordinary prisoner. He took his risks rather than go along, saying grace as a war correspondent. We had great admiration for him."[61]

While Fairbanks won a Silver Star for his gallantry at Ventotene, Steinbeck was also recommended for the same medal but was not eligible to receive it because he was not a member of the armed forces. Writing to Gwyn shortly before he returned to the States, Steinbeck describes his keen awareness of his brush with death: "But it is strange how you must do it. No one can do it for you. And the dark gentleman was very near. I think I wrote you about one particular night when I felt his breath."[62]

Although Steinbeck did everything in his power to serve his government during World War II, he was not a hawk, as the word is commonly understood to mean one who prefers war as a way of addressing international problems. His introduction to *Once There Was a War* adopts the pessimistic position, inspired by his ecological speculations, that if humankind is so stupid as to let another world war happen, "we do not, in a biologic sense, deserve survival. Many other species have disappeared from the earth through errors in mutational judgment."[63] He also makes clear to his readers that the journalistic "accounts and stories" were written under the strictures of censorship imposed by what he calls "The War Effort."

In 1944 he wrote Dook Sheffield, "You will laugh to think that for a year and a half I tried to get into the army but was blackballed from this largest club in the world." Steinbeck claimed to be happy to have been blackballed because as a correspondent he got "too much of a look" at war, whereas if he had been in the army he probably would have been "guarding a bridge in Santa Fe."[64]

Whatever experience Steinbeck gained, his service to the country was not without its costs. On the Salerno beachhead he had been hit in the neck, head, and back by a fifty-gallon oil drum that had been blown into the air during the bombardment. He had twisted his ankle when jumping out of a landing craft, and both eardrums had burst, leaving him barely able to hear. He also suffered periodic blackouts and some loss of memory. Months later Steinbeck wrote to Sheffield about his "nervousness, dreams, sleeplessness."[65] Although Steinbeck did not have a name for it, his symptoms resemble what psychiatrists now call post-traumatic stress disorder (PTSD). Steinbeck theorizes prophetically that about fifty thousand men might be suffering from similar symptoms and that there would be "a frightening amount of it after the war."⁶⁶ (For a discussion of PTSD in Steinbeck's work, see chapter 14.) His prescription for dealing with the war-induced trauma was to turn his attention back to simpler, happy-go-lucky times. In 1944 he wrote *Cannery Row,* which he describes as a "kind of fun book that never mentions the war and it is a relief to work on."⁶⁷

Steinbeck spent the last years of the war in Mexico, where he worked on various projects. It was there that he heard of the deaths of President Roosevelt and his friend Ernie Pyle. Pyle had accepted an assignment reporting from the Pacific Theater that Steinbeck had declined. In an unpublished memorial piece, Steinbeck writes, "War was everything Ernie Pyle didn't like. He hated filth and he hated cruelty."⁶⁸ Parini writes that on VE Day Steinbeck "celebrated the victory with a display of fireworks in his Mexican garden" and by drinking large quantities of Mexican beer.⁶⁹ Though he welcomed the news of Hermann Goering's capture, Steinbeck complained that many of those celebrating the war's end were never involved in it.

Steinbeck ironically juxtaposes the mundane activities of his civilian life and the cataclysmic world events. As he puts it, "The death of Hitler and I write 2000 words on the Wizard of Maine."⁷⁰ On VJ Day Steinbeck was living in New York City, where he heard a radio broadcast of General Douglas MacArthur speaking from the deck of the battleship *Missouri.* The *Herald Tribune* offered Steinbeck a chance to cover the impending war crimes trials in Europe, but Steinbeck was committed to his writing projects in Mexico. That country was the site for a number of Steinbeck's pre– and post–World War II projects. His insistence on using a Mexican director and actors rather than a Hollywood production company for the filming of *The Pearl* and his research and writing about Emiliano Zapata as a heroic figure and fighter for liberty suggest that his patriotism was not narrowly nationalistic. (For further discussion of Steinbeck's work on Mexico, see chapter 4, by Adrienne Akins Warfield, and chapter 9, by Marijane Osborn.)

Although Steinbeck wanted to serve his country when he felt it was imperiled, his experience of war led him to see it as "cosmic foolishness."⁷¹ His beliefs can be described as a conscious patriotism because, to borrow a phrase from Schaar, he felt "deeply indebted for those gifts, grateful to the people and places through which they came and determined to defend the legacy against enemies and pass it unspoiled to those who will come after."⁷² Steinbeck's connections to the land were deeply rooted, and they spawned a kind of natural patriotism compatible with a generous humanism and ecological convictions. (For further discussion of Steinbeck's connection to the land, see chapter 6, by Michael T. Gibbons.) Therefore, it stands to reason that when the clouds of a fascist threat loomed large from Europe and the Japanese attacked Pearl Harbor, Steinbeck did everything in his power to serve his country, even though he had to fight his government to do so.

Notes

1. Steinbeck's patriotism is in keeping with the historical context of a worldwide battle between democracy and fascism. Charles Taylor argues that a citizen democracy can exist only if its citizens are convinced of its importance and that therefore "we need patriotism as well as cosmopolitanism" in the modern world. Taylor, "Why Democracy Needs Patriotism," in *For the Love of Country*, ed. Martha Nussbaum (Boston: Beacon Press, 1996), 119–21.

2. John Steinbeck, *The Log from the Sea of Cortez* (New York: Viking, 1941), 85.

3. Jackson J. Benson, *The True Adventures of John Steinbeck, Writer* (New York: Viking, 1984), 23–24. The Steinbeck family was, however, caught up in the war effort. In *East of Eden* Steinbeck presents a charming remembrance of his mother's "Amazon-like" efforts selling Liberty Bonds. Steinbeck, *East of Eden* (New York: Viking, 1952), 173–78.

4. John Steinbeck, *Steinbeck: A Life in Letters*, ed. Elaine Steinbeck and Robert Wallsten (New York: Viking, 1975), 194.

5. Ibid., 205.

6. Ibid., 206.

7. Ibid., 211.

8. Dr. Melvyn Knisely, the chair of anatomy at the University of Chicago, was the originator of this psychological weapon. Steinbeck later wrote to Archibald MacLeish that the president liked the plan but the government's moneymen, Lord Lothian and Henry Morgenthau, did not. Jackson Benson opines, "It may have been that the contamination of anybody's money, even the enemy's, was too terrible a thing, by their gods, to even contemplate." Benson, *True Adventures*, 465.

9. Roy Simmonds, *John Steinbeck: The War Years, 1939–1945* (Lewisburg, Penn.: Bucknell University Press, 1996), 93.

10. Benson says that it is not clear if Steinbeck was offered a paid post and turned it down or if he volunteered to do work as an unpaid consultant. Benson, *True Adventures*, 487.

11. Simmonds, *John Steinbeck*, 93.

12. Steinbeck, *Life in Letters*, 244.

13. Benson notes that Steinbeck undertook a series of unpaid jobs for the government during the war years. Among them were positions in the Office of War Information, the Writers' War Board, and the Air Force. Benson, *True Adventures*, 487.

14. John Steinbeck, *Travels with Charley* (New York: Viking Press, 1962), 198.

15. Simmonds, *John Steinbeck*, 94. Simmonds cites, among others, Herbert Mitgang, *Dangerous Dossiers: Exposing the Secret War against America's Greatest Authors* (New York: Donald I. Fine, 1988), 71–79; and Jack Sirica, "The U.S. Army vs. John Steinbeck," *San Jose Mercury News*, June 2, 1984, 1A, 12A.

16. Thomas Fensch, ed., *Top Secret: The FBI Files on John Steinbeck* (Santa Teresa, N.M.: New Century Books, 2002), 6–7.

17. At the Yalta Conference Roosevelt would cede large parts of Eastern Europe to Soviet domination.

18. For more about these and other ideas concerning *The Moon Is Down*, see James H. Meredith, *Understanding the Literature of World War II: A Student Casebook to Issues, Sources, and Historical Documents* (Westport, Conn.: Greenwood, 1999): 124–29.

19. Steinbeck, *Life in Letters*, 67.

20. Donald V. Coers, *John Steinbeck as Propagandist:* The Moon Is Down *Goes to War* (Tuscaloosa: University of Alabama Press, 1991), xi.

21. Ibid. Coers describes the American reception to the book on 13–18.

22. Ibid., 138.

23. James H. Meredith, introduction to *Bombs Away: The Story of a Bomber Team*, by John Steinbeck (New York: Penguin, 2009), xii.

24. Rodney P. Rice, "Group Man Goes to War: Elements of Propaganda in John Steinbeck's *Bombs Away*," *War, Literature and the Arts: An International Journal of the Humanities* 15, nos. 1 and 2 (2002): 178–93.

25. Meredith, introduction, xii.

26. For the larger military implications of *Bombs Away*, see Rice, "Group Man Goes to War," 190.

27. John Steinbeck, *Bombs Away: The Story of a Bomber Team* (New York: Paragon House, 1990), 17.

28. Ibid., 23.

29. Ibid., 111–12.

30. Ibid., 114.

31. Carlos Baker, *Ernest Hemingway: A Life Story* (New York: Scribners, 1969), 371.

32. Simmonds, *John Steinbeck*, 131.

33. Steinbeck, *Log from the Sea of Cortez*, 267.

34. Ibid., 268.

35. Ibid., 369.

36. Ibid., 270.

37. Fensch, *Top Secret*, 12.

38. Jay Parini, *John Steinbeck: A Biography* (London: Heineman, 1994), 327.

39. Fensch, *Top Secret*, 14.

40. Ibid.

41. Ibid., 17.

42. Ibid., 21.

43. Ibid., 27.

44. Ibid., 23.

45. Ibid., 25.

46. Quoted in Simmonds, *John Steinbeck*, 143.

47. Steinbeck, *Life in Letters*, 250.

48. Ibid.

49. The marriage took place on March 29 in New Orleans. He telegrammed Toby Street on April 5 that he had been accredited as a war correspondent for the *Herald Tribune*, and he was set to leave in mid-April. Of course, he did not anticipate the additional bureaucracy and bungling that would keep him home until June. Still, he was originally ready to leave his new bride less than a month after the marriage.

50. Steinbeck, *Life in Letters*, 256.

51. John Steinbeck, *Once There Was a War* (New York: Viking Press, 1958), 3.

52. Ibid., 9.

53. Ibid., 25.

54. Mimi Reisel Gladstein details the differing routes and styles of these two famous World War II reporters in "Mr. Novelist Goes to War: Hemingway and Steinbeck as Front Line Correspondents," *War, Literature and the Arts: An International Journal of the Humanities*, 15, nos. 1 and 2 (2003): 258–65.

55. Steinbeck, *Once There Was a War*, 65.

56. John Steinbeck, "Acceptance Speech," in *Nobel Prize Library: Faulkner, O'Neill, Steinbeck* (New York: Helvetica Press, 1971), 206.

57. Jack Schaar, *Legitimacy and the Modern State* (New Brunswick, N.J.: Transaction Books, 1981), 304.

58. Steinbeck, *Once There Was a War*, 75.

59. Ibid., 143.

60. Roy Simmonds carefully reports the exact dates and extent of Steinbeck's participation in the Salerno landing and describes the capture of Ventotene and then Capri. Simmonds, *John Steinbeck*, 188–98.

61. Quoted in Benson, *True Adventures*, 532.

62. Ibid., 538.
63. Steinbeck, *Once There Was a War*, vi.
64. Steinbeck, *Life in Letters*, 268.
65. Ibid., 268.
66. Ibid., 269.
67. Ibid., 270.
68. Quoted in Simmonds, *John Steinbeck*, 266.
69. Parini, *John Steinbeck*, 355.
70. Quoted in Simmonds, *John Steinbeck*, 269.
71. Steinbeck, *Life in Letters*, 269.
72. Schaar, *Legitimacy and the Modern State*, 288.

CHAPTER 13

John Steinbeck's Shifting View of America: From *Travels with Charley* to *America and Americans*

Robert S. Hughes

WHEN PETER LISCA IN *The Wide World of John Steinbeck* includes *Travels with Charley* (1962) and *America and Americans* (1966) among the "serious defeats" of Steinbeck's later career, he reiterates a position that others have long held.[1] Whether or not one accepts this notion of a decline in Steinbeck's powers, these two neglected works provide a compendium of his life, thought, and art found nowhere else in his canon. They treat a most unwieldy subject—the entire American nation and its people—with contrasting approaches. Perhaps most interesting, though, is the shift these volumes reveal in Steinbeck's view of his country and his role as an American writer. After all, the central question he asks in both is, "What are Americans like today?"[2] Returning more than two decades after *The Grapes of Wrath* (1939) to rediscover his homeland, Steinbeck is, in a sense, "(Re)-Reading America."[3] In this essay I explore the relationship between his travelogue and his collection of essays, investigate their autobiographical and patriotic impetus, and discuss the events between the publication of the two works that led to Steinbeck's new perspective on himself and America.

Perhaps more than most writers, Steinbeck tenaciously guarded his private life and kept himself and his family out of his writings. It was only during his later years, when fame transformed him into an international celebrity and failing health forced him to acknowledge his mortality, that he succumbed to the autobiographical urge. In the early 1960s Steinbeck told Carlton Sheffield that he had contemplated writing an autobiography, though he never undertook one.[1] He wrote fiction based in part on his life: the short stories "His Father" (1949), "The Affair at &, Rue de M—" (1955),

"The Summer Before" (1955), and "Reunion at the Quiet Hotel" (1958) as well as the novels *East of Eden* (1952) and *The Winter of Our Discontent* (1961). *Travels with Charley* and *America and Americans* remain the most conventionally autobiographical of his writing. Not surprisingly, the *San Francisco Chronicle* calls *Travels with Charley* "as close to autobiography as anything Steinbeck has written," and Jackson J. Benson says of the subsequent volume, "Those who would understand . . . [Steinbeck's] canon from beginning to end, would do well to read *America and Americans*."[5] In each work Steinbeck holds a mirror up to himself as much as to his country. In *Travels with Charley* he characterizes the United States as a "macrocosm of microcosm me," explaining that while he "found matters to criticize and deplore" in the nation, "they were tendencies equally present in myself."[6] Similarly, in *America and Americans*, when Steinbeck says Americans are "a restless, a dissatisfied, a searching people," he reflects on his own often footloose and unsettled life.[7]

Steinbeck also had patriotic motives for writing the two books. From his letters to Adlai Stevenson and others, we can see that Steinbeck was deeply concerned about social unrest in the United States. In late 1959, after returning from England, where he had been working on his translation of the King Arthur legend, Steinbeck reports to Stevenson two disturbing impressions of America: first, a creeping, all-pervading nerve gas of immorality that starts in the nursery and does not stop until it reaches the highest offices, both corporate and governmental; and second, a nervous restlessness, a hunger, thirst, a yearning for something unknown—perhaps morality. Steinbeck concludes, "Someone has to reinspect our system and that soon."[8] His concern for what he perceived to be the degeneracy of America began to emerge in his writings. *The Winter of Our Discontent* (1961), which he completed just before his European travels, makes evident his alarm over a morally bankrupt America and foreshadows his further commentary on the nation in *Travels with Charley* and *America and Americans*. (For further discussion of this theme in *The Winter of Discontent*, see chapter 14, by Simon Stow.)

Contrasts in Form and Style

Although the two books share autobiographical and patriotic origins, they differ in form. Steinbeck characterizes *Travels with Charley*—which recounts his three-month, ten-thousand-mile, thirty-four-state tour of America—as a "little book of ambulatory memoirs" and "a most relaxed and personal account, somewhat like an extended letter but exploring many fields."[9] His friend Carlton Sheffield, in a letter to this author, explains that *Travels with Charley* was "originally designed as a series of narrative essays for *Holiday* magazine . . . verified by a footnote or editor's comment in *Letters of E. B. White*." The note observes,

> *Holiday* asked White to drive coast to coast, as he had done in 1922, and write some pieces about America. He accepted, but got only as far as Gale-town, Pennsylvania.
>
> "I discovered that I was traveling so fast that I might as well be home in bed, and I didn't see any way to slow down, so I gave up the idea . . ." he wrote his brother Stanley at the time. The assignment was passed on to John Steinbeck, who made the trip and wrote *Travels with Charley*.[10]

Sheffield thus raises the question as to whether Steinbeck himself conceived of his odyssey across America, as has been generally assumed, or whether the idea for the trip was suggested to him by *Holiday,* where the text appeared serially in three installments from July 1961 through February 1962. In either case, Steinbeck hints at the form of his travelogue through his use of the Spanish word *vacilando,* meaning to wander with an announced direction, not caring greatly whether one holds the course.[11] "I was born lost," Steinbeck tells us, "and take no pleasure in being found."[12] Reflecting this, Steinbeck in his darker moods calls *Travels with Charley* a "formless, shapeless, aimless . . . haphazard thing."[13]

Considering the desultory intent of Steinbeck's journey, we might expect the text to be equally wandering. Yet, while loose and episodic in its structure, *Travels with Charley* is unified by the circular path of Steinbeck's ongoing journey, by his continuing commentary on the national landscape, and especially by the antics of his charming companion. Called by the *Atlantic* "one of the most civilized and attractive dogs in literature," Steinbeck's aging poodle lends the volume, according to Benson, "its imaginative center and much of its flavor."[14] Charley accomplishes this in three ways. First, he functions as a social ambassador, helping Steinbeck establish contact with strangers who become the subjects of his book. Steinbeck reveals to the reader Charley's magic: "I release him, and he drifts toward the objective, or rather to whatever the objective may be preparing for dinner. I retrieve him so that he will not be a nuisance to my neighbors—et voila!"[15] Second, during their thirty-four-state odyssey Charley gives Steinbeck the opportunity to initiate a kind of "dialogue" about America. He confesses, "I found I was talking aloud to Charley. He likes the idea but the practice makes him sleepy."[16] This "dialogue" between master and dog, in turn, is overheard by the reader. The technique adds liveliness to what might otherwise be an unrelieved lecture on America. Charley functions finally as an example of a reasonable and sane living creature. Occasionally, when pointing out human folly and cruelty, Steinbeck contrasts Charley's sanity to the insanity of human beings. After witnessing an instance of racism in New Orleans, for example, Steinbeck observes, "It would be difficult to explain to a dog the good and moral purpose of a thousand humans gathered to curse one tiny human. . . . I am convinced that basically dogs think humans are nuts."[17]

Despite the unity Charley lends *Travels,* Steinbeck's tour of America turns out to be somewhat eccentric. He avoids nearly every major city in America. He bypasses Hartford and Providence, drives through Minneapolis and St. Paul without stopping, and avoids Cleveland, Toledo, South Bend, and other "great hives of production" along the Great Lakes.[18] He notes, perhaps as a justification, that people in cities "have points of difference, but in some ways they are alike."[19] Whenever he approaches the fringes of a city his litany of complaints begins: "The new American finds his challenge and his love in traffic-choked streets, skies nested in smog, choking with the acids of industry, the screech of rubber and houses leashed in against one another while the townlets wither a time and die."[20] He complains bitterly how "progress" has irrevocably changed Seattle, though he still finds a warm spot in his heart for San Francisco.[21]

Compounding this minimalist coverage of urban America, Steinbeck skips lightly over entire regions of the country. His uncertain health and low spirits at this time were no doubt partly responsible. Little more than halfway through the trip he confesses, "I was no longer hearing or seeing. . . . Like a man who goes on stuffing food after he is filled, I felt helpless to assimilate what was fed in through my eyes."[22] Consequently, during the final quarter of his journey, between New Mexico and Manhattan, Steinbeck stops only twice.

As a corollary to his revulsion for most U.S. cities, Steinbeck announces his preference for the back roads of America: "I stayed as much as possible on secondary roads where there was much to see and hear and smell, and avoided the great wide traffic slashes."[23] The people he meets generally hail from these outposts of America. Noting this, the *New York Times Book Review* says of *Travels with Charley*, "This is a book about Steinbeck's America and for all the fascination of the volume, that America is hardly coincident with the United States in the Sixties."[24] Steinbeck himself admits, "I cannot commend this account as an America that you will find."[25] Still, "What I set down here is true until someone else passes that way and rearranges the world in his own style."[26] Perhaps Steinbeck felt compelled to qualify his "search" for America because one of his "main but secret reasons" for the journey was entirely personal: to prove that despite his recent serious illness and professional setbacks he was still a vigorous man and talented artist.[27] Steinbeck tells Elizabeth Otis, "What I am proposing is not a little trip or reporting, but a frantic last attempt to save my life and the integrity of my creative pulse."[28]

In its 1962 review of *Travels with Charley*, the *Times Literary Supplement* anticipated by some four years the publication of *America and Americans*. The reviewer laments the sketchy quality of the travelogue and concludes that Steinbeck's "deepest impressions of modern America will probably not be put on paper until he has had more time to digest his experiences for future novels."[29] In *America and Americans* Steinbeck adds material on the ethnic origins of the nation, sexuality, child rearing, the aged, corporations, the U.S. Constitution, the presidency, and more. Viking president Thomas Guinzberg originally asked Steinbeck to write an introduction to a folio-sized collection of photographs distilling the spirit of the nation. As Steinbeck developed his introduction, the "short, 'commercial' job" evolved into a series of nine topical essays inspecting the whole nation and its people.[30] In keeping with the photographic theme of the volume, Steinbeck attempted to capture the spirit of America, yet he admits in the foreword that his essays also consist of his own "opinions, unashamed and individual."[31] "I may have to run for my life when it [America] comes out," he told John Huston and Gladys Hill. "I am taking 'the American' apart like a watch to see what makes him tick and some very curious things are emerging."[32]

Although *America and Americans* and *Travels with Charley* share a common subject, *America and Americans* is in many ways an entirely different book. It represents more than a mere rethinking and recasting of material Steinbeck uncovered during his three-month odyssey around the United States. The text, only one-third the length of the earlier travelogue, often resembles Steinbeck's occasional essays for *Newsday, Saturday Review,* and other newspapers and magazines. His description of teenage gangs "engaging in their 'rumbles' which are really wars" in the nation's cities, for example, recalls his *Saturday Review* article "Some Thoughts on Juvenile Delinquency."[33] His focus on civil rights echoes his earlier magazine article on the nobility of black Americans, "Atque Vale."[34] His thoughts on growing old bring to mind a 1958 essay, "The Easiest Way to Die."[35] And Steinbeck's suggestion that television and film present a distorted image of America reflects his *Saturday Review* piece "Madison Avenue and the Election," in which he equates endorsing political candidates on TV with selling breakfast cereal.[36]

Steinbeck also recycles material from earlier writings: *Pastures of Heaven* (1932); the Japanese spy club sketch in "Junius Maltby"; *The Grapes of Wrath* (1939), with an allusion to Rose of Sharon giving her breast to a starving man; *The Log from The Sea of Cortez* (1951), in the frequent biological perspective of the American people ("Perhaps we will have to inspect mankind as a species"); and *Travels with Charley,* with the cameo of a black man who, for fear of a rape accusation, passes by a drunken white woman who has slipped on a New York sidewalk.[37] When we recall his borrowings from journalistic pieces as well as previous narratives, *America and Americans* begins to look like a Steinbeck pastiche.

These extensive borrowings as well as the volume's essay format differentiate *America and Americans* from *Travels with Charley.* The narrative structure of the travelogue reminds us occasionally of Steinbeck's novels—William Rivers in the *Saturday Review* calls *Travels* a "novelist's-eye view of the U.S."[38] *America and Americans* lacks such a continuous story line, save a few narrative anecdotes and reminiscences sprinkled throughout the largely expository text. For this reason, each book touches us differently. *Travels with Charley,* with its novel-like odyssey of a beloved American writer and his dog, functions as a warm and penetrating nonfictional tale; *America and Americans,* in contrast, resembles a series of colorful and provocative editorials.

Differences in Political Message

Steinbeck seeks in both volumes to answer the question, "What are Americans like today?"[39] In *Travels with Charley* Steinbeck approaches this question tentatively, often phrasing his assumptions in the interrogative: "Could it be that Americans are a restless people, a mobile people, never satisfied with where they are as a matter of selection?" or "Perhaps we have over-rated roots as a psychic need. Maybe the greater urge, the deeper and more ancient is the need, the will, the hunger to be somewhere else."[10] That Steinbeck is unsure of these lines of thought is obvious from his manner of expression. Yet he seems to be struggling toward a hypothesis.

One of Steinbeck's problems in reaching a conclusion is the odd assortment of evidence he uncovers on his trip. He describes more than three dozen individual Americans, beginning with the neighbor boy on Long Island who yearns to accompany him in Rocinante, his camper, and ending with the black college student who rides with him to Montgomery, Alabama.[11] He meets farmers, waitresses, veterinarians, gas-station attendants, state troopers, immigration officials, truckers, mobile-home owners, hitchhikers, and an itinerant actor, among others. This collection of citizens is hardly representative of the nation as a whole, yet Steinbeck attempts to make generalizations about all Americans. He credits those he meets with being unique individuals, and at the same time he detects common traits. "The American identity is an exact and provable thing," he says.[42] Yet he fails to elaborate. The more he inspects Americans, the less sure he is what they are. "It appeared to me increasingly paradoxical," Steinbeck says, "and it has been my experience that when paradox crops up too often for comfort, it means certain factors are missing in the equation."[13]

Although Steinbeck is unable to solve this equation, he makes several broad judgments about the Americans he meets. In *America and Americans* he applauds some of his new acquaintances—such as the gas-station "saint" who on a rainy Sunday in Oregon finds two heavy-duty tires for Steinbeck's truck, and the brave father at a New Orleans school who escorts his daughter through a crowd of jeering bigots.[11] In *Travels with Charley* favorable portraits are the exception rather than the rule. More frequently Steinbeck presents us with malcontents, and Americans appear unhappy where they are. Steinbeck's disappointment inevitably seeps through the pages of the narrative. Among the negative traits he reports, perhaps the most disheartening is that Americans no longer have "guts."[15] Across the country, even during an election year, Steinbeck finds no opinions, "no arguments, no discussion."[16] He laments, "I didn't hear many convictions."[47]

This complacency bothers Steinbeck, as we can see from his commentary on the individual Americans he meets. In Bangor, Maine, Steinbeck meets a waitress in a "sponge-off apron" who "wasn't happy, but then she wasn't unhappy. She wasn't anything." This causes Steinbeck's spirits to sink. After a depressing encounter with her, he speculates, "Strange how one person can . . . drain off energy and joy, can suck pleasure dry and get no sustenance from it. Such people spread a grayness in the air about them."[48] In addition, Steinbeck meets the stout "bull bitch" woman whose Pomeranian bites him on the hand; "Lonesome Harry," whose loveless love affair at the Ambassador East in Chicago saddens Steinbeck; the "young and troubled" or "very old spry" (he can't decide which) waitress on U.S. 10 who chides him for getting lost outside Minneapolis; the elderly Spokane veterinarian whose shaking hands and alcoholic breath provoke Charley's "veiled contempt"; and the racist hitchhiker whom Steinbeck picks up in the South and quickly boots from his truck.[49] These dark cameos, by their graphic immediacy and frequent repetition, emphasize the less seemly side of the American character. Though such sketches reveal obliquely Steinbeck's attitude toward his people, he seems unable to express his findings in objective terms, and therefore he fails to explain what these individual portraits amount to in the aggregate.

In *America and Americans* Steinbeck's response to the implicit question "What are Americans like today?" is more direct, definite, and favorable. While he speaks hesitantly about the American character in *Travels with Charley*, with "perhaps," "maybe," and "could it be," in *America and Americans* he becomes more confident and less ambiguous.[50] Americans, he concludes, are "a restless, a dissatisfied, a searching people."[51] Steinbeck also deals more assuredly with the several paradoxes of American life he left unanswered in *Travels with Charley*. "Americans seem to live and breathe and function by paradox," he says.[52] We believe our government is "weak, stupid, overbearing, dishonest, and inefficient, and at the same time we are deeply convinced that it is the best government in the world." Though Americans "trample friends, relatives, and strangers" to achieve financial security, they are unhappy once they attain it and contribute their money to "foundations and charities."[53] Though they are remarkably kind and hospitable and open with both guests and strangers, they make "a wide circle around the man dying on the pavement."[54] And though the "home dream" is their most deeply ingrained illusion, few American families stay "in one place for more than five years."[55] Discussing a wide range of such paradoxes, Steinbeck eventually comes to the realization that the people themselves are paradoxical—their character reflecting the paradoxical nature of American life.

In *America and Americans* Steinbeck does not mask the darker side of American life and its sometimes unpredictable and dangerous fringe elements. He talks frankly about "screwballs," "assassins," "Haywire Mothers," misers, showoffs, and eccentrics.[56] His diatribe against spoiled American children and their naïve parents (he calls his observations of their failings "an exact description of what has been happening to Americans") are unforgiving, as are his descriptions of "illiterate child-women, all hair and false bosoms" and paranoid retired Americans on fixed incomes.[57] Steinbeck once again recognizes the national complacency that he discovered during his earlier cross-country tour but finds assurance in the American people's restlessness: "We are not satisfied. Our restlessness perhaps inherited from the hungry immigrants of our ancestry is still with us."[58]

The sometimes irreverent yet positive tone of *America and Americans* differs from the recurrent pessimism of *Travels with Charley.* Steinbeck's disillusionment over the nation in *Travels* (when he told Pascal Covici that he saw "haunting decay" in America) is supplanted by a more deliberate and reasoned approach in the later volume.[59] The occasional mood swings, depression, and loneliness that colored his highly impressionistic view in the travelogue give way in *America and Americans* to steadier observations and more thorough analyses. The pessimism in *Travels with Charley* emanates primarily from Steinbeck's disappointment over the "strangulation" of the nation—especially the cities—by a dubious progress, the "aimless and pointless ant-hill activity" he sees along the way, and the disappearance of what he calls "the people."[60] One of Steinbeck's errands on his first trip is to "find out where the People have gone."[61] What he discovers are "very few contented" Americans.[62] As he told Adlai Stevenson, "Having too many THINGS they spend their hours and money on the couch searching for a soul."[63]

Besides the polluted environment and loss of "the People," Steinbeck's spirits are also dampened in *Travels with Charley* by the Thanksgiving "orgy" he endures in Texas and the racial prejudice he observes in the South.[64] Perhaps most disturbing, though, is his California homecoming, where he fights over politics with his family and is nearly drawn into a Monterey barroom brawl. He is reminded of Thomas Wolfe's truism, "you can't go home again," and tells a few old friends, "What we knew is dead . . . and maybe the greatest part of what we were is dead."[65]

Disappointed with the America he finds, Steinbeck spends increasingly more of his time in *Travels with Charley* looking back, measuring present America against its past. The result is a mixture of nostalgia for the country as he remembers it twenty-five years earlier, disapproval for how it has changed, and apprehension about its future. Confessing that it sounds as though he "bemoans an older time," he argues, "I have never resisted change, even when it has been called progress, and yet I felt resentment toward strangers swamping what I thought of as my country with noise and clutter and the inevitable rings of junk."[66]

Although Steinbeck exposes some national failings in *America and Americans*, the reader never doubts his faith in the American people to solve their problems and endure. Steinbeck even sounds somewhat defensive about the country in his foreword, where he recalls how foreign visitors have promulgated dubious "opinions" about the nation and its people, opinions too often accepted by Americans. Although Steinbeck does not attempt to "refute the sausage-like propaganda which is ground out in our disfavor," he nonetheless champions America, saying that his book is "inspired by curiosity, impatience, some anger, and a passionate love of America and the Americans."[67] The nation, in Steinbeck's eyes, is many things but finally "unspeakably dear, and very beautiful."[68] Steinbeck attacks cherished illusions, yet this strong statement of affirmation underlies the entire book.

There is good reason to believe that Steinbeck's patriotic stance in *America and Americans* stems from his increased involvement in national affairs during the years between the publication of the two works. As Tetsumaro Hayashi has shown in *John Steinbeck and the Vietnam War*, after winning the Nobel Prize in 1962 and becoming the friend, confidante, and cultural ambassador of two American presidents (Kennedy and Johnson), Steinbeck found himself increasingly inclined to defend his nation and its policies.[69] He lambasted Communist insurgents in South Vietnam (where his two sons were stationed) and damned both racial bigots and "Peaceniks" at home. America, as Steinbeck knew and loved it, was being attacked on several fronts. In the early 1960s he desired merely to become reacquainted with America. His new position of influence prompted him in *America and Americans* not only to analyze the nation but also to defend it. He felt a new, more profound responsibility to the nation, an urgent call to become the prophet and patriot his country needed. That he had prophecy in mind after his trip across America is evident from his July 1961 letter to Pascal Covici: "Well, there was once a man named Isaiah—and what he saw in his time was not unlike what I have seen. . . . We have no prophecy now, nor any prophets."[70]

In a despairing moment in *America and Americans* Steinbeck asks, "Why are we on this verge of moral and hence nervous collapse?"[71] Yet unlike his bleak outlook in *Travels with Charley,* Steinbeck now conveys newfound hope. He recognizes the 1960s as a turning point: "We have reached the end of a road and have no new path to take."[72] He envisions a future in which Americans, by virtue of their restless character, will survive and continue to flourish. While Steinbeck does not underestimate the dangers facing America in the mid-1960s, he also discerns the traits necessary to overcome them. His closing statement, "We have failed sometimes . . . but we have never slipped back—never" may sound like an exaggeration in light of the argument Steinbeck has been building from the beginning of the book.[73] Still, his optimism seems consistent and genuine. Although Sanford E. Marovitz calls this concluding line "sheer optimism, in no way justified by anything in the volume that has come before it," Steinbeck nevertheless asserts that Americans will never slip back because they will never be satisfied.[74] His experiences between the writing of *Travels with Charley* and *America and Americans* had rekindled his "hope and confidence" in America.[75] Fittingly, then, he concludes the last volume published during his lifetime on a note of sincere optimism.

Besides his published letters and parts of a few other works, Steinbeck's most intimate record of himself and his art is preserved in *Travels with Charley* and *America and Americans.* While both works are autobiographical, they diverge in form, tone, technique, and coverage of topics. *Travels with Charley* recounts a national odyssey conducted in part for "secret" personal reasons. The book illustrates Steinbeck's novelistic skill. He places Charley at the book's imaginative center, and the dog acts as a sounding board for his master's observations on America. In addition, Steinbeck's eye for finding subjects and his ability to sketch them evocatively result in memorable glimpses of rural and small-town America, with some disparaging asides on cities. Steinbeck finds little to cheer or encourage him about his homeland, and he is unable to explain to his own satisfaction what Americans are like.

Perhaps because of his recent illness and his fears about losing his artistic powers, Steinbeck looks back nostalgically at a bygone America and looks unfavorably on the present one that he cannot fully understand or approve.

Although in some ways *America and Americans* comprises a pastiche of Steinbeck's earlier writings, it analyzes more thoroughly than does *Travels with Charley* the nation and its people. Steinbeck discusses issues he neglected in the earlier book. While each of the nine essays focuses on the less positive aspects of American life, Steinbeck's underlying tone is affirmative and optimistic. In addition, he discovers that the paradoxes of American life that befuddled him in *Travels with Charley* can be traced to a central paradox within all Americans—they are "a restless, a dissatisfied, a searching people."[76] These qualities prove to be saving graces.

Notes

1. Peter Lisca, *The Wide World of John Steinbeck* (New York: Gordian Press, 1981), 301–3.

2. John Steinbeck, *Travels with Charley: In Search of America* (New York: Penguin, 1980), 241.

3. Geralyn Stecker, "Reading Steinbeck (Re)-Reading America: *Travels with Charley* and *America and Americans*," in *After* The Grapes of Wrath: *Essays on John Steinbeck in Honor of Tetsumaro Hayashi*, ed. Donald V. Coers, Robert De Mott, and Paul D. Ruffin (Athens: Ohio University Press, 1995), 214.

4. John Steinbeck, *Steinbeck: A Life in Letters*, ed. Elaine Steinbeck and Robert Wallsten (New York: Viking, 1975), 798.

5. William Hogan, "Class Tells All in Steinbeck's Diary," review of *Travels with Charley*, by John Steinbeck, *San Francisco Chronicle*, July 29, 1962, 24; Jackson J. Benson, *The True Adventures of John Steinbeck, Writer* (New York: Viking, 1984), 968.

6. Steinbeck, *Travels with Charley*, 207. See also Douglas Dowland, "'Macrocosm of Microcosm Me': Steinbeck's *Travels with Charley*," *Literature Interpretation Theory* 16 (2005): 311–31.

7. John Steinbeck, America and Americans *and Selected Nonfiction*, ed. Susan Shillinglaw and Jackson J. Benson (New York: Viking, 2002), 32.

8. Steinbeck, *Life in Letters*, 651–53.

9. Ibid., 702.

10. E. B. White, *Letters of E. B. White*, ed. Dorothy Guth (New York: Harper and Row, 1976), 339.

11. Steinbeck, *Travels with Charley*, 63.

12. Ibid., 70.

13. Steinbeck, *Life in Letters*, 702.

14. Edward Weeks, "Seeing Our Country Close," review of *Travels with Charley*, by John Steinbeck, *Atlantic Monthly*, August 1962, 137; Benson, *True Adventures*, 884.

15. Steinbeck, *Travels with Charley*, 65.

16. Ibid., 140.

17. Ibid., 267.

18. Ibid., 108.

19. Ibid., 25–26.

20. Ibid., 72.

21. Ibid., 180.

22. Ibid., 219.

23. Ibid., 95.

24. Review of *Travels with Charley*, by John Steinbeck, *New York Times*, July 26, 1962, 5.

25. Steinbeck, *Travels with Charley*, 77.

26. Ibid., 76.

27. Ibid., 19–20.

28. Steinbeck, *Life in Letters*, 699.

29. Review of *Travels with Charley*, by John Steinbeck, *Times Literary Supplement*, November 2, 1962, 843.

30. Benson, *True Adventures*, 955.

31. John Steinbeck, *America and Americans* (New York: Bantam, 1968), 8.

32. Steinbeck, *Life in Letters*, 807.

33. Steinbeck, *America and Americans*, 41; John Steinbeck, "Some Thoughts on Juvenile Delinquency," *Saturday Review*, May 28, 1955, 22.

34. Steinbeck, *America and Americans*, 50, 70–77; John Steinbeck, "Atque Vale," *Saturday Review*, July 23, 1960, 13.

35. Steinbeck, *America and Americans*, 117; John Steinbeck, "The Easiest Way to Die," *Saturday Review*, August 23, 1958, 12, 37.

36. Steinbeck, *America and Americans*, 165; John Steinbeck, "Madison Avenue and the Election," *Saturday Review*, March 31, 1956, 11.

37. Steinbeck, *America and Americans*, 90, 118, 168, 77.

38. William Rivers, "The Peripatetic Poodle," review of *Travels with Charley*, by John Steinbeck, *Saturday Review*, September 11, 1962, 31.

39. Ibid., 241.

40. Ibid., 103, 104.

41. Ibid., 270.

42. Ibid., 208.

43. Ibid., 242.

44. Steinbeck, *America and Americans*, 186.

45. Ibid., 168.

46. Ibid., 31.

47. Ibid., 169.

48. Ibid., 45, 46.

49. Ibid., 40–41, 116–19, 130, 179, 267–70.

50. Steinbeck, *Travels with Charley*, 103–4.

51. Steinbeck, *America and Americans*, 32.

52. Ibid., 33.

53. Ibid., 32.

54. Ibid., 33.

55. Ibid., 35.

56. Ibid., 93, 91, 92, 95.

57. Ibid., 115, 117, 93.

58. Ibid., 177.

59. Steinbeck, *Life in Letters*, 703.

60. Steinbeck, *Travels with Charley*, 195, 169; Steinbeck, *Life in Letters*, 703.

61. Steinbeck, *Travels with Charley*, 169.

62. Ibid., 26.

63. Steinbeck, *Life in Letters*, 652.

64. Steinbeck, *Travels with Charley*, 233–40, 245–71.

65. Ibid., 205, 201.

66. Ibid., 181, 194.

67. Steinbeck, *America and Americans*, 8.

68. Ibid., 9.

69. Tetsumaro Hayashi, *John Steinbeck and the Vietnam War (Part I)*, Steinbeck Monograph Series 12 (Muncie, Ind.: Steinbeck Research Institute, 1986).

70. Steinbeck, *Life in Letters*, 703.

71. Steinbeck, *America and Americans*, 173.

72. Ibid., 173–74.

73. Ibid., 221.

74. Sanford E. Marovitz, "The Expository Prose of John Steinbeck," pt. 2, *Steinbeck Quarterly* 7 (Summer–Fall 1974): 100.

75. Steinbeck, *America and Americans*, 177.

76. Ibid., 32.

CHAPTER 14

"Can You Honestly Love a Dishonest Thing?" The Tragic Patriotism of *The Winter of Our Discontent*

Simon Stow

JOHN STEINBECK'S FINAL NOVEL, *The Winter of Our Discontent*, is a literary enigma. While the Nobel Prize Committee cited it as evidence of his continued importance as a writer, many of Steinbeck's contemporary critics dismissed it as a minor work from a journeyman author whose best days were behind him.[1] More recently a number of commentators have sought to rehabilitate the book and, with it, the later-Steinbeck's literary reputation.[2] In what follows I will bracket this debate, except insofar as it touches on the political argument of the essay, and concentrate instead on how the novel works to offer a tragic vision of America that, while critiquing the nation, nevertheless draws on a particular kind of love of country that it not only depicts but also seeks to engender in the reader.

The essay begins with an account of the ways in which *tragedy* and *tragic* are employed in the subsequent analysis. It then lays out the claims of a number of political theorists who argue that patriotism is incompatible with democratic politics. Central to their argument is the claim that patriotism necessarily excuses a nation of even its most egregious flaws and encourages its citizens to overlook the inevitable costs and conflicts of democratic life in favor of a perceived higher unity. It is a claim that would seem to be supported by the critical consensus that the novel's final act—in which its main protagonist, Ethan Hawley, steps back from the brink of suicide—is redemptive of both character and nation. By way of alternative, I offer a tragic reading of the novel and its final act, in which Ethan's decision appears hopeful but not optimistic. Arguing that a tragic worldview is necessarily dualistic, I identify the origins of the novel's worldview in the wartime experiences of both John Steinbeck and his character. This dual perspective is made possible by, and permits, a nonredemptive and democratically productive form of patriotism, one that can support an always ongoing critique of nation.

"Apart from the Tragedy and Human Waste"

Tragedy, as Robert Pirro points out, is a highly contestable concept. It is employed in a myriad of contexts: philosophical, literary, political, journalistic, and vernacular.[3] For many, as Terry Eagleton notes, tragedy simply means "very sad."[4] Here the terms *tragedy* and *tragic* draw on a definition and distinction suggested by J. G. Finlayson's work on Greek drama. It is a distinction between tragedy as *condition* and tragedy as *response*.[5] Tragedy as condition entails an understanding of the world as one of irreconcilable conflicts, frustrated agency, human suffering, and paradoxical demands. It is a world in which what is gained is marked by what is lost.[6] Tragedy as response shares this worldview and seeks to provide humanity with a coping strategy for the inevitable circumstances of its existence.[7]

Greek theater offered its audiences a democratic pedagogy: a way to engage with, reflect on, and live with the inevitable costs and conflicts of democratic life and politics. It was a complex ritual that played a key role in the polis. Indeed, Christian Meier argues that "attic democracy was *as* dependent on tragedy as upon its councils and assemblies."[8] Central to its pedagogical function was the cultivation of ambivalence, what Richard Seaford defines as "the presence of duality over unity."[9] The Greek word *theatron*, from which we get the modern word *theater*, has been translated as "seeing place."[10] While many characters in Greek drama were literally or figuratively blind—most often because of their hubristic excess—the theater allowed its audiences to see the inevitably negative consequences of such blindness. Underpinning this democratic pedagogy was the notion of "discrepant awareness," what one character sees or knows that another character does not or what the audience sees or knows that the characters do not.[11]

It was, however, not only the plays themselves that sought to generate ambivalence in their audiences but also their setting in the Great Dionysia, the Athenian springtime theatrical festival. There the religious and civic rituals that opened the festival and celebrated the city's strengths were tellingly juxtaposed with plays—both tragic and comedic—that problematized those same values.[12] That Steinbeck's bleak portrayal of New Baytown and its inhabitants is set between two holidays—the religious Good Friday and the civic July 4—might be thought to suggest a similar dynamic at work in *The Winter of Our Discontent.*

Tragedy as response then sought to cultivate in its audience an ambivalence of perspective, one that promoted a worldview that defied any simple categorization. It was neither a ritual of overcoming nor one of redemption. Both are denied by the recognition of the inevitability of tragedy as condition. Rather this ambivalence was, in the words of Paul Gilroy, "suffering made useful, made productive, not redemptive."[13] Many contemporary critics argue, however, that it is precisely this ambivalence that makes patriotism impossible.

"The Dignity of Pure Disinterested Patriots"

While patriotism has, in recent years, become central to American political discourse, it has fared less well among political theorists. George Kateb and Steven Johnston are just two of the thinkers who identify what they believe to be an inherent tension in the relationship between democracy and patriotism.[14] Both thinkers associate patriotism with a singular vision, a parochial worldview, an uncritical devotion to an abstract entity, and ultimately, with killing and/or self-sacrificing death.

Describing patriotism as "a self-concern that inevitably passes into licensed self-preference," George Kateb suggests the ways it inhibits critical reflection about the self or nation that is central to democratic politics.[15] A moral principle, he argues, "[must] be conceived as universalist and asks for consistent application; it aims at respect for persons or individuals, not abstract entities of the imagination."[16] Patriotism, he suggests, is a mistake because its partiality of perspective promotes nationalism and necrophilia. "A good patriot," Kateb observes, "does not want people in other countries to be patriots."[17] Arguing that patriotism is a group narcissism that promotes jealousy—one that needs enemies in order to define itself—Kateb declares that there is not "much difference, at least in effects, between patriotism and nationalism" and that this close relative to nationalism leads inexorably to death.[18] "Patriotism," he asserts, "is a readiness to die and kill for what is largely a figment of the imagination. For this figment, one commits oneself to a militarized and continuously politicized conception of life. . . . Patriotism is, from its nature, a commitment to the system of premature, violent death."[19] All of which, he writes, is predicated on a "falsely sanitized or falsely heroized" narrative of nation.[20]

Kateb's claims about dishonesty, jealousy, necrophilia, and singularity of vision are echoed in Steven Johnston's work. Patriotism, according to Johnston, "feeds on death." As such, any attempt to theorize "healthy forms of patriotism" is inevitably doomed to failure.[21] Indeed, the intoxicating power of patriotism is so great, Johnston argues, that even Socrates, the wisest man in Athens, willingly chose his own death over life in exile.[22] Such problematic choices, Johnston suggests, are the result of patriotism's blindly narcissistic outlook. By placing certain values—such as the life of a people or the identity of the nation as a perpetual project—beyond question, patriotism promotes a willingness to overlook the disparities between a nation's professed ideals and its political realities.[23] Thus any attempt to build a critical acknowledgment of a nation's failings into an expression of national pride, Johnston argues, inevitably devolves into self-congratulation, giving that magnanimous nation yet another reason to love itself.[24] Indeed, much of Johnston's argument rests on an extended reflection on the impossibilities or misplacement of love in democratic politics.[25] Fourth of July parades, the pledge of allegiance, and war memorials, he argues, all suggest the ways in which patriotism demands persistent inculcation. Citizens are, and must be, repeatedly taught to love their country. For Johnston, this reveals a contradiction. "Perhaps," he writes, "a political order that must make a point of fostering patriotism does not deserve the love it represents."[26] Patriotic love is, he suggests, uncritical, manufactured, and destructive. "Exclusivity, among other things, is what renders love special. Should it fade, transfer, or die out, love becomes capable of the most horrendous crimes. Thus love," he writes, "is intrinsically bound up with the intense passion of jealousy."[27] This passion, Johnston argues, makes patriotism ultimately "a politics of hate."[28] It is the "Manichean logic" of this hate, jealousy, and exclusivity that makes patriotism antagonistic, and thus anathema, to democracy.[29] As such, he dismisses the idea that patriotism might be tragic and thus open to engaged debate.[30] Its outlook is, he suggests, unequivocal and univocal.[31]

"An Unmitigated, Unredeemable Rascal"

Evidence for the claim that patriotism promotes a willingness to overlook a nation's flaws can be found in much of the commentary on Steinbeck's *The Winter of Our Discontent*. For, even as a number of scholars acknowledge the bleakness of Steinbeck's picture of New Baytown—and by extension America—they nevertheless seek to let America off Steinbeck's critical hook by presenting the book's deeply ambiguous ending as redemptive, both of Ethan and of his nation.

"Ethan," Michael J. Meyer argues, "finds the potential for redemption in the Hawley talisman which his daughter Ellen has secreted away in his coat pocket."[32] Indeed, Meyer sees national and personal redemption as a persistent theme in Steinbeck's work and draws a parallel between the endings of *The Winter of Our Discontent* and *The Grapes of Wrath*: "Just as the positive act of Rosasharn's breast-feeding the indigent man who is starving in the barn in *The Grapes of Wrath* encourages readers to believe that brotherhood and caring will eventually overcome evil and will once again be valued by the Okies as well as the Californians, so Ethan's refusal to commit suicide in order to maintain the light offers an optimistic outlook and a conviction that Mammon will never completely conquer America. Instead, the forces of good . . . will triumph over the forces of evil."[33] Such moments of redemption, Meyer suggests, situate Steinbeck within the tradition of the jeremiad: a form of speech in which a community is repeatedly condemned for its sins. What distinguishes the *American* jeremiad from its predecessors is the promise of redemption. "In their case," writes Sacvan Bercovitch of the early Americans, "they believed God's punishments were *corrective, not destructive*. Here, as nowhere else, His vengeance was a sign of love, a father's rod used to improve the errant child. In short, their punishments confirmed their promise."[34] Thus, even as Jonathan Edwards condemns the community in his famous sermon and paradigmatic jeremiad, "Sinners in the Hands of an Angry God," he holds out the hope that the damned might nevertheless secure the possibility (but only the *possibility*) of salvation by submitting themselves to the demands of church doctrine.

According to Meyer's reading of the novel, Steinbeck condemns the nation but holds out hope for change. Steinbeck is the father and his readers his wayward children. Certainly this would seem to be the implication of the scolding paternalism of the novel's epigraph. "Readers," writes Steinbeck, "seeking to identify the fictional people and places described would do better to inspect their own communities and search their own hearts, for this book is about a large part of America today." In the epigraph, Susan Shillinglaw argues, Steinbeck suggests that his novel "is a parable of corruption and redemption."[35] This is also the view of Hiroshi Kaname and Barbara A. Heavilin, who identify in Steinbeck's novel a "satirical but loving patriotism" that nevertheless redeems the nation.[36] "Ethan," they write, "like the American people as a whole whom he symbolizes, does not slip backwards into the darkness, but rather steps forward into a light that may be shining dimly but which, nevertheless, is still shining."[37] Indeed, for Kaname and Heavilin the redemptive nature of the novel, and of Steinbeck's entire oeuvre, is never in doubt. "Like those of Emerson and Whitman," they write, "the works of John Steinbeck reveal his unabashed love for his country and its people, his belief that they shall long endure."[38] Briefly acknowledging and then choosing to ignore the less than positive picture of America painted in the novel, they conclude that with *The Winter of Our Discontent* "as patriot and bard Steinbeck . . . has written a paean to the American people."[39]

The idea that the novel is one of punishment and redemption finds its fullest expression perhaps in Stephen K. George's essay on *The Winter of Our Discontent.* George finds parallels between Ethan's decision to live and the decision of those who—on George's account at least—chose to give their lives on September 11, 2001: "The final redemptive act at the novel's end, when Ethan rejects suicide and struggles out of the sea to return the family talisman to its new owner, his daughter Ellen, has been played out again in the sacrifice of firefighters, police, rescue workers, and even civilians aboard a plane over Pennsylvania, all of whom gave their lives—some figuratively, some literally—in reaffirming what is best about America."[40] Setting aside what it might mean to give one's life figuratively, George's comparison of Ethan's actions with those of the 9/11 responders and passengers on Flight 93 would seem to provide the best evidence for Kateb's and Johnston's claims that patriotism clouds the careful deliberation and good judgment necessary for democratic politics.

It is perhaps not Steinbeck who is what Kaname and Heavilin call an "unabashed patriot"—and here it is useful to recall that *unabashed* is a synonym for *shameless,* just as *paean* means *hymn of victory*—but rather those who would read his novel, and his broader body of work, as necessarily redemptive. For even as they acknowledge Steinbeck's critique of America, these scholars suggest, in the manner identified by Johnston, that the very existence of the critique is what makes the nation not only worthy of its citizens' love but also beyond meaningful reproach. In this they not only negate Steinbeck's critique but also deny his tragic vision.

"A Little Hope, Even Hopeless Hope, Never Hurt Anybody"

As a number of essays in this volume have made clear, Steinbeck was deeply committed to promoting progressive social change through his literature and journalism. As such, any suggestion that he might have a tragic worldview—his commitment to theater notwithstanding (see chapter 3, by Donna Kornhaber)—would seem to be an anathema to this widely held view of Steinbeck and his art. Indeed, many on the political Left contend that a tragic worldview is diametrically opposed to political action. Writing in 1944, C. Wright Mills accused American intellectuals of a "political failure of nerve" and argued that a tragic view of life promoted a retreat from political responsibility, thereby making "one's goal simply that of understanding."[41] A tragic sensibility, it has been suggested, promotes a debilitating fatalism, or nihilism counterproductive to political action. It is perhaps for this reason that so many commentators on *The Winter of Our Discontent* have been keen to identify what they perceive to be the—albeit sometimes qualified—hope that underpins Steinbeck's final literary work. For if Steinbeck's later vision of America is a tragic one, he would appear to have nothing to offer his country except nihilism.

Given Steinbeck's largely negative account of New Baytown, and by extension America, populated by the corrupt, the conniving, and the condemned, such an apparently nihilistic perspective is perhaps not too hard to discern. However, rather than engaging with the depth and complexity of Steinbeck's work and facing the hard truths his characters face—and must continue to face—many Steinbeck scholars impose an overly simplistic account of hope on the novel. It is an interpretation in which, as Meyer's work illustrates, hope is understood as synonymous with optimism. In his account of the American jeremiad, for example, Meyer glosses over the contingency of redemption and fails to recognize that while salvation is possible, it is far from secured.[42] Similarly, his account of the ending of *The Grapes of Wrath* fails to recognize that the hope is possible only because of the death of a child: that what is gained is marked by what is lost. There is, however, a richer understanding of hope within the tradition of American political thought, one that, far from being synonymous with optimism, recognizes and embraces the tragedy of human existence. Viewing Steinbeck's last novel through this lens reveals much about his dualistic vision of America.

"What the American public always wants," William Dean Howells famously observed, "is a tragedy with a happy ending."[43] Tragedies do not, however, have happy endings; such territory is the purview of melodrama.[44] Tragedies may have what Paul Gilroy calls "productive" endings.[45] Such endings leave the viewer or the reader with a deeper understanding of the tragedy of condition. They do not, however, necessarily rob her of the impetus to seek to alleviate those conditions, even as she recognizes the impossibility of their being overcome.

Cornel West—a leading theorist of the relationship between a "tragic sense" and social hope—calls tragedy "a kind of 'Good Friday' state of existence in which one is seemingly forever on the cross"—appropriate enough for a novel that begins at Easter. The crucified are, West suggests, "sustained by a hope against hope for a potential and possible triumphant state of affairs."[46] The apparently paradoxical relationship between hope, an understanding of tragedy as condition, and political agency is resolved by an understanding of the *nature* of the hope—the "hope against hope" or a "hopeless hope"—that West, W. E. B. Du Bois, and indeed, Steinbeck's Ethan Hawley, all identify.[47] Such hope does not entail an expectation of fulfillment but rather constitutes what Eddie Glaude Jr. has called "a regulative ideal toward which we aspire but which ultimately defies historical fulfillment."[48] It is an ideal that, even as we recognize it is unattainable, continues to regulate our behavior. We might think, for example, of the "more perfect union" promised by the U.S. Constitution, the tragic dimensions of which have been articulated by orators from Abraham Lincoln to Barack Obama.[49]

It is perhaps no surprise that the leading theorists of this tragic "hope against hope" are African American.[50] The insider/outsider perspective of being black in the United States, argued Du Bois, permitted African Americans what he called a "second sight," a perspective that, Robert Gooding-Williams observes, permits one "to see the world as it is disclosed to a social group different from one's own . . . thus as it is ordinarily not available to be seen."[51] Given the relative absence of black Americans from Steinbeck's work—the brief cameo offered by the two "Negro ladies" in the grocery store in *The Winter of Our Discontent* is indicative of their peripheral role in the America he describes—turning to an African American tradition to explain the tragic hope of Steinbeck's patriotic vision may seem something of a stretch.[52] What connects Steinbeck's novel to this black tragic outlook is the dual perspectives that both embody and seek to inculcate in their audiences.[53]

The Greek word *theoros,* from which we derive the modern word *theory,* referred both to an activity of watching and judging—such as in the theater—and to a person whose job it was to visit other city-states and report back on their activities. As the history of political theory suggests, journeys and return—such as for de Tocqueville—or the insider/outsider perspective of exile—such as for Thucydides and Machiavelli—permit a complex and critical perspective on the theorists' own community.[54] Implicit in both understandings of the term *theoros* is, then, a dual perspective, one that we see not only in Ethan Hawley but also in the construction of the novel.

"For Myself, I Can Double Think"

The Winter of Our Discontent employs two narrative voices: a third-person narrator who appears in the first two chapters of each section of the novel and the first-person perspective of Ethan Hawley. Steinbeck's technique has drawn criticism from, among others, Warren French, who argues that the switch in perspectives produced "the destruction of any consistent identification between Hawley and the reader."[55] Stephen George, however, says—albeit anachronistically—that the novel offers a "deliberate use of postmodern techniques, primarily with the narrative voice."[56] George cites John Ditsky, who, noting the multiple references to mirrors in the text, concludes that it is "a novel about mirrors."[57] While few except George would be willing to ascribe to Steinbeck the narrative strategies of postmodernism, the playfulness of Nabokov, or even the identity games and persistent narrative misdirection of Philip Roth—all of whom are far more thoroughgoing in their approach than Steinbeck in his brief foray into this experimental narrative territory—there is, nevertheless, a duality to Steinbeck's approach that may serve two functions.

First, perhaps the switch between narrators is meant to alert the reader to the perspectival nature of any story. It may be an approach that Steinbeck employs but never quite resolves to his own satisfaction. Whereas his heavy-handed didacticism in the novel's epigraph—where Steinbeck more or less suggests that the reader sit in a corner and think about what he or she has done—implies an allegorical quality to the text, Ethan Hawley's later observation—that the man who tells stories "must think of who is hearing or reading, for a story has as many versions as it has readers. Everyone takes what he wants or can from it and thus changes it to his measure. Some pick out parts and reject the rest, some strain the story through their mesh of prejudice, some paint it with their own delight"—suggests the author's tragic recognition that his work might fall on deaf ears.[58] Indeed, the persistence of misrecognition and an inability of characters to make themselves heard or understood, or themselves to hear or understand—itself a key aspect of Greek tragedy—is central to the novel. Had, for example, Ethan been able to hear his daughter, or had she been able to express more clearly her concerns about her brother's plagiarism—a failure that, despite the ellipti-cal nature of her approach, she blames on him: "You never listen, really listen"—the family's embarrassment over Allen's cheating might have been avoided.[59]

Second, Steinbeck may have meant this narrative dualism to reflect Ethan's own dualistic worldview: his own theoretical perspective. Ethan observes, "I wonder about people who say they haven't time to think. For myself, I can double think. I find that weighing vegetables, passing the time of day with customers, fighting or loving Mary, coping with the chil-dren—none of these prevents a second and continuing layer of thinking, wondering, conjecturing. Surely this must be true of everyone. Maybe not having time to think is not having the wish to think."[60] Ethan is, unlike many characters in the novel, unable to turn off his thoughts. He lives with a persistent dualism: in his job—happy but unhappy; in his family relation-ships—loving but unloving; and in his community—engaged with its values but aware of their corrupt foundation. Steinbeck uses Ethan's narration to demonstrate and cultivate a discrepant awareness, showing how what certain characters believe to be true is far from being the case. Mary, for example, understands very little about her husband. "When I am troubled," Ethan observes, "I play a game of silly so that my dear will not catch trouble from me. She hasn't found out yet, or if she has, I'll never know it."[61] Mary does not understand that the silliness masks her husband's anger and de-pression. "I am glad you are silly again," she declares. "It's awful when you're gloomy." As in Greek tragedy, she is, however, sometimes aware enough to recognize a gulf between them, even as she is unable to name it. "I never know what you're thinking," she observes.[62]

That Ethan epitomizes the dualistic perspective—and perhaps the ambivalence of his creator—that is displayed in the tragic sense outlined by Cornel West and others raises the question of the origins of his perspective. Why, that is, is he able to offer insight into New Baytown, and by extension America, that most of the other characters in the text cannot?[63] Tellingly, many scholars regard Greek tragedy as a ritual of mourning and homecoming for the citizen-soldiers who made up the polity.[64] Given this, and the novel's multiple references to Ethan's military and wartime experiences, it would appear that it is the main narrator's status as a veteran that affords him the ambivalent perspective of the *theoros*. Identifying the importance of this experience to Ethan's worldview—and indeed, to that of his creator—not only highlights a much-overlooked but important aspect of the novel, but it also permits critical reflection on the questions of patriotism and redemption that have dominated the novel's critical reception.

"Much of My Talk Is Addressed to People Who Are Dead"

Speaking of her brother's return from his stint reporting on World War II, Steinbeck's sister observed, "John wasn't himself when he got home. The humor was gone, the play knocked right out of him. The war changed him." The view was widely shared among his family and friends.[65] (For a discussion of Steinbeck's wartime experiences, see chapter 12, by Mimi R. Gladstein and James H. Meredith.) Tom Brokaw's popular 1998 book *The Greatest Generation* venerates those who fought the war and returned home to build a better, more just, and more equitable America. Brokaw writes, "When the war was over, the men and women who had been involved, in uniform and in civilian capacities, joined in joyous and short-lived celebrations, then immediately began the task of rebuilding their lives . . . battle-scarred and exhausted, but oh so happy to be home. The war had taught them what mattered most in their lives and they wanted now to settle down and live."[66] Brokaw's narrative has, however, come to obscure the rather more complicated experiences of wartime returnees, such as Steinbeck, and indeed, of the polity to which they were returning. Newspaper and magazine stories of the period expressed the anxiety felt by the general public, asking questions such as "Will your boy be a killer when he returns home?" and suggesting that veterans should spend time in reorientation camps before they were permitted back into society.[67] The much-vaunted veterans' benefits, including the GI Bill, were, moreover, frequently resented by the civilian population. A 1946 article in the *Saturday Evening Post* declared that the bill had proved to be "a tempting invitation to the shirker, the goldbricker, and the occasional crook."[68] Little wonder, perhaps, that a 1947 poll found that one-third of all veterans felt estranged from civilian life; and another, that 20 percent of veterans felt "completely hostile to civilians."[69] Similarly, narratives of return more complicated than those described by Brokaw were offered by William Wyler's 1946 film *The Best Years of Our Lives,* by Sloan Wilson's 1955 novel *The Man in the Gray Flannel Suit,* and by the 1956 film adaption of the novel, starring Gregory Peck. *The Winter of Our Discontent* seems to be a novel in a similar vein.

The novel's multiple references to combat, war, and killing make manifest the centrality of Ethan's wartime experiences to his ambivalence about America. Although the term post-traumatic stress disorder (PTSD) did not become a part of the *Diagnostic and Statistical Manual of the American Psychology Association* until 1980, it was but a belated recognition of a long-standing phenomenon depicted by the Greeks in plays such as *Ajax* and *Herakles* and identified as "soldier's heart" during the American Civil War, and as "shell-shock" in World War I. Ethan displays multiple symptoms of the disorder and *nearly* admits as much. "When it was going on," he observes of the war, "I'm not sure I knew its agony because I was busy and unutterably tired, but afterward that unit of a day and a night and a day came back to me over and over again in my night thoughts until it was like that insanity they call battle fatigue and once named shell-shock."[70] Despite his reluctance to admit the psychological impact of his wartime experiences—he expresses a disdain for "assembly-line psychoanalysts"— Ethan displays many of the diagnostic symptoms of post-traumatic stress disorder.[71]

As with many veterans, Ethan has trouble sleeping. "I fight off sleep," he declares, "at the same time craving it."[72] Much of his introspective and critical reflection takes place on long walks in the very early hours of the morning. Tellingly, such walks repeatedly take him past the war memorial on which his name is inscribed (unusually, perhaps) as a survivor of the conflict.[73] After he notes that the dead are listed below the living, Ethan's suicidal thoughts—also illustrated by his partial recitation of the "to be, or not to be" speech from *Hamlet* and his wading into the ocean at the end of the novel—rise to the surface.[74] "For a brief moment, I wished I could be with them in the lower files."[75] When Ethan does sleep, he is troubled by dreams of his military experiences. "Early in the morning a flight of [jets] boomed through and I jumped awake, a little trembly," he observes. "They must have made me dream of those German 88-milimeter all-purpose rifles we used to admire and fear so much."[76]

The extent to which Ethan struggles with his war experiences is suggested by his efforts to compartmentalize them. He recounts the—decidedly Nietzschean—method employed by his sergeant, who suggested that instead of trying to block out the horrors of war, one should embrace them.[77] Similarly, recounting the method of avoidance employed by his commander—"the best officer I ever had"—Ethan observes that he employs the same method when his "attention should be as uninterrupted as possible."[78] This suggests, perhaps, that much of his lack of focus and introspection are symptomatic of a man haunted, as he admits, by "ghosts."[79]

That Ethan is unsuccessful in his attempts to deal with his war experiences is suggested by his not-infrequent anger and panic attacks. Twice in the first chapter alone Ethan is quick to anger, first with Mr. Baker the banker, and second with his boss, Marullo.[80] We are told that "Ethan's top blew-off with a bang."[81] Later Ethan struggles to contain himself in a disagreement with his wife, Mary: "The intent to wound raises rage. I could feel the fever rise in me. Ugly, desperate words moved up like venom. I felt a sour hatefulness."[82] Likewise, during a conversation with Mary and Margie Young-Hunt, Ethan struggles to contain what seems to be a flashback or panic attack: "A flare of searing pain formed in my bowels and moved upward until it speared and tore at the place just under my ribs. A great wind roared in my ears and drove me like a helpless ship, dismasted before it could shorten sail. I tasted bitter salt and I saw a pulsing heaving room. Every warning signal screamed danger, screamed havoc, screamed shock. It caught me as I passed behind my ladies' chairs and doubled me over in quaking agony, and just as suddenly it was gone."[83]

During Ethan's panic attack he refers to his *two* ladies—Mary *and* Margie Young-Hunt. This reveals a further problem that Ethan shares with many veterans, particularly those of the Second World War: their marriage to and postwar alienation from spouses whom they hardly knew at the time of their wedding. Ethan declares, "I can see both of us, maybe more clearly now than then, a nervous, frightened Second Lieutenant Hawley with a weekend pass, and the soft, petal-cheeked, sweet-smelling darling of a girl. . . . How serious we were, how deadly serious. I was going to be killed and she was prepared to devote her life to my heroic memory. It was one of a million identical dreams of a million olive uniforms and cotton prints."[84] The marriage was based, in part, on Ethan's idea of what women should be rather than who Mary was. "Even if I hadn't wanted to marry Mary," he observes, "her constancy would have forced me to for the perpetuation of the world dream of fair and faithful women."[85] It is perhaps telling that Ethan seems to have a greater understanding with Margie Young-Hunt. She too recognizes the dual nature of New Baytown—the disparity between the professed morals of its community pillars and their private sexual conduct—and has herself experienced violence at the hands of men.[86]

Given Ethan's frequent bitterness about his war service—"When I joined up to fight the foe, I didn't know him," he observes of the enemy, here personified by the Italian store owner Marullo. "When I came back he was here. When I went broke, he took over the store and gave me a job."[87] Ethan (and his creator) might be thought to have sympathy with at least some of the arguments offered by Kateb and Johnston. Certainly, he is plagued by memories of the kind of killing that Kateb and Johnston identify as the direct product of patriotism. Although Ethan declares, "I don't feel guilt for the German lives I took," his denial seems more like that of a man attempting to suppress his wartime memories, trying to rationalize that which he feels or knows to be wrong.[88] Indeed, this suppression of moral feeling is central to his later success in business. It is success that is predicated on his ability to rationalize his actions toward both Danny Taylor—the guilt for which he tellingly accepts "as one accepts a wound in successful combat"—and Marullo.[89] "He was," Ethan declares of his former boss, "a foreigner, a wop, a criminal, a tyrant, a squeezer of the poor, a bastard, and eight kinds of son of a bitch. I having destroyed him, it was only natural that his faults and crimes should become blindingly apparent to me."[90] Ethan recognizes that this demonization of the enemy makes it possible for men such as himself to become killers. "How do you get ordinary Joes to slaughter people in a war?" he asks. The verb *slaughter*—which he uses more than once when discussing the war—suggests far more violence than the term *killing* might. "Well, it helps if the enemy looks different or talks different. But then how about civil war? Well the Yankees ate babies and the Rebs starved prisoners. That helps."[91]

Like Odysseus returned from the Trojan War, then, Ethan reflects on his birthplace, disguised, in his case, as a mild-mannered, well-meaning shop clerk. But it is clear that beneath this exterior lies a damaged individual whose interior monologue reveals a dualistic perspective on New Baytown. This dualism defies any categorization of the novel as simply redemptive of either Ethan or America.

"You've Got Every Right to Be Proud"

Central to Steinbeck's vision in *The Winter of Our Discontent* is the notion that the highest values of American society have tainted origins. The narrator repeatedly advances the Augustinian notion that social and political respectability are a simple matter of success, rather than an indicator of moral worth. In Augustine's *The City of God* a pirate asks an emperor, "What thou meanest by seizing the whole earth; but because I do it with a petty ship, I am called a robber, whilst thou who dost it with a great fleet art styled an emperor."[92] Ethan Hawley returns to that theme throughout the novel. He observes of his ancestors, "They successfully combined piracy and puritanism, which aren't so unalike when you come right down to it. Both had a strong dislike for opposition and both had a roving eye for other people's property."[93] Similarly, Ethan—contra Johnston, perhaps—acknowledges the double-edged nature of patriotism: "My ancestors, those highly revered ship-owners and captains, surely had commissions to raid commerce in the Revolution and again in 1812. Very patriotic and virtuous. But to the British they were pirates, and what they took they kept. That's how the family fortune started that was lost by my father. That's where the money that makes money came from. We can be proud of it."[94] The searing irony in the last sentence of this passage is repeated throughout the novel. Ethan recalls that many of America's greatest families obtained their exalted status through unscrupulous means, such as selling beef to the British while America was still at war with the mother nation or selling defective rifles to the army—an even greater irony for Ethan, perhaps, in that his father lost the family fortune by investing in munitions.[95] Similarly, Ethan turns repeatedly to the suggestion that Mr. Baker's bank fortune was predicated upon insurance fraud: the deliberate razing of the ship the *Belle-Adair,* which was jointly owned by Mr. Baker and Ethan's grandfathers.[96]

Ethan's Augustinian awareness of the tainted origins of the commercial successes upon which the nation, and New Baytown, was built is linked to his sardonic observations about the nature of morality. "If the laws of thinking are the laws of things," observes Ethan early on in the novel, "then morals are relative too, and manner and sin—that's relative too in a relative universe. Has to be. No getting away from it."[97] Later, Ethan tells his son, in a tone of bitter irony, "Allen! There are unchanging rules of conduct, of courtesy, of honesty, yes even of energy. It's time I taught you to give them lip service at least."[98] Similarly, Ethan, contemplating the actions that would return his family fortune, asks himself, "What are morals? Are they simply words?"[99] Looking outward beyond America, he returns again to the notion that might makes right: "To most of the world I remember how, when Hitler moved unchecked and triumphant, many honorable men sought and found virtues in him. And Mussolini made the trains run on time, and Vichy collaborated for the good of France, and whatever else Stalin was, he was strong. Strength and success—they are above morality, above criticism."[100] It is perhaps telling that the novel moves toward July 4, a holiday that, as Willie the cop notes, has become corrupted: "The glorious Fourth is always a mess. Coming on a Monday, there'll be just that much more accidents and fights and drunks—out of town drunks."[101] That it is July 4, 1960, the day on which the U.S. flag with the fiftieth star, representing Hawaii, was first raised is perhaps even more telling, given Ethan's comments about the respectability of power and about the history of colonial expansion that led to Hawaii's entry into the union.[102]

In a May 1960 letter to Frank and Fatima Loesser, Steinbeck notes his early preparations for the book that would become *Travels with Charley.* "I'm going to learn about my own country," he writes. "I've lost the flavor and taste and sound of it."[103] Having returned from an extended stay in England, Steinbeck had found himself at odds with his country. His insider/outsider perspective is suggested by a comment upon a visit to California. "Tom Wolfe was right. You can't go home again because home has ceased to exist except in the mothballs of memory."[104] This dual perspective drives the novel. Steinbeck's own status as a *theoros* informs the perspective of the novel's narrator. Given the rather bleak vision of America depicted in the novel—certainly compared to the more positive, albeit qualified, vision in *Travels with Charley* and *America and Americans* (see chapter 13, by Robert Hughes)—the question of whether *The Winter of Discontent* can in any way be considered a patriotic novel might legitimately be asked.

In light of the text's unrelenting criticism of corruption, commercialism, the absence of integrity, and the fundamental dishonesty of New Baytown and America, it is not entirely clear that the Steinbeck of *The Winter of Discontent* could be said to love his country. It is perhaps for this reason that many critics have placed so much hermeneutic weight on the rather thin reed of Ethan's decision to live at the end of the novel. Critics suggest that Ethan finds something for which to live, most obviously his daughter Ellen. Nevertheless, such a reading oversimplifies an emotionally complex relationship. Ethan declares of his daughter, "I do love her, and that's odd because she is everything I detest in anyone else."[105] His statement resembles the kind of uncritical love that Johnston believes is inherent to patriotism: the willingness to overlook fault. But Ethan also observes, "I love her, but I am somewhat in fear of her because I don't understand her."[106] It is a comment that might just as easily apply to his nation.

It would appear that there is a rather more complex love underpinning Steinbeck's depiction of his country than that which would make the ending of the novel simply redemptive, one that suggests patriotism—whose root is the Latin word *patria,* for father—might better be perceived of as a familial rather than a romantic attachment. Viewed from this perspective Steinbeck's nonredemptive, tragic love of country becomes evident.

"Can You Honestly Love a Dishonest Thing?"

"We are ashamed," Isaiah Berlin once observed, "of what our brothers or our friends do; of what strangers do we might disapprove, but we do not feel ashamed."[107] Berlin's observation suggests that the palpable sense of anger over and disappointment in America that pervades *The Winter of Our Discontent* could come only from one attached to the nation. Were Steinbeck not so connected, perhaps, the vision of America that he presents in the novel might be less indignant and, indeed, more redemptive. Steinbeck seems to recognize, however, that the love that underpins patriotism is not, as Kateb and Johnston would have it, romantic but familial. As such, it carries with it recognition of the flaws of the love object rather than simply the idealized vision that Johnston and Kateb ascribe to romantic love. Given

Steinbeck's own tangled and complex family life, it is perhaps not too much of a stretch to suggest that he was aware of the tragic difficulties of this kind of love.

In the case of Ellen, for example, the redemptive version of Ethan's decision to live—"Else another light might go out"—misses his own fear of his daughter.[108] Ellen is far from the perfect light that would make the tale redemptive. Her decision to alert the authorities to her brother's plagiarism might, for example, be regarded as morally praiseworthy, as evidence of a decency and goodness that is otherwise lacking in New Baytown. Yet such an account overlooks the manner in which she exposes Allen: not quietly to her parents but in the most humiliating way possible. Indeed, the pleasure that she takes in setting up Allen's exposure—the cruelty of her act, paralleling the similarly underhanded actions of her father when having Marullo deported—is suggested by her apparent excitement at what initially appears to be Allen's success: "'You'd think it was Ellen had won honorable mention,' Mary said. 'She's even prouder than if *she* was the celebrity. Look at the cake she baked.' It was a tall white cake with HERO written on its top in red, green, yellow, and blue letters."[109] Ellen takes similar pleasure in deceiving her father: "'I do love you,' she said. 'Isn't it exciting? And isn't Allen wonderful? It's like he's born to it.'" "And this," observes Ethan, "was the girl I had thought very selfish and a little mean."[110] The light that purportedly redeems Ethan and the novel has, perhaps, already gone out, if indeed it ever really shone.

In this way, even if Ethan believes that his daughter is a source of redemption—and it is not clear that this is indeed the case—Steinbeck appears to appeal over the heads of his characters to suggest otherwise to his reader. In this the discrepant awareness between what the reader knows and what the characters know suggests the novel's tragic vision. Steinbeck is hopeful but not optimistic about America. His is perhaps a rage against the dying of the light, a hope against hope. Even as he recognizes the possibilities of misinterpretation—evidenced, perhaps, by those who see the novel's ending as optimistic rather than as tragically hopeful—Steinbeck remains an engaged artist whose work aims at bringing the country he desires into being, even as he acknowledges that the odds are against him. In this he challenges both himself and the reader to do better. A 1959 letter to Adlai Stevenson perhaps best captures his awareness of the magnitude of the task. His invitation to Stevenson in the final sentence is the challenge to us, his readers: "Someone has to reinspect our system and that soon. We can't expect to raise our children to be good and honorable men when the city, the state, the government, the corporations all offer higher rewards for chicanery and deceit than probity and truth. On all levels it is rigged, Adlai. Maybe nothing can be done about it, but I am stupid enough and naively hopeful enough to want to try. How about you?"[111]

Notes

I wish to thank Cyrus Ernesto Zirakzadeh and the anonymous reviewers for the University Press of Kentucky for their helpful comments on an earlier version of this essay.

1. See, for example, "Books: Damnation of Ethan Hawley," review of *The Winter of Our Discontent*, by John Steinbeck, *Time*, June 23, 1961, http://www.time.com/time/magazine/article/0,9171,894545,00.html.

2. Stephen K. George, "The Contemporary Nature of Steinbeck's *Winter*: Artistry, Integrity, and September 11," in *A John Steinbeck Reader: Essays in Honor of Stephen K. George*, ed. Barbara Heavilin (Lanham, Md.: Scarecrow Press, 2009), 11–21; and the essays in Barbara Heavilin, ed., *Steinbeck Yearbook*, vol. 1, *The Winter of Our Discontent* (Lewiston, N.Y.: Edwin Mellen Press, 2000).

3. Robert C. Pirro, *The Politics of Tragedy and Democratic Citizenship* (New York: Continuum, 2011).

4. Terry Eagleton, *Sweet Violence: The Idea of the Tragic* (Oxford: Blackwell, 2003), 1.

5. The terms are my own, but they draw on Finlayson's work. James Finlayson, "Conflict and Resolution in Hegel's Theory of the Tragic," *Journal of the History of Philosophy* 37, no. 3 (1999): 493–520. I am grateful to Joel Schwartz for drawing this essay to my attention.

6. I am grateful to Steven Johnston for this formulation.

7. Simon Stow, "Agonistic Homegoing: Frederick Douglass, Joseph Lowery, and the Democratic Value of African American Public Mourning," *American Political Science Review* 104, no. 4 (2010): 682.

8. Christian Meier, *The Political Art of Greek Tragedy*, trans. Andrew Webber (Baltimore: Johns Hopkins University Press, 1993), 219; emphasis in the original.

9. Richard Seaford, "Historicizing Tragic Ambivalence: The Vote of Athena," in *History, Tragedy, Theory: Dialogues on Athenian Drama*, ed. Barbara Goff (Austin: University of Texas Press, 1995), 202.

10. Christopher Rocco, *Tragedy and Enlightenment: Athenian Political*

Thought and the Dilemmas of Modernity (Berkeley: University of California Press), 110.

11. Froma I. Zeitlin, "Playing the Other: Theater, Theatricality, and the Feminine in Greek Drama," *Representations* 11 (1985): 75.

12. Simon Goldhill, *Love, Sex, and Tragedy: How the Ancient World Shapes Our Lives* (Chicago: Chicago University Press, 2004).

13. Paul Gilroy, *Darker than Blue: On the Moral Economies of Black Atlantic Culture* (Cambridge, Mass.: Belknap Press of Harvard University Press, 2010), 150.

14. For an extended discussion of the costs and benefits of patriotism to democratic politics, see Martha Nussbaum, *For Love of Country*, ed. Joshua Cohen (Boston: Beacon Press, 2002).

15. George Kateb, *Patriotism and Other Mistakes* (New Haven, Conn.: Yale University Press, 2006), 9.

16. Ibid.

17. Ibid., 10.

18. Ibid., 9.

19. Ibid., 8.

20. Ibid.

21. Steven Johnston, *The Truth about Patriotism* (Durham, N.C.: Duke University Press, 2007), 162–63.

22. Ibid., 64–88.

23. Ibid., 23.

24. Ibid., 32.

25. Ibid., 165.

26. Ibid., 25.

27. Steven Johnston, "This Patriotism Which Is Not One," *Polity* 34, no. 3 (2002), 307.

28. Ibid., 312.

29. Johnston, *Truth about Patriotism*, 13.

30. Although Johnston seems to qualify this claim somewhat in a later article: Steven Johnston, "American Dionysia," *Contemporary Political Theory* 8, no. 3 (2009): 255–75.

31. Johnston, *Truth about Patriotism*, 59.

32. Michael J. Meyer, "American Jeremiads: *The Winter of Our Discontent* and *Into The Woods*," *Theory in Action* 3, no. 1 (January 2010): 92.

33. Michael J. Meyer, "In $$$$ We Trust: Steinbeck's Jeremiad against Mammon in *The Winter of Our Discontent*," in Heavilin, *Steinbeck Yearbook*, 135.

34. Sacvan Bercovitch, *The American Jeremiad* (Madison: University of Wisconsin Press, 1978), 8.

35. Susan Shillinglaw, introduction to John Steinbeck, *The Winter of Our Discontent* (New York: Penguin Books, 2008), i.

36. Hiroshi Kaname and Barbara A. Heavilin, "John Steinbeck's Patriotism in *The Winter of Our Discontent*," in Heavilin, *Steinbeck Yearbook*, 173.

37. Ibid., 183.

38. Ibid., 173.

39. Ibid., 182.

40. George, "Contemporary Nature," 19. While there can be little doubt that 9/11 first responders displayed great bravery and devotion to duty, the suggestion that they "gave their lives" suggests a willingness to die that belies the communication problems and poor emergency planning that, in many cases, led to their deaths. See Jim Dwyer and Kevin Flynn, *102 Minutes: The Untold Story of the Fight to Survive inside the Twin Towers* (New York: New York Times Books, 2005).

41. C. Wright Mills, "The Social Role of the Intellectual" (1944), quoted in Pirro, *Politics of Tragedy*, 15.

42. See, for example, George Shulman, *American Prophecy: Race and Redemption in American Culture* (Minneapolis: University of Minnesota Press, 2008).

43. Quoted in Edith Wharton, *A Backward Glance* (New York: Scribner's, 1933), 147.

44. See, for example, Elisabeth Anker, "Villains, Victims, and Heroes: Media, Melodrama, and September 11," *Journal of Communication* 55 (2005): 22–37.

45. Paul Gilroy, *Darker Than Blue: On the Moral Economies of Black Atlantic Culture* (Cambridge, Mass.: Belknap Press of Harvard University Press, 2010), 150.

46. Cornel West, "Prophetic Christian as Organic Intellectual: Martin Luther King, Jr.," in *The Cornel West Reader* (New York: Basic Books, 2000), 427.

47. Steinbeck, *The Winter of Our Discontent* (New York: Penguin Books), 78.

48. Eddie Glaude Jr., *Exodus! Race, Religion and Nation in Early Nineteenth-Century America* (Chicago: Chicago University Press, 2000), 112.

49. See Barack Obama, "A More Perfect Union," video and transcript of a speech delivered at Philadelphia, Penn., March 18, 2008, http://my.barackobama.com/page/content/hisownwords/.

50. Stow, "Agonistic Homegoing," 691.

51. W. E. B. Du Bois, *The Souls of Black Folk* (New York: Barnes and Noble, 2003), 9; Robert Gooding-Williams, *In the Shadow of Du Bois: Afro-modern Political Thought in America* (Cambridge, Mass.: Harvard University Press, 2009), 78.

52. Steinbeck, *Winter of Our Discontent*, 144. Though, in keeping with Kateb's and Johnston's critiques of patriotism, Ethan does observe that "the Army

discovered that black and white no longer fight each other when they have something else to fight in company" (224).

53. As I have argued elsewhere, in the case of African Americans this dual perspective—this tragic hope against hope—has been largely obscured in the mainstream of American politics by popular narratives of the civil rights struggle in which the hopes of black Americans are thought to have been fulfilled by the civil rights movement, by the election of America's first black president, and/or by the emergence of a supposedly postracial nation. Stow, "Agonistic Homegoing," 684. A myriad of statistics pointing to ongoing race-based inequalities in the United States and the reservations expressed by Cornel West and Tavis Smiley, among others, about the benefits to African Americans of the election of the first black president suggest, nevertheless, that such ambivalence does and should persist. Don Terry, "A Delicate Balancing Act for the Black Agenda," *New York Times,* March 19, 2010, http://www.nytimes.com/2010/03/19/us/19cncagenda .html?scp=3&sq=tavis%20smiley%20Barack%20obama&st=cse.

54. See, for example, Patrick Deneen, *The Odyssey of Political Theory: The Politics of Departure and Return* (Lanham, Md.: Rowman and Littlefield, 2003).

55. Warren French, "Steinbeck's Winter Tale," *Modern Fiction Studies* 2 (1965): 66–74.

56. George, "Contemporary Nature," 13. While George is perhaps right to situate the novel among a group of novels from the 1950s and 1960s that employed experimental narrative forms, the use of the term *postmodern* to describe them is too casual and historically problematic. See François Cusset, *French Theory: How Foucault, Derrida, Deleuze, and Co. Transformed the Intellectual Life of the United States* (Minneapolis: University of Minnesota Press, 2008).

57. John Ditsky, "The Devil Quotes Scripture: Biblical Misattribution and *The Winter of Our Discontent,*" *San Jose Studies* 15, no. 2 (1989): 19–28. There are ten references to mirrors and to what they reveal in a text that is less than three hundred pages long.

58. Steinbeck, *Winter of Our Discontent,* 70.

59. Ibid., 149.

60. Ibid., 186.

61. Ibid., 44.

62. Ibid., 55.

63. With the exception, perhaps, of Margie Young-Hunt, the character with whom Ethan has most in common.

64. See Jonathan Shay, *Odysseus in America: Combat Trauma and the Trials of Homecoming* (New York: Scribner, 2002).

65. Quoted in Jay Parini, *John Steinbeck: A Biography* (London: Heinemann, 1994), 338.

66. Tom Brokaw, *The Greatest Generation* (New York: Random House, 1998), xix–xx.

67. Thomas Childers, *Soldier from the War Returning: The Greatest Generation's Troubled Homecoming from World War II* (Boston: Houghton, Mifflin, Harcourt, 2009), 6.

68. Ibid., 217. Similarly, the paper asked, "Are we making a bum out of G.I. Joe?" (8).

69. Ibid., 8.

70. Steinbeck, *Winter of Our Discontent*, 89.

71. Ibid., 154. Much of this description of PTSD is drawn from Shay, *Odysseus in America*.

72. Steinbeck, *Winter of Our Discontent*, 35.

73. Ibid., 48, 203.

74. Ibid., 122.

75. Ibid., 203.

76. Ibid., 154.

77. Ibid., 90.

78. Ibid., 190–91.

79. Ibid., 61.

80. Ibid., 14.

81. Ibid., 21.

82. Ibid., 113.

83. Ibid., 77.

84. Ibid., 39.

85. Ibid.

86. Ibid., 159.

87. Ibid., 179.

88. Ibid., 92.

89. Ibid., 216.

90. Ibid., 219.

91. Ibid., 56.

92. St. Augustine, *The Political Writings* (Washington, D.C.: Regnery, 2002), 30. See also Hannah Arendt's observation, "Whatever brotherhood human beings may be capable of has grown out of fratricide, whatever political organization men may have achieved has its origins in crime." *On Revolution* (New York: Penguin Books, 1990), 20.

93. Steinbeck, *Winter of Our Discontent*, 37.

94. Ibid., 57.

95. Ibid., 107.

96. Ibid., 251.

97. Ibid., 56–57.

98. Ibid., 120.

99. Ibid., 187.

100. Ibid.

101. Ibid., 204.

102. See Noenoe K. Silva, *Aloha Betrayed: Native Hawaiian Resistance to American Colonialism* (Durham, N.C.: Duke University Press, 2004).

103. Quoted in Parini, *John Steinbeck*, 503.

104. Quoted in ibid., 512.

105. Steinbeck, *Winter of Our Discontent*, 75.

106. Ibid., 125.

107. Quoted in Yael Tamir, *Liberal Nationalism* (Princeton, N.J.: Princeton University Press, 1993), 98.

108. Steinbeck, *Winter of Our Discontent*, 276.

109. Ibid., 259.

110. Ibid., 261.

111. John Steinbeck, America and Americans *and Selected Nonfiction*, ed. Susan Shillinglaw and Jackson J. Benson (New York: Penguin Books, 2002), 109.

Acknowledgments

FIRST AND FOREMOST the editors wish to thank Steve Wrinn at the University Press of Kentucky. Steve's enthusiasm for the project sustained us through a number of setbacks. In addition, his kindness and compassion when each of us experienced sudden and unexpected losses in our immediate families demonstrated that not only is he a wonderful editor, but he is also a thoroughly decent human being. Steve was ably assisted at Kentucky by Allison Webster, to whom we are grateful for dealing with our (many) queries and concerns with admirable efficiency and good humor. We also wish to thank the anonymous readers at Kentucky for their close engagement with the text, for the sharing of their expertise, and for making many wonderful suggestions that greatly enhanced the finished product.

Our second greatest debt is to our contributors. We have been blessed with a collection of thoughtful and provocative essays from scholars in a wide variety of disciplines. A number of the contributors have been on board with this project for longer than we care to admit, and we thank them for their perseverance. At times we have undoubtedly tried their patience with seemingly endless editorial suggestions and follow-up questions. We hope, nevertheless, that they will agree that the outcome was worth it.

Additional thanks are due to Peter Van Coutren, Sabrina Nichols, and Rachel Collier at the Martha Heasley Cox Center for Steinbeck Studies at San Jose State University for providing us with the photograph of John Steinbeck that graces the book's cover. Thanks also go to Mona Okada at Grubman Indursky & Shire, P.C., for helping us to secure the rights to include lyrics to three songs by Bruce Springsteen.

Individually, Ernie wishes to thank *all* the friends and family members who have encouraged him over the years in his study of literature and political thought and who have offered ideas, good fellowship, and even citations related to this particular project. He is especially grateful that his partner of almost forty years, Barbara Zirakzadeh, has been willing to talk at all hours about books and the nature of reading and writing. She has enriched his life in so many ways. In graduate school, classmates and teachers—in particular, Hanna Pitkin, Giuseppe Di Palma, Michael McCann, Donald Downs, George Shulman, Michael MacDonald, and the late Ernie Haas, Michael Rogin, and Alexander George—taught him how to combine intellectual honesty, creativity, and playfulness. For those lessons, he will always be in their debt. At the University of Connecticut Ernie has met scores of energetic and unorthodox graduate students and colleagues—including faculty members in the departments of English, history, philosophy, political science, and sociology—who have helped his interdisciplinary tendencies flourish. Ernie and Simon Stow met by chance on an airport shuttle and immediately began chatting about trends and tendencies in American political culture. Simon's deep love for popular culture and his wicked sense of humor have made this publication personally fun for Ernie in addition to being a precious opportunity for intellectual growth. Three people who over the decades have cheered whenever Ernie writes and who freely shared their views on America and Americans are his mother (Refugio Flores Zirakzadeh), his daughter (Vanessa Marie Zirakzadeh), and his cherished friend and colleague (Howard Reiter). All three have passed away, but they live on in his heart.

Simon wishes to express his thanks to Caroline Hanley, John and Sandra Hanley, and Graham and Christine Stow for their continued love and support and to Daisy, Baxter, and Bluebell, both for their company and for serving as a welcome distraction during the writing and editing process. For Simon, the biggest delight of this project has been getting to know Ernie Zirakzadeh, whom he admires greatly; he is glad that they have become friends. Steven Johnston is both a wonderful friend and his fiercest interlocutor; John Seery has provided friendship, mentoring, and continued inspiration; and George Shulman showed him a way to think about literature and politics that made this book possible; he thanks them all. At William and Mary he is fortunate enough to have colleagues who are also friends. David Dessler, Chris Nemacheck, Ron (and, of course, Patricia) Rapoport, Joel Schwartz, and Mike Tierney have not only helped him navigate many of the travails he experienced during the writing and editing of this volume, but they also make coming in to work fun and exciting. He is extremely lucky to know them. He would also like to thank his friends Kip Kantelo, Jon and Karen Wood, and especially Ara Osterweil, whose frequent complaint "I can't believe you are still talking about that Steinbeck book" helped push him on to the end.

Finally, this book is dedicated to Michael Rogin (1937–2001), who taught both Ernie and Simon—almost twenty years apart—at the University of California, Berkeley. The best teachers are those who show their students a new way of seeing the world, one that changes both them and their understanding of it. Mike was such a figure. His work continues to inspire us; indeed, "Ambivalent American," one of the phrases that we use to describe John Steinbeck in this volume, could just as easily be used to describe Mike. Both were committed to interrogating their nation in ways that highlighted its paradoxes, hypocrisies, and complexities. We hope that in collating this volume we might have captured some of the passion and playfulness that not only illuminated Mike's work but also proved so influential for us in our own teaching and scholarship.

Cyrus Ernesto Zirakzadeh
Simon Stow

Selected Bibliography

Below are resources for readers interested in the politics and political vision of John Steinbeck. Examples of both classic studies and contemporary research are listed. While by no means a complete record of all the academic work undertaken on Steinbeck and his politics, the selected bibliography indicates the range of themes and disciplinary approaches that scholars have pursued and applied. For more extensive lists of the writings used in the making of this book, please see the endnotes to the individual chapters.

Writings by John Steinbeck

Steinbeck, John. *America and Americans and Selected Nonfiction.* Edited by Susan Shillinglaw and Jackson J. Benson. New York: Viking Penguin, 2002.

———. *Bombs Away: The Story of a Bomber Team.* New York: Viking Press, 1942.

———. *The Grapes of Wrath and Other Writings, 1936–1941:* The Long Valley / The Grapes of Wrath / The Log from the Sea of Cortez / The Harvest Gypsies. Edited by Robert DeMott and Elaine Steinbeck. New York: Library of America, 1996.

———. *Novels, 1942–1952:* The Moon Is Down / Cannery Row / The Pearl / East of Eden. Edited by Robert DeMott. New York: Library of America, 2001.

———. *Novels and Stories, 1932–1937:* The Pastures of Heaven / To a God Unknown / Tortilla Flat / In Dubious Battle / Of Mice and Men. Edited by Robert DeMott and Elaine Steinbeck. New York: Library of America, 1994.

———. *A Russian Journal.* New York: Viking Press, 1948.

———. *Speech Accepting the Nobel Prize for Literature.* New York: Viking Press, 1962.

———. *Steinbeck: A Life in Letters.* Edited by Elaine Steinbeck and Robert Wallsten. New York: Viking Penguin, 1975.

———. *Steinbeck in Vietnam: Dispatches from the War.* Edited by Thomas E. Barden. Charlottesville: University of Virginia Press, 2012.

———. Travels with Charley *and Later Novels, 1947–1962:* The Wayward Bus / Burning Bright / Sweet Thursday / The Winter of Our Discontent / Travels with Charley in Search of America. Edited by Robert DeMott and Brian Railsback. New York: Library of America, 2007.

———. *Working Days: The Journals of* The Grapes of Wrath, *1938–1941.* Edited by Robert DeMott. New York: Viking Penguin, 1989.

———. *Zapata.* Edited by Robert E. Morsberger. New York: Viking Penguin, 1993.

Biographies of John Steinbeck

Benson, Jackson J. *Looking for Steinbeck's Ghost.* Norman: University of Oklahoma Press, 1988.

———. *The True Adventures of John Steinbeck, Writer.* New York: Viking Press, 1984.

Kiernan, Thomas. *The Intricate Music: A Biography of John Steinbeck.* Boston: Little, Brown, 1979.

Parini, Jay. *John Steinbeck: A Biography.* New York: Henry Holt, 1995.

St. Pierre, Brian. *John Steinbeck: The California Years.* San Francisco: Chronicle Books, 1983.

Valjean, Nelson. *John Steinbeck, the Errant Knight: An Intimate Biography of His California Years.* San Francisco: Chronicle Books, 1975.

On Steinbeck's Politics and Political Visions

Astro, Richard. *John Steinbeck and Edward F. Ricketts: The Shaping of a Novelist.* Minneapolis: University of Minnesota Press, 1973.

Barry, Michael G. "Degrees of Mediation and Their Political Value in Steinbeck's *The Grapes of Wrath.*" In *The Steinbeck Question: New Essays in Criticism,* edited by Donald R. Noble, 108–24. Troy, N.Y.: Whitston, 1993.

Benson, Jackson J. "Through a Political Glass Darkly: The Example of John Steinbeck." *Studies in American Fiction* 12 (Spring 1984): 45–59.

———. "'To Tom, Who Lived It': John Steinbeck and the Man from Weedpatch." *Journal of Modern Literature* 5, no. 2 (April 1976): 151–210.

Benson, Jackson J., and Anne Loftis. "John Steinbeck and Farm Labor Unionization: The Background of *In Dubious Battle*." *American Literature* 52 (May 1980): 194–223.

Britch, Carroll, and Cliff Lewis. "Shadow of the Indian in the Fiction of John Steinbeck." *MELUS: The Journal of the Society for the Study of the Multi-Ethnic Literature of the United States* 11 (1984): 39–58.

Cook, Sylvia J. "Steinbeck, the People, and the Party." *Steinbeck Quarterly* 15 (Winter–Spring 1982): 11–23.

Donohue, Agnes McNeil, ed. *A Casebook on* The Grapes of Wrath. New York: Crowell, 1968.

Eisinger, Chester E. "Jeffersonian Agrarianism in *The Grapes of Wrath*." *University of Kansas City Review* 14 (Winter 1947): 149–54.

Evans, Thomas G. "Interpersonal Dilemmas: The Collision of Modernist and Popular Traditions in Two Political Novels, *The Grapes of Wrath* and *Ragtime*." *South Atlantic Review* 52 (1987): 71–85.

George, Stephen K. *The Moral Philosophy of John Steinbeck*. Lanham, Md.: Scarecrow Press, 2005.

Gold, Christina Sheehan. "Changing Perceptions of Homelessness: John Steinbeck, Carey McWilliams, and California during the 1930s." In *Beyond Boundaries: Rereading John Steinbeck*, edited by Susan Shillinglaw and Kevin Hearle, 47–65. Tuscaloosa: University of Alabama Press, 2002.

Hearle, Kevin. "These Are American People: The Spectre of Eugenics in *Their Blood Is Strong* and *The Grapes of Wrath*." In *Beyond Boundaries: Rereading John Steinbeck*, edited by Susan Shillinglaw and Kevin Hearle, 243–55. Tuscaloosa: University of Alabama Press, 2002.

Jones, Claude E. "Proletarian Writing and John Steinbeck." *Sewanee Review* 48 (October 1940): 445–56.

Loftis, Anne. *Witnesses to the Struggle: Imaging the 1930s California Labor Movement*. Reno: University of Nevada Press, 1998.

Lojek, Helen. "Jim Casy: Politico of the New Jerusalem." *Steinbeck Quarterly* 15 (Winter–Spring 1982): 30–37.

McKay, Nellie Y. "'Happy[?]-Wife-and-Motherdom': The Portrayal of Ma Joad in John Steinbeck's *The Grapes of Wrath*." In *New Essays on* The Grapes of Wrath, edited by David Wyatt, 47–70. Cambridge: Cambridge University Press, 1990.

Motley, Warren. "From Patriarchy to Matriarchy: Ma Joad's Role in *The Grapes of Wrath*." *American Literature* 53 (1978): 397–412.

Owen, Lewis. "Reconsideration: 'Grandpa Killed Indians, Pa Killed Snakes': Steinbeck and the American Indian." *MELUS: The Journal of the Society for the Study of the Multi-Ethnic Literature of the United States* 15 (1988): 85–92.

―――. "Writing 'in Costume': The Missing Voices of *In Dubious Battle.*" In *John Steinbeck: The Years of Greatness, 1936–1939*, edited by Tetsumaro Hayashi, 77–94. Tuscaloosa: University of Alabama Press, 1993.

Pressman, Richard S. "'Them's Horses—We're Men': Social Tendency and Counter-Tendency in *The Grapes of Wrath.*" *Steinbeck Quarterly* 19 (Summer/Fall 1986): 71–79.

Railton, Stephen. "Pilgrims' Politics: Steinbeck's Art of Conversion." In *New Essays on* The Grapes of Wrath, edited by David Wyatt, 27–46. Cambridge: Cambridge University Press, 1990.

Shockley, Martin. "The Reception of *The Grapes of Wrath* in Oklahoma." *American Literature* 15 (January 1944): 351–61.

Starr, Kevin. *Endangered Dreams: The Great Depression in California.* Oxford: Oxford University Press, 1996.

Tedlock, E. W., Jr., and C. V. Wicker, eds. *Steinbeck and His Critics: A Record of Twenty-Five Years.* Albuquerque: University of New Mexico Press, 1957.

Tetsumaro, Hayashi. "John Steinbeck as Lyndon B. Johnson's Speech Writer." In *A John Steinbeck Reader: Essays in Honor of Stephen K. George*, edited by Barbara A. Heavilin, 105–17. Lanham, Md.: Scarecrow Press, 2009.

Timmerman, John H. *John Steinbeck's Fiction: The Aesthetics of the Road Taken.* Norman: University of Oklahoma Press, 1986.

Trachtenberg, Stanley. "John Steinbeck and the Fate of Protest." *North Dakota Quarterly* 41 (Spring 1973): 5–11.

Wartzman, Rick. *Obscene in the Extreme: The Burning and Banning of John Steinbeck's* The Grapes of Wrath. New York: PublicAffairs, 2008.

Wyatt, David. Introduction to *New Essays on* The Grapes of Wrath, edited by David Wyatt, 1–26. Cambridge: Cambridge University Press, 1990.

Zirakzadeh, Cyrus Ernesto. "John Steinbeck on the Political Capacities of Everyday Folk: Moms, Reds, and Ma Joad's Revolt." *Polity* 36 (2004): 595–618.

Contributors

Adrienne Akins Warfield is assistant professor of English at Mars Hill University in Mars Hill, North Carolina. She has published articles on twentieth-century American literature and culture in the *Southern Literary Journal, Critique: Studies in Contemporary Fiction, Mississippi Quarterly, Journal of the Short Story in English, Southern Quarterly,* and other journals.

Michael T. Gibbons is associate professor in the Department of Government and International Affairs at the University of South Florida in Tampa. He teaches courses on religion and politics, politics and the military, and contemporary political theory. His primary research interests focus on the American founding and contemporary political theory. His current research includes a book on Richard Rorty. He is the editor in chief of *Blackwell's Encyclopedia of Political Thought,* eight volumes, forthcoming in 2013.

Mimi R. Gladstein is professor of English and theatre arts at the University of Texas at El Paso, where she has served as associate dean of liberal arts, chair of the English Department, and chair of the Theatre, Dance, and Film Department. She is the author of five books and the coeditor of two, one of which, *The Last Supper of Chicano Heroes: Selected Works of José Antonio Burciaga,* won an American Book Award, a Southwest Book Award, and a Latino Book Award. Gladstein is former president of the John Steinbeck Society of America.

Roxanne Harde is associate professor of English and McCalla University Professor at the University of Alberta, Augustana Faculty. She studies American literature and culture and teaches courses in feminist literary theory and American literature. She has recently published *Reading the Boss: Interdisciplinary Approaches to the Works of Bruce Springsteen*, and her essays have appeared in several journals, including *Christianity and Literature, Legacy, Studies in Puritan American Spirituality, Critique, Feminist Theology, Mosaic*, and in several edited collections.

Robert S. Hughes earned a PhD in English at Indiana University and taught American literature, film, writing, and popular fiction at the University of Hawai'i at Mānoa. He left the university in 2008 to write full time. His nonfiction publications include *Beyond* The Red Pony*: A Reader's Companion to Steinbeck's Complete Short Stories*—also translated into Japanese; *John Steinbeck: A Study of the Short Fiction;* and numerous essays and reviews. He is also the author of a series of detective novels that have been optioned for television.

Donna Kornhaber is assistant professor in the Department of English at the University of Texas at Austin, where she teaches classes in film history and theory, American drama, and the modern American novel. She received her PhD from Columbia University and her MFA in dramatic writing from the Tisch School of the Arts at New York University.

James H. Meredith retired from the U.S. Air Force as a lieutenant colonel in 2004 after twenty-five years of service. He was professor of English at the Air Force Academy. He is the author of *Understanding the Literature of World War II* (1999); *Understanding the Literature of World War I* (2004); "Fitzgerald and War," in *A Historical Guide to F. Scott Fitzgerald* (2004); and "*Tender Is the Night* and the Calculus of Modern War," in *Twenty-First-Century Readings of* Tender Is the Night (2007). In addition to being a contributing editor of *War, Literature, and the Arts: An International Journal of the Arts*, he is also president of the Ernest Hemingway Foundation and Society.

Lauren Onkey is vice president of education and public programs at the Rock and Roll Hall of Fame and Museum in Cleveland, Ohio. Prior to that she was associate professor of English at Ball State University. Her research and teaching explore the intersection of popular music with cultural studies, literature, and women's studies. Her book *Blackness and Transatlantic Irish Identity: Celtic Soul Brothers* was published by Routledge in 2009.

Marijane Osborn is a recently retired professor in the English Department at the University of California in Davis and recipient of a Phi Beta Kappa teaching award. Author of several books on *Beowulf* and Chaucer and numerous articles on "real things" in Old English poetry (from invading Viking ships to tame bees), she has also published articles on Melville, D. H. Lawrence, and C. S. Lewis, among other modern writers, and has translated a great deal of poetry as well as publishing some of her own. A favorite among her own books is one she coauthored with Gillian Overing, *Landscape of Desire*, though currently she is happy about her part in *Beowulf and Lejre*, edited by John D. Niles.

Simon Stow is associate professor in the Department of Government at the College of William and Mary. He is the author of *Republic of Readers? The Literary Turn in Political Thought and Analysis* (State University of New York Press, 2007). His work has appeared in the *American Political Science Review; Perspectives on Politics; Theory & Event; Philosophy and Literature;* and several edited volumes.

James R. Swensen is assistant professor of art history and the history of photography at Brigham Young University. He is in the process of completing a manuscript on the connections between *The Grapes of Wrath* and the photography of the Farm Security Administration.

Zoe Trodd is professor and chair of American literature in the Department of American and Canadian Studies at the University of Nottingham, where she focuses on American and African American protest literature. She has taught at Columbia University and the University of North Carolina, Chapel Hill, and has a PhD from Harvard University's History of American Civilization Department. Her books include *American Protest Literature* (2006), *To Plead Our Own Cause* (2009), and *The Tribunal: Responses to John Brown and the Harpers Ferry Raid* (2012).

Rick Wartzman is executive director of the Drucker Institute at Claremont Graduate University. He is the coauthor (with Mark Arax) of *The King of California: J. G. Boswell and the Making of a Secret American Empire,* the author of *Obscene in the Extreme: The Burning and Banning of John Steinbeck's* The Grapes of Wrath, the editor of *The Drucker Lectures: Essential Lessons on Management, Society, and Economy,* and the author of *What Would Drucker Do Now?,* a collection of columns for *Bloomberg Businessweek.* Wartzman also serves on the editorial board of *Boom: A Journal of California,* a quarterly on the life of the state published by the University of California Press.

Charles Williams is assistant professor in interdisciplinary arts and sciences at the University of Washington, Tacoma, where he teaches political science and labor studies. His research focuses on liberal political culture and the New Deal labor movement, including "Reconsidering CIO Political Culture: Briggs Local 212 and the Sources of Militancy in the Early UAW," *Labor: Studies in Working-Class History of the Americas* 7, no. 4 (Winter 2010).

Cyrus Ernesto Zirakzadeh is professor of political science at the University of Connecticut. His research on social movements, theories of workplace democracy, and contemporary representations of politics in literature and film have appeared in numerous edited books and journals, among them *Polity, Social Movement Studies, West European Politics, Journal of Theoretical Politics, Review of Politics,* and *Comparative Studies in Society and History.* He is the author of three books, including *Social Movements in Politics: A Comparative Study,* which received a 1998 *Choice* Outstanding Academic Book Award. Since 2010 he has been the editor in chief of the journal *Polity.*

Index

Page numbers in *italics* refer to photographs.

POLITICAL COMPANIONS
TO GREAT AMERICAN AUTHORS

SERIES EDITOR
Patrick J. Deneen, University of Notre Dame

CPSIA information can be obtained at www.ICGtesting.com
Printed in the USA
BVOW01s0435280814

364546BV00002B/68/P

9 780813 147390